MW00477107

POISONS AND
POISONERS

POISONS AND POISONERS

With Historical Accounts of
Some Famous Mysteries in
Ancient and Modern Times

C. J. S. THOMPSON

BARNES
&NOBLE
BOOKS
NEW YORK

TO
SIR WILLIAM H. WILLCOX
K.C.I.E., C.B., C.M.G., M.D., F.R.C.P. (LOND.)
As a slight appreciation of the eminent services
he has rendered to Toxicology and
Medicine, and his valuable
assistance.

This edition published by Barnes & Noble, Inc.

1993 Barnes & Noble Books

ISBN 1-56619-210-0
Printed and bound in the United States of America

M 9 8 7 6 5 4 3 2 1

CONTENTS

CONTENTS

POISONS AND POISONERS

CHAPTER I

WHAT IS A POISON ?

POISONS, those subtle and silent weapons capable of destroying life mysteriously, secretly and without violence, have ever had a peculiar fascination for mankind.

They have played so large a part in history at various periods, also in romance as well as crime, that the subject must be regarded as one of great human interest.

To define the meaning of the word poison with exactitude is a matter of some difficulty, for there is no legal definition of what constitutes a poison. The *New English Dictionary* describes a poison as, " any substance which when introduced into or absorbed by a living organism, destroys life or injures health, irrespective of mechanical means or direct thermal changes. Further, it is popularly applied to a substance capable of destroying life by rapid action and when taken in a small quantity. The more scientific use is recognized in the phrase ' slow poison ', indicating the cumulative effect of a deleterious drug or agent taken for a length of time ".

These definitions are not however altogether satisfactory, for although a substance which produces serious effects when taken in small quantities may rightly be regarded as a poison, there are certain substances which have actually been known to cause death that are not classed as poisons.

If a person dies from the effects of an overdose of saltpetre or a minute quantity of arsenic, the responsibility of the person who criminally administers it is the same; therefore, each substance must be regarded as a poison differing from the other only in its degrees of activity and perhaps in its mode of operation.

John Hunter realised this when writing on poisons over a century ago; he hazarded the idea, that " perhaps hereafter the meaning of the word poison may be lost and we shall only say the person took too much of such a substance. We never call those substances poisons that act mechanically ; thus if a person swallowed a piece of glass which afterwards killed him, we should not call it a poison, we should say he had his stomach or intestines wounded by the sharp edges of the glass and that death was the consequence. Hair swallowed whole produces no ill effect, but hair cut into very fine pieces produces very ill effects."

According to law, it is an act of poisoning if the substance criminally administered destroys life whatever may be its nature or mode of operation. If death is not the consequence then the person accused may be tried for the attempt to murder by poison.

The word poison, which appears to have been originally employed for a potion or draught prepared with a deadly or deleterious drug or ingredient, is used in that sense in English literature as early as 1230, where a reference is made in Hali Meid, to " Makien puison and bale ". In Trevisa Higden (Rolls) 1387, mention is made of " Venym and poyson " and in 1395, Purvey writes of " poisoning men with garbli venym ". The words venym, venum or bane, though no doubt originally applied to the poison of serpents, appear to have also been used for any poisonous or noxious substance which had the effect of a poison and was capable of destroying life.

For our purpose the substances that may be considered as poisons may be roughly grouped as follows : mineral poisons, corrosives and irritants (acids and alkalies), gaseous, poisonous carbon compounds, and poisons of vegetable and animal origin.

Although the Pharmacy Act of 1908 did not define the meaning of the word poison, it formulated a schedule of substances which should be deemed and labelled poisons within the Act, and laid down regulations for the keeping, dispensing and selling of those enumerated.

Later, the advancement of chemistry and the discovery of new substances led to further legislation in the shape of the Dangerous Drugs Act of 1920 which was designed to regulate the importation, manufacture, sale and use of opium and other dangerous drugs. This Act renders it unlawful for any person to import or bring into the United Kingdom any raw opium except under licence and into approved ports, and also prohibits the use of preparation of opium for smoking. It also places restrictions on cocaine, morphine, heroin and other similar substances and authorises their possession and keeping only to certain qualified persons. Further, the prescribing of such drugs is regulated and their importation prohibited except under licence.

Thus briefly are the laws at present in force respecting poisonous substances in this country. How far they safeguard the public is a matter of opinion but it is generally admitted that the regulations respecting the sale of preparations of arsenic require urgent amendment.

The historical survey that will be found in the following pages does not pretend to be a complete history of poisons, but has been confined as far as possible to those that have been employed for criminal purposes throughout the ages, together with accounts of some notable trials and poison mysteries that are still unsolved.

CHAPTER II

POISONS USED BY PRIMITIVE MAN

Our knowledge of the use of poisons by primitive man is chiefly derived from archælogical research which shows that from the earliest times, in every age and in every inhabited part of the globe, he has endeavoured by some means or other, to make the weapons he employed more deadly to his enemies or his prey. When injured in a tribal fray by a flint arrow-head or stone axe, he doubtless began to seek for something more subtle to wreak vengeance on his foe.

In his search for curative substances he doubtless discovered noxious ones, which he found were capable of producing unpleasant effects when applied to the point of a weapon destined to enter the internal economy of man or animals. He probably also observed that the arrow or spear-head on which the blood of former victims had dried caused wounds which might prove fatal, owing to the action of what are now called septic poisons. This may have led him to experiment with snake-venoms, and the juices of plants, until he discovered something of even a more deadly character. That he observed the poisonous effects of plants and herbs on animal life is evident from the names given to them in early times. Instances of these are perpetuated in cowbane (the water hemlock), which often has a fatal effect on cattle ; sowbane, so called, says Parkinson in his Herbal, as it was observed to kill swine ; wolf's bane, leopard's bane, henbane, and many others which might be mentioned, show that primitive man must have been aware of the evil effects of these plants on the animal whose name he associated with them.

In primeval times both the poisonous and medicinal properties of plants appear to have been first discovered and kept secret by the most observant and intelligent members of pastoral and nomadic tribes. The possessor of such secrets wielded an immense power over his fellows and often combined the office of medicine-man and priest. He reserved to himself as much as possible the knowledge which he had acquired of plants and their uses, and particularly those which would produce stupor, delirium and death, for by these means he was enabled to exert a greater influence over his fellows.

The study, therefore, of the poisons employed by primitive

races for destroying life in animals and man is one of considerable interest. Arrow-heads and spear-heads, worked with depressions, probably for holding poisons, have been found in cave remains of the palæolithic period in France. Laigneau is of the opinion that these weapons were first used to destroy large animals, such as the bison and reindeer, and were probably also used in tribal warfare.

The Greek word τοξικόν, used to denote poison, takes its origin from a word signifying a bow, which probably symbolized a poison-tipped arrow and the Greek toxican, from which the word toxicology is derived, is believed to have been used for the poisonous substance into which the arrow-heads were dipped.

It seems but a natural sequence, that man should have turned to his own account the knowledge he acquired of the effects of the substances which proved deadly when introduced into the body, by either external or internal means, as in them he found a more secure and secret weapon by means of which he could rid himself of the objects of his jealousy, hatred or revenge.

Poisoned arrows are mentioned by several of the early writers, including Homer, Horace and Ovid. The latter tells how the blood of vipers was used to poison weapons, and there was a general belief that disease and death were sometimes caused by poisoned arrows shot by an offended deity, as instanced in the mythical story of Apollo, whose darts were supposed to smite man with pestilence.

The Scythians are known to have used poisons and mixed the venom they employed with human blood. Certain tribes of the Caucasus are said to have used viper-venom mixed with decomposed human blood serum. Aristotle and Strabo state that the Celts were accustomed to poison their arrows and weapons, while Pliny and Celsus refer to the practice among the Gauls. As late as the seventh century poisoned arrows were used by the Dacians and the Dalmatians on the shores of the Danube, and among the Goths it seems to have been a common custom.

Almost every savage tribe and people throughout the world have been found to have their own particular poison for this purpose, and there is little doubt that this method of making the wound caused by the weapons more deadly, has been practised from a period of great antiquity.

Although most of the substances employed and the methods of preparation are now known to us, there are others about which little or no information can be obtained. The secret of the poison used by many barbaric tribes is still jealously guarded and is only known to certain chiefs and their families, or the medicine-men of the tribes who pass on the knowledge to their successors.

The substances used for lethal purposes are both of animal and vegetable origin, and include poisonous insects and fish, snake-venoms and poisonous plants, which are used alone or mixed together. These substances are not equally effective, as the active principle by age tends to decompose, but if the poison be freshly prepared, as it often is, it generally proves fatal. Lewin, however, states that he found an arrow poison used by the Bushmen in Australia still active after remaining for ninety years in a Berlin museum.

The poisons used by the various tribes of Bushmen of Africa vary according to the district in which they live. Livingstone states that those who inhabited the Kalahari district used the entrails of a small caterpillar for poisoning their spears and arrows. When drawn over a sore, this insect, which is known to the natives as " Nga," causes the most excruciating agony, and those wounded by arrows smeared with this poison die slowly in a condition of violent delirium.

It has been identified as the leaf beetle, or the *Diamphidia simplex*. Lewin, who examined the insect, found in its body besides inert fatty acids, a toxalbumin which causes paralysis and finally death. Boehm, after examination, states that the poison from the larva also belongs to the toxalbumins. The poison grubs are of a pale flesh colour, similar to the silkworm and are about three-quarters of an inch in length. When a wound is made by an arrow poisoned with this exudation the most intolerable agony is caused, and it proves fatal.

Baines tells us that the natives squeeze the grub gradually between the forefinger and thumb, when a colourless fluid exudes which is smeared over the arrow-head, thus forming an imperceptible coating. Modern investigators who have studied the properties of this curious poison, state that its action strongly resembles some of the snake-venoms and that it will retain its properties for an indefinite time. Livingstone also mentions the curious fact, that the natives consider the best antidote to the poison is to swallow the grub.

A very powerful poison employed by other tribes of Bushmen for their arrow- and spear-heads is said by Burchell to be prepared from *Amaryllis disticha*, various species of Euphorbium and Acocanthera, alone or mixed with snake-venom, and a species of black spider or beetle poison.

The Somali prepare a deadly poison from various species of Acocanthera which they call Waba, Wabayo or Ouabaio, to which they sometimes add snake-venom.

The Ovambos of South-West Africa employ a species of Adenium as an arrow poison, while the seeds of the strophanthus (*Strophanthus hispidus* or *kombé*) are largely used by the tribes who inhabit the districts near the Congo and the Zambezi.

The arrow-poison of the Pygmies of Central Africa, in which the red ant forms an ingredient, is described by Stanley, and is so deadly that a single arrow has been known to kill an elephant.

According to a recent writer on Malay poisons,* native poisoners frequently use narcotic plants to stupefy their victims as a preliminary to robbing them. They also employ sand, powdered glass, quicklime and other powders to disconcert their pursuers. Some of them claim to be able to know a method of causing loss of voice lasting seven or eight days, by the administration of certain poisons by the mouth.

Gimlette asserts that two or three clinical cases have occurred in Kelantan, in which it was alleged that the witnesses in court could not give evidence for this reason.

Malay cunning is proverbial, but it is not generally known that the natives are accustomed to use poison by mixing it with honey, which is sometimes smeared on the under surface of a knife. The poisoner then shares a meal with his enemy and divides a water-melon in half with the poisoned blade, but he is careful to eat only the upper and harmless portion as his share of the fruit. This method is said to be common in Tregganu, where potassium cyanide is employed for the purpose.

The Malays are said to have a knowledge of slow poisons which they call " time-poisons," by means of which they can give a single dose of poison and time the death of the victim within three, six, or even twelve months, according to the dose and the particular combination used. Native experts, however, say that the idea of this " time-poison " is unfounded, but they know that the effect of certain deadly poisons is greatly accelerated or delayed if certain fruits or vegetables, such as water-melon or cucumbers happen to be eaten soon after the ingestion of the poison.

Some of the Malays believe that poisoned food can be recognized by the shadow of the right hand and fingers not being cast when eating rice. Others believe that a stirring rod of ivory will become darkened if poison has been put into the food, and in Perak a spoon made of the beak of a horn-bill† is said to turn black if touched by anything of a poisonous nature.

The Malays use several different vegetable poisons for their blow-pipe darts, many of which are extremely powerful, but curiously enough, some are poisonous to certain animals and not to others, and on the other hand many of the poisons used to destroy human life may be eaten with impunity by graminivorous animals. Thus, opium does not poison pigeons, tobacco and hemlock do not injure goats, and henbane can be eaten by rabbits. The Malay jungle natives have special markings on their blow-pipe darts, by means of which they differentiate their various poisons. That of the upas-tree is specially marked to distinguish it from the others.

The sap of the upas-tree (*Antiaris toxicaria*), the active

* *Malay Poisons and Charm Cures*, John D. Gimlette, M.R.C.S. 1923.

† For the use of horns as antidotes or indicators of poison, see page 47.

principle of which is called antiarin, is used by natives through-out the Eastern Archipelago, including Java and Borneo, as a poison for their darts. It is extremely powerful and will some-times cause death in thirty minutes after a wound has been received. It is often mixed with the venom of snakes, scorpions or centipedes and occasionally with arsenic.

The upas-tree sap is collected in primitive vessels fashioned from palm leaves, which are afterwards suspended a few feet above a fire. The boiling process is somewhat protracted and during the whole time the sap is continually stirred. During this operation the liquid is transformed into a thick viscid mass and in this condition it is withdrawn from the fire. When cold, the sap is a solid, hard, yet brittle substance, so before it is set, the leaf is rolled up with its soft contents, the two ends tied with rattan and the poison thus kept till it is required.

The darts, which are projected by the natives with blow-pipes, consist of strips of palmwood from 20 to 30 cm. in length are pointed at one end. A quantity of poison is removed from its palm-leaf receptacle and ground up until it is of the consistency of flour, it is then mixed with water, and stirred up until it becomes a thin paste which is smeared upon the points of the darts. The process of preparation takes place before a fire, and when completed the darts are placed with their points towards the fire until the upas sap has dried into the wood. When darts are required for larger game, the point of the weapon is split open and a thin metal wedge or plate is inserted and the whole point is then smeared over with the poison. The opposite end of the dart comprises a small conical butt made of the soft pith of the sago palm. The darts are carried in small bamboo quivers, which are fixed into the loin-cloth of the native, the points being protected by a piece of animal skin.

North American Indians employ a poison called " caramari," which they prepare from the roots of a plant found along the sea coast. It is prepared by being burnt in earthen pipkins and to the residue is added a species of spider, hairy worms, bats' wings, the head and tail of a fish called " teborino," toads and mancanillas. These substances are set over a fire and heated in pots till they come to the consistency of a paste.

The Choco Indians of Colombia, South America, use a poison which they extract from a tree frog which they hold on a stick near a fire, when the heat causes the glands of the skin to secrete the poisonous fluid.

The Jivaro Indians of the Amazon use a vegetable poison called " jambi " for their arrows, which is said to be made from a species of vine which grows in great profusion throughout the Upper Amazon zone. The process for extracting the poison as described by Up de Graff* is as follows :

* *Head Hunters of the Amazon*, F. W. Up de Graff. 1922.

" The vine is cut into sections a foot in length, and the thin, hard outer crust of bark is carefully removed by scraping. The main bark, white when first exposed to the air, turns brown in just the same way as an apple. This inner bark is scraped into fine shavings by means of shells and flints, and these are placed in a colander which rests upon a pot in which water is boiling. The water is poured over the contents of the colander repeatedly, until the constant action on it has drawn out the alkaloid, when the lifeless shavings are throw away and the residue is boiled down until it resembles, both in consistency, colour and smell, plain chocolate. While still warm, it is poured into a bamboo receptacle and when cool it becomes semi-solidified."

The head of the arrow is dipped in the " jambi " and dried in the sun or before the fire.

These arrows have a swift and painless effect on animals and birds of the forest, and after a wound from the poisoned dart projected from a blow-gun, so long as the skin is broken at any point, they are killed within about two minutes. Experiments carried out on domestic animals have proved that the poison acts painlessly, the effect being much the same as an overdose of morphine, but despite its proved deadliness " jambi " is never used by the Head Hunters in warfare.

One of the most curious preparations in use among the North American Indians is the so-called " Black Poison," the effects of which are well-known around the lakes of the Winnipeg basin and in the Swan River district. Some time after administration it changes the colour of the skin from brownish yellow or copper colour to a sooty black and at the same time causes hair to grow on unusual parts, such as the cheek bones. Its first effects are sickness, headache, and pains in the back and limbs. Afterwards, ulceration and sores break out in various parts of the body, chiefly over the joints and more particularly the knuckles. When prepared, the poison is said to be a brown snuff-like powder with a slight and rather sickening smell. A small quantity administered in food appears to be sufficient to produce these effects. It is said to be partly composed of *Rhus toxicodendron* mixed with a dried acrid matter secreted by the glands in the skin of a species of toad.

The Indian tribes indigenous to California have a curious method of using certain plants to stupefy or poison fish. One of the most effective is " soap root " (*Chlorogalum pomeridianum*.) Besides providing a substitute for soap, the crushed pulp is dropped into the water, generally into a small pool or stream, and then stirred. The fish are stupefied by the poison, float to the surface and are captured either by hand or in a basket. Another plant employed for the same purpose is known as " blue-curls," or vinegar weed (*Trichostemma lancerlatum*).

Other tribes of Indians in South America use curare, which they extract from a certain species of strychnos and other plants, which were first brought to England by Sir Walter Ralegh in 1595. Although a deadly poison when introduced into a wound or injected under the skin, curare is practically harmless when swallowed ; indeed Humbolt states the Indians lick it off their fingers and use it as a stomachic tonic.

The Ainos of Japan are said to have used a preparation made from aconite and tobacco, while the natives of the New Hebrides are stated to smear their arrows with damp earth containing the tetanus bacillus which infects the person wounded by them.

Besides the use of poisons for offensive purposes, the institution of trial by ordeal still exists among barbaric tribes, especially in Africa. The substances employed vary with the locality inhabited by the tribe. " Muavi," which is used by several tribes in Western Africa, is prepared by scraping the bark of a poisonous tree, known only to the witch-doctors. A decoction of the scrapings is made with water and the resulting draught, which is of a highly poisonous nature, is administered to the suspected person. The action of " muavi " is generally rapid ; vomiting is quickly caused, followed by convulsions and death. When both the accuser and the accused are seized with vomiting the natives declare that the draught has been badly prepared, and should the result not prove fatal to either party, the test is repeated. When the guilt of one of the parties has been established by death, his property is at once confiscated and his wife and children are killed. So great is the belief of the natives in the infallibility of the " muavi " test, that they never hesitate to submit themselves to the trial and are said frequently to volunteer to go through the ordeal in order to prove their innocence.

The Balantes and other tribes who inhabit the West Coast of Africa employ Sassy bark (*Erythroplæum Guineense*) for their trial by ordeal. They prepare the poison by mixing the finely scraped or powdered bark with powdered glass, together with the dried and powdered viscera of the victims of the preceding trial. When required for use, the mixture is made into a paste with water, about two spoonsful being administered for a dose.

It is customary for the chief of another tribe to preside at the ordeal trial, whose duty it is to see that it is properly carried out. Each person who undergoes the trial has to pay him a fee in cash or in kind, the latter usually taking the form of rice, chickens or goats. The preparer of the poison and his assistants also receive an honorarium. When one of the Balantes is accused of a crime or witchcraft he must undergo the trial, as after once being suspected he is no longer protected by the ties of blood and friendship, and a father may even denounce his son or a husband, his wife.

Other West African tribes use the Calabar bean, commonly

called the Ordeal bean, which contains a powerful poisonous principle called physostigmine, a drug which is of great value to ophthalmic surgeons in the treatment of the eyes. It is so powerful that a fiftieth part of a grain is considered to be a poisonous dose. It was customary at one time, in old Calabar and at the mouth of the Niger where the plant grows, to destroy it whenever found, a few only being preserved to supply seeds for judicial purposes, and of these seeds the store was kept in the custody of the native chief. Now, it is preserved and the beans exported to Europe on account of the value of their active principle in medicine.

Witchcraft plays an important part in the daily life of most African natives and to witchcraft they attribute every ill that befalls them. One kind is practised secretly by evil-doers and the other by the witch-doctors with the view of destroying the effects of the evil-doers. The witch-doctors or medicine-men are undoubtedly the most powerful individuals in their tribes ; they hold the lives of all in their hands, and are daily employed to satisfy the passions of their neighbours. According to native ideas, death or sickness never occurs through natural causes, but is always the result of somebody's act. When a person is accused of having practised witchcraft or of having committed any other crime, the Calabar bean or the trial by ordeal is used to decide the case, except when the accuser is a witch-doctor, when both the accuser and the accused have to submit to the test.

Roscoe in his book, *The Soul of Central Africa*, alludes to a mysterious poison prepared by the medicine-men of Ankole. It is a tribal custom that should the king feel ill, or through age find his strength failing him, it is his duty to end his life by taking a dose of poison. The ingredients for the fatal draught are always kept at hand by the royal medicine-man who stores them in a crocodile's egg. " It must have been a strong poison," says the explorer, " for it took effect rapidly, ending the king's life in a few moments. I could not, however, discover the ingredients ; the man absolutely refused to divulge the secret. The king thus experienced no lengthened illness, but passed away in a few minutes after swallowing the fatal potion and his body was at once prepared for the ceremony."

Thus to primitive and barbaric races in various parts of the world we owe much of our knowledge of the properties of many powerful vegetable poisons.

CHAPTER III

POISONS IN TRADITION AND MYTHOLOGY— POISONS USED BY THE ANCIENT ASSYRIANS AND EGYPTIANS—THE ATHENIAN STATE POISON— ROMAN POISONERS

SEVERAL mysterious poisons are referred to in the legends and sagas that have come down to us from the dim ages of the past.

The earliest known deity associated with poisons is Gula, whose name was revered by the Sumerians about 4500 B.C. She was known as " The Mistress of Charms and Spells," the " Terrible Goddess," " Controller of noxious poisons," and was the deified form of the sorceress. Medical schools at Borsippa and Sirpurra were under her protection. She is described on a cuneiform tablet, said to have been written about 1400 B.C., as :

" Gula, the woman, the mighty one, the prince of all women.
His seed with a poison not curable
Without issue ; in his body may she place
All the days of his life,
Blood and pus like water may he pour forth."

Ages ago, a mysterious country in the far North was supposed to be ruled and dominated by sorcerers and kindred beings, all of whom were said to be children of the Sun. Here dwelt Æëtes, Perses, Hecate, Medea and Circe. To Hecate is ascribed the foundation of sorcery and the discovery of poisonous plants. Her knowledge of magic and spells was supposed to be unequalled. She transmitted her power to Medea, whose wonderful exploits are described in early Greek mythology, and who by her magic arts subdued the dragon that guarded the golden fleece and assisted Jason to perform his famous deeds. Hecate's garden is described by the poets as being enclosed in lofty walls with thrice-folding doors of ebony which were guarded by terrible forms, and only those who bore the leavened rod of expiation and the concealed conciliatory offering could enter. Towering above was the temple of the dread sorceress, where the ghastly sacrifices were offered and all kinds of horrible spells worked.

According to tradition, after Medea's adventures with Jason she returned with him to Thessaly and on their arrival they found Æson, the father of Jason, and Pelias, his uncle, who had usurped the throne, both old and decrepit. Medea was requested to exert her magical powers to make the old man young again, an operation which she is said to have speedily performed by infusing the juice of certain potent plants into his veins, and thus foreshadowing a recent operation for rejuvenating the old by means of injecting the solution of a certain gland.

Medea became the wife of Ægeus, king of Athens, whose son Theseus had been brought up in exile and who resolved to return to Athens to claim his rights. Medea, hearing of this, and for some reason greatly resenting it, prepared a poisoned goblet and gave it to Ægeus at an entertainment which he gave to Theseus, with the intent that he should hand it to his son. At the critical moment the king cast his eyes on the sword of Theseus, recognizing it as the weapon which he had given to his son when a child, directing that it should be brought by him when a man as a token of the mystery of his birth. The king at once threw the goblet from him and embraced his son, and according to the story, Medea fled from Athens in a chariot drawn by dragons.

Circe's charms were more seductive and romantic. She is said to have been endowed with exquisite beauty, which she employed to allure travellers to her territory. On their landing she entreated and enticed them to drink from her enchanted cup, but no sooner was the draught swallowed than the unfortunate stranger was turned into a hog and driven by the magician to her sty where he still retained the consciousness of what he had been and lived to repent his folly.

These mythological stories tend to show that some knowledge of poisonous substances existed in very remote times.

Leaving the period of tradition there is evidence from ancient records that the Assyrians possessed a considerable knowledge of poisonous substances, both of mineral and vegetable origin, at least three thousand years ago. From these records inscribed in cuneiform on clay tablets, we know that they employed such mineral poisons as orpiment the yellow trisulphide of arsenic, antimony oxide, copper acetate, lead, litharge, mercury and verdigris, and among the vegetable poisonous plants mentioned are poppy, aconite, mandragora, henbane and hemp.

From ancient papyri that have been discovered there is evidence that the ancient Egyptians also must have had a considerable knowledge of drugs. Some of their earliest deities, especially the god Thoth, are associated with the genesis of science, arts and magic. Thoth is reputed to have been the author of six divine works dealing with these subjects. He was identified by the Greeks with Hermes Trismegistos or the "thrice great," to whom they attributed the foundation of the science of alchemy.

Menes, the earliest Egyptian king of whom we have record, is said to have studied the properties of plants, and other Egyptian rulers cultivated the art of medicine, probably through the priests who were the chief practitioners of the art of healing in ancient Egypt. They apparently gathered a knowledge of certain poisonous substances both vegetable and mineral, were learned in the art of alchemy, and initiated votaries into its mysteries in their centres of science in the temples. The secrets taught were forbidden to be revealed under penalty of death and therefore probably many of the discoveries they made were lost to posterity. There is however sufficient evidence from various papyri to prove that they were conversant with crude arsenic, antimony, copper, copper vitriol, verdigris, lead, lead vitriol, red lead, opium, mandrake and other poisonous substances. This knowledge was probably handed down by oral tradition as part of the priest-craft for centuries before it was committed to writing.

Attalus Phylometer, the last King of Pergamus, is said to have studied the poisonous properties of plants and to have been acquainted with aconite, hemlock, henbane and hellebore.

The earliest known record of the actual preparation of a substance for lethal purposes, is mentioned in an Egyptian papyrus preserved in the Louvre in which the following sentence occurs ; as translated by Duteuil : " Pronounce not the name of I.A.O. under the penalty of the peach."* The Egyptians were probably the first people to practice the art of distillation and so discovered that from the kernels of the peach they could extract that powerful poison which we now call prussic acid. We know that peach stones contain 2.85 per cent of amygdalin, which in the presence of emulsion and water, breaks up into prussic acid and other compounds.

The Hebrews in ancient times were also acquainted with poisonous substances. Crude arsenic was known to them as " Sam ", aconite as " Boschka ", and they are also said to have known of the poisonous properties of ergot which they called " Son ".

The only mention of poison being used for the purpose of suicide in the Bible, occurs in the apochryphal book of Maccabees in which the following is recorded concerning Ptolemeus that was called Macrom :

" Whereupon being accused of (the king's) friends before Eupator and called traitor at every word, because he had left Cyprus that Philometor had committed unto him, and departed to Antiochus Epiphanes, and seeing that he was in no honourable

*I.A.O. is believed to represent Jah the ancient Hebrew name for God.

place, he was so discouraged that he poisoned himself and died."*

Coming to times of early culture in Greece, we find the knowledge of poisonous substances had considerably increased. The ancient Greeks knew of arsenic in the form of realgar and orpiment, also antimony, mercury, gold, silver, copper and lead and probably had a knowledge of their properties, as they recommended hot oil as an antidote in a case of poisoning and mention other means to promote vomiting and preventing poison being absorbed into the system.

Of the vegetable poisons known and used by the Greeks, hemlock appears to have been chiefly employed. They looked upon suicide under certain conditions as a noble act, and sanctioned the use of the poison-cup by those who desired to terminate their existence on earth. They also employed poison as a means of execution. The State Poison was chiefly composed of a species of hemlock called cicuta, the seeds of which were pounded in a mortar as the first step in preparation. Several of the early historians, including Plato, describe the action of the plant used, but its identification has long been a matter of dispute. From all accounts the poison draught does not appear to have been either very powerful or rapid in its action, as a second dose was often required before it proved fatal.

At the death of Phocion it is recorded that " having drunk all the hemlock juice, the quantity was found insufficient and the executioner refused to prepare more unless he was paid twelve drachmas." When Seneca wished to end his life, a friend and physician, at his request, procured for him some of the Athenian State Poison, but when he took it the effect was inadequate.

The circumstances attending the death of Socrates, which happened in the year 402 B.C., are thus recounted by Plato :

" When the fatal cup was brought, he asked what it was necessary for him to do. ' Nothing more,' replied the servant of the judges, ' than as soon as you have drunk of the draught, to walk about until you find your legs become weary and afterwards lie down upon your bed.'

" He took the cup without any emotion or change in his countenance and, looking at him in a steady and assured manner:

" ' Well ! ' said he, ' what say you of this drink ? '

" ' May a libation be made out of it ? '

" Upon being told that there was only enough for one dose, ' At least,' said he, ' we may pray to the gods as is our duty and implore them to make our exit from this world and our last stage happy, which is what I most ardently beg of them.'

*II Maccabees, chap. X, ver. 13.

" Having spoken these words he remained silent for some time and then drank off the whole draught.

" After reproving his friends for indulging in loud lamentations, he continued to walk about as he had been directed until he found his legs grow weary. Then he lay down upon his back and the person who had administered the poison went up to him and examined for a little time his feet and legs, and then squeezing his foot strongly, asked whether he felt him ? Socrates replied that he did not. He then did the same to his legs, and proceeding upwards in this way, showed us that he was cold and stiff, and he afterwards approached him and said to us that when the effect of the poison reached the heart Socrates would depart. And now the lower parts of his body were cold, when he uncovered himself and said, which were his last words : ' Crito, we owe Æsculapius a cock. Pay the debt and do not forget it.'

" ' It shall be done,' replied Crito. ' But consider whether you have anything else to say.'

" Socrates answered in the negative, but was in a short time convulsed. The man then uncovered him ; his eyes were fixed and when Crito observed this, he closed his eyelids and his mouth."

The poison, which is given the general name of φάρμακον by Plato, is termed κώνειον by Xenophon in relating the execution of Theramenes, whose death occurred but forty years after Socrates. The same word is again used by Plutarch in describing the State Poison by which Phocion fell a victim to the Athenians in the year B.C. 317.

Aristophanes, who was contemporary with Socrates, furnishes further evidence that the State Poison was commonly known in Athens by the name κώνειον, for in " The Frogs," which was acted many years before his death, the following allusion to the poison occurs :

HERCULES : Then there is a short and beaten road—that by the mortar.

BACCHUS : Speakest thou of hemlock, then ?

HERCULES : Most certainly.

BACCHUS : A journey cold and winterly forsooth, for it immediately congeals the shins.

Pliny and the other Latin authors use the word cicuta when alluding to the State Poison of the Greeks. Dioscorides (*circa* A.D. 40) in his work on Materia Medica, describing the cicuta, says it has a knotted stem and likens it to fennel. " Its branches shoot with umbels at their summits, while it bears a whitish flower with a heavy smell and a fruit like that of anise, but whiter." From this it was evidently an umbelliferous plant. Pliny refers to the spots on the stem, which further identifies the plant as the *Conium maculatum*, or hemlock.

According to Sibthorpe, *Conium maculatum* grows in various parts of Greece and in the vicinity of Athens, and no other poisonous umbelliferous plant grows in that country.

In addition to this, Pliny states that the cicuta (described by him as the Athenian State Poison) grows in Attica and at Megara, and describes the seeds and leaves as particularly fatal when drunk in wine, the former producing the most deadly effects.

This seems conclusive evidence that the cicuta of the Greeks was the plant we know as *Conium maculatum*.

The clinical effects of the drug as graphically described by Plutarch are identical with those produced by conium or hemlock. He mentions the coldness of the extremities, concluding with its influence on the brain, which would account for the strangeness of the last words of Socrates, referring to a sacrifice to the deity who presided over the Medical Art.

It is probable that opium was sometimes combined with hemlock, judging from the statement of Theophrastus, who was born only twenty-eight years after the death of Socrates.

He says : " Thrasyas, the Mantinian, stated that by making use of the juices of cicuta, the poppy and such other things, he had discovered a substance which occasioned death easily and without pain, and so portable and minute that the weight of a δραχμή (about sixty grains) was sufficient and absolutely irremediable."

For the effects of this compound there is absolutely no cure, and it will keep any length of time without losing its virtue at all. He used to gather his hemlock, not just anywhere, but at Susa, or some other cold and shady spot ; and so too with the other ingredients. His pupil Alexias was also clever and no less skilful than his master, being also versed in the science of medicine generally.

" At last Eudemus, the vendor of drugs, who had a high reputation in his business, after making a wager that he would experience no effect before sunset, drank quite a moderate dose, and it proved too strong for his power of resistance : while the Chian Eudemus took a draught of hellebore and was not purged. And on one occasion he said that in a single day he took two and twenty draughts in the market-place as he sat at his stall, and did not leave the place till it was evening, and then he went home and had a bath and dined, and was not sick. However, this man was able to hold out because he had provided himself with an antidote ; for he said that after the seventh dose he took a draught of tart vinegar with pumice-stone dust in it, and later on took a draught of the same in wine in like manner ;

and that the virtue of the pumice-stone dust is so great that if one puts it into a boiling pot of wine it causes it to cease to boil, not merely for the moment, but altogether, clearly because it has a drying effect and it catches the vapour and passes it off. It was by this antidote that Eudemus was able to contain himself in spite of the large quantity of hellebore which he took."

That a powerful preparation, certain in effect, was required at the time of the death of Socrates, is evident from the caution of the executioner, who states that none of the contents of the cup could be spared. Judging from all accounts, and the evidence afforded by the description of its action, there seems little doubt that the Athenian State Poison consisted of hemlock, probably in the form of the concentrated juice expressed from the leaves, to which a proportion of poppy juice was added to render its action more certain.

A curious custom prevailed among the ancient inhabitants of the island of Ceos in which poison played a part. When the old men found they were no longer of service to the State and began to feel life a burden, they assembled at a banquet of death and, with their heads crowned with chaplets, cheerfully drained the poison-cup. A relic of this early custom was once practised at Marseilles, where a poison was kept by the public authorities, of which hemlock was an ingredient. A dose of this was allowed by the magistrates to anyone who could bring a sufficient reason why he should deserve death. Valerius Maximus observes : " This custom came from Greece, particularly from the island of Ceos, where I saw an example of it in a woman of great quality who, having lived very happy ninety years, obtained leave to die in this way, lest by living longer she should happen to see a change of her good fortune."

The reputed poisonous property of bull's blood is recorded by various ancient writers, and it is stated that Æson, Midas King of Phrygia, Plutarch and Themistocles the Athenian leader employed it as a means of suicide. It is probable that some strong poisonous vegetable substance such as cicuta was mixed with it.

The symptoms and signs which were accepted in early times as evidence of poisoning, are sufficiently crude to inspire us with considerable doubt as to the reliability of many of the stories narrated. That there were certain post-mortem appearances which were generally considered as evidence of death by poison is recorded by Cicero, Tacitus and other early writers. In the account given by Suetonius of the death of Germanicus, who was poisoned by Piso at the instance of Tiberius, they are enumerated as " livid spots on the face and body, and foam at the mouth." It was further generally believed that worms could not generate in the bodies of persons who had died from the effects of poison.

Dioscorides throws a further light on the poisons of antiquity in his work on Materia Medica, which for fifteen centuries or more remained the chief authority on that subject. He mentions cantharides, and copper, mercury, lead and arsenic among the mineral substances.

The animal poisons include toads, salamanders, poisonous snakes, a peculiar kind of honey, and the blood of the ox, probably used after it had decomposed. The sea-hare is frequently alluded to by the ancient Greeks, and was evidently regarded by them as capable of producing a very powerful poison. Domitian is said to have administered it to Titus. It is supposed to have been one of the genus Aplysia, among the gasteropods, and is described by the old writers as a " dreadful object which was neither to be touched nor looked upon with safety."

The poisonous plants enumerated by Dioscorides include the poppy, black and white hellebore, henbane, mandragora, hemlock, elaterium, the juices of a species of euphorbia and apocynae. The black and white hellebore were known to the Romans and used by them as an insecticide, and Pliny states that the Gauls used a preparation of veratrum to poison their arrows. Although arsenic, in the form of the native realgar and orpiment, was employed by the Greeks as a caustic and for removing hair from the face, no mention is made of it being used internally or as a poison. Copper, mercury, and lead were also used in medical treatment.

The study of poisons was forbidden in the early Christian era, and Galen mentions the fact that only a few philosophers dared treat the subject in their works.

Theophrastus states that the poison of most subtle operation of his time was extracted from wolf's bane (aconite) ; no antidote had been discovered to this poison and it was a capital crime to have in one's possession the plant from which it was extracted. He tells us that in Ethiopia " there grows a certain deadly root, with which the people smear their arrows," and " In Scythia there are others some of which kill at once those who eat them, some after an interval shorter or longer, so that in the latter case men have a lingering death."

Livy records that about 200 B.C. several persons of distinction died in a mysterious way in Rome. At first it was thought that they had succumbed to plague, but Quintus Fabius Maximus is said to have been informed by a female slave, that the persons had been poisoned and that she could reveal the names of the guilty. The matter was laid before the Consuls and the Senate. The stipulated pardon was granted, and, guided by the slave, the officers of justice are said to have discovered the poisoners, among whom were women belonging to the noblest families of Rome. Twenty in all were seized ; two of them, Cornelia

and Sergia, undertook to speak for the rest, and declared that
the drugs they had prepared were medicinal. They were told
that to prove this, the preparation they had made would be
tried on themselves and to this test they agreed. After drinking
the draughts it is said they all died. One hundred and seventy
more of the noblest ladies of Rome were seized, on similar
information and condemned, and " before that day," says Livy,
" There was never an inquest on poisoning. To mark this
memorable example of what had never been done before, it was
resolved to have a nail driven into the Temple of Jupiter.

" A dictator was appointed for that mystic duty, a master of
the horse, and he drove a nail into the Temple of Jupiter, after
which a stop was put to poisoning for two or three centuries."

Unfortunately, however, in spite of this, the method of taking
life by poisons did not die out but apparently increased and
became frequent in Rome under the early Emperors.

Women, who not only dealt in poisons, but also practised as
poisoners for due reward were common in Rome. Among
these nefarious practitioners in crime was Locusta, who appears
to have been the personification of a fiendish poisoner. She was
a slave who had been condemned to death in a case which had
been proved against her, but her life had been spared in order
that she might be employed as a poisoner in the service of the
State. She appears to have been appointed as a kind of un-
official poisoner-in-ordinary to Nero who took great interest in
her experiments.

One of her duties was to train pupils so that her secrets should
not be lost, and the Emperor encouraged her to add to her
knowledge by experimenting on slaves who were liberally
supplied for the purpose.

She is said to have been commissioned by Agrippina to kill
the Emperor Claudius, and was instructed to prepare a poisonous
dish which was to have a gradual effect. It was to be so compounded that it would destroy the Emperor's reason, lest in the
course of his proposed illness he should take measures to
supplant Nero by Britannicus. Locusta undertook to fulfil this
commission and the dish took the form of prepared mushrooms
of which the Emperor was particularly fond. He was taken ill
shortly after eating them and had to be carried from the table,
but as this was an incident that often occurred after his dinner,
little notice was taken of it. His physician gave him an emetic
and he was recovering, but when Agrippina heard of it she at
once sent for Locusta and commanded her to use something
stronger. She then prepared a poisoned feather and under the
pretence of applying it to his throat to induce further vomiting,
she introduced a lethal dose and completed her infamous work.

To Locusta also is attributed the murder of Britannicus whom
Nero wished to remove from his path. It is stated that by threats

and blows she was compelled to prepare a powerful poisonous draught in his presence. According to Suetonius, it was first tried on a kid but the animal survived five hours. She was then ordered to make it stronger which she did by boiling it, until it was powerful enough to kill a pig. According to the story, the crime was committed when Britannicus was dining with his brother and the Imperial family, when, as was the custom, hot water was brought round by slaves to the table, the water being heated to varied degrees to suit the taste of the drinker. The cup handed to Britannicus was purposely made too hot and he handed it back to the slave to be made cooler. This presented the opportunity to add the fatal dose, for no sooner had he swallowed the draught than he fell back gasping for breath.

His mother, Agrippina and Octavia his sister became terror-stricken, but Nero unmoved calmly remarked, that he often had such fits in his youth without danger and the meal proceeded.

There is a curious tradition that has survived from ancient times, that if a body rapidly decomposes after sudden death, the individual has succumbed to poison ; thus it is recorded that when Britannicus died, the Romans attempted to conceal his discoloured face by the use of paint, no doubt to prevent rumours spreading that he had been poisoned.

The poisonous properties of certain fungi were known in Roman times, as Nicander refers to them as the " evil fermentations of the earth," and recommends vinegar and alkaline carbonates as antidotes.

With regard to the knowledge of powerful poisons of rapid action at this period it is recorded that during the reign of Tiberius, a Roman noble accused of high treason swallowed a poison and immediately fell dead at the feet of the senators.

CHAPTER IV

POISONS USED BY THE PERSIANS, HINDUS AND CHINESE IN ANCIENT TIMES

In the early ages the knowledge of poisonous substances appears to have been more general among Eastern races than among nations in the West.

The Persians in ancient times are said to have studied with care the art of poisoning. Plutarch and Ctesias relate that Queen Parysatis, the mother of Cyrus the younger, during the reign of Artaxerxes II (405-359 B.C.), poisoned her daughter-in-law Statira by means of a knife, one side of the blade being smeared with venom. A bird was set before the two queens at supper and was divided by the poisoned knife ; Parysatis ate her half with impunity, but Statira died. Such is the story, but there is no evidence to corroborate it. The Carthaginians were apparently also skilled in the art of poisons, and it is related that they killed Regulus, the Roman general, by this means.

With reference to the use of poisons in Persia the poet Nizámi in his *Treasury of Secrets*, relates a story of rivalry between two court physicians which finally reached such a point that they challenged one another to a duel or ordeal by poison. It was agreed that each should take a poison supplied by his antagonist, of which he should then endeavour to counteract the effects by a suitable antidote. The first prepared a poisonous draught " the fierceness of which would have melted black stone " ; his rival drained the cup and at once took an antidote which rendered it innocuous. It was now his turn, and he picked a rose from the garden, breathed an incantation over it, and bade his antagonist smell it, whereupon the latter at once fell down dead. That his death was due simply to fear and not to any poisonous or magical property of the rose is clearly indicated by the poet :

" Through this rose which the spell-breather had given him
Fear overmastered the foe and he gave up the ghost.
That one by treatment expelled the poison from his body,
While this one died of a rose from fear."

An incident which happened to the army led by Mark Antony against the Parthians, and described by Plutarch, is said to have been caused by aconite. At one time during the expedition, the soldiers, being very short of provisions, sought for roots and pot-herbs and found some that brought on madness and death. " The eater immediately lost all memory and would busy himself in turning over every stone he met with, as if on some important pursuit. The camp was full of unhappy men digging up and removing stones, till at last they were carried off by bilious vomiting. Whole numbers perished, and the Parthians still continued to harass them. Antony is said to have frequently exclaimed : ' Oh ! the ten thousand ! ' alluding to the army which Xenophon led in retreat both a longer way and through more numerous conflicts and yet led in safety."

There is a story told of Alexander the Great that after crossing the Cydenus, he was seized with a fever and was warned by Parmenio in a letter not to take the medicine which his physician offered to him for fear of poison. The physician's name was Philip, and Alexander so trusted him that he gave him the letter to read, scanning his face meanwhile. The calm air of the physician satisfied the ailing conqueror and assured him that he might safely drink the potion.

Strabo says that in the march of Alexander's army through the country of Gedrasia in India, " many beasts of burden were lost from having eaten a plant resembling the laurel or bay."

The death of Alexander the Great, like that of many other rulers, is ascribed by some historians to poison, but from Littré's investigations it would appear that the great Emperor, debilitated by his drinking habits, contracted malarial fever in the marshes round Babylon and died after an illness of eleven days.

In India and the Far East, poisons have been used from very early times, not only for the destruction of human life, but also for destroying animals. Arsenic, aconite, opium and many other poisonous mineral and vegetable substances were employed for this purpose.

The Hindus have many curious traditions concerning poisons, and like the Western nations, attribute to some the property of causing a lingering death which can be controlled by the will of the poisoner. The knowledge of the substances employed is guarded with great secrecy and even now are not fully known. Blyth mentions a mysterious substance known in India, called *Mucor phycomyces*, which is said to be a species of fungus. When the spores are administered in warm water they are said to attach themselves to the throat and speedily develop and grow, with the result that in a few weeks the respiratory organs are attacked and the victim is rapidly carried off as if by a fatal disease. Nine active or virulent poisonous substances are mentioned by the ancient writers on Hindu medicine. Some of them are at present still unidentified while others, there appears to be little doubt, were varieties of aconite, opium, *cannabis indica datura stramonium*, the roots of *nerium odorum* and *gloriosa superba*; the milky juices of *calatropis gigantea* and *euphorbia neriifolia* are also mentioned, together with arsenic (orpiment) and snake-venom.

Besides these, many other plants with poisonous properties have been known to the Hindus for centuries past. The roots and leaves of the Indian Oleander (*nerium odorum*), a plant with beautiful and attractive flowers which is found growing at an altitude of 6500 feet in the Himalayas, contain a powerful poisonous principle which has a rapid action on the heart. The root of the climbing lily (*gloriosa superba*) yields a poisonous alkaloid allied to colchicine, which has caused death within four hours. The deadly nightshade and henbane are both to be found growing in India and the leaves of the latter in some districts are smoked like ganja for their narcotic effects.

Aconite, of which various species are common in India, was originally used as an arrow-poison or placed in the drinking pools to kill animals. Nux vomica is also largely distributed in the country from the seeds of which strychnine and brucine are obtained.

The attractive scarlet seeds of the jequirity (*abrus precatorius*) popularly known as prayer-beads, contain a poisonous principle whose action is similar to snake-venom.

There are many other poisonous plants known to the natives in addition to those mentioned, including the *cleisanthus collinus*, all the parts of which are deadly but especially the capsule. A couple of the fruits have been known to cause death in four or five hours.

Most of the early Sanscrit manuscripts are written on paper prepared with orpiment (arsenic) to preserve them from the ravages of insects.

The three varieties of datura that yield atropine are said to have formerly been employed in India for putting an end to domestic quarrels. To this practice may be traced the origin of Suttee or widow-burning, as the Brahmins found from experience that by making a wife's life co-terminous with that of her husband, the average husband lived longer. The diamond had a reputation as a poison among the Hindus. When prepared by roasting seven times in a furnace and reducing it to powder, it was also used medicinally as a tonic in doses of one grain.

Both the Chinese and Japanese, from early times down to the present day, have studied the action of poisons.

The Chou Ritual, which is said to date from 246 B.C. and which still exists under the title of " The Chou Ritual, Chou li," contains a detailed account of the State medical service which comprised five departments. Among the medicaments used by its members was a group called Five Poisons (*wu tu*). They cannot all be identified but they appear to have included cinnabar (mercury), realgar (arsenic), green vitriol (copper sulphate), and loadstone.

According to a commentator,* they were heated together in an earthenware crucible for three days and nights. The fumes arising therefrom were then caught on a bunch of feathers. The compounds thus collected probably consisted of the sulphides of mercury and arsenic, and were used externally.

The Chinese are said to have employed gold leaf for suicidal purposes from a time of great antiquity and until recent times, when a high official put an end to his life, it was officially announced that he had " taken gold-leaf."

At the time of the death of the Emperor Kwang Su, the cause of which was enveloped in mystery, it was rumoured that he did not die from natural causes but committed suicide by request. For some time previous to his death it is said that the Emperor had led a miserable existence and was simply a ruler in name. The Dowager-Empress Tzu Hsi had resolved that her nephew should precede her to the tomb. She therefore convoked the Grand Council and as a result of this conclave, it was announced that Kwang Su was dangerously ill from heart disease, but the offers of the foreign legations to send their medical officers for his relief were firmly declined.

According to the story, " at ten o'clock next morning the Chief Eunuch with two confidential attendants, entered the Little Palace where the Emperor was confined, and after ordering everybody to leave the room, he declared to Kwang Su that the Empress was dying and that it was needful for him to predecease her.

" He then deposited on a table, pills of opium, a packet of gold-leaf and some yellow silk plaited cord, promising to return in three hours time. He told the Emperor that if he found that neither the opium or the gold-leaf had been used, it would be his painful duty to strangle him with the silken cord. Meanwhile, the two executioners would watch the door of the room." It should be explained that to cause death, a piece of fine gold-leaf is placed over the lips and the breath being deeply drawn inwards, it passes into the throat and obstructs the glottis thereby causing suffocation.

" When the Chief Eunuch returned at one o'clock he found the opium pills had disappeared and Kwang Su stretched unconscious on his couch but still breathing. It was stated, that he died at five o'clock and the three-year-old Pou Yi was at once brought to the Imperial Palace and proclaimed Emperor."

* *Pestilence and Leechcraft in Ancient China.* W. P. Yetts.

The Japanese are said to import from China certain powerful poisons prepared by the Chinese medicine-men, the secret of which is only known to them. They are thought to be a mixture of both animal and mineral poisons as they have a very deadly effect though their exact composition is unknown.

CHAPTER V

ANCIENT ANTIDOTES TO POISON—EARLY LAWS AND REGULATIONS RESPECTING POISONS

SOON after man discovered the properties of poisonous substances he began to seek for some means to prevent their fatal action and counteract their effects. He also sought to find protection against the bites of venomous reptiles, animals and mad dogs and doubtless experimented with drugs for this purpose. Homer (900 B.C.) in the " Odyssey " in his account of Ulysses' men, alludes to a plant which Hermes recommended him to take when he set out to rescue his followers :

" Then take the antidote the Gods provide
The plant I give through all the direful power
Shall guard thee and avert the evil hour."

This is supposed to refer to a herb called moli or molu which is frequently mentioned by ancient writers. It is alluded to by Theophrastus, Dioscorides, Pliny and Galen and is thought to have been a species of allium. It is described by some, as a plant having an onion or squill-like odour which was said to grow in Arcadia and Campania.

The Hindus, like other ancient peoples, also had an idea of a general antidote for poisons as expressed by the word " *agada* ".

Apparently the ambition of the early Greek physicians was to discover a universal antidote to all poisons, and many of them devoted years, and spent a great part of their lives in endeavouring to find it.

These antidotes were called by the Greeks alexipharmica or theriacs, the former word being derived from the Greek " alexipharmakos ", meaning that " which keeps off poison " and the noun " antipharmakon ", an antidote. Theriac, which meant something pertaining to poisonous reptiles, eventually became applied to the antidote itself and came to mean a treacle or confection used against poisons generally.

One of the earliest writers on the subject was Nicander of Colophon (185-135 B.C.) who was physician to Attalus, King of Bithynia, under whom he is said to have secured special facilities for studying poisons, being allowed to experiment on condemned criminals. He was an hereditary priest of Apollo of Clarus.

He wrote a great work consisting of a thousand hexameters on Theriaca, dealing with the bites of venomous animals and six hundred hexameters on Alexipharmica, which treats of poisonous substances when swallowed and the use of emetics.

The name Theriaca which was afterwards applied to an actual substance therefore differed from the alexipharmica, which came to be regarded more as a method of treatment. This division was afterwards adopted by all the subsequent writers on the subject, including Dioscorides, Galen, Aetius, Paulus Aegineta, Avicenna and Rhazes.

From the first century, Theriaca was regarded as a very important compound, and in the endeavour to secure the most effective combination for the purpose, the most extraordinary formulæ containing a large number of ingredients, were devised by various physicians. The general treatment recommended by Nicander for the bites of all venomous animals was sucking the wound, applying cupping vessels to it, cauteries and leeches, and afterwards administering stimulating medicines.

Respecting the sucking of a wound, he gives an important injunction that the person who sucks the wound should not be fasting, from which it may be gathered that he was aware of the physiological fact that the vessels absorb more readily when in an empty state.

Nicander's particular remedies were such drugs as birthwort, alkanet, and Theriaca of vipers, which was prepared with a great many aromatic roots and fruits, including ginger, cinnamon, myrrh, iris and gentian.

In his work he mentions twenty-two poisonous substances including aconite (wolf's bane), litharge (lead oxide), buprestis (a beetle resembling cantharides), ceruse (white lead), conium (hemlock), cantharides, hyoscyamus (henbane), ixias (probably a species of chameleon), coagulated milk, sea-hare, poppy (opium), pharicum (probably a composition of agaric), the red toad and marsh frog, the salamander, bull's blood, taxus (yew), and toxicum (an unknown poison). As general antidotes he recommends warm oil, warm water and mallow or linseed tea to excite vomiting.

From this list we have some idea of the knowledge of poisons in the second century before the Christian era. Most of the substances enumerated are of vegetable or animal origin, few of the soluble mineral poisons being known at that time.

Galen noticed that opium after being dissolved in a small quantity of wine, produced stronger effects than when given alone, and that when a larger draught of wine was given, it proved an antidote by counteracting the narcotic powers of the opium. He states that he once cured a person reduced to the last stage of coma by the administration of strong wine.

Dioscorides also dealt very largely with this subject, and, like

Nicander directs that " the person who sucks the poisoned wound be not fasting and that he shall keep some oil in his mouth." The wound was then to be fomented with a sponge and scarified or cut out, a method on which there is no improvement at the present time. Cauterization with fire is another method which Dioscorides recommends, and for the bite of a venomous serpent known to be deadly, he advises immediate amputation to save life.

According to Pliny and Galen, the formula for the first Theriaca against the bites of all venomous animals was inscribed in verse on a stone in the temple of Asklepios on the island of Cos. It contained wild thyme, opoponax, aniseed, fennel, parsley, meum and ammi. These were to be beaten up with meal of fitches (*ervum ervilla*), passed through a sieve, kneaded with wine, cut into lozenges of the weight of half a denarius (30 grammes), one to be placed in three cyathi (about five ounces) of wine and swallowed.

The next Theriaca in antiquity was that originated by Antiochus III, King of Syria and Babylon, who flourished about 223 B.C. He is said to have devised a preparation that rendered a person proof against the bites of all venomous animals and reptiles except the asp.

Mithridates VI, King of Pontus in Asia Minor (120-63 B.C.), who is said to have lived in constant apprehension of being poisoned by his enemies, then began to study the subject. In order to render himself immune, he devised an antidote which he took together with small doses of poisonous substances daily, and thus believed he had made himself poison-proof. The formula for this antidote, which was called Mithridatum, he committed to writing and kept it strictly guarded. He carried on warfare with the Romans for many years but was finally defeated by Pompey, and not wishing to fall into the hands of his enemies put an end to his life. After the conquest, Pompey is said to have captured the coveted formula which he discovered among the secret papers of the king.

Mithridatum was found to consist of fifty-four ingredients and was prepared in the form of a confection or electuary. Judging from the numerous drugs it contained it was more likely to harm than to heal or protect the individual who took it.

Pliny throws a light on some of the poisons known to Mithridates and mentions " the blood of a duck found in a certain district of Pontus, which was supposed to live on poisonous food, and the blood of this duck was afterwards used in the preparation of the Mithridatum, because it fed on poisonous plants and suffered no harm."

Another antidote is attributed to Zopyros, a Greek physician of Alexandria who lived about 80 B.C. He called it " Ambrosia " and it contained frankincense, galbanum, pepper, and other aromatics made into a confection with boiled honey. A piece the size of an Egyptian bean was directed to be swallowed washed down with a draught of wine.

Equally celebrated at a later period, was the Theriaca of Philon of Tarsus who flourished in the early part of the first century of the Christian era. He also recorded his formula in symbolic Greek verse. Galen states that Philon's Theriaca had a great reputation for a long time and was one of the most famous preparations of its kind.

It contained such curious substances as " the red hair of a lad whose blood had been shed on the fields of Mercury," which was possibly symbolic language for suffering, and certain drugs the names of which are disguised in mystic terms. The whole of the mixture was to be made into a conserve with " the work of the Daughters of the Bull of Athens " which is supposed to mean Attic honey.

The Theriaca Philonium survived over 1,700 years and has an interesting history. It passed into many of the pharmacopœias of Europe, remaining in the *London Pharmacopœia* from 1618 until 1746, when it was composed of opium, pepper, ginger, caraway, syrup, honey and wine. Until 1746 it was called " Philonium Romanum," but its name was afterwards changed to " Philonium Londonense," and syrup of poppies was substituted for the honey. It is probable that this mixture was originally intended as a remedy for a peculiar form of colic which became epidemic in Rome when Philon flourished there. Philon's formula formed the basis of what was afterwards known as Confection of Opium which remained in the *London Pharmacopœia* until 1867.

The Theriaca which eclipsed all others in fame and popularity however, was that originated by Andromachus, physician to Nero (A.D. 37-68). So greatly did the Emperor appreciate his physician's efforts to devise a universal antidote, that he raised him to the dignity of Archiatrus. The Theriaca of Andromachus was claimed to be an improvement on that of Mithridates, until then the greatest antidote in Roman pharmacy. He added vipers to the compound and called his Theriaca " *Galene*", because " those who had been poisoned or bitten by some venomous creature were cured by its use and made tranquil." Like other physicians of his time, Andromachus wrote his formula and described its virtues in Greek verse, which he dedicated to Nero. He claimed that it would " counteract all poisons and bites of venomous animals and that it would also relieve all pain, weakness of the stomach, asthma, difficulty of breathing, phthisis, colic, jaundice, dropsy, weakness of sight, inflammation of the bladder and kidneys, and plague." The dose was a piece as large as a broad bean, which was to be taken in the morning or if administered in the evening he says : " it will relieve the patient in whom the dark night always increases the suffering and will restore all disturbed functions." It was indeed a panacea for all ills.

Galen states that he tested this antidote by giving it to a number of fowls to which he had first administered a poison. Those to which the Theriaca had been given survived, but all the others died. He says that it resisted poison and venomous bites and cured a great many diseases. The original formula contained no less than seventy-three ingredients, including dried vipers the preparation of which he describes in detail. The vipers were to be chosen and caught in the spring or autumn; their heads, tails and skin being removed, they were to be soaked in salt and water then cooked, and after the flesh had been separated from the bones, the former was to be mixed with bread crumbs then made into small lozenges and dried. This remarkable concoction remained in popular use throughout the Middle Ages and is still made and sold in the pharmacies in Italy and also in the drug bazaars of Constantinople and other cities in the Near East.

About the year A.D. 50 the Theriaca of Damocrates became famous. This was similar to the compound of Andromachus, the formula for which Damocrates, a Greek physician then living in Rome, translated into verse. Other formulæ were originated by Nicolaus of Salerno, Amando, Arnauld and Abano, each of whom added something to the original formula. These preparations may be said to have reached their zenith in the sixteenth century when Pietro Andrea Matthiolus, the commentator of Dioscorides, published another formula which consisted of no less than *two hundred and fifty* separate substances including dried vipers, pearls, red coral and emeralds. This formula in a modified form was included in the *London Pharmacopœia* of 1618 and remained an official remedy until 1746.

Several cities became celebrated for the manufacture of Theriaca, including Cairo, Constantinople, Florence, Genoa, Bologna and Venice. The Theriaca of Venice or Treacle as it was called, which contained sixty-one ingredients, had a reputation throughout Europe and was included in the *London Pharmacopœia* down to 1746. In Bologna, the mixing of the Theriaca was carried out with great ceremony in the courtyard of the ancient Archiginnasio in the presence of the chief officials of the city. The ingredients were mixed under the supervision of the medical professors of the University to ensure of it being faithfully and properly compounded. From the fourteenth to the seventeenth century it was regarded as a remedy for plague and was used in great quantities. Evelyn, in his Diary, March 23, 1646, thus alludes to the Theriaca of Venice :

" Having packed up my purchases of books, pictures, casts, treacle, etc. (the making and extraordinary ceremony whereof

I had been curious to observe, for it is extremely pompous and worth seeing) I departed from Venice."

The great consumption of this medicament in the sixteenth century is evidenced by Morgan, Apothecary to Queen Elizabeth, who in a pamphlet insists that a product that he had made had been compared with other "theriacle" brought from Constantinople and Venice and had been commended.

"It is very lamentable to consider," he writes, "that straungers doe dayly send into England a false and naughty kinde of Mithridatium and Threacle in great barrelles more than a thousand weight in a year, and vtter ye same at a lowe price for 3*d*., and 4*d*. a pound, to ye great hurt of Her Majesties subjects and no small gaine to straungers purses."

In 1612, it is recorded that the Master and Wardens of the Grocers' Company of London marked that "a filthy and unwholesome baggage composition was being brought into this Realm as Tryacle of Genoa, made only of the rotten garble and refuse outcast of all kinds of spices and drugs, hand overhead with a little filthy molasses and tarre to worke it up withal." This was communicated to the College of Physicians, and they set about not only to devise their own formula, but to superintend its manufacture, which was then entrusted to William Besse, an apothecary in the Poultry. Besse was made to take a "corporal oath" before the Lord Mayor, and every year when he made the confection had to show the ingredients and the product to the College of Physicians. His treacle was sold at not above 2*s*. 8*d*. per lb. or 2*d*. per ounce.

Later, in the seventeenth century, Theriaca was officially made in public by the Society of Apothecaries at their house in Water Lane. According to their records, in "1772, five hundred pounds of Venicc Treacle publicly made and potted, was sealed with the Company's Seal."

The use, however, of this medicament in Great Britain goes back to a much earlier period. It was recommended to Alfred the Great by Helia, the Patriarch of Jerusalem, according to an Anglo-Saxon MS. of the eleventh century. It is again mentioned by Foucher de Chartres in 1124, who states it was used in the first Crusade. It is recorded in a Close Roll of King John in 1208, and a "triacle box du pere apelle une Hakette garniz d'or" is mentioned amongst the precious effects of Henry V.

Prosper Alpinus, a famous physician of Padua, who travelled in Egypt in 1591, refers to the manufacture of Theriaca in Cairo and states that it was only allowed to be made in public, and that the ceremony was performed once a year in the Mosque of Morestan by the chief apothecary of the city in the presence of all the physicians. He states that at that time Italians, Germans, Poles, Flemings, Englishmen and Frenchmen came to Cairo to purchase this true Theriaca.

Much more might be written describing the making of this ancient and interesting medicament, which has a literature of its own, but it will be sufficient to quote one more account from the Regulations and Statutes of Montpellier, where the compounding was also carried out with great ceremony.

According to a report by Laurens Catelan, Master Apothecary in Ordinary to Monseigneur the Prince of Condé, it was required that the preparation should be made in public in the presence of the very illustrious professors of the famous Faculty of Medicine, so that they might have the opportunity of censuring or approving the ingredients, and that the public might therefore be sure of the virtue of these important medicines. In the old pharmacies in Italy to-day, large marble vases capable of holding from fifty to sixty pounds are still to be found in which the Theriaca is kept.

It may well be asked what was the rationale of administering these extraordinary compounds which survived for centuries. All that can be said is, that these complex mixtures of gums, balsams and aromatic substances would probably have some antiseptic action on the alimentary canal and internal organs. They were generally directed to be given with wine which would aid their action and, at any rate, would produce a reviving and stimulating effect on the individual, but no real antidotal properties can be ascribed to them.

The search for antidotes to poison was not confined entirely to the Old World, for according to the *Carolina Gazette* of May 9, 1750, the General Assembly, the Governing Body of the Colony, authorized the publication of " Nigger Caeser's cure for poison." The General Assembly had purchased Nigger Caeser's freedom, who was apparently a slave, and granted him £100 a year for life as the price of his formula, which consisted of roots of plantain and wild hore-hound, 3 oz. boiled together in 2 quarts of water down to 1 quart and strained. Of this, one-third was to be given every morning fasting for three consecutive mornings. Certain dieting was also required, and it is stated that if in the three days' treatment no benefit had resulted, it was a sign that the patient had either not been poisoned at all or had been by such poisons as Caeser's antidote would not remedy.

Judging from the earliest laws on record, criminal poisoning does not appear to have been common amongst the ancient Egyptians or Hebrews. The first law against criminal poisoning was passed by Sulla in Rome in the year 82 B.C. and it continued in force until the fall of the Empire. The penalty was confiscation of property and exile or exposure to wild beasts.

One of Cicero's finest orations was his defence of Cluentius, who was charged with poisoning in 66 B.C.

In the time of Justinian (A.D. 483-565) the aid of the physician was called in specially during the investigation of crime. Accord-

ing to the institutes or laws of that period, those who by odious
arts, whether by poison or by " magical whispers " (incanta-
tions), took away the life of another, were punished with death.
A contract for the sale of a poison was also held to be void
" on the analogy of the contracts of partnership and agency
which have no power to deal with improper matters."

It seems appropriate that the earliest law to regulate the sale of
poisons in mediaeval times should have been enacted in Italy.
Thus as early as 1365, a statute was passed in Siena rendering it
illegal to sell red arsenic or corrosive sublimate to any slave,
freed or otherwise, or to any servant or person under twenty
years of age. These poisons could only be sold to an adult
who was well known to the apothecary. There was also a law
in Perugia in 1378 which enacted that a person could not obtain
a poison without the express permission of a doctor, which
permit should state the purpose for which it was intended to be
used. The statutes of Genoa (1488) amongst other items demanded that in no medicament should substitution be allowed,
or as the statute reads " Ponere quid pro quo " without the
doctor's express permission. The pharmacist was to be careful
that honey was not substituted for sugar, nor that the latter
should serve as a cover for the former, and that he should put
neither rice nor starch in anything composed of sugar, in whole
or in part.

In early times there is little doubt that many people died
from the effects of poison without suspicion. On the other hand
many more succumbed to the sudden effects of latent and un-
recognized diseases, such as aneurism, peritonitis and others, of
which practically nothing was known, whose deaths were wrong-
fully attributed to poison. Before the period of judicial post-
mortem examination, the practice was to expose the bodies for
inspection to those who were believed to be able to form a
sufficiently accurate judgment for themselves as to the cause
of death.

It was believed that poisonous substances had a peculiar
action on the heart and were capable of altering its substance
in such a manner that it resisted the action of a funeral pyre
and remained unconsumed. When the heart resisted the pyre
it was regarded as unmistakable evidence that the person had
perished by poison. If, in addition, the body from any cause
rapidly decomposed, such a sign was at once believed to be
conclusive of death from poison. This belief prevailed to a
greater or lesser extent down to the middle of the seventeenth
century.

CHAPTER VI

PROTECTIVE METHODS EMPLOYED AGAINST POISONING—SACRED SEALED EARTH OR TERRA SIGILLATA — POISON-CUPS — POISON CHARMS— THE TOADSTONE—UNICORN'S HORN—RHINOS- CEROS HORN—ASSAY CUPS—BEZOAR STONES

AMONG the famous medicaments of antiquity reputed to be effective in counteracting poisons was terra sigillata or " sacred sealed earth," a peculiar clay which originally came from the Isle of Lemnos. Its reputation dates from the time of Herodotus, and it continues in use in Turkey and some parts of the East to-day. This red clay was formerly excavated from the side of a certain hill with great ceremony, in the presence of the principal inhabitants of the island. The ceremony was originally associa- ted with the worship of Diana and was carried out on May 6, each year. This particular earth was not allowed to be dug by anyone on any other day of the year except that formally set apart for the operation.

According to Dioscorides, the clay was made into a paste, with goats' blood, in his time, and the Greeks stamped or sealed the earth with a representation of Diana, one of the goddesses associated with healing, and this seal was regarded as sacred. It had a universal reputation as an antidote to all poisons, and a poisoned liquid drunk from a cup made from the clay was believed to be rendered harmless. The seal was stamped upon it to prove its being genuine.

So great was the demand for the famous Terra Sigillata of Lemnos from the thirteenth to the fifteenth century that many other earths, for which similar properties were claimed, were exploited and recommended in books on medicine of the period. Thus a terra sigillata was made in Cilicia (Silesia), also in several districts of Italy, in Malta and in Palestine. In England a clay was found which was said to have the same properties. It entered into the composition of many important remedies, including the Theriaca of Andromachus, and was regarded generally as being an antidote against all deadly poisons.

An analysis made some years ago showed that terra sigillata was composed of oxides of iron, aluminium, and magnesia, with a proportion of silicates. It was thus an astringent and absorbent earth, its chief virtues probably being, like many other ancient remedies, chiefly due to the mystery surrounding its origin and the superstition connected with its source.*

A curious account of how its value was once tested is recorded in the following grant dated 1580, made by Prince William, the Landgrave of Hesse, to Andreas Bertoldus of Oschatz :

Be it knowen unto all persons, that an honest man called Bertold of Oschatz, came into the presence of the most noble Prince and Lord, the Lord William Landgraue of Hesse Court of Catzenelnbogen Ditz, Ziegenheim and Nidda, etc., our gracious Lord and prince, and in humble manner declared unto him, that hee had found in an olde mine of Golde within the dominion of Schneidnitz, a new kinde of earth, which is a present help and a most notable remedie against all manner of poysons and sundrie diseases, which earth having a stampe upon it he offered to sell unto his Excellencie : who not trusting the man upon his bare worde, committed the matter to his Phisitions Maurice Thauer, and Laurence Hyper : Commanding them to make a perfect tryall of the saide earth, whereupon the saide Doctors in Phisicke to satisfie their Prince, did make a double proffe of the deadliest poysons that might be, which were, Mercurie Sublimate, Aconitum, Nereum and Apocynum, and of some one of these they gave halfe a dramme a peece to eight dogges, to foure of them they gave the earth, after the poyson, and to the other foure the poyson alone : of these foure that tooke it alone, the first that tooke Apocynum : dyed within halfe an houre, the second that had taken Nereum died within foure houres : the third that swallowed Mercurie, died within nine houres after. And although they all did call up some part of the poyson, yet after most cruell tormentes with crampes and trembling they died : the fourth dogge that eat Aconitum, systeyned thirteene great panges of the crampe, so as every man thought hee woulde have died with his fellowes, yet lived he the first day, and having half of the dose of this medicine given him, he thoroughly recovered. The other foure dogges to whom the poysons before named with the like quantities of this Terra Sigillata was given, for three houres after the receiving of it, were very sicke and feeble, especially one of them to whom the double quantitie of Aconitum by negligence was given, vomited thrise : the next day they were all well and did eate their meate greedily, so as there appeared scarse any token of poyson.

* See " Terra Sigillata, a famous Medicament of Ancient Times," C. J. S. Thompson, *Proceedings* 17th *International Congress of Medicine*, London, 1913.

When thus his Highnesse had seene the experience of this earth to bee so present a remedie against such deadly poysons, and that the saide Andreas Bertold had humbly craved his letters of credite, both in the favour of man and advancement of the truth, that others might have knowledge, he denied not to graunt them : But commanded that his letter, testimonial sealed with his Highnesse his privie seale, and subscribed with the handes of the foresaid Doctors, in whose presence this triall was made, should be given unto him. Which we the above named Doctors upon our allegiance to his Highnesse, and for the furtherance of the truth, because we found it as hath beene declared to be true and unseyned, most willingly have done. Given the XXVIII of July, the yeare of our Lorde 1580.

MAURITIUS THAUER, D.
LAURENCIUS HYPERIUS, M.D.
IOHAN KRUG.

Petrus Oponus or Petri de Abano (1250-1303) wrote a work entitled " De Remediis Venenorum " in the thirteenth century, in which he records the following poisons known in his time. He mentions mercury, gypsum, copper, iron rust, magnetite (magnetic stone), lapis lazuli, arsenic sublimate, litharge, lead, realgar, cateputia juice, cucumber juice, usnea, coriander juice, mandragora, poppy, opium, scammony, aconite, oleander juice, hellebore juice, mezereon juice, fool's-parsley, briony, nux vomica, colocynth, laurel berries, poppy, cicuta, serpentary and cantharides.

Certain charms were believed to act as antidotes to poison and the two following quotations are taken from a MS. by Petrus Hispanus (Pope John XXI) in the fourteenth century :

CONTRA VENENUM

" Scribe nota nostra i lamina loctonus ut alio quoque
comodo et lana et dari biber et abent scribi
cum moro ut cumque nio alio nota sit nota et sine
scripta 7 lineis past."

" Zaare. Zaare Zaam, Zaare
Zaare ssleqer Bohorum, nabarayn
Uessally—uessredaza—asseyan—Haurahe
reamue—ayn latinume quene :
draytery, nuyyeri, quibari, yeh ay
hahanny ymkatrum hanitanery vnerym
caruhe tahuene cehue beyne
et Lana cuz aqua . . . dame bibere."

The so-called Toadstone has from early times been reputed
to possess the property of counteracting the effect of poisons.
These stones were believed to be found in the heads of old
toads which, when caught, were placed on a red cloth and the
stone recovered through the mouth. Pomet, who wrote in the
seventeenth century, threw doubt on this source of origin
and states that "toad stones are found in the mountains or
plains, although he would not dispute that they might have been
bred in the heads of old toads." He describes two kinds,
"the round and the long : the former being of a deep grey
inclining to blue ; the long being redder grey with reddish
spots. It is false that they change colour and sweat when they
approach the cup wherein there is poison."

Lemery, a French writer of the same period, in describing
these stones, states that when applied to the sting or bite of
venomous beasts, they draw out the poison. They were usually
set and worn as rings and regarded as of great value. They
were generally mounted so that the back of the stone could
touch the skin, and were said to notify the presence of poison
by producing a sensation of heat in the finger at the point of
contact.

A toadstone ring is described by Jones which he attributes
to the fossil palatal tooth of a species of Ray that is believed
to be a specific in cases of kidney disease when immersed in
water and drunk by the patient. In the inventory of the Duc
de Berry mention is made of a toadstone in a ring of gold, and
similar rings are alluded to in the records of the Duke of Burgundy.

Fenton, writing in 1569, says, " Toadstones being used in
rings, give forewarning of venom " ; and in Ben Jonson's
" Fox " they are referred to as follows :

" Were you enamoured on his copper rings,
    His saffron jewel, with the toadstone in't ? "

Lupton, in his *Thousand Notable Things*, goes as far as to
give a method of obtaining the stone from the toad :

" Put a great or overgrown toad (first bruised in divers
places) into an earthen pot ; put the same into an ants' hillock,
and cover the same with earth, which toad at length the ants
will eat, so that the bones of the toad and stone will be left in
the pot."

Another writer, however, states that the stone should be
obtained while the toad is living, and this may be done by simply
placing him upon a piece of scarlet cloth, " wherewithal they

are much delighted, so that, while they stretch out themselves as it were in sport upon that cloth, they cast out the stone of their head, but instantly they sup it up again, unless it be taken from them through some secret hole in the same cloth."

The scarlet cloth, however, did not always perform this miracle, for Boetius relates how he watched a whole night an old toad he had laid on a red cloth to see him cast forth the stone, but the toad was stubborn, and left him nothing to gratify the great pangs of his whole night's restlessness.

The Londesborough Collection included a specimen of a toadstone ring described as being of metal gilt, having upon it the figure of a toad swallowing a serpent. Another set with a large greyish-brown stone mounted in silver bears an inscription on the inside of the ring, " God cureth me."

According to an inventory of the jewels belonging to Mary Queen of Scots at Fotheringhay in 1586, there was " a little silver bottle containing a Stone medicinable against poison."

The so-called horn of the unicorn, which was in reality the tusk of the Narwhal, has been associated with mysterious properties since the time of Aristotle, Pliny and other ancient writers. Ctesias (about 390 B.C.) was the first to record the wonderful properties attributed to it. " Drinking vessels," he says, " were made of the horn and those who used them were protected against poisons, convulsions and epilepsy, provided that, just before or just after taking poison, they drank wine or water from the cup made from it. Other writers declared that poisoned wounds could be cured by merely holding the horn of the unicorn close to the wound.

These horns were considered of great value and in the Middle Ages are said to have been worth about ten times the price of gold. In 1553, a unicorn's horn was brought to the King of France which was valued at £20,000 sterling, and one presented to Charles I, supposed to be the largest then known, measured seven feet long and weighed 13 lb.

Edward IV gave to the Duke of Burgundy a gold cup set with jewels, with a piece of unicorn's horn worked into the metal ; and one large horn in the possession of the City of Dresden was valued at 75,000 thalers. A piece of this horn was occasionally sawn off to be used for medicinal purposes, and it was a city regulation that two persons of princely rank should be present whenever this operation was performed.

In the sixteenth century these horns were so rare that Dr. Racq, a physician of Florence, recorded that a German merchant sold one of them to the Pope for 4,000 livres. Ambròise Paré wrote a treatise on the unicorn's horn and its remedial properties, and Thomas Bartholinus published a work entitled : " Observations on the Unicorn Horn " in 1678, which dealt with its medicinal uses only.

Although it was considered of such great value, the horn was utilized for making goblets mounted in gold, and walking sticks, to which were ascribed remarkable virtues, the greatest of which, according to writers on natural history of the time, was its " resistance to all manner of poysons."

Before the seventeenth century the genuine unicorn's horn was supposed to be black or dark in colour, and Boetius de Boodt records that he saw a horn in Venice at the close of the sixteenth century which was said to be a genuine unicorn horn, but he believed it to be that of a gazelle. However, in the seventeenth century it came to be universally agreed that the genuine unicorn's horns were long, and of an ivory-like colour, tapering towards the tip with curling staves. Several of these horns are still kept among other treasures in churches and monasteries in Europe. One of the most famous and frequently mentioned, was the horn preserved in the Monastery of St. Denis, near Paris. Cardanus, who described it in the sixteenth century, says that he saw it when he visited the monastery while on a journey in France. He states " it was so long that he could not reach the tip when he placed it at his side ; it was not particularly thick, becoming gradually thinner towards the tip and curling like a snail's shell. The colour was that of a hartshorn." This horn was greatly venerated and was included in the inventory of treasures consisting of gold and precious stones and holy relics of the monastery.

Two unicorn's horns were preserved at St. Mark's in Venice, and in the sixteenth century were exhibited to the people once a year on Ascension Day, together with the other treasures of the Duomo.

There is frequent mention in records, of ducal cups of unicorn's horn which were used as drinking vessels by those whose lives were sought by poisoners. The effect of the poison was believed to be neutralized on coming into contact with the horn. A cup of this kind is preserved at Rosenberg which dates from the early part of the seventeenth century.

Gesner states that the rich put a piece of horn in their cups to protect themselves and to cure themselves, " but it must be a fresh piece and not one the properties of which have been exhausted by often being placed in drinks. It loses its virtue like plants do."

Ambrôise Paré doubted the value of unicorn's horn as an antidote and says : " after making a trial thereof yet could never find any good success in the use against poisons. Chapelaine, the chief physician to King Charles IX often used to say, that he would very willingly take away that custom of dipping a piece of unicorn's horn in the King's cup, but he knew that opinion to be so deeply ingrafted in the minds of men that he feared that it would scarce be impugned by reason."

Pomet, writing in the seventeenth century, says : " We ought to undeceive those who believe what we now call the unicorn's horn was the horn of a land animal whereof mention was made in the Old Testament, since it is nothing but the horn of the Narwhal and, as to the choice of it, ought to be the whitest, largest and finest."

It is recorded in 1650 that a certain well in Venice was remarkable for its fresh water on account of two pieces of unicorn's horn being concealed at the bottom.

Horns were used in early times as drinking vessels, not only on account of their suitability in shape, but also with the idea that they could impart their supposed health-giving properties to the liquid placed in them.

In Denmark, in the seventeenth century, unicorn's horn was sold in the apothecaries' shops and was much esteemed by Danish physicians on account of its medicinal properties. In 1593 there is a record that some physicians in Vienna in order to prove the efficacy of unicorn's horn as an antidote to poisons, experimented on a dog who was first given a dose of arsenic followed by one of unicorn's horn, and the dog subsequently recovered, while dogs to which arsenic had been given alone died from the effects. Similar tests were said to have been carried out in Copenhagen in 1636, as the result of which it was recorded that " unicorn's horn is an antidote against poisons, just as those seen at Paris and elsewhere."

On October 31 of that year, Drs. Fincke, Worm and Scheele met in the house of an apothecary called Johannes Woldenberg in Copenhagen and undertook the following experiment. Two pigeons and two cats were dosed with arsenic and corrosive sublimate. Unfortunately for the experiment, the pigeon which received both the poison and the antidote of unicorn's horn, vomited the latter and died some hours afterwards. The cat which was given sublimate but no antidote, is said to have died after a short interval, while the cat which in addition to the poison was given a small dose of unicorn's horn lived until the middle of the night. These and similar attempts to prove the value of the horn were made in Europe during the seventeenth century. It was said to be efficacious in plague and fever because they had certain symptoms in common with those produced by poisons and were called " poisonous diseases."

The Coronation Chair of the Royal house of Denmark in the seventeenth century was partly composed of unicorn's horns, which are said to have been used on account of their great value, and as being more precious than gold. The making of this curious chair was commenced by Frederick III, " the columns supporting it being composed of Narwhal's teeth and the chair covered with the horn wherever possible, the same being used for the supports for the arms." In the time

of Frederick III and Christian V this chair was considered one
of the most wonderful and valuable objects in the kingdom,
and was celebrated both in history and story. On June 7, 1671,
Christian V in magnificent robes was crowned in it, and the
feet of the throne were guarded by two silver lions. The bishop
who crowned the king in the Castle of Fredericksborg in his
address said : " Of mighty King Solomon, history bears witness
that he built a throne of ivory and covered it with the finest
gold ; Your Majesty is also sitting on a costly throne which in
the glory of its material and shape is like unto King Solomon's
throne, and the like thereof cannot be found in any kingdom."

From a time of great antiquity the horn of the Indian
rhinoceros has been reputed to possess the power of absorbing
poisonous substances brought into contact with it.

The Chinese fashioned these horns, which they still value
very highly, into cups which are sometimes ornamented with
beautiful carving. The tradition in China concerning the horn
was not so much that it acted as an antidote to poison, but that
it gave a sure indication when any liquid placed in it contained
a poisonous substance. When a poisoned liquid was allowed
to stand in the horn the latter was said to sweat and change
colour. It is not therefore to be wondered that the great
Emperors of the East, whose lives were frequently attempted by
poison, chose these horns as drinking cups.

Rudolf II of Germany (1575-1612) fashioned a cup of
rhinoceros horn for his own use, which is now preserved in the
National Museum at Copenhagen. Several other vessels of
rhinoceros horn are mentioned in Danish records, one being
described as : "a little flat dish of rhinoceros horn with a gilt
foot and then gilded, with an Indian underneath."

Lemery says : " The horn and nails of the animal are both
used in medicine and contain in them a good deal of volatile
salt and oil which are useful to resist poison."

Pomet declares that " the horn is highly alkalescent and is
also good against malignant fevers and destroys malignant acids
which stir up the most pernicious diseases."

There have been certain periods in the world's history when
every eminent personage, king, prince, minister or favourite,
was deemed in danger of poison, and when not a particle of
food was swallowed by them until it had first been tasted.

The traditions attached to the horn of the rhinoceros must
have come to Europe at an early period, as we find that cups
made from the horn, called " assay cups " were used in England
as early as the fifteenth century in the time of Edward
V.

The earliest allusion to the assay cups, which were made
both from the horn of the rhinoceros and the unicorn, is in
Russell's *Book of Nurture*, 1480, in which it is stated :

" Credence and tastynge is used
for drede of poysenynge
to all officers ysworne and grete
othe by chargynge."

It was customary for the esquire in attendance on a distinguished person to first test the wine by drinking some from his assay cup. Hall, in his Chronicle (1550), refers to this custom as follows :

" The esquier whiche was accustomed to sewe and take the assaye before kyng Rychard."

" The Maior of London claymed to serue the quene with a cuppe of golde and a cuppe of assay of the same."

and Gutch in 1530 alludes to :

" Two little Cuppis of asseye silvar and gilt."

" Tasters " were often employed in the castles of nobles and houses of the wealthy to taste the wine before it was handed to their masters, and dishes made of electron, which were believed to become tarnished if poisonous food was placed upon them, were frequently used at table. Beakers of Venetian glass which were warranted to fly into atoms if poisoned wine was placed in them, were also among the detectors used in the sixteenth century, when the dread of poison was greater than the assassin's dagger.

In the British Museum is the base of a poison-cup made from the terra sigillata of Malta, stamped with the image of St. Paul holding a staff around which a serpent is entwined, and encircling the figure are the words PIETRA. D.S. PAULO. CONTRA VELENO.

The chalky earth or clay of which it is composed, was taken from the sides and floor of the cave in which St. Paul is said to have taken refuge, after he was shipwrecked on the coast of Malta. It was believed to have the property of resisting poisons.

Embedded in the bottom of the cup are several coloured stones that have been known in Malta for centuries as " Serpent's eyes ". They were believed to have been fashioned by nature to perpetuate St. Paul's miracle when he escaped death after the viper " Fastened on his hand."

" Serpent's eyes " were also believed to have the property of averting the effects of poisons and their addition to the cup was no doubt due to the idea, that they would thus render it more powerful as an antidote to any poisonous liquid that might be placed in it.

It is on account of its association with medicine, the rhinoceros was adopted as the crest of the Society of Apothecaries of London when it was founded in 1617.

The Chinese, who appear to have ever been suspicious of being poisoned, also made little cups of glass about $1\frac{1}{2}$ in. high which they believed would crack if a poisoned liquid were poured into them.

In India certain bowls of pottery with a light greenish glaze, called Gherian ware, are made which are said to break into pieces if touched by poisoned food or liquid. They were introduced into Northern India by Mohammed Ghori in the twelfth century from whom they take their name.

Another substance which was regarded with great veneration as an antidote to poisons, especially in the East, was the bezoar stone, a calculus found in the intestines of Persian wild goats, cows, a species of ape and other animals. These stones vary in size from that of a small egg down to a hazelnut, and are of a yellowish brown colour.

Pomet says : " If you would have the finest and best oriental bezoar, you must choose that which is shining, of a pleasant scent, tending to that of ambergris. The shape is of no consequence, whether round, smooth or rough, and whether white, yellow or grey, but the principal colour is usually an olive."

Bezoar was introduced into Eastern medicine by the Arabs, but its reputation is of much greater antiquity. The name is said to be of Persian origin and derived from the word " *pad-zahr*," " an expeller of poisons," and is mentioned first by Avenzoar, an Arab physician of Seville, about the year A.D. 1140.

Bezoar was known to the Hebrews in ancient times as " *Bel Zaard* " which means the " Master," or " every cure for poisons."

There are several varieties of these stones, the most esteemed being the Oriental, which come from Persia. On dividing the calculus, it appears to have been formed by a deposit of calcium phosphate round some nucleus, such as hair or the stone of a fruit. One that is still preserved in the Museum of St. Bartholomew's Hospital has a date stone as the nucleus. It was believed that the special virtues of the stone were due to some unknown plant on which the animal had fed.

The Occidental, another variety of bezoar stone, is said to be obtained from the llamas of Peru, and a European variety is got from the chamois of the Swiss mountains, but these varieties never commanded the great value as did those from the Orient, which are said by early writers to have been sold for ten times their weight in gold. The Occidental bezoar stone is usually much larger than the Oriental and has a dull surface.

Lemery mentions a bezoar stone obtained from the hog, which is of a whitish colour inclining to green. It is said to be produced in the gall of certain swine in India and is very highly esteemed by the natives.

All varieties of bezoar had a reputation for counteracting the effects of poison. They were generally preserved in elaborate cases of pierced gold with a chain attached so that they could be suspended in wine or liquid before it was drunk. " The Portuguese above all nations," says a writer of the seventeenth century, " drive a great trade with bezoar, because they are always on their guard and watching one another for fear of poison."

As well as being an antidote to poison, the bezoar came to be regarded as a valuable remedy for fevers and was also applied externally in skin diseases. It was given internally in doses of 4 to 16 grains and, in Portugal, in time of plague, the stones were loaned to sufferers at about the equivalent of 10s. a day.

Ambròise Paré, when surgeon to Charles IX of France, relates that one day, when the king was at Clermont, a Spanish nobleman brought him a bezoar stone which he assured him was an antidote to all poisons. The king sent for Paré and asked him if he knew any substance which would annul the effects of any poison. Paré said that could not be, for there were many sorts of poisons which acted in very different ways. The Spanish nobleman, however, maintained that this stone was a universal antidote and as the king was eager to test the question, the Provost of the Palace was sent for and asked if he had any criminal in his charge condemned to death. He replied that he had a cook who had stolen two silver dishes, who was to be hanged the next day. The offer was thereupon made to the cook that he should take a poison and the alleged antidote immediately afterwards, and if he escaped with his life he should go free. The cook gladly consented, and an apothecary was ordered to prepare a deadly draught and administer it, to be followed by a dose of the bezoar. This was done. The poor wretch lived for about seven hours in terrible agony which Paré tried in vain to relieve. After his death Paré made an autopsy which showed that the antidote had no effect at all. It was sublimate which had been given. "And," the writer concludes, " the king commanded that the stone should be thrown into the fire ; which was done."

Three bezoar stones were sent by the Shah of Persia, as a royal gift, to the Emperor Napoleon a little over a century ago.

A stone called Draconites, described by Albertus Magnus (1193-1280) as a shining black stone of pyramidal shape, was also believed to be antidote to all kinds of poisons.

A cup or goblet made of electrum, an alloy composed of gold and silver known to the ancients, according to Pliny, had the property of revealing any poisonous liquid which was placed in it, by exhibiting certain circles like rainbows in the liquid, which it also kept sparkling and hissing as if on fire.

CHAPTER VII

POISONS TRIED ON MAN

FROM an early period science has been gradually built up by experimental methods and even the ancients were cognizant of the fact that the remedial properties of a substance could only be proved by actual experiment. Not only animals but human beings were utilized for this purpose by many famous physicians in the Middle Ages. Criminals who had been condemned to death were generally selected when available.

It is stated by Pierre Fabre, in the *History of the Apostles*, that the Apostle John was present at the execution of two criminals by poison in the public forum at Ephesus.

Vivisection of the live human subject was practised by the Alexandrian school in the time of the Ptolemies. Erasistratos and Herophilos, pupils of Chrysippos of Cnidos, are said to have experimented upon 600 condemned criminals handed over to them by Ptolemy Soter. They opened the abdomens of some of these men to study the movements of the colon and those of the muscle of the diaphragm on the inspiration of air ; they also opened the chests of the others to study the cardiac movements. Their conduct, however, met with the reprobation of their contemporaries. Celsus and Galen reproached Herophilos with " cruel and useless sacrifices " and of " inhuman feeling," while Tertullian called him roundly " an executioner who gave lingering death with refined cruelty." The Court physicians of Attalus, King of Pergamus, and Mithridates, King of Pontus, were authorized in virtue of their office to try poisons upon criminals, and were accused by their jealous colleagues of pluming themselves upon their privileges, while less favoured practitioners were compelled to be content to experiment upon cocks and dogs.

An allusion to the use of animals for the purpose of physiological experiment is to be found in a document still preserved in the Venetian secret archives, which is dated 1432. It states : " Trial has been made on three porcine animals of certain venoms found in the chancery sent very long ago from Vicenza which have been proved not to be good."

This document affords interesting proof that the Italians at that period made tests with poisons on animals and were thus in advance of other European nations in their knowledge of poisonous substances.

Brassavola of Ferrara studied little known and doubtful remedies by testing their effects on criminals, and Fallopius, his pupil, who eventually made such important physiological discoveries, followed his master's example. It is recorded that Cosimo de Medici, Grand Duke of Tuscany, on one occasion ordered the magistrates of Pisa to hand over two men to Fallopius, " in order that he may put them to death in whatever way he pleases, and then anatomize them." Fallopius, however, seeing the men were condemned to death, seems to have acted with both dignity and humanity. He gave them opium ; one died and the other recovered. Cosimo pardoned him, but, if we may believe contemporary records, Fallopius did not : he gave the man eight grains more, and this time he died.

At Bologna, poisons were habitually administered to criminals without their knowledge to obviate the perturbing influence of fear upon natural toxic effects. Arsenic was employed in the same way at Mantua and Florence. Even princes of the Church did not show themselves above taking part in these experiments. The Cardinal-Archbishop of Ravenna, with the permission of Duke Ercole II, tried the effects of corrosive sublimate (!) as an antidote, though this seems rather like cutting off a child's head to cure it of squinting. Pope Clement VII's experiment with a secret oil which was given to certain unfortunate Corsicans as an antidote to the aconite they administered judicially, may be cited as a more humane effort in the cause of science, and was, no doubt, considered to have been partially successful, as one of the victims survived the aconite and received a free pardon.

Dr. Harris, who was physician-in-ordinary to Charles II, gives an account of one Pontæus, apparently a contemporary, who is described as the first mountebank who ever appeared on a stage in England. This performer issued a challenge to the physicians of Oxford to prepare the rankest poison they could contrive, and he undertook that one of his servants should take it and recover. Thus would he demonstrate the marvellous virtues of the Orvietan he had for sale. The medical practitioners of Oxford accepted the challenge, and decided on aqua fortis. Pontæus's man drank off on the stage what they brought him, fell down as dead, was carried off, and reappeared the next day no worse for his experience. Dr. Harris explains that previous to the test the man had well greased his mouth and gullet with 2 or 3 lb. of fresh butter, and that after getting him behind the scenes more butter was administered, and then warm water, which made him sick. Another member of the charlatan's staff next washed his hands in molten lead before the spectators. His hands were immediately violently inflamed, and his sufferings were obvious to the crowd, if not appreciated by himself.

Some of the professor's famous green ointment was then applied to the almost skinless flesh, and the hands were carefully bandaged. Next day the bandages were removed, and the hands were scarcely even inflamed. It transpired afterwards that the molten lead was warm quicksilver placed in a ladle painted red, and when the man dipped his hands in the metal he was concealing in them some vermilion, which he rubbed over the flesh under the quicksilver.

François Ranchin, Professor and Chancellor of the Faculty of Montpellier in the eighteenth century, wrote that experiments upon human beings were worthy of approval and had been held in high honour by the ancients.

English surgeons in the eighteenth century were also willing to avail themselves when the opportunity offered, to experiment on a condemned criminal.

In 1731 a man named Charles Ray was reprieved on condition that William Cheselden, the famous anatomist and surgeon, should perforate the drum of his ear in order to ascertain if it would cause deafness. The unfortunate subject, however, was taken ill with fever before the experiment could be performed, and the operation was abandoned.

Again, in 1763 another condemned man was offered a reprieve on condition that he consented to have one of his legs amputated to test the power of a new styptic. Fortunately, perhaps, for him, he died before the experiment could be performed. Four years later one John Benham is reported to have been reprieved for a similar purpose, but when Pierce, the inventor of the styptic, waited upon the Secretary of State to make arrangements, he was informed that His Majesty the King was of the opinion that it was quite improper to try such an experiment.

In more recent times seven condemned criminals in France were innoculated with the plague, but only one contracted the disease, and a certain German professor inoculated a man with carbuncle, which brought upon him the denunciations of his professional brethren.

On the ethics of such experiments much diversity of opinion exists, but only when the subjects voluntarily submit themselves, as was recently done in connexion with the researches on yellow fever, can such a course be in any way justified.

CHAPTER VIII

SOME ANCIENT VEGETABLE POISONS—POISONS USED BY WITCHES—THE MANDRAKE—ACONITE, " THE QUEEN MOTHER OF POISONS "

MANY curious superstitions are associated with certain poisonous plants which have been handed down to us from past ages. The mysterious properties, especially of those which caused sleep or by supposed magical powers concealed in them produced delirium, were attributed by the ancients to a spirit or demon which dwelt in the roots of the plants, and various rites and ceremonies were connected with their gathering. The real cause of their physiological effect on the body was of course unknown, but the narcotic effects, which from experience were found to produce insensibility, dreams and frenzy, made a deep impression on the mind.

The hallucinations of the witches which we read about in the Middle Ages, may be compared with those of the medicine-men of many savage tribes to-day. In all probability these effects were produced by the action of various drugs which they knew were capable of causing hallucinations and temporary insanity. Weak-minded women, who probably formed the greater part of the class known as witches, made use of an unguent with which they anointed themselves in preparation for the so-called " witches' Sabbath." Johannes Wierius, who was a witness of such a gathering, recorded in 1566 the composition of the witches' ointment and states it contained such powerful narcotic poisons as mandrake, belladonna, henbane and stramonium. The absorption of this unguent was followed by unconsciousness and sleep, and on being awakened the person so anointed was fully assured that she had visited the " Sabbath."

They were also aware of the poisonous effects of other plants and knew that the fumes of henbane, stramonium and poppy would cause stupefication and even hallucinations, when inhaled in confined places.

Among the secrets of witches and sorcerers included in the *Grand Grimoire* is a preparation called " The Composition of Death or the Philosophical Stone." It is directed to be prepared as follows : " Mix together in a new glazed pot, 1 lb. of Red

Copper and 10 ounces of Nitric Acid. Allow them to boil for one and a half hours, after which take 3 ounces of Verdigris and boil together for an hour. Then add 2½ ounces of arsenic and boil for an hour, and 3 ounces of Oak bark, well powdered and boil for an hour. Add twenty ounces of Rose water and boil for twelve minutes and finally three ounces of black soot and boil altogether. Remove the pot before it burns, allow it to stand and cool, then transfer it to a closed vessel."

The frenzies into which the sorcerers of the Middle Ages worked themselves may also be attributed to the action of various substances with delirient properties.

There is probably no plant around which clusters more legendary lore and superstition than the mandrake (*mandragora officinalis*). Sufficient has been recorded about it to fill volumes, and between the years 1510 and 1850 no less than twenty-two treatises are known to have been written on the subject.

It was known to the Babylonians over 3,000 years ago, and their women carried a mandrake root as a charm against sterility. The ancient Egyptians called it " The Phallus of the Field " and held it in the highest esteem. The Greeks surrounded it with strange traditions, and in Eastern Europe, Arabia, Palestine and Syria, it has been associated with mysterious rites and customs from time immemorial.

Theophrastus (300 B.C.) the earliest writer on botany, alludes to the mandrake and mentions its property of inducing sleep and its use in the composition of love-philtres. Demosthenes, the Athenian orator, is stated to have compared his lethargic hearers to those who had eaten it. The early Greeks bestowed on it the name of Circeium, derived from the name of the witch Circe, as they believed that an evil spirit dwelt in the root. Pliny, in alluding to the mandrake, states that " he who would undertake the office of uprooting it should stand with his back to the wind, and before he begins to dig, make three circles round the plant with the point of a sword, and then turning to the west proceed to dig it up." In other countries the gathering of the root was believed to be attended with great danger to the individual who was sufficiently daring to pull it from the ground.

The Greeks believed that when dragged from the earth the root gave a dreadful shriek and struck dead the person who had the presumption to pull it up. They therefore adopted the following ingenious method of obtaining it. A dog was allowed to fast, and was then brought near the plant round which a cord was fastened. The end was then tied to the tail of the dog. The gatherer would then place some food within a few feet of the hungry animal, who in his struggles to reach it would uproot the plant and be immediately killed by the evil spirit. At the moment of uprooting the gatherer generally sounded a horn, in order to drown the shriek of the demon that dwelt in the plant.

The mandrake is thought to be the plant mentioned in the Book of Genesis, which was called by the ancient Hebrews " Dudaïm," and when found by Reuben, was carried by him to his mother. The inducement which tempted Leah to part with it proves the value set upon it at this time. Maundrell found it used in the neighbourhood of Aleppo as described in the Bible and states that the Arabs call it " *tuphac el sheitan*." The Greeks sometimes alluded to Venus as *Mandragoritis* and the fruit of the plant was popularly termed " place of love." Pythagoras calls the mandrake "*Anthropomorphum*," while Columella terms it " *semihomo*," and in the Middle Ages the fruit was sometimes called " Devil's Apple," " Devil's Testicle " or "Love Apple."

Dioscorides refers to the mandrake in the first century, and mentions its use for love-charms and philtres. In the earliest MS. of his work, written in the fifth century which is still preserved in Vienna, there is a drawing in colour depicting Euresis, the goddess of discovery, presenting the author with a mandrake root. The root is represented in human form with five leaves growing out of the head, and near by on the ground is a dog expiring in the agonies of death.

Josephus mentions the custom in a Jewish village of pulling up the root by means of a dog, which was killed by the shriek from the demon which resided in it. This tradition appears to have been attached to the gathering of the mandrake in nearly every country where it was known.

Many of the traditions and superstitions connected with the plant appear to have arisen from the curious natural shape of the root, which often bears a strong resemblance to the human form. This similitude was turned to account by those who dealt in it, as they found they obtained a greater value after manipulating it to make the features and limbs more perfectly resemble a man or a woman.

Beyond the effects attributed to it by tradition, the mandrake has undoubted powerful narcotic properties. Its active principle, mandragorine was discovered by Ahrens, and is said to be a mixture of bases of which hyoscyamine is the chief, mixed with scopolamine.

The ancients attributed powerful aphrodisiacal virtues to the plant and claimed that it could produce a condition of sexual excitement which was often attributed to natural and magical powers, and for this reason included it in the composition of their love-philtres. It was among the more important narcotic drugs employed for producing anæsthesia, and Dioscorides gives the formula for a wine made by infusing the root in Cyprus wine, which was directed to be administered before amputation of a limb or before the application of a hot cautery.

Pliny remarks that mandrake " is taken against serpents and before cutting and puncture, lest they be felt. Sometimes the smell is sufficient," and Apuleius, writing in the second century, claims that half an ounce with wine is sufficient to make a person insensible, even to the pain of amputation.

Lyman suggests that it was mandragora wine mixed with myrrh that was offered to Christ on the Cross, as it was commonly given to those who suffered death by crucifixion to allay in some degree their terrible agonies.

Shakespeare alludes to the mandragora and its properties in several of his plays. Thus we have Cleopatra asking for the drug that she may " sleep out this great gap of time " while her Antony is away, and Iago, whilst the poison begins to work in the mind of Othello, exclaims :

> " Not poppy, nor mandragora
> Nor all the drowsy syrups of this world
> Shall ever medicine thee to that sweet sleep."

In the sixteenth century the Germans called these human-like roots *Abrunes* or *Alraun*. They were considered of considerable value and treated with the greatest veneration. After fashioning them as near as possible to the form of a man or woman, they dressed them every day and consulted them as oracles. Abrunes were introduced into England in the time of Henry VIII, and met with ready purchasers. To increase their value and importance, the roots were said by the vendors to be produced from the flesh of criminals which fell from the gibbet, and that they only grew beneath the gallows :

Lord Bacon notices their use in the following words :

" Some plants there are, but rare, that have a morsie or downie root and likewise that have a number of threads like beards, as mandrakes, whereof witches and impostours make an ugly image, giving it the form of a face at the top of the root, and these strings to make a broad beard down to the foot."

Madame de Genlis remarks that " the mandrake roots should be wrapped in a sheet, for that then they will bring increasing good luck."

The plant is still used medicinally in China, where it is said to be employed by the Mandarins, who believe it will give them increased intellectual powers and prolong their lives.

The origin of *Alraun*, the name given by the Germans to the mandrake root, has been variously explained. Tacitus speaks of a formidable people among the Germans called Aurinia, believed to be endowed with magical powers, and " some attribute Allrun to their name on account of their use of the plant in

sorcery. They are the same of whom Aventinus speaks as
loose-haired, bare-legged witches who would slay a man,
drink his blood from his skull and divine the future from his
mangled remains." There is some reason to believe, however,
that the word is simply a later form of the Gothic Allrune, and
that it is related to rune. The French word *Mandragloire* is
simply a part of the Greek word Mandragora, blended with the
name of the old French fairy Magloire.

Both in Germany and France the mandrake was said to
spring up where the presence of a criminal had polluted the
ground. It was sure to be found near a gallows, and so was
popularly called in Germany *Galgemannlein*. It was to be
gathered in the way described by Josephus, but, it was added,
" one must sign the cross three times over the plant before
pulling it up. Having got the root it must be bathed every
Friday, kept in a white cloth in a box and then it would procure
manifold benefits."

There is a letter still preserved from a burgess of Leipzig
to his brother at Riga written in 1675, which is interesting as
showing the popular ideas concerning the mandrake at that time.
It reads :

" Brotherly love and truth and all good wishes to thee dear
brother.   I have thy letter and have made out from it enough
to understand that thou dear brother in thy home affairs hast
suffered great sorrow ; that thy children, cows, swine, sheep
and horses, have all died ; thy wine and beer soured in thy
cellar, and thy provender destroyed and that thou dwellest with
thy wife in great contention ; which is all grievous to hear.
I have therefore gone to those who understand such things to
find what is needed and have asked them why thou art so
unlucky. They have told me that these evils proceed not from
God but from wicked people ; and they know what will help
thee.   If thou hast a Mandrake (*Allruniken odor Erdmannikin*)
and bring it into thy house, thou shalt have good fortune. So
I have taken the pains for thy sake to go to those who have
such things and to our executioner have paid 64 thalers and a
piece of gold drinkgelt to his servant, and this (Mandrake) dear
brother I send thee, and thou must keep it as I shall tell in this
letter.   When thou hast the Erdman in thy house let it rest
three days without approaching it ; then place it in warm water.
With the water afterwards sprinkle the animals and sills of the
house going all over, and soon it shall go better with thee and
thou shalt come to thy own if thou serve Erdmannikin right.
Bathe it four times every year and as often wrap it in silk cloth
and lay it among thy best things and thou need do no more.
The Bath in which it has been bathed is especially good. If a
woman is in child pain and cannot bear, if she drinks a spoonful

she will be delivered with joy and thankfulness. And when thou goest to law put Erdman under thy right arm and thou shalt succeed whether right or wrong. Now dear brother this Erdmannikin I send with all love and faith to thee for a happy new year. Let it be kept and it may do the same for thy childrens children. God keep thee—Leipzig, Sunday before fastnight, 75. Hans, N."

It is certainly remarkable that in 1675 so much as seventy-five thalers could be obtained for one of these little figures. It is probable that the dealing in them had become very secret on account of the danger incurred of being suspected of witch-craft as in 1630 three women were executed in Hamburg on this account.

Matthiolus, in his commentary on Dioscorides, describes the great ingenuity which had been reached in the carving of the root into the human semblance, and the training of little shoots from seeds planted in it which were manipulated so as to look like hair. The same ingenuity appears to have been employed to invest each figure with a marvellous legend of its origin or potency.

A haunted place was formerly shown in Lower Würtemberg where a merchant of Ulm tried vainly to get rid of his Gal-gemannlein, and for a long time a house stood in Frankfort which was avoided because it had been the habitation of a baker-woman who had perished horribly with a mandrake in her possession, which she had long tried to abandon.

This diabolical phase of the superstition was especially strong in France and England. It was believed by many that Joan of Arc had one of these mandrake figures in her possession, and she was even asked by the judge at her trial whether this was not the case ; but she disclaimed any knowledge of the mandrake. At Romorantin, Margaret Ragum Bouchery, the wife of a Moor, was hanged as a witch in 1603, the charge against her being that she kept and fed daily a living mandrake fiend which was stated to be in the form of a female ape.

Superstitions concerning the mandrake were common in the South of England, and it was believed that it had a human heart at its root. It was said in some places to be perpetually watched by Satan, and if it was pulled up at certain holy times and with certain invocations, the Evil Spirit would appear to do the bidding of the practitioner. In the mining regions of Germany the mandrake was supposed to reach down to the cobolds beneath the earth, and shrieked when it was torn up. In Silesia, Thuringia, the Tyrol and Bohemia, it is still connected with the idea of subterranean treasures, and in the Hartz, mandrake decoction is poured on animals to prevent swellings.

In 1429 the use of mandrakes as amulets was so general in

France that Friar Richard furiously denounced them and vast
numbers were burned. La Fontaine's fable " La Mandragore,"
copied from Machiavel's comedy of the same title, turns upon
the supposed potency of the plant to produce children. The
Tyrolese believe that it not only reveals hidden treasures, but
also renders the possessor proof against blows. In the Alpine
regions it is laid on the bed to prevent nightmare, and carried
as a charm to protect the mountaineer against robbers and bad
weather.

In Iceland the mandrake is called *Thjofarot* (thieves' root)
and is believed to spring from the froth of the mouth of one
who has been hanged or the cairn where he has been buried.

In some parts of Kent the mandrake is said to be still carried
by women to prevent sterility, and the same superstition survives
in Greece, where pieces of the root are worn by young people as
love-charms. Mandrake roots are also carried by women in
Syria and Turkey to promote fecundity and may still be bought
in the drug shops.

Among other poisonous plants known to the ancients, aconite
may rightly be claimed to be one of the most important. It
has been called the " Queen Mother of Poisons " and has been
a matter of comment and note by early historians for over two
thousand years. Species of the plant were known as wolf's
bane, leopard's bane, and women's bane. Its root was compared by some of the ancient botanists to sea crabfish, by others
to a scorpion ; " for," says one writer, " the root doth turn
and crook inward in manner of a scorpion's taile." Various
origins are given to the name aconite ; some attribute it to
the fact that it grows quite naturally upon bare and naked rocks
which the Greeks call Aconas. Theophrastus says the name is
derived from Aconæ, " a certain towne, neer to which it groweth
abundantly." It is also said to have been derived from the
Greek word for javelin or arrow, because " some barbarous
nations employed the juice to poison their arrows and spears."

In early times a number of poisonous plants were described
under the name of aconite as well as the *Aconitum napellus*, the
species now employed in medicine.

Its deadly effects are alluded to by Ovid, Virgil and Juvenal.
Plutarch, in referring to the death of Orodes, says : " He fell
into a disease that became a dropsie after he had lost his son
Pacorus who was slain in a battle by the Romans. Phraates,
his second son, thinking to set his father forwards gave him a
drink of the juice of Aconitum. The dropsie received the poison
and the one drave the other out of Orodes' body and set him on
foot again."

Hanbury says the ancients were well aware of the poisonous
properties of aconite, though the various species were not more

exactly distinguished until the close of the Middle Ages. It was used by the Chinese in ancient times and is still employed by the less civilized of the hill tribes of India as an arrow poison. It is said also to have been used for the same purpose by the aborigines of ancient Gaul. It is mentioned in the well-known ancient Welsh MS. of " The Physicians of Myddvai," written in the thirteenth century, as " one of the plants that every physician is to grow."

Matthiolus relates the results of certain experiments carried out by order of Pope Clement VII, on the persons of two criminals condemned to death, for the purpose of testing the value of an antidote to aconite, which he describes as the most deadly of all known poisons. One of the criminals was used as a test and the other for a control experiment.

The root, which contains the largest proportion of the active principle called aconitine, has often caused fatal results in being mistaken for that of horse-radish. It had rarely been used for criminal purposes until Lamson in 1881 employed the alkaloid to take the life of Percy Malcolm John. In connexion with aconitine it is related that Dr. Christison, the famous toxicologist, who was professor of Medical Jurisprudence at the University of Edinburgh, when giving evidence in a certain case as to the recognition of poisonous substances sought for in the body after death, said to the judge, " My Lord, there is but one deadly agent of this kind which we cannot satisfactorily trace in the human body after death, and that is—" when the Judge sharply interrupted him with : " Stop, stop, please, Dr. Christison. It is much better that the public should not know it." Years afterwards it was vividly recalled to the memory of his then student class, that Lamson, who was a member of his audience as a medical student, and exceptionally assiduous in note-taking, was present on one of the occasions when Professor Christison was explaining to his class that the real name of the poison which the Court had prevented him from naming was aconitine.

It is satisfactory to note that toxicology has advanced since the days of Christison, for Sir Thomas Stevenson, who gave evidence for the Crown at Lamson's trial, was able to prove by clinical tests that his victim had been poisoned by aconitine.

The aconite now used for medicinal purposes is derived from the *Aconitum napellus*, chiefly grown in Britain. It is also found in the mountainous districts of the temperate parts of the northern hemisphere. It grows on the Alps, the Pyrenees, the mountains of Germany and Austria and also in Denmark and Sweden. On the Himalayas it is found at 10,000 to 16,000 feet above the sea-level. Both the root and the leaves are used medicinally. Aconite contains several alkaloids, all of which are powerful poisons. The chief of these aconitine is one of the most deadly poisons known, the fiftieth part of a grain of which has nearly caused death.   Indian aconite known as " *Bish* " is chiefly derived from *Aconitum ferox*, a native of high altitude in the Himalaya regions.   It is mentioned by the Persian physician, Alhervi, in the tenth century, and also by many early Arabian writers on medicine.   Ali Ben Isa pronounced it to be the most rapid of deadly poisons, and describes the symptoms with tolerable correctness.   The chief symptoms of poisoning by aconite are heat, numbness and tingling in the mouth and throat, giddiness, and loss of muscular power.   The pupils become dilated, the skin cold and pulse feeble, with oppressed breathing and dread of approaching death.   Finally, numbness and paralysis come on, rapidly followed by death in a few sudden gasps.   The poison being extremely rapid in effect, immediate action is absolutely necessary to save life.

CHAPTER IX

HEMLOCK — HELLEBORE — HENBANE — OPIUM — BELLADONNA—FOXGLOVE—STRAMONIUM — NUX VOMICA

HEMLOCK or cicuta was a classical poison well-known in ancient times and has had an evil reputation from an early period. References are made to it in Greek literature from the fourth century before the Christian era.

Its use by the Greeks as a State poison has already been dealt with. Dioscorides describes it as " a very evil, dangerous, hurtful and poisonous herb, insomuch that whosoever taketh it into his body dieth remediless, except the party drink some wine before the venom hath taken the heart." Pliny declares that even serpents flee from its leaves.

It was used in Anglo-Saxon medicine and is mentioned in the Vocabulary of Alfric as early as the tenth century, the name hemlock being derived from the Anglo-Saxon words " hem," border or shore and " leac."

Its chief active principle, conine, is a colourless oily liquid which resembles nicotine in its action.

Hellebore or Melampus root, like Hemlock, has been associated with mystery and evil throughout the ages. The poet Campbell thus refers to its reputation :

" By the witches' tower,
Where Hellebore and Hemlock seem to weave
Round its dark vaults a melancholy bower
For spirits of the dead at night's enchanted hour."

It is supposed to have taken its name from Melampus, a traditionary physician who is said to have cured the daughters of Proetus, King of Argus, of mental derangement and leprosy, by administering the root.

On the other hand, Pliny states that the daughters of Proetus were restored to their senses by drinking the milk of goats that had fed on hellebore. Melampus is reputed to have flourished at Pylus about 1530 B.C., and after his time the plant was generally known as Melampus root and later as Christmas Rose.

The root of the black hellebore was used by the ancients to hallow their dwellings and they believed that by strewing it about it would drive away evil spirits. The ceremony of laying it was performed with great devotion and accompanied with the chanting of solemn hymns. Cattle were also blessed with hellebore in the same manner, to keep them free from the spells of the wicked. For these purposes it was dug up with solemn religious ceremonies. A circle was drawn round the plant with a sword ; then, turning to the East, a humble prayer was finally offered up by the devotee to Apollo and Aesculap was asked leave to dig up the root. The flight of an eagle was looked for during the ceremony, for should this bird approach near the spot during the celebration of the rite, it was considered to predict the certain death of the person who uprooted the plant in the course of the year. Others ate garlic previous to the rite, which was supposed to counteract the poisonous effluvia of the plant. Dioscorides relates that when Carneades, the Cyrenaic philosopher, undertook to answer the books of Zeno, he sharpened his wit and quickened his spirit by purging his head with powdered hellebore, and it is of this plant Juvenal sarcastically observes " Misers need a double dose of hellebore." It is stated that the Gauls never went to the chase without rubbing the point of their arrows with this herb, believing that it would render the game killed with them more tender.

Hyoscyamus, commonly called henbane, is a herb which has been employed in medicine from early times. Over three thousand years ago it was used by the Bablyonians to r elieve toothache, and the use of the seeds for this purpose still survives in country districts in England.

Gerard writing in the sixteenth century says," the seed was used by quack-doctors to cause worms to come forth of the teeth by burning them in a chafing dish of coles, the party holding his mouth over the fume thereof, persuading the patient that those small creepers come out of his mouth."

Benedictus Crispus, Archbishop of Milan, in a work written shortly before A.D. 681, alludes to it under the names of hyoscamus and symphoniaca, and in the tenth century its virtues are recorded in the works of Macer Floridus. In the early Anglo-Saxon manuscripts it is called henbell and sometimes belene. In a French herbal of the fifteenth century it is called hanibane or hanebane. It has been employed from ancient times as a sedative and anodyne for producing sleep, although hallucinations sometimes accompany its use. In the Middle Ages it was known among the peasantry of Germany as " Devil's eye," and the Piedmontese have a tradition that if a hare be sprinkled with henbane juice, all the other hares in the district will desert it.

Its chief active principles are hyoscyamine and hyoscine, both of which are very powerful poisons. There is an old tradition that once in the refectory of an ancient monastery, the monks were served in error by the cook with henbane instead of some harmless vegetable. After partaking of the dish they were seized with the most extraordinary hallucinations. At midnight one monk sounded the bell for matins, while others walked in the chapel and opened their books, but could not read. Others sang roystering drinking songs and performed mountebank antics, which convulsed the others with uncontrollable laughter, and the pious monastery for the nonce was turned into a lunatic asylum.

There are few drugs used to-day with a more interesting history than opium. It figures not only in history but also in romance and crime. It has been associated with the acquisition of wealth and prosperity and with the most terrible degradation. Opium has been the cause of war, of bitter feeling and punishments. Whilst it has enslaved many with the most pleasurable hallucinations and relieved the most agonizing pains, it is capable of reducing human beings to the level of the beasts.

It is mentioned in the Papyrus Ebers, one of the earliest records of medicine, as having been known and used by the Egyptians about 1550 years B.C. It is described by Theophrastus as having been used by the Greeks 300 years B.C. and is supposed to have formed the chief ingredient in the potion known as " Nepenthe " which Helen of Troy gave to the guests of Menelaus to drive away their care. This conjecture receives support from Homer, who states that Nepenthe was obtained from Thebes, the ancient capital of Egypt. According to Prosper Alpinus, the Egyptians were practised opium eaters and were often faint and languid through the want of it. They prepared and drank it in the form of " Cretic Wine," which they flavoured by the addition of pepper and other aromatics. Scribonius Largus (A.D. 40) mentions the method of preparing opium and points out that the true drug is derived from the capsules of the poppy and not from the foliage of the plant.

Dioscorides, in the same century, describes how the capsules from which the drug is collected should be cut and the milky juices collected, and one can infer from his statements that the collection of opium was at that time a source of industry in Asia Minor. Pliny gives an account of " opion," while it is also mentioned by Celsus, a Roman medical writer of the first century, and by several other Latin authors, who allude to it by the quaint name of " poppy tears."

It was well known to the Arabs, who transmitted their knowledge of its properties first to the Persians and then to other nations of the East. In India its introduction would appear to be connected with the spread of Mahommedanism, and may have been favoured by their prohibition of the use of wine. The earliest mention of opium in connexion with India occurs in the travels of Barbosa, who visited Calicut and the

Malabar Coast in 1511, and who gives it a prominent place with other valuable drugs. Pyres, the first ambassador from Europe to China in 1516, speaks of the opium of Egypt, Cambay, and the kingdom of Coûs (Kus Bahar, S.W. Bhotan in Bengal), and states it was eaten by " the kings and lords, and even the common people, though not so much because it costs dear." In the fifteenth and sixteenth centuries its praises were also sung by poets of the Far East.

It is believed that opium was introduced by the Arabs into both India and China, as they are known to have traded with the southern parts of the empire as early as the ninth century. In the eighteenth century the Chinese marketed the drug in their junks as a return cargo from India. It was at that time almost exclusively used as a remedy for dysentery, but the trade grew and in 1787, the importation reached a thousand chests.

In 1780 the East India Company opened an opium depôt with two small vessels at Lark's Bay, Macao. The Chinese authorities began to complain of these two ships in 1793, but the traffic still increased, until they issued an edict forbidding any vessel having opium on board to enter the Canton River. This led to political differences which culminated in the war called the " Opium War." It was concluded by the Treaty of Nankin, after which five ports of China were opened to foreign trade, opium being admitted as a legalized import in 1858.

Opium smoking does not appear to have been practised in China until the latter part of the seventeenth century, but within a hundred years it spread like the tentacles of an octopus over the entire empire. At this time the authorities became greatly alarmed at the injurious effects among the people following the abuse of opium. Suicides became frequent and the high officials and all classes were becoming rapid slaves to the habit. The sale rose from 2,300 chests in 1788 to 17,500 in 1836. The first edict against it was issued in 1796 and since that time in spite of many others, the traffic has increased and is still carried on. In 1879 in the State of Amoy and its adjacent towns, the proportion of opium smokers was estimated at from fifteen to twenty per cent of the total population.

With regard to the introduction of opium into India, the Moslems having once established its use, began to make it a source of income. The Great Mogul monopolized the opium production and trade, and derived an immense income from its sale.

The drug is employed in various forms, according to the class of people who consume it. In India it is largely used in the crude state, and is sold at about two annas a drachm, in small square pieces. The opium eater will take two or three grains and roll them into the form of a pill between his fingers, and then chew or swallow it, often twenty times in the day. It is also used in a liquid form called *Kusamba*, made by macerating opium in rose-water ; others boil it with milk, then collect the cream and eat it. The varieties for smoking are known as *Chundoo* and *Mudat*, the former being a very impure extract of a fairly stiff consistency, and the latter made from the refuse of *Chundoo*, of which it largely consists. From two to four grains a day may be called a moderate use of the crude drug. The poorer people regularly give it to children up to two years of age to keep them quiet, also as a preventive against such complaints as enteritis, which is very common in the East ; and so before youth is reached they become inured to its action. Licences to sell the drug are sold to the highest bidder at the opium auctions, the licensee having the privilege of supplying a certain number of small dealers.

The Chinese smoker usually lays himself down on his side, with his head supported by a pillow. On the straw mat beside him, between his doubled-up knees and his nose, a small glass oil lamp, covered with a glass shade, is burning. Close to this is a tray, containing a small round box, holding the drug, a straight piece of wire used for manipulating it, a knife to scrape up the fragments, and the pipe used for smoking. The latter is about two feet long, with a nose of about half an inch in diameter, and is not unlike the stem of a flute before it is fitted. About two inches from the bottom of the tube is a closed cup or bowl of earthenware or stone, having a central perforation. To charge the pipe, a small portion of the drug (weighing a few grains) is picked up with the wire, kneaded and rolled in the closed surface of the cup, then heated in the flame of the lamp till it swells. This is rolled up and again manipulated, then finally placed in the aperture in the surface of the bowl. It is then lighted from the lamp, and the smoke drawn into the lungs through the tube till the first charge is exhausted.

It is stated that opium provides the Chinese war-lords, now battling for supremacy, with the means of carrying on the fight. There is still an enormous demand for the drug in spite of all the efforts to suppress the traffic. It was recently estimated that in Peking alone £10,000 a day is spent in opium and one person in every ten is said to be addicted to opium-smoking.

So great is the need of the war-lords for money that they have compelled starving peasants to plant the poppy even in the famine areas.

According to a recent account :

" Military leaders in Shensi and Kansu are not willing to send their opium through Feng Yu-hsiang's territory, as there is no assurance that it would arrive safely. If it escaped the bandits, it is unlikely to escape seizure by Feng or other commanders whose need of the sinews of war is great. The war-lords have taken over the opium traffic almost entirely in several provinces, and the problem of transporting it safely to the markets is leading to much military activity. Travellers to Inner Mongolia have observed that large numbers of northern soldiers have been stationed along the caravan routes. These routes, traversed by motor cars as well as camels, are infested by bandits, but soldiers do not usually trouble them."

In Persia, at the present time, according to Wills, nine out of ten of the aged take from one to five grains of the drug daily. It is also largely used by the native physicians. It does not appear that the moderate use of Persian opium in the country itself is deleterious. Opium smoking is almost unknown, and when it is smoked, it is, as a rule, by a doctor's orders. The opium pill-box—a tiny box of silver—is as common in Persia as the snuff-box was once with us. Most men of forty in the middle and upper classes take from a grain to a grain and a half, divided into two pills, one in the afternoon and one at night. The majority of authorities agree that opium smoking as a habit is much more harmful and attended with much more demoralizing influences than opium eating ; but either habit is undoubtedly harmful to Europeans, and when once formed, is extremely difficult to break. The amount of alkaloids absorbed in the smoke is very small, both because the quantity of opium used in the pipe is minute and because most of the active principles in the drug are thus destroyed. Absorption however is rapid, and an immediate effect is produced. Professor Dixon states that the morphine in ten pipes contains about half a grain and 99 per cent of this is destroyed in combustion. After the first few whiffs to the novice, there is a feeling of elation, followed in the habitué by a feeling of lanquid ease, an exalted sense of superiority and later by a dreamy sleep. The habitué rapidly becomes a slave to the habit which clutches him like a vice. More pernicious even than smoking is the use of one of the derivatives of opium by injection, as the victim soon finds that to produce the desired effect the dose must be constantly increased until sufficient is used that would ordinarily kill half a dozen people.

Paracelsus is generally credited with being the originator of the word laudanum, the name by which tincture of opium is commonly known. Yet there seems little doubt the word was first applied to the gum of the cistus. Clusius, in his *Rariorum Plantarum Historia*, states : " The gum of the cistus is called in Greek and Latin, ladanum, and in shops laudanum." It is therefore very likely that the secret preparation originated by Paracelsus in the sixteenth century which he called laudanum, was composed of the gum of the cistus as well as opium, and that he adopted the name from the former ingredient.

Among the poisonous plants with powerful narcotic properties is belladonna (*atropa belladonna*) or deadly nightshade which is a native of Southern Europe but is often found growing wild in several of the Southern counties of England.

It cannot be identified with certainty earlier than the sixteenth century, where it is mentioned in the *Grand Herbier*, printed in Paris about 1504. In 1542, Leonard Fuchs included it in his *Historia Stirpium* and recognized its poisonous properties.

Matthiolus who noticed it a few years later, calls the plant *Solatrum majus* and says it is commonly called by the Venetians *Herba Bella donne*, because the Italian women use a distilled water of the plant as a cosmetic. Whether this is true or not, it was certainly used by women in several European countries on account of its property of enlarging the pupils of the eyes which they thought added to their beauty.

It began to be used in medicine about the middle of the last century.

In 1833, Mein prepared from the root, and Geiger and Hesse isolated from the leaves, the alkaloid called atropine, a powerful poison of which they contain a large proportion. Hubschmann claimed to have found another alkaloid in the plant in 1858, which he called Belladonnine.

Another plant of a highly poisonous nature which is commonly seen growing in our woods and gardens is the foxglove (*digitalis purpurea*) with its handsome spikes of purple or white flowers.

The name digitalis, from digitale, a thimble or finger stall, was given to the plant by Fuchs in 1542 who figured it in his " Herbal." The Germans called it *fingerhut*, while to the French it was known as *gantelée*.

In folk-lore it was regarded as the special flower of the fairies and its little bells were supposed to afford the tiny elves a safe retreat and hiding place. In Ireland it was called the " fairy cap " and in Wales it was known as " goblin's gloves."

The flower is also said to have been held in high favour by the witches who decorated their fingers with the largest bells and it was thus known in some parts of England as " witches bells " or " fairy folks glove."

Foxglove was used as an external remedy by the physicians of Wales as early as the thirteenth century. It became known as a remedial agent in the seventeenth century and was first included in the London Pharmacopœia in 1650.

Its value in reducing the heart's action was recognized by Dr. Withering of Birmingham in 1785, who also used it with advantage in cases of dropsy.

Its active principles are digitalin, digitalein and digitoxin, the latter being discovered by Schmiedeberg in 1874, but they are so highly poisonous that they are now but rarely used in medicine.

The stramonium (*datura stramonium*) or thornapple, which

contains the highly poisonous alkaloids, atropine and hyoscyamine, appears to have spread itself about the middle of the
fifteenth century from the regions near the Caspian Sea. We
know from Gerard, that it was cultivated in London near the
close of the sixteenth century. He tells us that he received the
seed from Constantinople. When dried, the leaves were smoked
to relieve asthma and were so used by the Nubians for other
chest troubles. Both the leaves and seeds contain daturine
which was discovered by Geiger and Hesse in 1833, and who
considered it to have the same composition as atropine, although
the latter is double as poisonous as the former.

Another variety of the plant known as the white-flowered
datura, is a native of India. It was used by the Arab physicians,
who were aware of its poisonous properties, from an early
period and called *datura alba*.

Garcia de Orta observed this plant in India in 1563 and states
that its flowers and seeds were put into food to intoxicate persons
it was designed to rob. Christoval Acosta in 1578 described
two varieties of the plant, the seeds of either being very poisonous
and were often administered with criminal intent. Graham states
it was used by Bombay thieves who administered it in order to
deprive their victims of the power of resistance.

It is an interesting fact that certain poisonous drugs act in
distinct antagonism to each other. Many years ago, Fraser
thus drew attention to the action of atropine and physostigmine
on the pupil of the eye and showed, that while the former
dilated it, the latter caused its contraction. Preyer also observed
that aconite and prussic acid were antagonistic and later,
Schmeidberg and Kopp proved that muscarin and atropine
were similarly opposed in their action.

Other investigators have shown the antagonism existing between chloroform, ether and chloral hydrate on the one hand
and strychnine on the other. It has been proved that very
large doses of strychnine can be borne by animals, including
man, if the spasm be kept under by ether, chloroform or chloral,
and there appears little doubt that life has been saved after
poisonous doses of strychnine by the use of these drugs.

Nux vomica from which strychnine is chiefly obtained was
not known to the ancients. It was first used in England about
1640 for poisoning dogs and birds.

The chief active principles, strychnine and brucine, both of
which are highly poisonous, were isolated by Pelletier and
Caventou from St. Ignatius bean in 1818–19. These alkaloids
are obtained from both sources.

CHAPTER X

DRUG INTOXICANTS AND
DELIRIANTS—HASHISH—MESCAL—A POISON CLUB

HASHISH, or Bhang, is the native name applied to the dried flowering tops of the Indian hemp, from which the resin has not been removed.

This plant which is cultivated largely in India, is now considered to be the same, botanically, as the *Cannabis sativa* of European cultivation. There is however great difference in their medicinal activity, that growing in India being much more powerful. Indian hemp is said to owe its properties to the alkaloid called trigonelline. *Ganja* is the native name for one part of the plant, and *Sidhi* for another part, which is much poorer in resin. The resinous principle is called *churrus* or *charas*, and the entire plant, cut during inflorescence, dried in the sun and pressed into bundles, is called *bhang*.

The method of using it in India is chiefly for smoking in combination with tobacco. For this purpose, a plug of tobacco is first placed at the bottom of the bowl of the pipe and on the top a small piece of hashish, while over this is put a piece of glowing charcoal. Another way is to knead the drug with the tobacco by the thumb of one hand and working it in the palm of the other, till they are thoroughly incorporated.

In India, both *ganja* and *churrus* are used for smoking, but not *bhang* or *sidhi*, and according to native accounts, the habit of smoking *ganja* is said to become part of a man's life. Under ordinary circumstances he has his smoke daily when his day's labour is over, and during the interval when he cooks his evening meal. Under extraordinary circumstances he takes it to sustain him in the midst of severe or prolonged exertion. It does not (as in opium smoking) affect his appetite, but enables the poorest to partake with a heartier appetite of their somewhat uninviting fare. It does not affect the digestion or interfere in the slightest degree with bodily or mental health, and the habit does not grow on the votary. Ganja-smoking appears to be only injurious when indulged in to excess by those who lead sedentary lives.

Simple infusions of the leaves and flowering tops are also much used for drinking purposes by old and young in India, the alcoholic form being a most active and dangerous intoxicant.

The drug is said to have been used in China to produce insensibility when performing operations as early as the year 220. The Persians employed it in the Middle Ages for the purpose of exciting the pugnacity and fanaticism of the soldiers during the wars of the Crusades.

In 1803 Visey, a French scientist, published a memoir on hashish, and attempted to prove that it was the Nepenthe of Homer ; there is little doubt, however, that the use of the drug was known to Galen.

Silvestin de Lacy contends that the word assassin is derived from " hashishin," a name given to a wild sect of Mohammedans who committed murder under its influence.

The Chinese herbal, *Rh-ya*, which dates from about the fifth century B.C., mentions the fact that the hemp plant is of two kinds, the one producing seeds and the other flowers only. Herodotus states that hemp grows in Scythia both wild and cultivated, and that the Thracians made garments from it which could hardly be distinguished from linen. He also describes " how the Scythians exposed themselves as in a bath " to the vapour of the seeds thrown on hot coals.

Bhang which consists of the entire plant dried and mixed with a few fruits is of a dark green colour. It has a peculiar odour but little taste. Mixed with flour or incorporated with sweetmeat it is called hashish. It is also smoked or taken infused in cold water. *Ganja* consists exclusively of the flowering shoots of the female plant, having a compound or glutinous appearance, and is brownish-green in colour. *Majun* is a name applied to a sweetmeat or confection, of which Indian hemp is the basis, but it may contain nux vomica, opium, cantharides, or frequently datura seeds, according to the purpose for which it is intended, whether as an aphrodisiac, a criminal excitant or deliriant.

Of the many curious experiences that have been written describing the effects of hashish, one of the most interesting is that given by Gautier, in which he relates his own experience of the drug.

" The Orientalists," he says, " have, in consequence of the interdiction of wine, sought that species of excitement which the Western nations derive from alcoholic drinks." He then proceeds to state how a few minutes after swallowing some of the preparation, a sudden overwhelming sensation took possession of him. It appeared to him that his body was dissolved, and that he had become transparent. He clearly saw in his stomach the hashish he had swallowed, under the form of an emerald, from which a thousand little sparks issued. His eyelashes were lengthened indefinitely, and rolled like threads of gold around ivory balls, which turned with inconceivable rapidity. Around him were sparklings of precious stones of all

colours, changes eternally produced, like the play of a kaleido-
scope. He every now and then saw his friends who were around
him disfigured as half men, half plants, some having the wings
of the ostrich, which they were constantly shaking. So strange
were these that he burst into fits of laughter, and, to join in the
apparent ridiculousness of the affair, he began by throwing the
cushions in the air, catching and turning them with the rapidity
of an Indian juggler. One gentleman spoke to him in Italian,
which the hashish transposed into Spanish. After a few minutes
he recovered his habitual calmness, without any bad effect, and
only with feelings of astonishment at what had passed. Half
an hour had scarcely elapsed before he again fell under the
influence of the drug. On this occasion the vision was more
complicated and extraordinary. In the air there were millions
of butterflies, confusedly luminous, shaking their wings like
fans. Gigantic flowers, with calices of crystal ; large peonies
upon beds of gold and silver rose and surrounded him with the
crackling sound that accompanies the explosion in the air of
fireworks. His hearing had acquired new power ; it was
enormously developed. He heard the noise of colours. Green,
red, blue, yellow sounds reached him in waves—a glass thrown
down, the creaking of a sofa, a word pronounced low, vibrated
and rolled within him like peals of thunder. His own voice
sounded so loud that he feared to speak lest he should knock
down the walls or explode like a rocket. More than five hundred
clocks struck the hour with fleeting silvery voices, and every
object touched gave a note like the harmonica or the Æolian
harp. He swam in an ocean of sound, where floated like aisles
of light some of the airs of " Lucia di Lammermoor " and the
" Barber of Seville." Never did similar bliss overwhelm him
with its waves ; he was lost in a wilderness of sweets ; he was
not himself ; he was relieved from consciousness, that feeling
which always pervades the mind ; and for the first time he
comprehended what might be the state of elementary beings,
of angels, of souls separated from the body. All his system
seemed infected with the fantastic colouring in which he was
plunged. Sounds, perfume, light, reached him only by minute
rays, in the midst of which he heard mystic currents whistling
along. According to his calculation, this state lasted about
three hundred years, for the sensations were so numerous and
so hurried one upon the other, that a real appreciation of time
was impossible. The paroxysm over, he was aware that it had
only lasted a *quarter of an hour*.

Another interesting account of the strange hallucinations
produced by the drug is related by Dr. Moreau, who, with two
friends, experimented with hashish.

" At first," he states, " I thought my companions were less
influenced by the drug than myself. Then, as the effect, I

fancied that the person who brought me the dose had given me some of more active quality. This, I thought to myself, was an imprudence and the involuntary idea presented itself that I might be poisoned. The idea became fixed ; I called out loudly to Dr. Roche : ' You are an assassin ; you have poisoned me ! ' This was received with shouts of laughter, and my lamentations excited mirth. I struggled for some time against the thought, but the greater the effort the more completely did it overcame me, till at last it took full possession of my mind. The extravagant conviction now came uppermost that I was dead, and upon the point of being buried ; my soul had left my body. In a few minutes I had gone through all the stages of delirium.

" These fixed ideas and erroneous convictions are apt to be produced, but they only last a few seconds, unless there is any physical disorder.

" The Orientalist, when he indulges in hashish retires into the depth of his harem ; no one is then admitted who cannot contribute to his enjoyment. He surrounds himself with his dancing girls, who perform their graceful evolutions before him to the sound of music ; gradually a new condition of the brain allows a series of illusions, arising from the external senses, to present themselves. The mind becomes overpowered by the brilliancy of gorgeous visions ; discrimination, comparison, reason, yield up their throne to dreams and phantoms which exhilarate and delight.

" The mind tries to understand what is the cause of the new delight, but it is in vain. It seems to know there is no reality."

Hardly two people appear to experience the same results from hashish. Upon some it has little effect, while upon others, especially women, it exerts extraordinary power. While one person says he imagined his body endowed with such elasticity that he fancied he could enter into a bottle and remain there at his ease, another fancied he had become the piston of a steam engine ; under the influence of the drug the ear lends itself more to the illusion than any other sense. Its first effect is one of intense exhilaration, almost amounting to delirium ; power of thought is soon lost, and the victim laughs, cries and sings or dances, all the time imagining he is acting rationally. The second stage is one of dreamy enjoyment followed by a dead stupor.

Of the ordinary physical effects of hashish, the first is a feeling of slight compression of the temporal bones and upper parts of the head. The respiration is gentle, the pulse is increased, and a gentle heat is felt all over the surface of the body. There is a sense of weight about the fore-part of the arms, and an occasional slight involuntary motion, as if to seek relief from it. There is a feeling of discomfort about the extremities, creating a feeling of uneasiness, and if the dose has been too large the usual symptoms of poisoning by Indian hemp show themselves. Flushes of heat seem to ascend to the head, even to the brain, which create considerable alarm. Singing in the ears is complained of ; then comes on a state of anxiety, almost of anguish, with a sense of constriction about the chest. The individual fancies he hears the beating of his heart with unaccustomed loudness ; but throughout the whole period it is the nervous system that is affected, and in this way the drug differs materially from opium, whose action on the muscular and digestive systems is most marked.

It is a remarkable fact that Indian hemp fails to produce the same intoxicating effects in this country that it does in warmer climates, and whether this is due to the loss of some volatile principle or difference in temperature, it is not yet determined. But would-be experimentalists in the effects of hashish would do well to remember that it may not be indulged in with impunity, and most authorities agree that the brain, even in India, becomes eventually disordered with frequent indulgence in the drug. Frequent intoxication leads to a condition of delirium, usually of a dangerous nature ; the moral nature becomes numbed, and the victim at last becomes unfit to pursue his ordinary avocation. It is stated by those who have had considerable experience in its use, that even during the dream of joy there is a consciousness that all is illusion ; there is at no period a belief that anything that dances before the senses or plays upon the imagination is real, and that when the mind recovers its equilibrium it knows that all is but a phantasm.

The Kiowa and other Mexican Indians use the fruit of the *Anhelonium Lewinii*, known as " mescal buttons," to produce a species of intoxication and stimulation during certain of their religious ceremonies. The effects of mescal, like Indian hemp, varies considerably in different individuals. They are very peculiar, and have been described in some detail by Lewin, Prentiss, Havelock Ellis and Morgan.

The eating of the fruit first results in a state of strange excitement and great exuberance of spirits, accompanied by volubility in speech. This is shortly followed by a stage of intoxication in which the sight is affected in a very extraordinary manner, consisting of a kaleidoscopic play of colours ever in motion, of every possible shade and tint, and these constantly changing. The pupils of the eyes are widely dilated, cutaneous sensation is blunted and thoughts seem to flash through the brain with extraordinary rapidity. The colour visions are generally only seen with closed eyes, but the colouring of all external objects is exaggerated. Sometimes there is also an indescribable sensation of dual existence.

The Mexican Indians treat this cactus with great veneration, gathering it with uncovered heads and amid clouds of incense.

The celebration of the rite is usually held on a Saturday night, when seated in a circle around a large camp fire, for the visions are said to be most intense by flickering firelight. The men pray for " a good intoxication," and then the leader passes the drug around. Throughout the night the men sit quietly round the fire in a state of reverie, absorbed in colour-visions, amid continual singing and beating of drums by assistants. The effects do not pass off till the following noon, when they get up and go about their business with apparently no depression or other after-effects.

After taking three of the " buttons " in small fragments by pouring boiling water on them twice and drinking the infusion thrice at intervals of an hour, Ellis states that the phenomena of mescal intoxication are merely the saturnalia of the specific senses and chiefly an orgy of vision.

After a transient consciousness of energy, he felt faint and giddy, pale violet shadows floated before him, suggesting, without any definite form, pictures. The air seemed to be filled with a vague perfume, then he saw glorious fields of jewels which sprang into flower-like shapes before his gaze, and then turned into butterfly forms.

" I was further impressed," he says, " not only by the brilliance and delicate beauty of their colours, but even more by their lovely and various textures."

A friend, to whom he gave some of the drug, experienced a pain at the heart and a sensation of imminent death, then with the suddenness of a neuralgic pain the back of his head seemed to open and emit streams of bright colour. " I had the sensation of the skin disappearing from the brow ; any movement sent out streams of blue flames of wondrous beauty."

The Mexicans also make a drink from the mescal, which is distilled from the juice of the plant, and during their social entertainments swallow it in copious draughts. Its effects are said to be highly intoxicating, and according to the reports of authorities 90 per cent of the crimes perpetrated in the ranches and villages are due to this poisonous liquid.

The properties of mescal are due to an alkaloid called mescaline which has been used in America as a drug, but its increasing employment as an intoxicant and deliriant is now said to be perturbing the police authorities in the large cities.

Popularly known as peyote, the intoxication produced by it is manifested by prolonged visual hallucinations, often followed by vertigo, headache, nausea and confusion of thought.

Visions begin within half an hour after taking the drug and are always brightly coloured and of dazzling brightness. Its influence varies in individuals and while some experience a gorgeous and multi-coloured pageantry, others see only a medley of geometrical designs.

Dr. Critchley who recently experimented with the drug upon a colleague and himself thus describes the effects :

" Some of the visual phenomena began about twenty-five minutes after 0.2 gramme of mescaline sulphate had been ingested. The hallucinatory images were at first simple in pattern and colour, and only visible when the eyes were closed. Later they became more complicated, and no longer comprised simple geometrical designs as at first, but took a three-dimensional form and were most brilliantly illuminated and coloured.

" The hallucinations now became apparent with the eyes open, though never to the same extent as when the eyes were closed. This bewildering state reached its maximum in ninety minutes and persisted at this level for several hours."

Large doses are said to produce complete paralysis and death is caused by respiratory failure.

While not a dangerous drug, mescal is undoubtedly habit-forming and is eventually harmful both mentally and physically.

A few years ago a secret club, the members of which undertook to record their experiences of certain poisons, was formed among some students in a university city in America.

This circle met periodically to carry out their experiments with mescal and their experiences are said to have resulted in a variety of impressions according to the nature of each individual.

One experience at the first meeting, is thus recorded by a member.

" The field of consciousness was a dense soft black. Suddenly from the right bounced the cathedral of Milan, pure and shining silver. As it hit solid ground, each little spire shot tremblingly upward and flattened again to its usual proportions.

" The Milan took another bounce toward the left and Rheims bounced into its place, both performing the same evolutions. One by one, all the gothics I had ever seen in Europe and many that my fervid imagination conceived of itself had passed in a dazzling procession of silver or jet. A noise in the next room finally broke the spell and the cathedrals that happened to be on the stage, shivered themselves into shards and thence into anentity. The experience left me trembling and breathless.

" The same night I also saw a magnificent tableau ; all the ensigns, eagles and banners of Imperial Rome, unbelievably colourful, sliding or rather flowing slowly from all sides towards the centre. And the centrepiece of this spectacle was a tiny cuckoo-bird, nodding his head drolly up and down and uttering the appropriate cry.

" Another symbolic vision was beheld by a much-travelled

musician of our set. He saw the interior of Notre Dame in the dusk of twilight, and heard the great organ playing softly, and a distinctly religious and mystic atmosphere pervading it all. Suspended from the roof was a diminutive pair of delicate pink corsets ! Paris indeed !

" The second meeting," says the writer, " was marked by a rather frightful experience for two of us. Mr. F. a classical scholar and a mystic, became imbued with the idea that he was two distinct persons, one ordering an act and one forbidding it.

" There were just two of them alone together, the other being a Mr. K. a musician, eccentric and tense-nerved. Suddenly F.'s eye fell upon a very keen-edged dagger which lay on the table. His evil demon immediately ordered him to cut his friend's throat and cast his blood to the winds with an incantation ; his good demon forbade it.   But while K. was frantic with anxiety (for F is an immense person) and K is slender, also paralysed on one side of his body, the evil demon was rapidly getting the best of the argument. Suddenly K. got an inspiration which probably saved F.'s life. Calling him to him sharply he told him that he was Kenosha, the god of all gods, supreme in power, and damning the act as obscure desecration of the Kenoshic mysteries, ordered him to stop immediately, put the dagger down and atone on his knees. The plan worked ; F. did as ordered and the demons returned not again that night.

" At the third meeting, H., a strange fellow, who though of scientific bent is in normal state rather high-strung almost to hysteria, had some very spectacular visions. In the principal of these he sat astride a comet blazing along through limitless space at a terrific speed, and, with a revolver of diamonds shot at the passing stars. When hit, each star burst with a tremendous crash of colour and sound, while he rode gaily on to the kingdom of No where."

These are but a few of the experiences of the members of this curious coterie, which are interesting as showing the effects and hallucinations produced by mescal.

CHAPTER XI

POISONOUS AND DEADLY FUNGI—SOME COMMON POISONOUS PLANTS

RESEARCH into manuscripts dealing with poisons written in the Middle Ages show that certain fungi " those evil fermentations of the earth that spring up in a night no man knows whither," played a more important part in criminal poisoning than is generally supposed.

The toxic properties of several varieties were known in the early Christian era and mention is made of them directly or indirectly in works on medicine from the fourteenth to the sixteenth century. The facts that they could so easily be obtained and when carefully dried and powdered could be mixed with food or wine no doubt led to their frequent use as secret poisons. In those days, there was little or no chance of the poison being discovered, the symptoms produced such as severe abdominal pain, vomiting, purging, dilated pupils, tetanic spasms and convulsions generally followed by rapid coma, might easily be mistaken, and doubtless were in some cases, for those of natural disease. On the other hand we now know that the clinical picture of fungus poisoning is not unlike the effects of arsenic.

There are at least twenty-five poisonous varieties of mushrooms, but the most deadly of all which accounts for more than ninety per cent of the deaths from fungi, is the *amanita phalloides*.

It owes its virulence to an active principle or alkaloid called amanita toxin.

Then there is the *amanita muscaria* with its bright red top studded with red spots, which contains at least three highly poisonous bodies called muscarin, myceto-atropine and choline. It produces intoxication, and fatal delirium, which is usually followed by death within twenty-four hours.

The *amanita muscaria* or fly agaric, so-called from its power of killing flies when it is steeped in milk, is an extremely deadly poison yet according to Dr. Lanesdorff the natives of Kamschatka and other parts of north-east Asia make a drink from it which is said to have extraordinary intoxicating effects.

The fungi are collected in the hottest months and dried in the air. They are sometimes rolled up and swallowed without chewing or they are eaten fresh in soups and sauces, but in this way they loose much of their intoxicating properties. Water drank after swallowing them augments their narcotic effects which are said to come on within one or two hours afterwards. Drunkenness and giddiness follow, as after taking alcohol. Cheerful emotions of the mind are first produced and the face becomes flushed. Involuntary words and actions follow, with sometimes an entire loss of consciousness.

It renders some persons remarkably active and stimulates muscular exertion, while on others a large dose produces violent spasmodic effects. At times the effects are very ludicrous to the onlooker, for when a person under the influence wishes to step over a straw or twig, he is seen to take a stride or a jump sufficient to clear the trunk of a tree. Talkative persons cannot keep silent and those fond of music are heard perpetually singing.

" The most singular effect of the amanita," says Lanesdorff, " is the influence it possesses over the urine to which it imparts an intoxicating quality which continues for a considerable time afterwards. For instance, a man moderately intoxicated one day, will by the next morning have slept himself sober, but his urine will be more powerfully intoxicating than on the previous day."

Besides the varieties of fungi mentioned there are the *agaricus semi-globatus* which is highly poisonous, *agaricus nicator*, the deadly agaric, which contains the toxic principles agaricine and phalline, and the poisonous chantarella, *cantharellus aurantiacus*, which is also a violent poison. Among the brightly coloured fungi, the purple-red *agaricus ruber*, which contains an alkaloid called agarythrine, is of a very dangerous character.

Girolamo Corraro of Verona, in his treatise on poisons written in the sixteenth century, alludes to the diabolical poisons used in his time which he had studied from the early authors. Among them he refers to the many species of fungi of which " Clusius mentions more than a dozen that are very poisonous and cause death whether from accident or purpose." The symptoms resulting by which such cases of poisoning may be recognized, he says, are difficulty of breathing, intense pain in the stomach and bowels, delirium, rigors, followed by syncope and death. The only antidote he knew for these poisonous fungi was the sylvester pear given in strong wine.

Another writer observes that external indications that death has been caused by poisonous fungi, are numerous violet coloured spots which afterwards appear on the skin over the whole body.

A certain cardinal who lived in Rome in the sixteenth century is said to have had granules prepared from the dried amanita muscaria which he kept in a secret receptacle in a ring.

The story of another poisonous fungus now known as ergot,

is one of historic interest and forms a page in the romance of science.

Ergot is a peculiar form of the fungus *Claviceps purpurea* which is developed in the ovaries of certain kinds of grasses but is now chiefly found in rye. It develops gradually in the ear of the rye and by the summer appears as a long, black, triangular " horn," some eight or ten often being found in one ear.

As early as the eleventh century it was observed by Sigebert de Gremblour, who remarked that an epidemic followed the consumption of damaged crops, but it was not until the end of the seventeenth century, that it was recognized as the cause of a terrible disease which had decimated mankind for centuries.

Epidemics of this disease known as St. Antony's or Holy fire, had been especially common in France, from the tenth century, and in one of these, forty thousand persons are said to have perished. Sigebert who describes the sufferings of the people attacked in 1089, says : " a great number were afflicted by a gruesome disease which caused their limbs to become as black as coal and from which the patients died miserably, or were reduced to an unhappy life, having lost hands and feet."

The relics of St. Antony were believed to have a miraculous effect on the sufferers, and so his name became associated with the malady.

Other saints were also regarded as healers and when the people of Paris were visited by an epidemic of this pestilential disease in 1129, St. Geneviève was invoked and her shrine was carried in a solemn procession through the streets so that the sick might be healed by touching it.

Germany, Flanders, Burgundy and other countries suffered from epidemics of the disease but England practically escaped.

About the sixteenth century it began to be noticed that these epidemics occurred at particular seasons of the year, and that certain provinces were more frequently visited than others. In the district of the Sologne in France it appeared to be specially prevalent and there the disease was almost entirely confined to the peasantry.

A contemporary writer describes the attack as beginning with intense pains in the legs and feet causing the victims to writhe and scream. A fire seemed to burn between the flesh and the bones. Sometimes the skin became livid and black or large blisters arose upon it. Gangrene of the limbs followed and a foot or hand would fall off, or the flesh of the whole limb would be destroyed to the bones.

The first suggestion that a fungus might be the cause of the disease, resulted from an investigation made by the Medical Faculty of Marburg following an outbreak in Hesse in 1597. Their conclusions led to the belief that the epidemic had been caused by the use of " spurred rye." This was followed by the observations of Thuillier, physician to the Duke of Sully, who expressed the belief that ergot or spurred rye was the cause of the disease which had decimated some parts of France in 1630. He noted that the intensity of the epidemic was in proportion to the amount of contaminated grain consumed, and proved the poisonous nature of ergot by experiments on birds and animals.

In 1709 there was an outbreak of the disease in Switzerland which spread to France, and the following year M. Noel, a surgeon of the Hôtel Dieu at Orleans, published his opinion that the disease was "produced by bad nourishment, particularly by the use of bread in which there was a great quantity of ergot."

The leading physicians of the time then began to recognize that ergot was largely the cause of the scourge and M. Fagon chief physician to the King of France, stigmatized it as " a king of monsters in vegetation, which a particular sort of rye sown in March, is more apt to produce than what is sown in autumn and which often abounds in moist, cold countries and in wet seasons."

There were severe epidemics of the disease in Sweden, Russia, France and Flanders in 1746 and 1747. The pain suffered by the victims in these outbreaks is said to have been terribly violent, and many in their agonies hurled themselves against the walls or even threw themselves in to the water.

The immunity of the people of Great Britain to the disease, and its freedom from such epidemics, was obviously due to the fact that rye was seldom grown and rarely used for making bread in this country.

By the end of the eighteenth century it was generally concluded that the eating of rye contaminated with ergot was the cause of the gangrenous disease which came to be called ergotism.

It has not yet been completely stamped out in some countries, for as late as 1883 and 1888 there were outbreaks in Russia, but its now comparative disappearance is owing to greater care being exercised in the cultivation of rye and other cereals in which the fungus develops.

Ergot is now only employed in medicine, and thus through scientific investigation and research, what was once the cause of terrible suffering and death has been transformed into a medicinal agent of great value to the human race.

There are several plants often met with in our gardens and in the country which contain poisonous and irritant principles such as the common arum, that excites an intolerable sensation of burning and pricking in the tongue which will continue for several hours. The juice of white briony also, which has a nauseous bitter acrid taste, when applied to the skin for some time, will inflame and blister the part. From it the alkaloids veratrine and ceratine are obtained. The meadow crowfoot produces intense itching, redness and blisters when applied to the skin and acts as a poison if taken internally.

From the common meadow saffron, colchicine a poisonous alkaloid is obtained and from the Christmas rose, powerful principles called helleborin and jervine have been isolated. Several plants of the narcissus tribe, such as the musk-scented daffodil, the common double daffodil and the French daffodil, contain toxic principles including narcissine, an irritant poison, and the purple clematis yields one called clematine. The yellow toadflax, so common in our fields, contains two active principles called gratiolin and linarin and from the beautiful lily of the valley, the alkaloid convallarin is extracted which exerts a powerful action on the heart.

Several shrubs and trees are capable of yielding prussic acid including the seeds of various species of prunus, the yellow-flowered pea, the leaves of the common laurel, bitter almonds and the kernels of stone fruits such as the nectarine, damson, apricot and peach. They all contain principles which by contact with water produce an oil and prussic acid. The kernels of the peach in particular contain 2.85 per cent of amygdalin, which in the presence of emulsion and water breaks up into prussic acid and other compounds.

One of the myriapods (chilognathen) contains glands at the roots of the hairs which also secret prussic acid and when the insect is seized the poisonous secretion is poured out.

The volatile oil extracted from the common wormwood (*artemisia absinthium*) to which absinthe owes some of its properties, when taken in excess acts as a narcotic poison. It contains a principle called absinthic acid and the introduction of such a deleterious body into cocktails is to be greatly deprecated. Absinthe, which is a strong alcoholic mixture of the oils of aniseed and wormwood with aromatic flavourings, capable of forming a most enslaving habit, is now prohibited in France. It is a most insidious intoxicant the excessive use of which may induce epileptic attacks.

A mysterious poison, kept as a secret by some of the gipsy tribes which wander Europe is said to be composed of a certain poisonous fungus. When mixed with food it causes death in from two to three weeks after administration. The symptoms produced are said to resemble those of typhoid fever. A case of poisoning with this substance, which is known to the gipsies by the name of " dri " or " drei," was reported in London in 1864.

It is remarkable that certain animals and birds can consume plants and substances that are poisonous to man, with impunity. Thus storks and quails can feed on hemlock and aconite. Water hemlock can be eaten by oxen, goats, horses and sheep without apparent ill effects.

In human beings the state of health and disease have considerable influence over the action of poisons. Climate also has its effect and it is well known that natives of southern countries, especially those with warm climates, are more susceptible to narcotics and other vegetable poisons, than those who live in more northern and colder latitudes.

CHAPTER XII

TOBACCO AS A DRUG AND A POISON—POISONING WITH NICOTINE

IT is a curious fact that a plant which yields one of the most powerful poisons known, is in daily use by millions of people throughout all parts of the world. It affords an apt illustration of the truth that even the most poisonous substances have their beneficent as well as their evil uses, for to quote Richard Burton: " Tobacco divine, rare, superexcellent tobacco which goes farre beyond all their Panaceas, potable gold and Philosopher's stones, is a soveraign Remedy for all diseases."

The history of the tobacco plant (*nicotiana tabacum*) is so well-known it need not be recapitulated. A native of the New World, the practice of smoking the leaves has been widely diffused among the natives of South America from time immemorial.

Columbus appears to have seen the plant shortly before he landed in America when he called at ' Guanahani ' or San Salvador.

Las Cascus relates that when he landed in Cuba a few days later, two emissaries he sent to visit the King returned, stating they had seen " many people, men and women, going to and from their villages, and always the men with a brand in their hands and certain herbs in order to take their smokes."

The first description of the tobacco plant is that given by Gonzalo Fernandez de Oviedo y Valde in his work entitled *Historia General de las Indias*, printed in Seville in 1535.

By the end of the sixteenth century the custom of smoking was generally known throughout Spain and Portugal, from whence it passed into eastern Europe, Egypt and India.

Tobacco was brought to England in 1586 by Francis Drake in a ship which also carried Sir Walter Raleigh, but the plant had been introduced into France by André Trevet in 1556. In his book " *Singularites de la France Antarctique* " he describes tobacco and its use in Brazil and also the smoking of the herb by the Canadian Indians.

It was not grown in Europe until the middle of the sixteenth century when the seeds were first brought to Lisbon by Jean Nicot the French Ambassador and thence taken to France in 1561, as those of a valuable medicinal plant and presented to Catherine de' Medici.

In 1583, Charles Estienne claimed for it the first place among medicinal herbs " on account of its singular and almost Divine virtues."

It should be remembered that tobacco was first introduced into

Europe as a drug and was so regarded, as it took a place in the pharmacopœias and was sold by the apothecaries and druggists. An ointment prepared from tobacco leaves and lard was included in the *London Pharmacopœia* printed in 1618 and it remained an official drug until 1868.

Pomet writing in 1696 says : " Jean Nicot first brought it into France to the Queen Regent hence it was called the ' Queen's herb,' and also the ' Holy herb ' from its great virtues ; last of all Petum, which is the name the Indians give it and which was the first and the true name for tobacco."

It was originally used medicinally in the treatment of dropsy and palsy and in doses of from three to ten grains as an emetic. A medical writer at the beginning of the nineteenth century remarks " the smoke is used as a pleasant mode of losing time."

Early in the XIX century it was strongly recommended as a stimulating clyster for resusitating the apparently drowned, and the Royal Humane Society issued cases containing an elaborate apparatus consisting of bellows and syringes with instructions for using it.

Nicotine the chief alkaloid of tobacco was first isolated by Posselt and Reimann in 1828. It is a thin, oily liquid of a pale amber colour, with a peculiar acrid odour like stale tobacco smoke.

It is a most violent poison and Taylor records that he found a single drop killed a rabbit in three and a half minutes. Nicotine was found in the stomach and blood, and was clearly detected after a week in the tongue and soft parts of the throat.

According to another writer, " the Hottentots are said to kill snakes by putting a drop of the oil of tobacco on their tongues which causes instant death as if by an electric shock."

Both nicotine and oil nicotianin are soluble in water and readily absorbed by the skin. The toxic effects of tobacco smoking are due to several chemical compounds such as pyridine, picoline and lutidine, and even the leaf when applied to an abraided skin, may cause poisonous symptoms.

A case was recently recorded of two gardeners who had been using an insecticide to some fruit trees and were taken ill with vomiting a few hours afterwards. The solution was found to contain 3.7 per cent of nicotine, which on being brushed on the trees, had splashed the hands, arms and faces of the men and had so been absorbed into the system.

There are however but few cases on record of nicotine having been used with criminal intent, the most important being that of the Count and Countess Bocarmé who were charged and tried for poisoning the Countess's brother Gustav Fougnies, at the Château de Bitremont in Belgium in 1851. The accused couple belonged to one of the first families in Hainaut and after their marriage lived in great style at the Château de Bitremont and also in their town house in Brussels.

It transpired that they had been living much beyond their means, for the Countess before her marriage had exaggerated her patrimony, but they still hoped to retrieve their fortunes on the death of her father who was a wealthy man. This hope was not fulfilled as when he died he left most of his money to his son Gustav. Meanwhile, the Bocarmés got deeper into debt and at length planned to murder Gustav Fougnies so that they might come into his fortune.

In order to escape detection, the Count determined to prepare himself the poison he had decided to use, for which purpose he went to Ghent and under an assumed name obtained instruction in the art of distillation from a professor of chemistry in that city. After purchasing some retorts and the necessary apparatus, he returned to the château and practised distilling the essential oil of tobacco.

After he had obtained the desired result, the Bocarmés invited Gustav to dine with them at the château and the unsuspecting young man duly arrived. When the meal was over, it is said he went into the garden to see if his coach was ready for his return and during his absence, the Count seized the opportunity of mixing the poison with a glass of liqueur. On returning to the room, it is supposed he drank it off, as he gave a sudden cry for help, then collapsed and died in less than five minutes. Another account was furnished by a servant, who declared that he had seen the Count with a small phial in his hand, the contents of which he forcibly poured into Gustav's mouth while he held his head.

Although it was given out that Gustav Fougnies had died from apoplexy, suspicions were aroused and the Count and his wife were arrested.

The trial took place at the Assizes held at Hainaut and aroused intense interest throughout the country.

The possession of the poison, as well as the moral evidence, fixed the crime on the Count, who it was stated tried to alter the appearance of his victim after death in order to conceal his crime, by pouring some strong acid into the mouth and over the body. By this means he also sought to conceal or remove the odour of the nicotine.

At the trial, the Countess admitted they were ruined and hoped for the death of her brother so she might inherit his fortune.

M. Stas who made an analysis of the organs of the body, detected nicotine present to the extent of four decigrammes and also found traces in the tongue, throat, stomach, liver and lungs. He also affirmed that he had found nicotine in the wood of the floor near where Gustav Fougnies had been sitting.

Count Bocarmé was found guilty and condemned to death but his wife the Countess was acquitted.

CHAPTER XIII

SOME CLASSICAL MINERAL POISONS AND THEIR HISTORIES—ARSENIC—MERCURY—ANTIMONY

ARSENIC appears to have had an extraordinary fascination for the poisoner for centuries past and has, perhaps, been more frequently used for criminal purposes than any other poison. Through its history runs a vein of mystery and romance which has continued until the present day.

It is one of the most widely distributed elements and is found in many ores, soils and in mineral waters. It is rarely found native and occurs in nature usually associated with other minerals, in crystalline rocks and other schists, mainly in Siberia, Saxony, Transylvannia and Norway.

It was known to the Greeks as early as the fifth century before Christ. Hippocrates, the father of medicine, who flourished 460—377 B.C., used it as an external remedy for ulcers and similar disorders. It was known at that time in the form of sulphuret of arsenic or realgar, also as arsenic sulphide or orpiment which is found native in Greece and Hungary. Dioscorides knew it in its latter form and also mentions its properties when applied externally. At this period there is no allusion to its employment either as a poison or for internal treatment of disease.

The golden colour of orpiment caused many of the early alchemists to consider it the key to the Philosophers' Stone, and this is said to be grounded on some enigmatical phrase attributed to the Sibylline oracles. The Emperor Caligula (A.D. 12-41), according to Pliny, ordered a large quantity of orpiment to be melted and manipulated so that the gold it was supposed to contain could be extracted from it, but he was no doubt disappointed by the result.

Diocletian (A.D. 260) is said to have collected all the books dealing with the transmutation of metals possessed by the Egyptians whom he had conquered, and destroyed them ; but, when the Arabs overran Egypt, the Jews who fled to Europe carried with them the knowledge of science they had acquired from the Arabs and so kept the lamp of alchemy alive.

In the eighth century there arose the great Arab alchemist Jábir ibn Hâyyan, whose writings were known under the name of Geber. He is said to have been a native of Tarsus and believed to have been the first in Europe to obtain what is now known as white arsenic (arsenious acid) by heating realgar. He gave it the name which it still bears to distinguish it from orpiment or yellow arsenic. From his works we know that he was acquainted with crude arsenic and apparently knew, that under certain conditions, it deposited a dull silver coat when in contact with bright copper. His discovery was not without its disadvantages to mankind, as from this period probably dates the time when arsenic began to be used for criminal purposes. On the other hand, its medicinal properties, when properly administered, became known and recognized by physicians.

Before white arsenic or arsenious acid was known, most of the poisons recorded by the early writers had something peculiar in regard to their taste, smell or colour. White arsenic put a new instrument in the hands of the secret poisoner who sought for something powerful and tasteless for his evil designs.

White arsenic as it usually occurs, in pieces, is much less active than when in powder, and it is again more active in solution, while in gaseous form it is still more rapid and powerful in action. As a white crystalline powder it is but slightly soluble in cold water but fairly soluble in hot liquids. It is almost tasteless and in solution is colourless and odourless. It is prepared by roasting the ores and is used largely in glass-making, calico printing, and in the manufacture of pigments and enamels. No less than 2,346 tons of white arsenic were imported into Great Britain and Northern Ireland in 1929.

Although legally it cannot be sold unless it is first mixed with a proportion of soot or indigo, preparations of it in the shape of weed-killers and sheep-dip can be obtained without difficulty especially in country districts. When arsenic is dissolved in alkaline solutions it forms salts called arsenites which are the basis of many sheep-dips, and weed-killers and are also used for making fly-papers.

The large percentage of arsenic in these preparations renders them highly dangerous, a fact which the public are slow to recognize. Some of them contain as much as seventy per cent of arsenic and yet they are frequently handled by ignorant and careless people especially in agricultural districts, where they can be so easily obtained.

An extraordinary case of suicide by weed-killer was investigated by the Coroner for North Devon, at an inquest held on the body of a man in June 1928.

According to the evidence of the county analyst who made an examination of the organs and stomach, the man must have drink about a teacupful of the weed-killer, as no less than 328 grains of arsenic were found in his body. This is probably the largest amount ever recovered from the human body and shows that he must have swallowed sufficient to kill at least two hundred people.

It is in the sale of these products the law needs urgent amendment and their distribution should be entirely restricted to qualified chemists.

There is no cogent reason why all arsenical compounds, with the exception of those used in medicine, should not be rendered distinguishable by colour, taste or smell.

When arsenic is selected by the criminal it is on account of its colourless and tasteless nature and is usually administered in foods solid or liquid and generally in the guise of friendly solicitude. If then it was treated before sale so it would produce a distinctive colour or taste, the intended victim might be put on his guard.

This suggestion was made by a French chemist named Grimaud many years ago. He found by a series of experiments when arsenic was treated with a mixture of sulphate of iron and cyanure of potash it gave distinctive colour reactions. Thus to hot meat and soups, it gave a green bronze colour ; to hot or cold milk, an opal tint ; to red wine a violet colour ; to bread stuffs a deep blue, and to coffee a dirty yellow colour, and to other foods it also gave distinctive characteristics.

In India, arsenic has been commonly used for criminal purposes from ancient times down to the present. The reports of the analyst of the Bombay Government throw considerable light on the methods pursued by native poisoners. In most cases the poison is introduced into sweetmeats and generally distributed by a " strange woman " who has been met in the bazaar or street and who mysteriously disappears. This " strange woman " is found in nearly every analyst's report for the past fifty years and under much the same circumstances. Most of the cases are typical of the people among whom they occur, as instanced in the account of a man who went into a shop one day and entered into friendly conversation with a stranger he met there. By way of thanking him, the stranger presented him with some sweets for distribution among his friends. The result was that five men and a boy were poisoned, and the obliging stranger has never been heard of since.

It is difficult to account for the rationale of such cases, but still they occur and the professional poisoner in India—for there are many such—is rarely caught or even suspected. In many instances, crimes of this kind are taken little notice of by the community and sometimes the criminal apparently thinks nothing of poisoning a whole family in order to make sure of his victim. The utter absence of motive in many cases could point to the conclusion that they are largely the result of homicidal mania.

In the Middle Ages there was a prevalent idea that all poisonous substances possessed a powerful and mutual elective attraction for each other, and if a poison was worn suspended round the neck it would intercept and absorb all other noxious matter and even preserve the body from contagion of disease. During the Great Plague of London amulets containing arsenic were worn suspended over the region of the heart and were thus believed to preserve the wearer from infection.

It is characteristic of arsenic, antimony and mercury that their presence may be detected and demonstrated years after they have been taken into the body. Many cases might be cited in corroboration of this, but the following is one of peculiar interest. A wealthy farmer died and was buried in the grave where his father had been interred thirty-five years previously. An examination of certain of the bones of the father revealed particles of a metallic-looking substance which were collected, and on analysis proved to be mercury. It had thus been preserved in the remains for more than a third of a century, the probability being that he had been in the habit of taking it medicinally during the latter part of his life. Another case worthy of note came under the notice of a Bristol analyst, in which he found abundant traces of arsenic in the remains of young children after they had been buried for eight years.

A curious case, proving how the advance of science may influence the rendering of justice, was shown in a striking way by a decision of the Judicial Committee of the revision of trials in France in February, 1904. Twenty-five years previously, one Dauval, a chemist, had been found guilty of the murder of his wife by poisoning her with arsenic and was sentenced to transportation for life. Scientific evidence having since come to light, tending to show that he was innocent of the crime, he was granted a free pardon eighteen months previous to the meeting of the Judicial Committee. The evidence on which Dauval was found guilty was purely scientific, and later investigation showed that evidence to be open to doubt. At the trial in 1879, all the expert witnesses swore that the quantity of arsenic— one milligramme—found in the body of Dauval's wife after the post-mortem examination, could not possibly have existed in the system under natural circumstances. It was held to be proved that the presence of such a quantity of the poison was incompatible with life. Since the trial Gautier and Bertrand and other scientific workers have demonstrated that the quantity of arsenic mentioned can, and frequently does, exist in the human body in a normal condition. The presumption thus set up in Dauval's defence was that the presence of arsenic in his wife's remains was owing to her having been in the habit of taking the drug in medicinal doses.

A curious story was related by the late Sir Richard Quain that came under his notice which would have proved a profound mystery to this day but for his practical knowledge and acumen. He was asked to make a post-mortem examination on the body of a man who was by trade a stone-mason. To continue the story in his own words : " One day, on coming in to his dinner, he went into the scullery, washed his hands, and going into the kitchen he said to his wife, ' It is all over ; I have taken poison.' ' What have you taken ? ' ' Arsenic,' he replied, and she at once took him off to the Western General Dispensary.

" The senior surgeon was out when they got there, but two young students of his happened to be in, who thought it was a very important case, and they would treat it pretty actively. So they gave him tartar emetic, pumped out the stomach, and pumped oxide of iron into it, and performed a good many other operations. The poor man was extremely ill and died in twenty-four hours. The coroner's beadle went to the chemist and said : ' How did you come to sell this man poison ? ' He replied, ' I sold him no poison ; I thought he was off his head when he came.' ' What did you give him ? ' ' Oh, I gave him some alum and cream of tartar and labelled it poison.' " " He swallowed this in the belief it was arsenic," says Sir Richard. " When I made the post-mortem examination, to my amazement I found a great deal of *arsenic* in the stomach. This was rather puzzling. I said if it is in the stomach it ought to go farther down. So I searched the intestines, but there was no trace of arsenic anywhere. The simple explanation of it was this, these two young fellows, horrified to find the man had died without taking arsenic after all, pumped some into the stomach."

Another instance that terminated in a less tragic manner, in which a would-be suicide was frustrated by a watchful chemist, happened some years ago. One morning a tall, decently-dressed man, of seafaring aspect, entered a chemist's shop in the neighbourhood of the docks of a northern seaport, and in a solemn and confidential manner asked for a shilling's worth of *strong* laudanum.

" For what purpose do you require it ? " asked the chemist.

" Well, you see, sir," the man explained, " I've just come off a voyage from 'Frisco, and I find my sweetheart has gone off with Jim, you see, sir, and now it's all up with me. Give me a strong dose please, and if you don't think a shilling's worth will be enough——"

" But, my good man——" interrupted the chemist.

" I'll shoot myself if not, sir, I will," replied the man, thrusting his hand into his pocket.

" All right, then," said the chemist ; and seeing that argument was useless, he proceeded to mix an innocent but nauseous draught of aloes.

" Now put in a shilling's worth of arsenic."

" Very well," replied the chemist, adding some harmless magnesia.

" And you might as well throw in a shilling's worth of prussic acid," said the broken-hearted lover.

The chemist carefully measured a little essence of almonds into the glass and handed it to the would-be suicide. He paid, swallowed it at one draught, and solemnly walked out of the shop. Crossing the street, which was quiet at the time, he deliberately laid himself flat on his back on the footpath and closed his eyes. A group of children gathered round, and stood gazing with their eyes and mouths open in wonderment, and an occasional passer-by stopped a moment, cast a glance at the unwonted sight and then passed on. After lying thus quite motionless for about five minutes, he suddenly raised his head, took a look round, then with one bound jumped to his feet and made off as fast as he could run.

A parallel case occurred quite recently at Dartmouth, when a naval stoker after a quarrel with his fiancée, entered a chemist's shop and asked for an ounce of strychnine. The chemist, noting his excited manner and becoming suspicious, to pacify him gave him an ounce of borax which he took away, and obtaining a glass, mixed it with water and went out on the cliffs and drank it. Finding it only made him feel very unwell he resolved to throw himself over the cliffs into the sea, but the police arrived just in time to prevent him and found the glass with the remains of borax in it at his side. In this case it ended in a charge of attempted suicide.

Arsenic has been the favourite medium of female poisoners from early times, and in two celebrated poison cases of recent years, in which women were accused of murder by the administration of arsenic, it has been pleaded that the poison had been used by them for cosmetic purposes. The effect of arsenic on the skin is well known, and also that it is frequently used by women externally to improve the complexion. That this practice may lead to the taking of arsenic as a confirmed habit there is also evidence to prove, and there are many cases recorded where the habit of taking arsenic in solution has thus been contracted by women.

Formerly, many cases of chronic arsenical poisoning have resulted from the use of arsenic in making cheap green wall-papers and green sweets (both coloured by Scheele's green or hydrogen copper arsenite). Arsenic in wall-papers has been known to give off a poisonous gas during warm damp weather and a case which had a fatal result was reported a few months ago. The victim, the wife of a professor at Vienna University, some three years ago began to suffer from a skin trouble, which became more and more serious until it led to her death. A chemical examination of the wall-paper in one of the rooms she occupied showed that it contained in every sixteen square inches, seven-tenths of a milligram of arsenic. Arsenic has also been found in artificial flowers, in carpets, furs, dress fabrics dyed with aniline dyes, and in black stockings. Murrell examined a number of coloured tobacco and cigarette cartons and found arsenic in one-third of them. Used as an insecticide for spraying fruit, it remains on the skins. In these minute doses it seldom does any harm, but it may produce chronic poisoning, with loss of hair, neuritis and other harmful results.

Arsenic has ever had a peculiar attraction for the criminal poisoner for we find that it was employed in twenty out of forty attempts of murder in recent years.

In nine, it was administered in medicine, in three it was given in food, three in wine or beer, four in coffee or tea and one in chocolate.

In France, according to statistics kept for twenty-one years, between 1851 and 1871, out of 1,000 attempts at poisoning, in 331 arsenic was the medium used.

Arsenic is poisonous to all animals with a central nervous system (brain or spinal cord) and to most of the higher plants. Mice show the greatest resistance and next come hedgehogs, rabbits, dogs and cats. When it is taken for some time it finds its way into the hair within about two weeks and remains there for years.

The alleged practice of eating arsenic or taking it as a habit, has long been a matter of discussion, and as far back as the early part of the last century toxicologists were sceptical as to the statement that the inhabitants of Styria, and other parts of Hungary where arsenic is found, had contracted the regular habit of taking the drug until they had almost become immune to its effects.

In 1865, Maclagan of Edinburgh visited Styria for the purpose of investigating these statements, and in an account of his visit given in the *Edinburgh Medical Journal*, 1865, he affirms that while he was staying at the village of Legist in Middle Styria, two men were brought to him and in his presence, one took about 4½ and the other 6 grains of white arsenic. He brought back samples of what they had swallowed, and on testing it found them to be white arsenic. It was taken by one man on a piece of bread, and by the other was washed down with a draught of water. How extensively the habit existed in the district Maclagan was not able to ascertain, but he mentions that the peasants called it Hydrach or Huttereich. One of the men took a dose about twice a week, the other generally once a week, and he learned they had commenced the habit with doses of less than a grain. The effect was said to be tonic and stimulant and it was believed to aid the respiration when climbing. Once having acquired the habit, like that of other poisons, an occasional dose was much missed if omitted.

Arsenic has been a subject of interest to some of our most eminent chemists, one of whom at least, fell a victim to it. The first to make an accurate investigation of its chemical nature was Georg Brandt, a Swede, in 1773. The famous Swedish chemist Scheele (1742-1786) also worked on the subject, and discovered arsenic acid in 1775, and impure arseniuretted hydrogen. Soubeiran, the French chemist, together with Pfaff, succeeded in obtaining pure arseniuretted hydrogen, but so little was known of its deadly effects that in 1815, Gehlen, a professor of chemistry at Munich, died owing to inhaling a minute quantity of the pure gas. Both Berzelius (1779-1848) and Bunsen contributed much to the scientific knowledge of arsenic, and the latter in 1842 discovered an organic radical containing arsenic and methyl, which became known as cacodyl, the salts of which have since been introduced into medicine for certain diseases with satisfactory results.

From the end of the eighteenth century the founders of the modern science of toxicology, Orfila, Raspail, Christison, Taylor and Thomas Stevenson, devoted the best part of their lives to the discovery of new and accurate tests for poisons. Orfila (1787-1853) did his best to make their detection a matter of certainty, by insisting that poisons should be looked for in other parts of the body and not only in the alimentary canal. It was in his time that the three principal tests by liquid reagents became known.

Robert Christison (1797-1882) worked under Orfila in Paris, and devoted much attention to methods of testing for arsenic. He was professor of medical jurisprudence in the University of Edinburgh until 1882, and was called as toxicological expert at the trial of Madeleine Smith and in other famous cases.

Reinsch, who developed the test of the deposition of metallic arsenic on a bright copper plate, published his results in 1842, and this was followed by Marsh with his still more important test with nascent hydrogen in 1846. Fresenius and von Babo discovered a method for the systematic search of the organic matter of the viscera in 1844, and in 1850, Stas published his process by which alkaline poisons could be extracted from the viscera.

Thus as the science of toxicology has progressed the chances of the criminal poisoner being undetected have grown smaller and smaller.

A story is told of a distinguished medical professor who used to impress on his students that they should never dismiss from their minds the possibility of murder in the case of a mysterious illness, however little suspicious the circumstances might be. He used to give an illustration from his own experience in a case where he was called in consultation by a local practitioner, who was baffled by the illness of the wife of a clergyman. The professor, after the consultation, asked the husband, " Has the possibility of poisoning occurred to you ? " " It has," was his reply, " and I have been so careful to guard against it that I have actually made it a practice to prepare my wife's food myself." " Then I dismiss the thought," replied the doctor, " but as I have already taken a sample of the food in the bedroom, I may as well have it analysed as a matter of form." The clergyman thanked the physician for his scrupulous care, the latter returned to London, and the former shot himself. According to the story, the truth of which is not vouched for, the wife recovered and erected a memorial to her husband in the parish church.

Mercury, one of the most fascinating of all the elements, has traditions that carry it back to an unknown period of antiquity. In the form of sulphide it is recorded in the Paprus Ebers (1550 B.C.) as being used by the ancient Egyptians, but it is said to have been known at an even earlier date in the form of quicksilver in China and India.

The metal was probably named after the Roman divinity Mercury on account of its volatile nature and its elusive properties when handled. It has the peculiar property of absorbing other metals and forming amalgams. As well as being found native, it was obtained by the ancients by sublimation from cinnabar, the oxide. By the alchemists it was represented by the same sign as the planet Mercury. It is alluded to by Theophrastus in the fourth century B.C., but it is to Dioscorides in the first century A.D. it owes the name of hydrargyrum or fluid silver.

For a long period the liquid metal was believed to be poisonous and the native quicksilver was thought to be different from hydrargyrum obtained from the sulphide. Berthelot has shown that the protochloride of mercury was prepared and known as far back as the time of Democritus in the fifth century B.C. In 1386 Chaucer alludes to it as " quick-silver yclept mercurie."

The Arabs, who doubtless derived their knowledge of the metal from the Greeks, were much attracted by it, and Geber describes perchloride of mercury, also the red oxide. Avicenna, the Arab physician, was the first to doubt the poisonous properties of the metal itself, and noted that many persons swallowed it without any ill effects, as it passed through the body unchanged. Fallopius (1523-1562) records that shepherds gave quicksilver to sheep and cattle to expel worms, and Brassovola (1500-1555) says that he had given it to children in doses from two to twenty grains for the expulsion of worms.

About 1497 it was first used in the treatment of syphilis, by inunction or in the form of plasters and fumigation. Beringario de Carpi of Bologna, who lived in the early part of the sixteenth century, is said to have made large sums of money

from his treatment of syphilis by inunction with mercurial ointment. John Vigo advised fumigation in obstinate cases. The
first to record its use internally was Peter Matthiolus, the
commentator of Dioscorides (1501-1577). Paracelsus popu-
larized its use, and since the sixteenth century the value of
mercury and its salts have come to be recognized throughout
the world.

Robert Boyle, who was born in 1627, and is regarded as
the father of chemistry in Great Britain, commenced his experiments in a little laboratory in Oxford in 1653. He afterwards
founded the Royal Society, and used to make the oxide by
heating mercury in a bottle fitted with a stopper provided with a
narrow tube by which air was admitted. The product was
known as " Boyle's Hell," on account of the belief that it caused
the metal to suffer extreme agonies.

The many ways in which mercury can be transformed and the
numerous products which can be made from it, have had a
fascination for chemists throughout the ages. Homberg
(c. 1675), a German chemist, found that by putting a little
mercury into a bottle and attaching it to the wheel of a mill,
the metal was turned into a blackish powder (protoxide). It
is to Sir Theodore Turquet de Mayerne that we owe the
popularity of calomel, or subchloride of mercury, for medicinal
purposes. Mayerne was the favourite physician of Henry IV of
France, but being compelled to leave Paris, he settled in London
and served in the same capacity to James I and Charles I.

Pouqueville, physician to the French Army in Egypt, who was
a prisoner at Constantinople in 1798, relates the following story
concerning an old Turk named Suleiman Yeyen, who used to
swallow perchloride of mercury, commonly called corrosive
sublimate, a powerful poison, in enormous doses.

" When I was there," he says, " he was supposed to be nearly
a hundred years old. In early life he had habituated himself to
taking opium but notwithstanding that he constantly increased
the dose, he ceased to feel the desired effect and so tried sublimate, the effects of which he had heard highly spoken of.
For thirty years this old man never ceased to take it daily and the
quantity he could now bear exceeded a drachm. At this time
he came into the shop of a Jewish apothecary and asked for a
drachm of sublimate which he swallowed immediately having
first mixed it in a glass of water. The apothecary, terrified and
fearing that he should be accused of poisoning a Turk, immediately shut up his shop, reproaching himself bitterly, but his
surprise was very great when the next day the Turk came again
and asked for a like dose of the poison."

Mercury has been credited with certain occult properties,
and in the seventeenth and eighteenth centuries it was a common
practice in London, to carry in the pocket a quill filled with

quicksilver and sealed at the end, as a protection against rheumatism. This superstition has survived to the present day, and in some chemists' shops in the City little glass tubes containing mercury, sealed and placed in wash-leather bags, are still sold and carried in the belief that they will ward off attacks of pain.

Antimony has played an important part, both in medicine and chemistry, from a very early period. Known to the ancients as " stibium " or " stimmi," the native sulphide was used by women in Egypt and in the East for darkening the eyebrows and eyelids over three thousand years ago. Arab women still use it in the form of " kohl," finely ground, for making lines between the eyelids, which they regard as an aid to beauty. It was a favourite metal with the alchemists, who hoped to obtain from it a remedy for all ills. They soon discovered how readily it formed alloys with other metals, and found it a simple matter to make salts of the metal. They knew that by simply heating crude antimony in a crucible they would sometimes get a vitreous substance, in consequence of some of the silica of the crucible combining with the metal. They found that by digesting it in wine, the tartar of the wine formed a tartrate of antimony, and by other processes they got various salts which they discovered to have medicinal properties.

The white oxychloride which was called " Algaroth's powder " or the " mercury of life " was one of the most popular emetics in the sixteenth century and was introduced by Victor Algarotti, a physician of Verona. Another celebrated antimony compound was Kermes Mineral, which is said to have been discovered by Glauber about 1651. The process for making this orange-red powder was kept secret, and wonderful cures are declared to have been effected by it.

In the seventeenth century it was probably one of the most popular remedies in France for ague, dropsy, smallpox, syphilis and other diseases. Louis XV bought the formula for its preparation from La Ligerie for a considerable sum in 1720.

In the early part of the seventeenth century, Mynsicht is said to have re-discovered the properties of tartar emetic, which has probably been more frequently used in medicine than any other salt of antimony. It was regarded at one time as a specific for fevers, but more especially employed for its emetic properties.

In the sixteenth and seventeenth centuries cups were made of an alloy of antimony and tin, called " antimony cups " (pocula emetica). A cup, when filled with wine, was allowed to stand for some little time and become slightly impregnated with tartar emetic, and the liquid when drunk caused vomiting. These cups are said to have been frequently kept in monasteries, so that the monks who took too much wine could be punished by having to drink from the poculum emeticum.

In the seventeenth century Basil Valentine, who is believed to have been a German chemist named Johann Thölde, published a work entitled the " Triumphal Chariot of Antimony," in which he describes its virtues as a remedy, and the manner in which it could be prescribed. It was translated into English and published in London in 1678.

A curious case, which shows how by accidental means a poison found its way into human remains after death, came to light some time ago in Yorkshire. After the death of a young man, who was certified to have died of gastro-enteritis, his friends found that they could not obtain an order to cremate the body until a partial post-mortem examination had been made. This was done and a small quantity of antimonious oxide was found, which was supposed to have contributed to the cause of death.

A further examination was therefore ordered, and the organs of the body were sent to the Home Office analyst. He found that these were entirely free from antimony, but he discovered that antimonious oxide was present in the rubber rings of old pickle jars which had been used to send the remains to London for examination. From this source the organs had become contaminated and the certificate that death resulted from natural causes was confirmed.

It is probable that in this case if the analyst had not found antimony present in the rubber bands of the stoppers of the glass jars—which of course should not have been used—it might have been declared that the man had died from the effects of antimonial poisoning, as presumably he had been actually taking antimony in the form of medicine and the result might have been another unsolved poison mystery.

One of the peculiarities of antimony when given in large doses is its property of preserving the tissues of the body after death. In the Klosowski case, the body of one of his victims, whom he had poisoned with antimony, was exhumed after five years, and was found to be completely mummified and as well preserved as if it had only been buried a few days.

CHAPTER XIV

THE POISON LORE OF TOADS AND SPIDERS—
THE POISON OF THE SALAMANDER

FROM early times the toad has had an unenviable reputation for evil and has been suspected of poisonous properties. Some of the early historians attribute the death of King John of England to a friar who squeezed the secretion of a toad into his cup of wine. The story is probably fictitious, but there is some ground for the evil reputation that has so long been associated with this unlovely reptile. The venom of some toads is believed to possess poisonous properties in certain countries throughout the world, and some species are said to be particularly virulent. A few years ago, Phisalix and Bertrand undertook an investigation to ascertain if there was any truth in the story of the poisonous properties attributed to toads. They succeeded in extracting two powerful principles from the parotid gland and skin of the common toad. One of these, phrynine, was found to act on the heart in a similar manner to digitalis, and the other known as bufotenine, exercised a powerful paralysing action on the nerve centres.

The *Ceratophrys ornata*, a toad found in South America, is of a very poisonous nature. It will bite anything that comes in its way and then hang on with the tenacity of a bulldog, poisoning the blood with its glandular secretion. Death may follow its bite, and it has been known to kill a horse by gripping him by the nose, while the animal was cropping grass.

Shakespeare alludes to the evil reputation of the toad in two of his plays and the

> " Toad, that under cold stone,
> Days and nights went thirty-one
> Swelter'd venom sleeping got,"

formed an ingredient in the witches' hell-broth in " Macbeth." When dropped into the wine-cup it was believed to act with deadly effect on those who drank its contents.

In connexion with the poison of the toad there is an interesting record on a medical diploma preserved in the Library of Ferrara, which was granted to one Generoso Marini in 1642. Marini appears to have made an application for a diploma of medicine and the judges who had the power of granting such degrees, ordered him to produce some efficient proofs of his capability to practise the healing art. Marini agreed to comply with their demand and the result is recorded on his diploma, which was discovered by Cittadella among the archives of Ferrara some years ago ; it reads as follows :—

" Having publicly examined and approved the science and knowledge of medicine of Signor Generoso Marini, and his possession of the wonderful secret called ' Orvietano,' which he exhibited on the stage built in the centre of this our city of Ferrara, in presence of its entire population, so remarkable for their civilisation and learning, and in presence of many foreigners and other classes of people, we hereby certify that, also in our presence, as well as that of the city authorities, he took several living toads, not those of his own providing, but from a great number of toads, which had been caught in fields in the locality by persons who were strangers to him, and which were only handed to him at the moment of making the experiment. An officer of the court then selected from the number of toads collected, five of the largest, which the said Generoso Marini placed on a bench before him, and in presence of all assembled spectators, he, with a large knife, cut all the said toads in half. Then, taking a drinking cup, he took in each hand one half of a dead toad, and squeezed from it all the juices and fluids it contained into the cup, and the same he did with the remainder. After mixing the contents together, he swallowed the whole, and then placing the cup on the bench he advanced to the edge of the stage, where for some minutes he remained stationary. Then he became pale as death and his limbs trembled and his body began to swell in a frightful and terrible manner ; and all the spectators began to believe that he would never recover from the poison he had swallowed, and that his death was certain. Suddenly taking from a jar by his side some of his celebrated ' Orvietano,' he placed a portion of it in his mouth and swallowed it. Instantly the effect of this wonderful medicine was to make him vomit the poison he had taken, and he stood before the spectators in the full enjoyment of health.

" The populace applauded him highly for the indisputable proof he had given of his talent, and he then invited many of the most learned of those present to accompany him to his house, and he there showed them his dispensary as well as his collection of antidotes, and among them a powder made from little vipers, a powerful remedy for curing every sort of fever, as he had proved by different experiments he had made on people of quality and virtue, all of whom he had cured of the fever from which they were suffering, etc.

" In consequence of the rare talent exhibited by Signr Generoso Marini, and as a proof of our love and respect for his wisdom, we have resolved by the authority placed in our hands publicly to reward him with a diploma so that he may be universally recognized, applauded and respected. In witness thereof we have set out hands and the public seal of the municipality of Ferrara.

" Data in Ferrara con grandissimo applauso il di 26 Luglio, 1642.

" JOANNES CAJETANUS MODONI,
Index sapientum Civitatis Ferrari.
" FRANCISCUS ALTRAMARI,
Cancellarium."

But although the toad under certain conditions was credited with poisonous properties, during the Middle Ages it was esteemed a valuable remedy for the plague and was employed for that purpose in Austria as late as the year 1712.

The country people of Brazil believe the milky secretion of the common toad possesses wonderful curative properties and use it externally as a cure for shingles. In these cases living toads are generally applied to the part affected.

The poisonous drug known as " Senso " in China and Japan is said to be composed of the dried poison from a species of toad. It has been found to contain cholesterol, the bufagin of Abel and Macht ; bufotenine, and a base resembling epinephrine. Bufagin causes a marked rise of blood pressure, and acts as a diuretic. It is toxic in small doses. Bufotenine acts as a local anæsthetic, causes convulsions of the medullary type, and is pharmacologically allied to picrotoxin. The base, resembling epinephrine, is a powerful poison.

There are some small red frogs known as poison-frogs in Costa Rica and Tropical America which have strawberry-coloured bodies and dark blue legs, specimens of which were to be seen in the Reptile house at the Zoo. They are the *Dendrobates tinctorius* and have the power when irritated of exuding a poisonous secretion from the skin which is without taste or smell.

The Indians of Colombia avoid handling these frogs as they are well aware that the secretion produces a painful rash. Although it has not been known to be fatal to human beings, the Indians use it as an arrow-poison when hunting and it is said to kill a deer or a jaguar in a few minutes and smaller animals or birds in a few seconds. These frogs are very tiny but a single one is said to provide sufficient venom to poison fifty arrows. This poisonous exudation serves to protect the reptiles against most mammals.

The secretion of the skin glands of the salamander (*salamandra maculosa*) contains a strong poison called salamandrine.

Certain species of spider possess poisonous properties, notably the *Chiracanthium nutrix* and the *Epeira diadema*.

The bite of the female of the former is distinctly venomous, and one milligramme of the juice of the latter variety injected into a cat resulted in death.

Some curious methods of the manner in which some Indian tribes of South America utilize a poisonous grass as a method of defence have been investigated by Bomain. He found that a belt of this plant formed a natural barrier between the Indian tribes who lived on each side of a range of mountains, where it flourished. Animals died as soon as they ate the poisonous grass, and thus a hostile tribe was prevented from encroaching on the territory of another.

On scientific investigation, it was discovered that a few hundred grains of the grass would kill a horse or a mule in an hour or two, the deadly effect being due to the production of prussic acid, which was caused by the decomposition of a glucosive under the influence of a ferment.

CHAPTER XV

POISONS IN MEDIAEVAL TIMES—THE "BOOK OF VENOMS"—PETER OF ABANO ON POISONS—SLOW AND TIME POISONS—THE POISONING OF FRANCESCO CENCI

OUR knowledge of the substances regarded as poisons from the ninth to the fifteenth century is derived from manuscripts that have come down to us from those periods, although few are devoted specially to the subject.

Arsenic, red oxide of mercury, corrosive sublimate, nitric and hydrochloric acids were known to the Arabs in the ninth century and in the twelfth century, Albertus Magnus described the preparation of the acetates of copper and lead.

One of the most interesting of the early treatises on poisons and poisonous animals was written by Johannes Egidius of Zamora, a Franciscan monk who lived about 1300. It is written on vellum and illuminated with ornamented initials and decorative borders. He first deals with the bites and stings of venomous animals and reptiles and the methods of treating them, including the bites of mad dogs and the stings of serpents and scorpions. Several of the vegetable drugs he describes as poisonous we know to be innocuous, but among the more potent venoms he includes aconite napellus, mandrake, opium, hellebore, and muscus (fungi).

Another manuscript in which we have a fuller list, is "The Book of Venoms" written by Magister Santes de Ardoynis in 1424. He describes three kinds of arsenic, viz., arsenic sublimate, yellow and red. He also includes silver, turpeth mineral among his mineral poisons ; aconite, hellebore, laurel, opium, briony, mandrake and agaricus among the vegetable, and cantharides, buprestis, sea-hare, leopard's gall, cat's brains, menstrual blood as animal poisons.

He recommends the Confection of Cleopatra as an antidote to many of these which he states can be made by macerating musk, aristolochia piper and scorpions in wine.

Still later, Maister Peter of Abano wrote a treatise on poisons which was first printed in 1470. How far the knowledge of these substances had increased by the end of the fifteenth century is evidenced from the fact that he enumerates seventy drugs that were then regarded as venoms. Among the more powerful are sublimated arsenic, litharge, the juices of water-hemlock, poppy, mandrake, mezereon, hellebore, and briony. He also mentions opium and nux vomica, poisonous fungi, cantharides, scorpions, bull's blood, brain of a cat, sea-hare, menstrual blood and the venom of serpents.

He describes the symptoms of poisoning by these substances and the antidotes that should be administered.

Ambrôise Paré, the famous French surgeon of the sixteenth century believed that " certain poisons worked by an occult and specifick property and have their essence from the stars and celestial influence which is apt to destroy the strength of man's body, because being taken but even in a small quantity, yet they are of so pernicious a quality that they kill almost in a moment." In spite of this he did not believe in the so-called slow or time poisons that were said to be used in his time. Concerning these he says : " There are no such as will kill in set limits of time according to the will and desire of men, but some kill sooner or later than others, because the subject upon which they light doth more or less resist or yield to their efficacy."

He enumerates the following substances as poisons known in his time : Rosealgar (arsenic) sublimate, verdigris, orpiment, litharge, lead, lime, scales of brass, and prepared antimony. Among the vegetable substances he includes hemlock, poppy, nightshade, henbane, and mandrake.

He calls the deadly nightshade, solanum manicum, and says, "the root drunk in the weight of one drachm in wine causeth vain and not unpleasing imagination, but double this quantity causeth destruction or alienation of the mind for three days, but four times so much kills." Poisonous vapours or gases were recognized in his period for he alludes to "certain vapours that were exhaled out of the earth " and states, that " a poison carried into the body by smell is the most rapid and effectual. He states that " Pope Clement VII was poisoned by the fume of a poisonous torch that was carried before him."

He tells the story of a " certain man not long ago, when he had put his nose and smelled a little into a pomander which was secretly poisoned, was presently taken with a vertigo and all his face swelled and unlesse he had gotten speedy helpe he had died shortly."

" Some affirm," he adds, " that there are prepared some poisons of such force that being anointed on the saddle they will kill the rider or if you anoint the stirrups therewith, they will send so deadly poisonous a qualitie into the rider through his boots, that he shall die thereof within a short time after, which things though they scarce be credible because such poisons touch not the naked skin."

From this it is evident that Ambrôise Paré did not altogether believe in the stories concerning the effects of the so-called slow and time poisons that were current in his time.

The belief that certain poisons could be so prepared that their administration controlled with such a degree of precision as to cause death at any given period, according to the will of the poisoner, has existed from ancient times. This idea was encouraged and fostered by the practitioners of alchemy and astrology, and others who professed to exercise magical powers. They also claimed a knowledge of certain lethal bodies which could be administered to the victims that would leave no trace behind them.

" Truly," says a writer of the seventeenth century, " this poisoning art called ' veneficium ' of all others is most abominable, as whereby (crime) may be committed where no suspicion may be gathered nor any resistance be made ; the strong cannot avoid the weak ; the wise cannot prevent the foolish, the godly cannot be preserved from the hands of the wicked ; children may thereby kill their parents, the servant the master, the wife her husband so privily, so uncurably, that of all other it hath been thought the most odious kind of murther."

The origin of the time or slow poison tradition may be found in the cunning which is usually associated with the poisoner. In order to avoid suspicion, the poison was probably first administered to the victim in minute quantities, then gradually increased, from time to time, until it was finally decided to give the lethal dose, and so the culminating time could be determined by the poisoner.

Theophrastus refers to a poison prepared from aconite which, he states, would produce its effects after two, three or six months, or even years, after it had been administered. Plutarch records that one of the Philips of Macedon caused such a poison to be given to Aratus King of Sicyon, which is said to have produced a gradual wasting of the whole body, accompanied by bleeding from the nose.

In Italy, during the Middle Ages, the highest dignitaries of the Church did not scruple to employ poisons in order to gain their ends, and statesmen used them as instruments of diplomacy. Princes and nobles became adepts in devising the most cunning methods of administering a lethal dose to those whom they wished removed from their paths. This subtle method for the destruction of human life seems to have specially appealed to the Latin races. When they desired to dispose of a dangerous enemy or an inconvenient rival, they saw no distinction between using poison and the dagger. Many notable personages are said to have fallen victims to the poisoner's craft, including Pope Victor II, Christopher I King of Denmark, and Henry VII of Germany.

With respect to the latter monarch, it is stated that on his return from Italy, where he had made many enemies both in Church and State, he stopped at the small town of Buon-

conventis to celebrate the festival of Easter. After receiving
the sacrament he fell suddenly ill and died in terrible agony.
The Sacred Elements of the Eucharist are said indeed to have
been sometimes utilised as a medium for this evil purpose. A
case occurred within recent years when the same method was
employed, proving that even to-day, in some remote parts of
Italy, the old craft of the poisoner still survives. A few years
ago, an aged priest named Donato Marulli, while celebrating
mass in his church in the village of Villamagua in Abruzzi,
fell writhing in agony on the altar steps. Consternation ensued
among the congregation present, who crowded round the
sacristan demanding explanations. Hearing suspicions of poisoning mentioned, he seized the chalice and drained the contents
to demonstrate that the priest's seizure was not due to the
consecrated cup, but in a few moments he collapsed in the same
manner. Suspicion afterwards fell on a young priest, who was
subsequently arrested. It was found that he had mixed corrosive
sublimate with the wine just before the celebration, the motive
being to get promoted as parish priest in the old man's stead.

The extent to which the belief in the extraordinary power
of poisons is instanced in the story of an association of women
that flourished at Cassalis in Italy in the year 1536. The
members are said to have poisoned whole families by
" smearing the posts and doors of their houses with a noxious
ointment and powder of which they prepared about forty crocks
for the purpose. The like villainy was practised at Genoa and
execution was done upon the offenders. Their art consisted in
poisoning cattle as well as men, for it is written by divers authors
that if wolves' dung be hidden in the mangers, racks, or else in
the hedges about the pastures where cattle go (through the
antipathy of the nature of the wolfe and other cattle) all the beasts
that favour the same do not only forbear to eat but run about as
though they were mad."

It need hardly be said that this story is simply a phase
of the witchcraft superstition so commonly believed at this
period.

On a careful investigation of the cases recorded of so-called
secret and slow poisonings mentioned by writers of the Middle
Ages, the substance employed in the majority of such cases was
probably arsenic. La Spara's mysterious elixir, that was the
cause of so many deaths in Rome in the seventeenth century,
was a preparation of arsenic, and so also was the famous Aqua
Toffana, which is said to have put an end to no less than six
hundred persons. It is improbable that any substances of a
toxic nature were used in mediaeval or earlier times that are
unknown to science to-day, and most of the stories of slow and
secret poisoning can be explained by the manner in which
the poison was given. A common phrase used by historians of

this period in closing the account of some personages of note was, " he died not without suspicion of venom."

The death of Niccolo Macchiavelli, whose abbreviated Christian name according to Macaulay, was the origin of the term " Old Nick " commonly applied to the universal enemy of mankind, is said to have been due to a magic potion. Henry Morley, however, gives another version, and states that, " having failed in health after his last reverses, Macchiavelli increased his ailment by an overdose of castor oil, a medicine then in particular repute, and died two days afterwards on June 22, 1527."

This statement is evidently an error, as castor oil (the oil expressed from the seeds of the *Ricinis communis*) was not in use as a medicinal agent until more than 200 years after Macchiavelli's death. The drug that Macchiavelli may have taken is the oil of castor, a product of the animal of that name which was often used in the fifteenth and sixteenth centuries. An interesting light is thrown on the composition of the so-called magic potion in a letter written by him to his friend Guicciardini on August 17, 1525, nearly two years before his death. He states :

" I send you twenty-five pills made for you already four days since ; you will find the receipt for them at the end of my letter. I tell you they have resuscitated me. Begin by taking one after supper ; if it has any effect you will cease ; if not, you will take two or three, but not beyond five. As for myself, two have always sufficed, and that only once a week, except when my head is heavy or my stomach loaded. . . . But let us return to the receipt for the pills :—

Aloes	–	–	–	–	–	–	drachm	$1\frac{1}{2}$
Carman. deos ? (Cardamom sem.)					–	,,	1
Saffron	–	–	–	–	–	–	,,	$\frac{1}{2}$
Myrrh	–	–	–	–	–	–	,,	$\frac{1}{2}$
Betony	–	–	–	–	–	–	,,	$\frac{1}{2}$
Pipinella	–	–	–	–	–	–	,,	$\frac{1}{2}$
Armenian bole	–	–	–	–	–	,,	$\frac{1}{2}$ "

Such was the medicine of which Macchiavelli ordinarily made use, and which Paul Jove calls an " enchanted potion," saying that " Macchiavelli, after having taken it, died mocking God, and pretending that he had, so to speak, become immortal."

These pills are a strong purgative taken in the dose pre-scribed, and it is possible that Macchiavelli, while in a weakened condition, may have overdosed himself with them, and so hastened his end.

Elisabetta Sirani, one of the famous women painters of the Bolognese school in the seventeenth century, is supposed to have been poisoned by her maid, and an interesting account of her illness and death is recorded in a manuscript in the Archives of Bologna. It states, that, " In Lent, 1665, she was seized with pains in her stomach. She grew thin and lost her colour so that every one wondered at it, for before she was healthy and robust. In the summer, about St. Bartholomew's Day, a redness with a little swelling appeared under her chin and jaw. These were cured with an ointment in a few days. On August 12 or 13 she was again seized with pain which was worse after eating. Her sister was in bed stricken with fever and the family physician Doctor Gallerati was attending her. Elisabetta complained to him. He said, ' it was no time to take medicine for the Sun was in Leo and that the pain was due to a little catarrh.' He advised her to take a little acid syrup early in the morning. Her aunt made the syrup and she took it two or three times, four teaspoonsful for a dose and seemed relieved.

" But the pains returned. Nevertheless, she went with her mother on August 24 to the Feast of the Porchetta, and when asked how she was, said she ' was all right when she didn't think about it.' On August 27 about two in the afternoon the pain returned with violence. She became ghastly and was bathed in cold perspiration. Her aunt with difficulty put her to bed. She could not lie flat, but was easier in a half sitting posture.

" She felt sick, but the emetics and clysters given had little effect. All through the night her relations applied hot cloths to her cold body. The pain continued and the extremities turned black.

" A little while before her death the pain seemed to lessen and go lower ; she began to move in bed, then fainted and died about eleven o'clock after being ill about thirty-three hours. After death her body swelled. The nose thickened, the features changed. She looked like a woman of sixty albeit she was but twenty-six years of age. She was given by her relatives : 1, Teriaca ; *2, Spetie di Elescoff in broth ; 3, Bezoar and oil of the Grand Duke against poison."

At her father's urgent request a post-mortem examination was made the day following Elisabetta's death. This, it is recorded, was carried out by Master Ludovico, Surgeon of the Ospedale della Morte, in the presence of six other physicians. Perforations were found in the stomach, which five out of the seven doctors, attributed to the action of a " corrosive poison." A Doctor Fabri introduced his finger into one of these perforations and found the circumference was surrounded by hardened tissue, and Dr. Gallerati, the family physician who had attended her, was of the opinion there was evidence of a " corrosive poison."

Suspicion fell upon a maidservant called Lucia Tolomelli, on the assertion of another domestic, that she had seen her

* A purgative electuary composed of scammony, cream of tartar and salt of tartar.

place a " brown powder " in some food. So Lucia was arrested on September 1, 1665, and charged with the murder of Elisabetta Sirani. After a protracted trial, the evidence was deemed insufficient and she was released, it being concluded that death had been due to natural causes.

There seems little doubt that this conclusion was correct and this gifted woman probably died from peritonitis.

In this case, as in many others when the physician was unable to diagnose the disease and was puzzled to account for a patient's death, he generally deemed it to be the result of a slow poison, which deduction formed a ready solution of the difficulty.

The story of the poisoning of Francesco Cenci in 1598, is told by Corrado Ricci in his " Beatrice Cenci " and shows how the ' silent weapon of death ' was used in Italian families at that period.

His family plotted his death in the first months of 1598 and soon decided to carry out their evil design. Giacomo relates how Olimpio when he returned to La Petrella told the others that he had bought some opium and " to Bernardo, Paolo and myself, showed a small lump which was somewhat yellowish or reddish. It was a lump no bigger than a small finger-nail and he said that he had bought it to give to Beatrice, and that Beatrice would know what to do with it, and she would serve it up to our father. And he told us it was opium, and he showed us also a reddish root which was half-a-finger long, and he told me he had it from a chemist who served the Cardinal Marc-antonio Colonna, and he said that this fellow was his great friend and he told us this root was a perfect poison, and the opium he told us he had bought for three or four pence from an apothecary through the aid of that chemist."

Beatrice however testified afterwards that " Olimpio gave her a lump of red stuff as big as one's nail but round, and she said to him what is this ? He answered, Giacomo gave me this and bids you to put it in his wine. You should dissolve it first in other wine or in water before you put it in the cup. For it was to be drunk and one would dissolve it by stirring it about with the finger in a dish or in the bowl before being put into the bottle, and Olimpio said it was opium."

Olimpio also showed the red root to Marzio Catalano and told him that Giacomo had given it to him together with a dose of opium.

However, their nefarious plans were upset, as Francesco became so suspicious that he would no longer touch food or drink unless Beatrice tasted it first, and thus " gave it credit as was said."

Finally, Beatrice and Olimpio decided to kill Cenci in his bed and to give out the tale that he had been killed by accident.

But the opium was not wasted, as it transpired that before

the deed was carried out, Beatrice endeavoured to stupefy him and according to the statement of Lucretzia his wife, she dissolved the opium in a little cup by pressing it down with her finger. She then put it in the wine, shaking the bottle, and then poured the wine into her father's wine-glass.

CHAPTER XVI

CURIOUS METHODS EMPLOYED BY SECRET POISONERS—WOMEN POISONERS—POISON RINGS—A POISON KNIFE

THE secret poisoner who endeavoured to kill his victim by the most subtle and cunning methods, unseen and mysterious, has been dreaded throughout the centuries. He was even more feared by kings, princes and nobles than the assassin with his poniard or dagger. The various methods employed, from the poisoned knife of Queen Parysatis, to the apparently innocent cup of tea of recent times, forms an interesting study. Food or drink appear to have been the favourite media and have been more commonly employed than any other method. The poisoned cake or wine recurs with monotonous frequency in the history of poisoning from the earliest times down to the present. Women especially seem to have had a predilection for this method of administering a lethal dose, a fact probably due to their control and direction of domestic matters, which rendered the introduction of a poisonous substance into food or drink an easy matter.

In early times some fell victims to their own evil designs, as instanced in the case of Rosamond, the wife of Alboin, King of Lombardy, in A.D. 573. It is stated that, wishing to rid herself of her husband, she gave him a cup of poisoned wine when he was coming from his bath. The king drank part, but suspecting its nature from the strange effect it produced, wisely insisted that she should drink the remainder, with the result that both died shortly afterwards.

Reginald Scot, who wrote *The Discovery of Witchcraft* in 1584, quaintly states his belief that " women were the first inventors and the greatest practisers of poysoning and more materially addicted and given thereunto than men."

Throughout the history of criminal poisoning there has always been a high percentage of women implicated and there are numerous accounts of female maniacs with whom the use of poison amounted to an obsession. With this class there is no suggestion of a motive, the object apparently being the destruction of life without reason.

Of this type was Van der Linden, a Dutch woman who poisoned one hundred and two people, and Hélène Jegado, who apparently regarded poisoning as a pastime and is said to have been responsible for twenty-six deaths.

From the time of the Marquise de Brinvilliers some women-poisoners have been found to possess an alluring charm combined with a fiend-like nature, capable of plotting a crime with an utter indifference to the physical pain and distress they purposely inflicted on others.

The motives actuating their crimes have generally proved to be greed of gain, jealousy or lust, while there have been others who appear to have acted from sheer love of notoriety and the power of possession.

American statistics show that five-eighths of the murders by poison in that country were the work of women; housewives, housekeepers, servants and nurses, and from statistics in France covering 21 years, between 1851 and 1871, the women accused of poisoning numbered 399, against 304 men, charged with the same offence. Out of 1,000 attempts, 331 were due to arsenic and 301 were due to phosphorus.

Some poisoners, not content with introducing the substance into wine or other drink, essayed to improve on this method by preparing a goblet or cup in such a way that it would impregnate any liquid that was placed in it. There is record of one François Belot, a Frenchman, who made a speciality of this method, and is said to have thus derived a considerable income. He fitly ended his days by being broken on the wheel on June 10, 1679.

According to a contemporary writer, Belot's special method consisted in cramming a toad with arsenic, placing it in a silver goblet, and after pricking its head, crushing it in the vessel. Whilst this operation was being performed he recited certain charms. According to his own account, which is still on record, of treating a cup with a toad in this way, " I know a secret," he says, " such that, in doctoring a cup with a toad, and what I put into it, if fifty persons chanced to drink from it afterwards, even if it were washed and rinsed, they would all be done for, and the cup could only be purified by throwing it into a hot fire. After having thus poisoned the cup, I should not try it upon a human being, but upon a dog, and I should entrust the cup to nobody." Belot's statements were evidently believed in his time, and he enjoyed a considerable reputation.

Another individual named Blessis flourished about the same period, who claimed to practise sorcery and magic. He went so far as to declare to the world, that he had discovered a method of manipulating mirrors in such a way that whoever looked into them would meet his death.

According to tradition, boots, gloves, shirts, and other articles of wearing apparel have been utilized by poisoners for carrying out their evil plans, and although many of these tales are purely legendary, it is possible that others may have had a substratum of truth. Tissot states that John, King of Castille, owed his death to wearing a pair of boots which were supposed to have been impregnated with poison by a Turk. Henry VI is said to have succumbed through wearing poisoned gloves, and Louis XIV and Pope Clement VII died after inhaling the fumes of a poisoned candle or torch.

The stories of poisoned shirts which, if contemporary records are to be believed, were not infrequently employed by poisoners in the seventeenth century, are within the bounds of possibility. Apparently corrosive sublimate, arsenic and cantharides were employed for this purpose. The shirt is said to have been prepared by soaking it in a strong solution of one of these poisons, the idea being to produce a violent dermatitis with ulceration, which would force the victim to take to his bed. " The physician would then be sent for," states a writer, " and would probably diagnose the case as due to syphilis, and prescribe mercury, with the effect of killing the patient in the end."

Such a case is recorded by Dr. Lucian Nass, who relates the story of Madame de Poulaillon, the wife of a wealthy man who was a good deal her senior. Desirous of ridding herself of her husband, she sought the counsel of one Marie Bosse, who told Madame that she should try the method of the poisoned shirt, which she herself would prepare. She then took one of her husband's shirts, together with a piece of arsenic " as big as an egg," to Bosse. She first washed it and then soaked the tail in a strong solution of arsenic, so that it only looked " a little rusty," as if it had been ill-washed, and was stiffer than usual. Bosse told her that only the lower part of the shirt had been thus prepared, and the effect would be to produce violent inflammation and intense pain.

Madame de Poulaillon is said to have given Bosse a sum of money, equal to £800 at the present day, for her services. The husband was, however, warned of the evil intended to him and had his wife arrested. The lady is said to have so fascinated her judges that a contemporary writer states " they were touched by her wit and by her grace and by the tones in which she spoke of her misfortunes and her crime, and though she confessed her guilt, and pronounced herself worthy of death, she was acquitted with applause."

A few years ago, Dr. Nass, with a view to ascertaining the truth of the assertions connected with the poisoned shirt, made some interesting experiments on a guinea-pig. He carefully shaved a portion of the left lumbar region and gently rubbed the skin with a paste containing arsenic in the proportion of one in ten. He repeated the operation several times during the day. Shortly afterwards the animal became prostrate, the eyes became dull, it assumed a cholera-like aspect and in forty-eight hours died. The skin on which the paste had been applied remained unchanged and unbroken, and showed no sign of ulceration. On examining the internal organs after death, fatty degeneration of the viscera was found and several marked symptoms of arsenical poisoning. This experiment does not, of course, prove the fact that a shirt impregnated with arsenic worn in direct contact with the skin would prove fatal, but it shows that arsenic may be introduced into the body simply by gentle friction on an unbroken skin, and that the effect of the poisoned shirt was possible.

The Duke of Savoy is said to have been one of the last victims of this method, and it is stated that when a shirt could not be procured a slipper was used, although it did not prove so effective. Apparently the primary object in this method was not to kill but to prostrate the patient in bed where he could be despatched at leisure under pretence of treatment.

Similar to the method of treating the shirt there is a legendary story in India of the Queen of Ganore, who is said to have killed Rajah Bukht by impregnating his marriage robes with poison. Chevers, who relates the story,* affirms that this form of poisoning is possible. " Anyone," he writes, " who has noticed how freely a robust person in India perspires through a thin garment, can understand that if the cloth were thoroughly impregnated with the cantharadine of that very powerful vesicant, the Telini, the result would be as dangerous as that of an extensive burn." He further states that Mr. Todd has published ample evidence in support of the idea that the deaths of several historical personages in India were caused by poisoned robes.

A curious case in which the poisoner attempted to prove that the medical treatment was responsible for the crime occurred in France a few years ago, when a woman was charged at the Paris Court of Assizes with attempting to murder her husband. It was known that the couple had lived unhappily together, and arrangements had been made for a divorce.

One morning the husband complained of a severe headache and his wife suggested a dose of antipyrine, which she gave him in some mineral water. He remarked to her at the time that the draught had a peculiar taste. Later in the day she administered sundry cups of coffee to him, but he grew rapidly worse and at night a doctor was summoned. He failed to diagnose the complaint, and called in other medical men, who were equally puzzled. One thing which they all noticed was a peculiar dilatation of the pupils of the patient's eyes.

A consultation was held the next day, and shortly afterwards one of the medical men received a note from the wife in which she stated that her husband was " black. He was dead, more dead than any man I ever saw."

* *Manual of Medical Jurisprudence in India.* Norman Chevers.

The doctor at once went to see the patient, and found him in a state of collapse. He bled him twice and injected caffeine, but he still remained motionless. After a time it occurred to the doctor that the patient's symptoms resembled those of atropine poisoning, and, resorting to other measures, he eventually brought him round. Then he remembered that the woman had previously asked him for some morphine for herself, and when he had refused it she requested some atropine for her dog's eyes. He wrote her a prescription for a solution of atropine, containing ten per cent of the drug, and took it to the chemist himself. On further inquiries it was proved that she had procured atropine upon various other occasions by copying the doctor's prescription and forging his signature.

At the trial the medical evidence was very conflicting, but the consensus of opinion was in favour of the theory that atropine had been administered in small, repeated doses. The accused woman declared in her defence, that atropine had been put into the medicine for her husband in mistake by the pharmacist who had dispensed it. There was no evidence to support this theory, and she was found guilty and sentenced to five years' penal servitude.

A case of poisoning through a boot came to light a few years ago when death was caused by the absorption of a poisonous boot-blacking. The victim, a young man, had been to a dance, and shortly afterwards became unconscious and died in four hours. For some time the cause of his death was a complete mystery, when a few days later a bottle of blacking was found in his room, with which it was discovered he had blacked his shoes on the evening of his death. The colouring had penetrated his socks and stained his feet and ankles. On analysis, the solvent in the blacking was found to consist of benzaldehyde, a poisonous liquid, often used in the manufacture of the cheap, strong-smelling perfumes and soaps so frequently used. It was no doubt rapidly absorbed by his hot feet when dancing, and so proved fatal.

A great deal of nonsense has been written concerning the so-called poison rings of the sixteenth and seventeenth century, which are generally taken to mean a finger ring containing a secret receptacle for carrying some poisonous substance. In the majority of cases it has been found that these receptacles were originally intended for hair kept as " memento mori " or for fragments of religious relics.

Other rings have been described as being fitted with a tiny envenomed spike by means of which the wearer could inoculate his victim by a grasp of the hand, as described in the following story published a few years ago in a Paris journal.

It stated that when examining an ancient ring he had picked up in the shop of an antiquity dealer in the Rue St. Honoré, a customer scratched his hand. While still talking to the dealer, in a few moments he suddenly felt an indescribable feeling, as if his whole body was paralysed to the finger-tips, and he became so ill that it was found necessary to send for a medical man. The doctor diagnosed it as a case of poisoning and after the prompt administration of an emetic the patient recovered. The medical man is then said to have examined the ring and found attached to it, inside, two tiny claws made of sharp steel, with grooves in them, which contained the poison. Having long resided in Venice, he recognized it as being what was formerly called the " annelo della morte " or " death ring," often used by Italians in the sixteenth and seventeenth centuries.

Outside the realm of fiction, however, there is little doubt that rings were used in ancient times as a medium for carrying poisons. This was sometimes done for the purpose of self-destruction. There are several specimens of rings with traditions attached to them which bear evidence of their authenticity.

In the troublous times of the Roman Emperors, when those who took a prominent part in public affairs were liable to be suddenly thrown into prison at the word of a capricious monarch, rings containing receptacles for poison are said to have been sometimes worn, so that the contents could be swallowed to save their wearer from torture, imprisonment or an ignominious death.

Rings of the Roman period were always wrought with the hammer, and never cast ; they were thus hollow and would easily afford a convenient receptacle for poison. Pliny records that when Marcus Crassus robbed the Capitol of the gold deposited there by Camillus, the custodian who was responsible for its safety " broke the stone of his ring " and died shortly afterwards.

An interesting Roman gem which might have been used for this purpose is in a London museum. It is an onyx upon which is engraved the head of a horned fawn. The stone itself has been hollowed out, forming a cavity sufficiently large to carry poison, to take which it would only be necessary to bite through the thin shell of the onyx and swallow the contents of the cavity.

Further mention of these hollowed gems is made in connexion with Heliogabalus, to whom it was foretold that he should die a violent death. It is said " he therefore prepared against such an emergency, halters twined with silk, and poison enclosed in rubies, sapphires and emeralds set in his rings to give him a choice of deaths." It is recorded of Demosthenes that having given up all hope of escaping from his enemies the Macedonians, he swallowed a poison which he carried about with him concealed in a stylus.

Hannibal is said to have taken his life in a similar manner, and when hunted and in dread of being delivered into the hands of the Romans by Prusias, King of Bithynia, took the poison which he always carried with him concealed in the hollow of a ring. Juvenal thus alludes to it in his Tenth Satire :

" Nor swords, nor spears, nor stones from engines hurl'd,
    Shall quell the man whose frown·alarm'd the world ;
    The vengeance due to Cannæ's fatal field,
    And floods of human gore—a ring shall yield."

Although these stories describe what happened in ages past, it is curious to note how history repeats itself, when we recall the tragic conclusion to the trial of Whittaker Wright in London some years ago. Immediately, when found guilty of the charges brought against him, either as he was listening to the judge's closing words or as he was leaving the scene of the trial, he swallowed, unobserved, some tablets of potassium cyanide which he had secreted about him, and died shortly afterwards within the precincts of the court.

Another instance of a similar refuge from persecuting fate is that of Condorcet, who was secretary to the Academy of Sciences of France, and who was proscribed by the Convention at the time of the Revolution. He took refuge in the house of a Madame Vernet in Paris, but fearing to compromise his protectress by a longer stay, he left his asylum with the intention of taking refuge in the country house of an old friend. Unfortunately, the friend was away and he wandered about sleeping at night in some stone quarries, but was at length arrested and taken to Bourg-la-Reine and lodged in prison. On the following morning, March 28, 1794, he was found dead in his cell, having swallowed some poison which he carried about in readiness for an emergency, concealed in his ring. On investigation, the poison was found to consist of opium and stramonium which had been specially prepared.

Motley records that in the conspiracies against the life of the Prince of Orange about the year 1582 under the influence of the Court of Spain, the young Lamoral Egmont, in return for the kindness shown to him by the Prince, attempted to destroy him at his own table by means of poison which he kept concealed in a ring. Philippe van Marnix, Lord of Saint Aldegonde, was to have been treated in the same way, and a hollow ring containing poison was said to have been found in Egmont's lodgings.

There are rings of the sixteenth and seventeenth century of Italian workmanship having traditions that they were used for the purpose of carrying poisons. Some are found with cavities and receptacles on the inside of the bezel, but it is improbable that they were ever used for this purpose. There are other rings extant, called poison rings, with small boxes placed at the back of a stone, but these rings could only have been used for containing a perfume or a small relic. The construction of a ring, claimed to have been used for the purpose, must show reasonable grounds that it could have been so employed. The most interesting ring of the kind known, is one that was formerly in the possession of the late Bishop of Ely. It passed from him to a clergyman in London, who was a well-known antiquary. He claimed that it once belonged to Cæsar Borgia, and from the workmanship there seems to be little doubt it was made about the XVI century. Made of gold, slightly enamelled, it bears the date of 1503, and round the inside are inscribed the words: " FAYS CEQUE DOYS AVIEN QUE POURRA." The bezel forms a hollow receptacle and on the front is engraved the name " Borgia," and in letters reversed are the words " COR UNUM UNA VIA." At the side of the bezel is a secret slide, which on being pushed reveals a cavity for holding poison.

Another gold ring of the late sixteenth century, formerly in the possession of an Italian nobleman, is said to have originally belonged to a member of the family, who was a prince of the Church. The bezel is elaborately wrought, and richly ornamented with dark blue enamel, picked out with red and white. It is apparently made in one piece, but a small portion in the centre has been cunningly made to open on a hinge, revealing a secret receptacle capable of holding a sufficient quantity of arsenic or corrosive sublimate to cause the death of two or three people.

Fairholt describes a jewelled ring of curious construction set with two rubies and a pyramidal diamond. The gold setting was richly engraved, and the collet securing the diamond opened with a spring, disclosing a somewhat large receptacle for " such virulent poisons as were concocted by Italian chemists in the sixteenth and seventeenth centuries."

One of the most curious rings of this kind was formerly in the possession of an Italian cardinal. It is beautifully wrought in fine gold and dates from the latter part of the sixteenth century. The shanks are partly enamelled in black and the bezel is rectangular ; at the side of it is a very minute knob with a groove which could be easily turned with the finger-nail without removing the ring from the finger. On turning the knob a cylindrical receptacle is revealed, which was most likely used for carrying some poisonous substance. There is a story told in connexion with this ring, that the secret receptacle was kept filled with tiny granules prepared from a deadly fungus, specially prepared for the owner. The secret receptacle of this ring is almost unnoticeable even when it has been opened.

There is a tradition that Lord Holland had in his collection at Holland House, a poison ring of the sixteenth century to which a curious story was attached. The bezel of the ring was formed by a carbuncle carved in the shape of a skull which was charged with the poison. It was said to have been sent to Mary Queen of Scots when she was a prisoner at Fotherinhay Castle.

Of all the inventions that were introduced for the purpose of secretly introducing poison to the human anatomy, the poison knife appears to have been the most diabolical.

We have recently had the opportunity of examining an example which was apparently made in the late sixteenth century. The knife is one that would probably be used for cutting bread or fruit, its total length being 6¾ inches. The blade, which tapers to a point, is of steel, 4 inches long and half an inch wide at the base. The handle of beaten silver is gilded and jewelled with three stones on each side set in raised mounts and at the end of the handle is an ornamental cap. There are two diamond-shaped emeralds and one square ruby on each side of the handle.

The mechanism is ingenious and is concealed inside the hollow handle. The blade works on a pivot which pierces the top of the handle and is fixed on the shank of the blade which also conceals three tiny spikes with sharp needle points. Thus, when the knife is held in the hand and the slightest pressure exerted on the cutting-side of the blade, the three sharp spikes, which are an eighth of an inch long, spring out and wound any part of the users' hand with which they come in contact. Directly the pressure on the handle is relaxed, the spikes totally disappear.

It is not clear if the intention was to introduce some poisonous substance into the blood-stream by means of the spikes or simply to allow them, if rusty, to do their work alone. In any case they would likely penetrate a vein and so might cause septic wounds.

A story related in a London newspaper some time ago is not without interest in this connexion. The writer says : " The police are searching for a man who is alleged to have poisoned a girl in London under extraordinary circumstances. The girl, who was a typist employed in a Fleet Street office, said that she was walking to her office when a well-dressed man overtook her and grasped her by the wrist. Directly she reached her office she was overcome by four fainting fits in succession. When she recovered she showed a small punctured wound in her wrist and the police were informed." Then follows a lengthy description of the wanted man. " In various parts of America," adds the writer, " similar reports of devices employed by persons connected with the White Slave Traffic have been made known.

When the victim faints in the street, the assailant who then passes as a relative or friend, calls a cab and drives off with the girl, the poison having been injected into the wrist by pressure from a poison ring ! "

The only finger rings known with a syringe attachment are those made about a century ago, from the bezel of which perfume might be ejected through a pin-hole aperture.

One of the most curious receptacles used for carrying poison was a wooden leg. Some years ago a man named Jasper Reed, who was once a member of a gang of international thieves, had his leg amputated while he was in prison for a theft of £480 from a bank in Antwerp. After his release he was lost sight of for a long time, until one day a wooden-legged cripple was arrested in a street in Antwerp in connexion with the theft of some bank-notes, and afterwards poisoned himself while in prison. A post-mortem examination of the body showed that he had killed him-self with potassium cyanide, and a bottle containing the poison was found concealed in a hollow receptacle in the wooden leg he was wearing.

The tradition that Pope Clement VII, one of the Medici, was poisoned in 1534 by the fumes of a torch impregnated with arsenic carried before him in a religious procession is within the realm of probability, if the torch or candle had been so prepared that it would give off a certain amount of arseniuretted hydrogen.

The poisoned flowers of mediaeval romance, although they have been discredited in the light of modern science, must not be dismissed as entirely improbable, as evidenced from the following curious case which occurred in London some years ago. A hawker with a barrow filled with bunches of lavender, was noticed talking wildly in a street in Stockwell. In a few minutes he was seen to fall insensible and was removed to Lambeth Infirmary, where he died shortly afterwards. The medical officer of the institution said he found the man was suffering from benzaldehyde poisoning, and in his pockets were discovered seventeen packets of lavender seeds and a bottle of oil of mirbane which he had evidently used to increase the perfume of the lavender he sold. The doctor stated that in his opinion, the man had been overcome by the vapour of the benzaldehyde he had inhaled from the lavender on his barrow.

In the military poison plot investigated in Austria in 1909, and referred to in detail elsewhere, the gaol authorities were at a loss to account for the prisoner's constant demand for flowers for pious purposes while he was on remand. It was only dis-covered by intercepted letters that he wanted them in order to smuggle poison into his cell, which he apparently succeeded in doing. He requested his wife to insert the poison in flowers which he asked for so he could place them on an altar which he had erected in his cell. The letter to his wife in which this was discovered reads : " I should like to commit suicide, but will not, as I must work for you and for the children. You can save me. Get me flowers and have some atropine or hyoscyamine. Victor or —— will obtain it for you, in liquid and solid. Put it carefully in a small quill and seal it up with wax. Put this quill in a carnation, the calyx will hold it well, then tie the calyx round with a thread as they do in florists' shops." It appears that some poison actually reached him in this ingenious manner.

A curious case in which a poisoned bed played an important part came to light in America a few years ago, when a woman named Mary Kelliher was tried at Boston on charges of poisoning her husband, three children, a sister and sister-in-law. These people died mysteriously during a period of three years ; but after the death of a daughter, in July, 1908, suspicion was aroused, and a post-mortem was held which disclosed the presence of arsenic in the body. The bodies of the other five persons were then exhumed, and arsenic was found in all. There was, however, no evidence connecting the woman with the administration of poison to her victims until it occurred to the District Attorney to examine some of the furniture in the bedroom. The mattress, on which all those of the family who had died had lain, was then cut open and carefully examined. In the hair stuffing considerable quantities of arsenic were discovered, which it was suggested had been specially impregnated, so the poison could be absorbed during sleep by the person lying on the bed. Ingenious as this suggestion for the prosecution was, Mrs. Kelliher was acquitted after being kept fifteen months in prison.

Probably the most deadly poison known to science to-day exists in the form of an innocent-looking white powder, which is highly dangerous even to handle. It emits a slight vapour even when exposed to the air, which if inhaled would cause instant death. It has been estimated that if three grains were diffused in a roomful of people it would kill every one present. It is hardly necessary to state that poisons of such great virulence as those revealed by modern chemical research were unknown to the chemists of the Middle Ages, and it is equally certain that the latter knew of few poisonous bodies that are not familiar to chemists of the present day.

A few months ago a statement appeared in the press announcing the discovery in the Transvaal of " the deadliest poison in existence." This astonishing discovery is said to have been made by some labourers working near the Pienaars River, who tasted some bulbs they found growing there, to " quench their thirst. All became violently ill and one died." While two natives were cutting up some of the bulbs, they were overcome and their lives only saved with the greatest difficulty.

We are told the scientific name of the poison is 'Adenia' and that " it leaves no traces behind in the organs of its victims—*one thousandth part of a grain is sufficient to kill an adult*." This extraordinary story was accepted by several leading newspapers in all seriousness.

POISON KNIFE (*see p.* 123).

CHAPTER XVII

LOVE-PHILTRES—POTIONS AND LOVE CHARMS

THE employment of certain substances having aphrodisiac properties in the form of charms or potions to incite the amatory passion has long been practised by both barbaric and civilized races. The idea involved in the use of love-philtres, as they were termed at a later period, was no doubt based to a certain extent on physiological principles and was probably first suggested by observation of the habits of the lower animals. The early Hebrews are said to have employed the fruits of the mandrake, which were known by the suggestive name of " love-apples," for this purpose.

The popularity of the *philtra* or *pocula amatoria* among the ancient Greeks and Romans at a later period can readily be understood in an age given to sensuality in its grossest forms. Medea was regarded as the greatest adept in the art of preparing philtres, and hence the term " Medei de herbae," used by Horace and Ovid to designate the substances generally used. Next in reputation came the Thessalian women, who were supposed to have acquired the art from Medea, and who were said to be versed in all the secrets relating to poison and sorcery.

Lucretius, the great philosophical poet of the Ciceronian era, is said to have written his poem entitled " On the Nature of Things " in the intervals of delirium occasioned by a philtre which had been secretly administered to him by his wife or his mistress, Lucilia, and it is stated that Lucullus, the Roman general, died in a state of delirium from a similar cause. Thus the effects of these potions were evidently often more serious than was contemplated by those who used them.

Ovid, the exponent of the amatory art, judging from some of his verse, was evidently no believer in this method of procuring affection so much practised by his contemporaries. He writes :

" Who so doth run to Hæmon arts
   I dub him for a dolt,
And giveth that which he doth pluck
   From forehead of a colt.
Medea's herbs will not procure
   That love shall lasting give,
No slibbersawces given to maids

To make them pale and wan
Will help ; such slibbersawces mar the minds of maid and
man,
And have in them a furious force of phrensie now and then."

Cornelius Nepos, Plutarch and other early writers also state
that the love-philtre was often indeed but a poison-cup, and
the death of the Emperor Lucius is quoted as having been due
to a draught of this description given to him at the instance of
Calisthenes.

That the effects of these philtres were often dangerous and
sometimes fatal is hardly to be wondered at, when we consider
the extraordinary nature of some of the substances used in their
composition. They were generally compounded with much
mystery by the old or wise women, who had a reputation for
sorcery, and they observed the greatest secrecy in their concoction.

Many of the ingredients were both grotesque and filthy, such
as " the hair that grew in the nether part of a wolf's tail, the
penis of a wolf, the brain of a cat, the brain of a newt, the brain
of a lizard, a certain fish called ' remora,' and the bones of a
green frog which had been left bare by ants." Young swallows
were buried in the earth and after a time disinterred. The
bodies of those that were found with open bills were believed to
provoke love, while those with closed beaks were given to produce
the opposite effect.

The testicles of certain animals were employed, selected doubtless for a physiological reason, and the menstrual blood, especially
that of a red-haired woman, was highly esteemed and was
believed to have powerful effects.

Poisonous properties were attributed to the blood of both men
and animals by the ancients. Herodotus states that Psam-
menitus, King of Egypt, was put to death by Cambyses by
means of a draught of bullock's blood. Themistocles, who
wished to die rather than fight against his countrymen, is also
said to have drunk a goblet of the blood of a sacrificial ox and
to have expired shortly afterwards. Zacutus Lusitanus relates
several instances of the evil effects resulting from drinking blood
and records the case of a student to whom was given in joke two
ounces of the blood of a red-haired woman, mixed with sugar,
with the result that he became insane.

In the Anglo-Saxon Leechdoms, an ointment composed of
goat's gall, incense, goat's dung and nettle seeds is recommended
as an application to the genital organs to promote passion.

Another substance highly esteemed as an ingredient in love-
philtres was the mysterious hippomanes, which is described
as " a growth found on the forehead of a newly born foal," to
which Ovid alludes in the lines previously quoted.

Love-philtres and charms were also used by Eastern nations, and the Hindus still employ mango, champac, jasmine, lotus and asoka for this purpose. According to Albertus Magnus, the most powerful herb for promoting love is the " Provinsa," the secret of which, he says, has been handed down from the Chaldeans. The Greeks called it Vorax and it is thought to be the same plant now known to the Sicilians as " *Pizzu'ngurdu*," to which they attribute remarkable properties. They believe that if given surreptitiously it will provoke an ardent passion in the heart of the coldest and most chaste woman. The Sicilians have also great faith in the power of hemp to secure the affection of those on whom they set their hearts, and they gather the plant with certain ceremonies.

" As touching this kind of witchcraft," says a writer of the sixteenth century, " the principall part thereof consisteth in certain confections prepared by lewd people to procure love which indeed are mere poisons, bereaving some of the benefit of the braine and some of the sense and understanding of the minde." Yet even such men as Van Helmont believed in the efficacy of the love-philtre. Writing in the seventeenth century, he says ; " I know a plant of common occurrence which if you rub and cherish it in the hand till it becomes warm, and take the hand of another and hold it until it becomes warm, that person will forthwith be stimulated with love for you and continue so for several days." Reginald Scot states, wolf's penis was an ingredient in the love-philtres of his time, and Frommaun mentions that human skull, coral, verbena, urine and leopard's dung were also employed in some of these concoctions.

The mandrake root, which was a common ingredient in love-philtres in ancient times, is still worn in some parts of France as a charm for that purpose, and in Germany a belief in the power of endive seed to influence the affections still exists. In Italy, basil was used to inflame the heart of the indifferent, and a young man who accepted a sprig of this plant from the hand of a maiden was sure to be inspired with love for her. Satyrion is another herb for which amatory properties were claimed, while certain species of orchis, when eaten fresh, were believed to inspire pure love, and when dried were employed to check illicit passion.

Of other plants employed in the composition of love-philtres, mention should be made of the cyclamen, carrot, purslane, cummin, maiden-hair, valerian, navel-wort, wild poppy, anemone, crocus, periwinkle, pansy and the root of the male fern, which has long had a reputation for inspiring the tender passion, although, curiously enough, its present use in medicine is as a vermifuge.

Even at the present day belief in the efficacy of love-charms has not yet died out in some parts of England. Among the

ignorant in some parts of the country "All Hallow E'en" is
dedicated to the performance of certain love charms, in which
the gum-resin called dragon's-blood and quicksilver play an important part. Quite recently, a Russian Jewess in the East End
of London was indicted with having obtained money by false
pretences from two women. From one, whose husband had
deserted her, she obtained money to purchase candles into which
she stuck pins which she said would attract the husband to his
home again. This charm, however, did not work satisfactorily,
and she insisted on having a nightdress, some sheets and pillow
cases which she said she could prepare with a secret process,
so that one night the wife would wake up and find her husband
beside her. "He would be wearing the nightdress, and the
pillow cases she had treated with something which would have
the wonderful power of preventing her husband ever again running away."

But all those charms failed, and even the final effort, in which
a magic liquid was sprinkled about the room and the wearing of
the clippings from the back of a black cat, proved useless in
restoring the missing husband.

To the other woman, who wished her intended husband to
come from Russia, this modern magician gave two curious
powders, with instructions that they were to be placed on the
end of a hairpin and consumed in a flame which would show
the man's love for her.

This modern witch's practice, which was said to be both large
and lucrative, was suspended while she remained nine months in
gaol, and afterwards deported to her native land.

Ginseng root, which has been used for centuries in China
to promote longevity, was also recommended as a love-charm.
It is believed by the Chinese to have the power of rejuvenating
the old and stimulating the senses of the young.

Among primitive peoples the love-philtre is still in vogue, and
P. A. Talbot found it generally used among the tribes in Southern
Nigeria, through which he travelled, especially among the
mysterious race called the Ibibios, who live in the Eket district
of the country. "It is a custom," he states, "for a love-potion
to be given by men and women to gain the hearts of those whom
they desire, or to wrest affection from rivals."

The numerous wives of each chieftain are constantly employing these potions in order to secure the husband's affection
and become his favourite.

The drugs used in these potions are guarded with the utmost
care and secrecy by the witch-doctor and are only known to
him. There is however, no doubt, that they are often capable
of producing frenzy and sometimes death.

A few years ago, an extraordinary story was revealed at the
trial of the wife of a wealthy man living at Lakewood, Ohio, who

was believed to have been murdered. It was stated during the trial that a spiritualistic practitioner had been called in by the lady, who had administered to the husband a magic potion or philtre which contained arsenic. If this failed, he was to have been assassinated.

CHAPTER XVIII

ROYAL AND HISTORIC POISONERS

POISON appears to have been employed as a political agent from an early period of history, and many stories have been handed down of royal personages who used this secret and deadly method of ridding themselves of troublesome individuals and removing enemies from their path. In the same way, they themselves sometimes became the victims of jealous rivals. The greatest craft and cunning were exerted in order to introduce poison into the human body, and there are many stories concerning the curious and subtle methods said to have been employed.

There are but few authenticated records of the use of poison in England for criminal purposes until the sixteenth century. According to tradition King John is said to have compassed the death of the unfortunate Maud FitzWalter by means of a poisoned egg.

The romantic story is thus related by Hepworth Dixon in *Her Majesty's Tower*. In the reign of King John the White Tower received one of the first and fairest of a long line of female victims, in the person of Maud FitzWalter, who was known to the troubadours of the time as Maud the Fair. The father of this beautiful girl was Robert, Lord FitzWalter, of Castle Baynard on the Thames, one of John's most powerful and greatest barons. The King, it is said, during a fit of violence or temper with the Queen, fell madly in love with the fair Maud. As neither the lady herself nor her father would listen to his disgraceful suit, the King is said to have seized her by force at Dunmow and brought her to the Tower. FitzWalter raised an outcry, on which the King sent troops into Castle Baynard and his other houses, and when the baron protested against these wrongs his royal master banished him from the realm. Fitz-Walter fled to France with his wife and other children, leaving poor Maud in the Tower, where she suffered a daily insult in the King's unlawful suit. She remained obdurate, however, and refused his offers. On her proud and scornful answer to his overtures being heard, John carried her up to the roof and locked her in the round turret, standing on the north-east angle of the keep. Maud's cage was the highest and chilliest den in the Tower, but neither cold, solitude nor hunger could break her resolve, and at last, in a rage of disappointed love, the King sent one of his minions to her room with a poisoned egg, of which the brave girl ate and died.

According to the French Chronicles, " After the death of Gaultier Giffard, Count Buckingham, in the early part of the twelfth century, Agnes his widow became enamoured with Robert Duke of Normandy, and attached herself to him in an illicit manner, shortly after which time his wife Sibylle died of poison."

One of the earliest recorded cases of secret poisoning in England is that of Sir Walter de Scotiney, who was convicted of poisoning the Abbot of Westminster and William, brother of the Earl of Gloucester. According to Leland's account, this happened during the meeting of a Parliament which had been convened at Winchester by Henry the Third about 1230. The story is told in the following words :

" The Abbot of Westminster and William brother of the Earl of Gloucester, a person of great worth and spirit, were both destroyed. The Earl of Gloucester himself languished under the effects of the poison and only escaped death with extreme difficulty, for the hair fell from his head and the nails from his fingers. They are said to have received into their bowels the deadly drug at the table of the Lord Edward, King Henry's eldest son, during breakfast. The Earl escaped destruction merely by the strength of his constitution with the loss of his hair, nails, skin and great injury to his teeth. These atrocious deeds struck the people with horror. The villainy was imputed to a certain knight, Walter de Scotiney, and at the appeal of the Countess de L'Isle he was seized, judged and drawn."

" In the same year and the latter end of February," the chronicler continues : " was apprehended at London Walter de Scotiney, the Chief Councillor of the Earl of Gloucester and his seneschal, being suspected of having given the poisonous potion to the Earl, who was himself hardly saved from the gate of death, and to his brother William de Clare who was really killed by it ; also was taken William de Bussey whose villainies if related must excite horror and astonishment. He was the seneschal and principal councillor of William de Valence. These men, although they had been under the safe custody of sureties, being now seized and brought before the judges were committed to a viler prison and put in chains."

In the records of Hugh de Bigot, the High Justiciar, it is stated :

" Coming to Winchester they brought Walter de Scotiney steward of the Earl of Gloucester to his trial for poisoning William de Clare the preceding year. Scotiney was convicted, condemned and executed."

The strict precautions taken by Royal personages against attempts at poisoning, are evidenced in the orders made by Henry VII for protecting the infant Prince of Wales. It was laid down by command that : " No person of whatsoever rank, except the regular attendants in the nursery should approach the cradle except with an order from the King's hand. The food given to the child was to be largely " assayed " and his clothes were to be washed by his own servants and no other hand might touch them. The material was to be subject to all tests. The Chamberlain and Vice-Chamberlain must be present morning and evening when the Prince was washed and dressed and nothing of any kind bought for the use of the nursery might be introduced until it was washed and perfumed."

The story of the Countess of Somerset, who was tried with others for the murder of Sir Thomas Overbury in the reign of James I, forms an interesting episode in the history of romantic poisoning. Robert Earl of Essex, son of Queen Elizabeth's favourite, and who afterwards became Commander-in-Chief of the Parliamentary forces, married, at the age of fourteen, Frances Howard, a younger daughter of the Earl of Suffolk, the bride being just a year younger than her husband. The match had been arranged and brought about through the influence of relatives, who thought it expedient that the youthful bridegroom should be sent off to travel on the Continent immediately after the marriage had taken place, and he remained away for three or four years. During this period the countess, who was brought up at Court, developed into a very beautiful woman, but seems to have been both unprincipled and capricious. On the return of the earl from his travels, she shrank from all advances on his part, and showed the utmost repugnance to her husband on all occasions. Their dispositions were entirely different. He loved retirement, and wished to live a quiet country life, while she, who had been bred at Court, and accustomed to adulation and intrigue, refused to leave town. The King about this time had a number of young men of distinguished appearance and good looks attached to the Court, and of these, one Robert Carr at length became an exclusive favourite. Between him and the self-willed young countess there sprang up an attachment, which, at least on her side, amounted to infatuation. Her opportunities for meeting her lover were short and rare, and in this emergency she applied to a Mrs. Turner, who introduced her to Simon Forman, a noted astrologer and magician at that time, and he, by images made of wax and other devices of the black art, undertook to procure the love of Carr for the lady. At the same time he was also to practise against the earl in the opposite direction. These measures, however, were too slow for the wayward countess, and having gone to the utmost lengths with her lover, she insisted on a divorce from her husband, and a legal marriage with Carr.

One of Carr's greatest friends was Sir Thomas Overbury, a young courtier, a man of honour and of a kindly disposition. He was much against the intimacy, and besought his friend to break it off, assuring him it would ruin his prospects and reputation if he married the lady. Carr unwisely made this known to the countess, who at once regarded Overbury as a bitter enemy, and resolved to do what she could to remove him from her path. The pair plotted together with evident success, for the unfortunate Sir Thomas was shortly afterwards committed to the Tower by an arbitrary mandate of the King, and was not allowed to see any visitors. Finally, his food was poisoned, and, after several unsuccessful attempts on his life, he at last died from the effects of poison. Cantharides, nitrate of silver, spiders, arsenic, and last of all, corrosive sublimate, are said to have been administered in turn to this unfortunate man. Meanwhile, the countess obtained a divorce from her husband on the ground of impotency, and married Carr, who was soon after made Earl of Somerset by King James.

Two years elapsed before the murder of Sir Thomas Overbury was brought to light, when the inferior criminals, Mrs. Turner and others, were convicted and executed ; but the Earl of Somerset and his countess, although found guilty with their accomplices, received the royal pardon. The happiness of the earl and countess, however, was not of long duration, as it is stated they " afterwards became so alienated from each other, that they resided for years under the same roof with the most careful precautions that they might not by any chance come into each other's presence." Mrs. Turner, implicated in the crime, is said to have been the first to introduce into England the yellow starch that was then applied to ladies' ruffs. Her last request was that she should be hanged in a ruff dyed with her own yellow starch, and her wish is said to have been duly carried out.

Whether Robert Dudley, Earl of Leicester, Prime Minister and favourite of Queen Elizabeth, was as black as he is painted by some of the historians of his time, it is difficult to judge. His ambition to marry his royal mistress, who, shrewd woman as she was, appears to have had no insight into his unscrupulous character, was apparently the cause of his attempting by insidious methods to move every human obstacle from his path. The death of his wife, Amy Robsart, a mystery which has never been completely solved was believed by some to be due to poison. Leicester was also suspected of causing the death of Lord Sheffield, and the Earl of Essex, another rival, is stated to have been the victim of his hatred.

The death of the latter peer is said, in the language of a contemporary chronicler, as having been due to " an extreme flux cause by an Italian Receit, the maker whereof was a surgeon that was then newly come to my Lord from Italy, a cunning man and sure in operation." The inventor of this recipe was known as Dr. Julio, who was said to be able " to make a man dye in what manner of sickness you will." Essex died when on his way back to England from Ireland, with the object, it is said, of revenging himself on Leicester for his domestic wrongs. " With the Earl of Essex, one Mrs. Alice Drakott, a godly gentle-woman, is also said to have been poisoned." This lady happened to be accompanying the earl on her way towards her own house, when after partaking of the same cup, she was also seized with violent pain and vomiting which continued until she died, a day or two before the earl succumbed. " When she was dead," says the chronicler, " her body was swollen into a monstrous bigness and deformity ; whereof the good earl, hearing the day following, lamented the case greatly, and said in the presence of his servants, ' Ah ! poor Alice, the cup was not prepared for thee, albeit it was thy hard fortune to taste thereof.' "

According to all accounts, Leicester's list of victims did not cease here, and, rightly or wrongly, the death of Cardinal Chatillian, who was taken suddenly ill and died in Canterbury, is also attributed to him. The Cardinal had accused the earl of preventing the marriage of the Queen to the King of France, and was journeying back to Dover when he was taken ill and died in a mysterious manner.

Another mysterious death at this time that occasioned con-siderable sensation was that of Sir Nicholas Throgmorton, a wealthy city magnate of Elizabeth's time. Sir Nicholas is said to have been an associate of Leicester's and the one who was ready to do his bidding in thwarting the doings of the Lord Treasurer, Sir William Cecil, who was thought by Leicester to be playing him false. He invited him one night to a supper at his house in London, and, just as the meal was served, hurriedly left for Court, to which he said he had been suddenly called by her Majesty. Sir Nicholas was told to proceed with the meal in his absence, which he did, but soon after was seized with violent vomiting, from which he never recovered. The story continues, that the day before his death he declared to a dear friend " all the circumstances and causes of his complaint, which he affirmed plainly to be poison given him in a sallet at supper, inveighing most earnestly against the earl's cruelty and bloody disposition, and affirming him to be the wickedest, most perilous and perfidi-ous man under heaven."

Whether Leicester was the unscrupulous villain he was made out to be or not, there is no evidence to prove. Many writers declare that he kept professional poisoners ready to do his will and carry out his designs. There seems little doubt that he had some needy physicians in his pay. His personal doctor, one Bayly, is said to have boasted of the fact that " he knew of poisons which might be so tempered that they should kill the party afterwards at what time it should be appointed."

An Italian doctor whom Leicester brought from Italy, is mentioned in several stories as one of the unscrupulous creatures employed by him who were ready to administer the " Italian Comfortive," as the poison was called, at his bidding. Those whose sudden deaths were attributed to Leicester's instrumentality were commonly said to have succumbed to " Leicester's cold."

It is probable, however, that Leicester was suspected of being the instigator of many murders which he may have had nothing to do with, as he made many enemies.

With reference to the sudden demise of Lord Sheffield, whose death is said to have been due to " Leicester's cold." A short time afterwards, the earl married his widow, but under pretence that the Queen would be offended at the marriage, compelled her to keep it secret. After some time, the more effectually to conceal the connexion, he required her to marry Sir Edward Stafford. This she refused to do, till under the gentle discipline of Leicester it is recorded that " her hair fell off and her nails fell out, and she did what was demanded of her to save her life." This story is certified by her own testimony on oath, and recorded by Sir William Dugdale.

The Earl of Sussex, his great rival, is also said to have been one of his victims. On his death-bed he is said to have warned his friends in the following words : " I am passing into another world and must now leave you to your good fortunes and to the Queen's grace and goodness ; but beware of the gipsy's son (Leicester) for he will be too hard for you all. You know the beast as well as I do."

Camden, the historian, who does not discredit many of these stories, asserts that Leicester actually proposed in Council that Mary Queen of Scots should be removed by poison. This statement is interesting in connexion with the story of Lord Holland's poison ring previously mentioned.

There was a curious mystery about the death of Prince Alexander, the son of Peter the Great, the story of which is related by Henry Bruce, an Englishman in Peter's service in 1782. Bruce states that he was at the citadel of St. Peter and St. Paul, where the Tsarevitch was imprisoned on a charge of lèse-majesté, the Tsar and Marshal Veide being also present. The latter ordered Bruce to go to the apothecary Beer, who lived close by, and tell him " the potion must be made strong, for the Prince was very bad indeed." The apothecary trembled and turned pale at the message, but refused to explain to Bruce why he was thus agitated. The Marshal, who had sent Bruce, followed him, and told Beer to " hurry, for the Prince had had an apoplectic fit." The apothecary handed him a silver cup, which the Marshal carried to the Prince, " staggering all the time like a drunken man." Half an hour after the Tsar left the citadel, gloomy, like all his retinue. Bruce was ordered to stay and dine at a table set for the Tsarevitch. " Two doctors and two surgeons dined apart. They were called in to the Prince ; he was in convulsions, and died at 5 p.m., after atrocious suffering. Bruce informed the Marshal, who told the Tsar. The viscera were removed by Peter the Great's orders before the body was coffined."

In India, when powdered glass is employed for lethal purposes, it is generally given with sherbet or some kind of food. It acts as a powerful irritant to the coats of the stomach or intestines and produces gastro-enteritis.

A celebrated case in which this substance was alleged to have been used occurred in India in 1874, when the Gaekwar or reigning prince of Baroda, was tried for attempting to kill the British political resident, Colonel Phayre, by administering powdered glass to him in sherbet. He was brought to trial before a court composed of three Indian and three English judges, and after a trial lasting thirty-five days the English judges pronounced for a conviction and the three Indian ones for an acquittal. In the end the Gaekwar was deposed and deported to Madras.

Both powdered glass and diamond dust have for centuries had the reputation of acting as powerful irritants. Benvenuto Cellini mentions in his Autobiography that an attempt was made on his life with powdered diamonds, but the person who was instructed to prepare the powder substituted an innocuous substance instead.

In India, glass bangles obtained from the bazaars, after being reduced to powder, are known to have been administered mixed with curry. The effect, naturally, depends on the size and sharpness of the particles, the larger and sharper having the more dangerous results and being more likely to set up some form of gastro-enteritis.

The symptoms produced are in the main due to damage to the mucous membrane of the alimentary canal resembling those of gastro-enteritis, accompanied by pain and vomiting, the latter being streaked with blood.

On the other hand, in curious contrast, in 1925 a medical practitioner wrote to the *Lancet*[*] recommending powdered glass as an efficient vermifuge and stated he had used it for that purpose in children and adults with uniform success.

* *The Lancet.* Feb. 19th, 1925.

CHAPTER XIX

POISON MYSTERIES IN EARLY SCOTTISH HISTORY

ACCORDING to historical records, Scotland had its poison mysteries in early times.

In the year 1332, Thomas Randolph, Earl of Moray, who on the death of Robert Bruce was appointed Regent during the minority of the young King David the Second, is said to have fallen a victim to poison.

Hector Boece, in his *Cronikles of Scotland*, boldly attributes his death to the malice of Edward III, King of England, who, he states, " tuk purpos to sla him be venome." The fatal draught is said to have been administered to the Earl by a monk who had been sent by the English King as a physician, with the result that the unfortunate Moray found " certaine dolouris ilk day mair increasing in his wame," and died very suddenly.

The Duke of Albany, younger son of James III, according to a chronicler, was also " posonit in oure Souverane lordis presens and palas," which caused " a sclandir and murmur rising in the cuntre," but by whom it was administered is not known.

In 1497 Margaret Drummond, mistress of James the Fourth, is said to have been poisoned, with her two sisters, at the instigation of the nobles who wished the king to marry.

In 1536 Jean Douglas, Lady Glamis, grand-daughter of " Bell-the-Cat," was tried for having removed her husband some years before *per intoxicationem*, and for having conspired to dispose in the same way of King James the V, who had put the whole Douglas family under ban. She was *convicta de arte et parte proditorie conspirationis et imaginationis interfectionis sive destructionis nobilissime personne serenissimi domini nostri Regis per pessimum venenum lie poysone*, and condemned to " be had to Castell hill of Edinburghe and their Byrnt in ane fyre to the deid, as ane Traytour."

Another case of alleged poisoning famous in Scottish history is that of the Earl of Atholl, Treasurer of the Kingdom, who died suddenly after a reconciliation feast given by the Regent, Morton. Atholl, a near kinsman of the King, was a Catholic ; Morton " a licentious man, but a fervent Protestant " : the two men were, besides, rivals in the State. It was generally

believed at the time that Atholl was poisoned by Morton, and
so clamorous did the popular indignation become that by order
of the Privy Council an inquest was held in the presence of the
King and his Councillors. Six surgeons were appointed to make
a post-mortem examination. James Owhegarty, " Ireland man
born leiche that ministratis medicine in the mouth and curis
outward be herbis," testified that the cause of death was " rank
venom " introduced by the mouth. The testimony of Alexander
Prestoun, " Doctour in Medicine," and George Boswell,
" Mediciner and Chirurgiane in Perty," was to the same effect.
Gilbert Moncrieff gave a more guarded opinion ; he considered
the humour in the stomach to be venomous, but was unable to
say whether it was exterior or interior grown within the body.
David Rattray, " Chirurgiane in Conpare," gave it as his opinion,
that death was caused by " ane extraordinarie poyson," adding
that " ane spune put in the humour change it in the cullour of
brass." R. Craig, " Burgess of Edinburgh, chirurgiane,"
cautiously opined that the Earl " to all appearance " had died of
poison. A non-medical witness thought that a red matter shown
to him by Dr. Prestoun was " a cauld poyson." Several ministers
also gave testimony, one of them stating that he saw " strange
and unnatural tokens in the stomach, black and red, as it were
the dregs of bread and wine mixed, and that he had heard the
dead man say " that he had got offence, and God forgive them
that had done it." Bernardino de Mendoza, the Spanish
Ambassador, writing to his King, gives the following description
of the inquest :

They had opened the body in the presence of five doctors,
three of whom said he had been poisoned, and two that he had
not. One of the latter, to assure them that he was right, by
proof, took some of the contents of the stomach on his finger,
and put it into his mouth. The effect was that in a few hours
he was thought to be dying. It is not known whether the
order to poison him came from Morton or some private person.

In the end " the physicians did upon their oath declare that
his death was not caused by any extraordinary means." The
result of the inquest did not, however, allay the general suspicion,
and Morton thought it necessary, when he was about to die on
the scaffold in 1581, to make a solemn declaration, that he
" would not for the Earldom of Atholl have either ministered
poison unto him or caused it to be ministered unto him."

Shortly after the death of Robert Stewart, Earl of Orkney,
who was an illegitimate brother of Queen Mary, a quarrel
arose between his eldest son Patrick and his younger brothers,
John, James, and William Stewart. Eventually the latter were
suspected of conspiring to poison their brother, who had succeeded to the title, and in 1596 we find the three brothers, John,
James and William, were brought to trial and accused of having

" conspyrit and dewysit how to murthour the said Patrick Erl of Orkney his brother, be poysoning or utherwayes be craft and guylt dealing," in November, 1593.

The Earl, it appears, captured his brother's servant, who confessed he was hired to do the deed. This confession, however, was only extorted from him after being tortured eleven days and nights in the " cashie-lawis," put in the " buitis " twice a day, and " skargeit with towis."

Tried on the charge of plotting to murder the Earl at a banquet in the house of David Moncriefis of Kirkwell in Orkney, John was acquitted.

Another Scottish noble, George Home, Earl of Dunbar, is said to have been poisoned by " tablets of Sugar given him for expelling the cold " by Secretary Cecil in 1611. A post-mortem examination was made by one Martin Souqir, a doctor, who is said to have tried the poison by laying his finger on the subject's heart and touching it with his tongue " (a curious clinical test for poison on which apparently great reliance was placed at that period), with the result that he died within a few days thereafter.

CHAPTER XX

THE ITALIAN SCHOOL OF POISONERS—
A PROFESSIONAL POISONER AND HIS FEES—
THE INFAMOUS TOFFANA

THE study of poisons for criminal purposes developed into a cult in Italy during the Middle Ages, and the Italian school of poisoners became known throughout Europe. There is an authentic record that its members were ready on receipt of certain fees to carry out murder by poison to order.

A document drawn up by Charles, King of Navarre, throws some light on the systematic manner in which the poisoning of obnoxious persons was carried out. It is in the form of a commission to one Wondreton to poison Charles VI, the Duke of Valois, brother of the King, and his uncles the Dukes of Berri, Burgundy and Bourbon. It reads :

" Go thou to Paris ; thou canst do great service if thou wilt. Do what I tell thee ; I will reward thee well. There is a thing which is called sublimed arsenic ; if a man eat a bit the size of a pea, he will never survive ; Thou wilt find it in Pampeluna, Bordeaux, Bayonne, and in all the good towns thou wilt pass at the apothecaries' shops. Take it, and powder it ; and when thou shalt be in the house of the King, of the Count de Valois his brother, and the Dukes of Berri, Burgundy and Bourbon, draw near and betake thyself to the kitchen, to the larder, to the cellar, or any other place where thy point can best be gained, and put the powder in the soups, meats, or wines ; provided that thou canst do it secretly. Otherwise do it not."

It is satisfactory to learn that the miscreant who was entrusted with this diabolical commission was detected in time, and executed in 1384.

There seems little doubt that some of the Italian alchemists of the fourteenth and fifteenth centuries studied the art of combining certain poisonous substances with the object of making them more virulent ; thus, Pierre le Bon of Ferrara, describes a poison he compounded, containing aconite and copper with the venom of toads.

Jagot expresses his belief with respect to the poisons used by the Borgias or their agents, that they knew of the toxic properties of the urine and saliva of certain animals which are sometimes very poisonous. He states that a mixture of the saliva and blood of the pig is extremely toxic and the method of allowing a pig to decompose and then treating it with arsenic, thus combining the ptomaines of putrefaction with the mineral poison, was well known to them.

From the fifteenth to the seventeenth century there were schools of poisoners both in Venice and Rome. The Venetian poisoners who first came into notoriety began their operations early in the sixteenth century. At that period the mania for poisoning had risen to such a degree that the governments of the States were formally recognizing secret assassination by poison, and considering the removal of emperors, princes and powerful nobles by this method. This is not a myth, as a record of the notorious Council of Ten which met to consider such plans, and an account of their proceedings, still exists. It gives the number of those who voted for and who voted against the proposed removal of certain persons, the reasons for their assassination and the sums paid for their execution. Thus these conspirators quietly and secretly arranged to take the lives of many prominent individuals who displeased them. When the deed had been carried out it was registered on the margin of their official record by the significant word " Factum."

On December 15th, 1543, John of Ragusa, a Franciscan brother, offered the Council a selection of poisons, and declared himself ready to remove any person out of the way whom they deemed objectionable. He openly stated his terms, which for the first successful case was to be a pension of 1,500 ducats a year, to be increased on the execution of future services. The Presidents, Guolando Duoda and Pietro Guiarini, placed this matter before the Council on January 4th, 1544, and on a division it was resolved to accept this patriotic offer, and to experiment first on the Emperor Maximilian. John, who had evidently reduced poisoning to a fine art, afterwards submitted the following regular graduated tariff to the Council :

For the great Sultan, 500 ducats.
For the King of Spain, 150 ducats, including the expenses of the journey, etc.
For the Duke of Milan, 60 ducats.
For the Marquis of Mantua, 50 ducats.
For the Pope, 100 ducats.

He further adds at the foot of the document, " The farther the journey, the more eminent the man, the more it is necessary to reward the toil and hardships undertaken, and the heavier must be the payment."

What may be called the Roman school of poisoners became prominent in the early sixteenth century, and their operations continued until the early part of the eighteenth century. During this period the magnitude and daring of their crimes struck terror into the hearts of the chief nobles and rulers of the country. The books on what were termed " secrets," printed in Italy about this time, consisting of formulæ of various descriptions, contain many allusions to poisons. In them stories are told of poisons supposed to be unknown, whose secrets died with their originators.

The mania for poisoning appears to have seized on all classes from the highest to the lowest, and no one who made an enemy was safe. Giovanni Battista Porta, who wrote a book entitled : *Neapolitani Magiæ Naturalis*, printed in Naples in 1589, made a careful study of the subject, and describes methods which were no doubt used in his time. He mentions various means for drugging wine, a favourite medium for administering poison. For this purpose belladonna root, nux vomica, aconite and hellebore were employed, all of which are very deadly in their effects. He gives a formula for compounding what he calls, " a very strong poison," named " Venenum Lupinum," which was composed of aconite, taxus baccata, caustic lime, arsenic, bitter almonds and powdered glass. These substances were to be mixed with honey into a stiff paste and made into pills the size of hazel nut. His method of poisoning a sleeping person was to make a mixture of hemlock juice, bruised stramonium, belladonna and opium, which was to be placed in a leaden box with a perfectly fitting lid, and allowed to ferment for several days. When this was done it was to be uncovered and placed under the nose of the intended victim while asleep. So long as the individual only smelt and did not swallow the compound, it could not have done much harm.

During the early part of the seventeenth century the southern parts of Italy, including Sicily, also appear to have been infested by unscrupulous practitioners in the use of poison, and Naples became a centre for this nefarious trade. The most notorious of these criminals whose name has been left on record is the woman named Toffana, who is said to have been responsible indirectly for the deaths of hundreds of people. About 1650, when she was little more than a girl, she began her evil career in Palermo, but in 1659, during the pontificate of Alexander VII, she removed to Naples and made it the centre of her operations. Whether she herself devised the poison which is associated with her name, or whether she obtained the knowledge from a confederate, is not known. Her method was to prepare a solution and bottle it in special phials bearing the representation of some saint, generally Saint Nicholas of Bari, who was associated with a medicinal spring, the water of which had a reputation for healing. Sometimes she used other names for her poisonous solution, such as " Aquetta di Napoli," " Manna of St. Nicholas di Bari," or " Aqua Toffana." These bottles of poison were freely sold, especially to women, reputedly as a cosmetic for application to the skin to improve the complexion, for which purpose, owing to its active constituent being arsenic, it probably proved effective. Anyone in the secret could buy the poison for its supposed external application, and Toffana took care only to deal with individuals after due safeguards had been built up. She changed her abode so frequently, and adopted so many disguises, that even when suspicion actually fell upon her after many mysterious deaths, detection was rendered very difficult. She cunningly worked on the minds of her customers who were susceptible to religious or superstitious influences, and those who were unaware of the origin of her deadly solution were told it was a certain miraculous liquid supposed to ooze from the tomb of St. Nicholas, a saint of healing.

Her preparations were doubtless bought by many in good faith in the belief that the liquid had miraculous properties, but those who knew the secret, especially women, who wished to rid themselves of their husbands, often used it for criminal purposes, and it is estimated that over six hundred persons were poisoned by her preparations in Naples and Rome. Two Popes and other Church dignitaries are said to have fallen victims to the poison, and it was not until after a long career, and when Toffana had reached the age of seventy, that she was found to be the originator of these wholesale crimes. In a letter addressed to Hoffman* by Garcelli, physician to the Emperor Charles VI of Austria, he informed him that being Governor of Naples at the time, he knew that the Aquetta di Napoli was the dread of every noble family in the city, and that the subject was investigated legally. He thus had the opportunity of examining all the documents, and found the poison to consist of a solution of arsenic, which was of such strength that from four to six drops in water or wine was said to kill an adult, and that it was colourless, transparent and tasteless.

When the manufacture and sale of the poison was at last traced to Toffana, she took refuge in a convent where, under the privileges of the place, she bade defiance for some time to the officers of justice, and continued to vend her solution from the very bosom of the Church until the scandal at length became too great to be tolerated. She was then dragged from her refuge and thrown into prison. A great outcry was raised by the clergy at this violation of their privileges, and the people, unwilling to be defrauded of their right to use the poison, joined in the clamour of the priests. It was only by circulating a report that she had poisoned the wells in the city, that the current of public sentiment could be turned against her. Being put to the rack she confessed her crimes, and named those who had afforded her protection. They were immediately arrested in

* *Medicina Rationalis Systematica*, i, 198.

various churches and monasteries. It was stated that the day before her last flight from justice, she had sent two boxes of her " manna " to Rome. They were found in the custom-house in that city. The archbishop still murmured at her being torn from a privileged asylum and accordingly the authorities contrived to have her strangled and thrown into the court-yard of the convent from which she had been taken in 1709. The sale of her preparations however, did not cease at her death, and, according to Keysler, who travelled in Southern Italy in the early part of the eighteenth century, the *aquetta* continued to be prepared in great quantities for some time afterwards.

There was naturally much mystery at the time as to the composition of Aqua Toffana and the most extraordinary properties were attributed to it. Its alleged effects are thus described by Behrens, a contemporary writer : " a certain indescribable change is felt in the whole body, which leads the person to complain to his physician. The physician examines and reflects, but finds no symptoms either external or internal, no vomiting, no inflammation, no fever. In short, he can only advise patience, strict regimen, and laxatives. The malady, however, creeps on, and the physician is again sent for. Still he cannot detect any symptoms of note. Meanwhile the poison takes firmer hold of the system ; languor, wearisomeness, and loathing of food continue ; the nobler organs gradually become torpid, and the lungs in particular at length begin to suffer. In a word, the malady from the first is incurable ; the unhappy victim pines away insensibly even in the hands of the physician, and thus he is brought to a miserable end through months or years, according to his enemy's desire."

Father Labat, in his *Travels in Italy*, observes that the association of the name of St. Nicholas of Bari with Aqua Toffana was a great advantage to her, as there was such a preparation in reality, a sacred water, and Toffana's solution, under the name " Manna of St. Nicholas di Bari," was able to pass the Custom-house with little scrutiny.

Toffana had many imitators, who continued to practise for some time after her death. A similar scheme was attempted with a poisonous preparation called " Aquetta di Perugia," which was also sold for cosmetic purposes. It is said to have been prepared by killing a hog, disjointing it, and strewing the pieces with white arsenic, which was well rubbed in, and finally collecting the juice which dropped from the meat itself.

This preparation was supposed to be a stronger and more powerful poison than arsenic, and more rapid in its action.

Some idea of the extent to which criminal poisoning was carried in Italy may be gathered from an account of a secret society of women that was formed in Rome in 1659. Many of the members were young married women belonging to some of the best and wealthiest families of that city. They apparently met together with the chief object of plotting to destroy the lives of their husbands or members of families connected with them. They gathered at regular intervals at the house of a woman called Hieronyma Spara, who was reputed to be a sorceress. She provided the members of the Society with the poison necessary for their purposes, and planned and instructed them how to use it.

Operations had been carried on for some time before the existence of the Society was discovered, " and," says a contemporary writer, " the hardened old hag passed the ordeal of the rack without confession, but another woman divulged the secrets of the sisterhood, and La Spara, together with twelve other women implicated, were hanged. Many others were publicly whipped through the streets of the city."

A curious story is told of D'Annuzio, the Italian poet, who became prominent in 1921 in the seizure of Fiume, which he held as dictator for some time. It is stated that when serving in the Italian Air Force, which he did with distinction during the war, it was his custom to carry a small bottle of a very powerful poison in his pocket to which he used to allude as " My Pharmic Liberator."   This poison which he is said to have had concocted for him in Venice, was made from a mediaeval recipe only known to the Venetian poisoners. It is said that when he was performing his memorable raid over Vienna the engines of his aeroplane stopped and restarted thrice over, and feeling certain that a descent over enemy territory was inevitable, he got his phial ready in order that the Austrians should not capture him alive. At that very moment he is said to have seen an apparition of his mother, who had died two years beforehand, who bade him cast away all fears and he would get through. According to the story he kept his phial of poison close at hand during the bombardment of Fiume, and his friends had to keep perpetual watch upon him during those critical hours.

CHAPTER XXI

THE MYSTERY OF THE BORGIA POISON

CONSIDERABLE mystery has ever enveloped the history of the Borgia family, whose name historians have linked with some of the most morbid stories of crime and secret poisoning of the Middle Ages. A great deal that has been written concerning their crimes is doubtless pure fiction, and it is only within recent years that owing to the discovery of certain contemporary documents, some light has been thrown upon the darksome deeds they are said to have perpetrated. From an examination of these records on the one hand, it would appear that certain members of the family were not so black as tradition has painted them, and on the other, there seems little doubt that some of the Borgias were guilty of terrible and sinister deeds, which were only too common in the times in which they lived.

The Borgias, who were of Spanish origin, migrated to Italy and came into notoriety in the time of Pope Calixtus III, about the year 1455. The first member to come into prominence was Rodrigo, who was born in 1431, and who began life as a soldier. Afterwards, through the influence of Calixtus he entered the priesthood, and finally rose to be the head of the Church under the title of Pope Alexander VI. He is said to have had five children by his mistress Vanozza de Cattanei, viz. : Pier Luigi, who died in infancy, Giovanni Duke of Gandia, Giffredo Count of Cariati, Cesare, afterwards Duke of Valentinois, and Lucrezia, who eventually became Duchess of Ferrara.

Alexander is described by contemporary writers as " a handsome man of majestic and kingly bearing," and is said to have looked " more like a Cæsar returned to life than a Vicar of Christ."

As his children grew up he loaded them with titles and honours. When he came to the papal chair, Cesare was about twenty-two years of age and Lucrezia between thirteen and fourteen. He recognized all of them in special Bulls, except Cesare, from whom (in order to bestow the purple on him) he wished to remove the stigma of his origin, and declared him to be the son of Vanozza and Domenico d'Arignano. This he proclaimed in a Bull dated October 17th, 1480.

In the early part of 1498 a youth was introduced to the household called Romano, whom the Pope declared was the son of Cesare. He created him Duke of Nepi, and presented him with large estates. According to documents discovered by Gregorovius, dated September 1, 1501, the Pope himself was the real father, and the maternity of this boy involves one of the most obscure mysteries of the history of the Borgias.

Before Alexander obtained the pontificate, he had betrothed Lucrezia to a Spanish gentleman, but he broke off the engagement with the evident object of marrying his daughter to a man of higher rank, and on June 12, 1493, Lucrezia was espoused to Giovanni Sforza, Lord of Pesaro. The marriage was by no means a happy one, and at the end of four years was dissolved by the Pope, who had other motives in view, for he soon arranged a fresh alliance between Lucrezia and Alfonso Duke of Bisceglie, the natural son of Alfonso II, King of Naples. The marriage took place, but soon after the birth of their first child, the Duke was attacked by several men and severely wounded. The tragic story is thus related by a chronicler :

" On the night of July 15 (1500) on which solemn ceremonies were taking place to celebrate the jubilee of the Pope, a young man staggered headlong into the pontifical apartments, endeavouring to stem with his hands a stream of blood which gushed from a large wound in his chest. It was the Duke of Bisceglie, Alfonso of Aragon, Lucrezia's second husband. Consternation was caused when it was spread abroad that a band of assassins in the pay of Cesare had attempted to assassinate him near the steps of St. Peter's when on his way to the celebration. The young man, who is said to have been of a kind and gentle nature, fell unconscious at the feet of the Pope. Lucrezia and his sister Sancia, who were standing by, both fainted away and were carried into a room of the tower behind the Pope's chambers. He is said to have been nursed by the two women and to have nearly recovered, when one night, in Lucrezia's absence, he was strangled with a cord in bed under the eyes of Cesare."

Lucrezia then retired for a time to an estate at Nepi. On her return to Rome, she appears to have acted as a kind of secretary to her father the Pope, and in about twelve months her betrothal to Alfonso d'Este, the eldest son of the Duke of Ferrara, was announced, and the marriage took place by proxy on December 20, 1502. Shortly afterwards she left Rome to take up her residence in Ferrara.

From father to children, who apparently put no restraint on their criminal and sensual instincts, it was not long before the most extraordinary stories were circulated about the Borgias. Cesare, in particular, appears to have been a degenerate of the worst possible type. He was first made bishop of Pampeluna and afterwards Cardinal of Valenza, and appears to have been even a worse character than his father. Tragedies in the family began in 1497 when Giovanni Duke of Gandia, the second son, was found in the Tiber, his body being pierced with ten wounds from a dagger. According to Scalona, suspicion rested on Sforza Count of Pesaro.

Cesare conceived a violent jealousy of an attendant in his sister's household, named Pedro Calderon, who was probably a Spaniard. In a fit of passion he is said to have pursued the man with a dagger right into the pontifical apartments and assassinated him in the presence of the Pope, " even so," says the chronicler, " that the pontifical garments were splashed with blood." According to Capello, " four hired ruffians carried his body to the Tiber, tied a large stone to his neck and threw him into the river."

Public feeling at length began to be aroused against the Borgias, but Alexander kept on his way serenely, in spite of the wave of contumely which seethed round the papal throne in Rome. Sannazaro's couplets, Pontano's epigrams, and the reports let drop by the Mantuan and Venetian ambassadors of the grave rumours but whispered in Rome, were followed by the accusations of bishops and even of some cardinals, but nothing was done.

In justice to the Borgias one must try to visualize the condition of the people of Rome at this period. Poison may be said to have become a common weapon in the social and political life of the country. For the politician it was a weapon which procured him office, for the theologian a secret method of removing an enemy from his path, and so on throughout the whole social strata. Superstition was rampant, and according to a writer of the time, even the worst criminals would make the sign of the Cross on passing before a church and supplicate the Madonna to give them help and profit in their crimes. Scarcely any value was attached to human life, and those in prominent positions lived in a constant state of insecurity. No wonder that vendors of amulets, talismans and antidotes to poison, flourished everywhere.

Apollinaire paints a lurid picture of the Borgias in the following account of a fête held in the vineyard of St. Peter-in-Chains :

" La Vanozza de Cattanei receives the cardinals and the ambassadors, and after being introduced to one another, the guests disperse about the vineyard and exchange conversation and courtesies. Later she disappears and joins Cesare in a room on the first floor of the building. She finds him with his sleeves rolled up, bent over a kneading trough, and absorbed in his task. This room was reserved for Vanozza and Cesare ; only the Pope shared with them the right of entry, no one else was allowed to cross the threshold. On the floor lay several large shallow copper dishes, some of which were entirely covered with verdigris, and from which a colourless-looking liquid was being evaporated. One of these dishes was always placed near the fire in order that the heat might hasten the evaporation.

" As La Vanozza enters Cesare remarks : ' Yet I forbade you to make a fire.'

" ' I only put a few live coals to hasten the result,' she replies. ' I did not make enough for it to be possible for the powder to scorch ; if I had not done it we should not have had the powder to-day ! '

" ' It is not so much for fear of its scorching, but because of the cinders which mix with the powder and render it less fine,' said Cesare. ' Happily Cardinal di Riaro is short-sighted. This is quite enough for him in any case, but for others, hand me the tart dish,' he continues. ' It should be dry by now.'

" La Vanozza lifts the heavy red copper dish by the two handles, and on it may be noticed a mouldiness, or greenish spots caused by a settling deposit. With a hare's paw Cesare collects this powder, then with an ivory knife he carefully scrapes the copper, and mixes the residue in a marble mortar. From it he takes in small pinches some of the powder and places it in another mortar of agate, and reduces it with a pestle to an impalpable dust until it is like a morsel of polished silver.

" ' Give me the " manna," ' says Cesare. La Vanozza hands him the arsenic which he calls by that name, and he mixes some with the powder in the mortar, passing the mixture again under the pestle until thoroughly incorporated, and then, his task completed, he stands erect and exclaims : ' God said " Let there be light " and there was light. We Borgias are able to say " Let it be night," and night it shall be.' He then remarks to Vanozza, ' It is time for luncheon.' La Vanozza leaves him and retraces her way ; when she is gone, the copper dish being empty, he pours urine in it in order to replace that which has evaporated, the salts of which he had just utilized. The salt which resulted, combined with the verdigris, were then mixed with arsenic and this formed the famous poison which the Borgias called ' La Cantarella.' ' That which the Borgias utilized in conjunction with arsenic without knowing it,' says Apollinaire, ' was phosphorus, a secret which had been divulged to the Borgias by a Spanish monk, who also knew the antidote for it, as well as an antidote for arsenic ; one sees, therefore, that they were well armed.' "

There is no evidence to prove the truth of Apollinaire's statements, and he may only have recorded the reports common at the time. These records are, however, interesting to compare with the statements made by contemporary historians.

An astrologer is said to have predicted to Alexander that he would never die so long as he carried on his person a box containing the Blessed Sacrament. This gold box is stated to have never left his person. On a certain day he is said to have invited those who had been nominated as cardinals to supper with him. Suspicious of their host the commanded guests were doubtful of acceptance, and only agreed to come on condition that the supper took place at the house of the Cardinal de Corneto. Alexander and his son Cesare are stated to have bribed the chief attendant of the Cardinal for a large sum and pledged him to serve a certain wine at dinner to which they had added poison. The evening arrived, and Alexander, as he entered the room, remembered he had forgotten the box containing the Blessed Sacrament. He at once ordered Monsignor Caraffa to fetch it.

Apollinaire, who records the story, continues : " While Caraffa obeyed, the Pope irritated by his forgetfulness, asked that a drink should be brought to him before seating himself at the table. The chamberlain in attendance said he would see the order was carried out, but it happened that the chief attendant whom the Pope and Cesare had bribed was absent at the moment, and the chamberlain who came for the wine was served by an underling who was in ignorance of the plot. A goblet was filled from the poisoned caraffe which had been prepared by Cesare and taken to the Pope. Directly after, Caraffa arrived, bringing with him the missing box. It was, however, too late ; the Pope had drunk some of the wine and was already feeling the effects of the poison. Cardinal Valentinois himself lay convulsed upon the ground, surrounded by the others kneeling round in absorbed awe and murmuring Pater Nosters. Alexander appeared to suffer greater agonies than the rest. Surgeons were called in and bled him without any effect, and he succumbed on the eighth day afterwards."

Sanuto gives another account of Alexander's death :

" The death of Pope Alexander VI," he states, " occurred in the following manner. The Cardinal Datary Arian de Corneto having one morning received a message from the Pontiff stating that he intended in company with his son Cesare, the Duke of Valentinois, that evening to pay the Cardinal a visit and to sup with him, and that they would bring their supper with them, was terrified at the intelligence, being fully impressed with the conviction that His Holiness or his son intended poisoning him to possess his treasure, the said Cardinal being very rich. Thinking rapidly over the matter he saw but one means of saving his life. He immediately sent to the head carver of the Pope requesting he would oblige him by visiting him as soon as possible. The carver obeyed the request and the Cardinal having conducted him to a private room placed in his hand ten golden ducats which he requested the said carver to accept as a proof of the love he bore him. After many objections and simulated repugnance the carver accepted the gift, stating that he did so from obedience to the orders of his Eminence. The

Cardinal then finding the carver willing to lend a ready ear to anything he might say, addressed him in the following manner : ' You perfectly well know the intentions of the Pope and that he and his son have determined that I shall die by poison, which will be administered to me this evening and I now humbly beg of you to spare my life.'

" After some demur the carver told him the manner in which it had been agreed between them that the poison should be administered.   After supper was over he had been ordered to place on the table three boxes of confectionery one of which was to be placed before the Pope, another before the Cardinal, and the third before the Duke of Valentinois, taking care to place the one containing the poison before his Excellency. The Cardinal begged and implored the said carver to change the manner in which the confectionaries were to be placed on the table so that the one containing the poison should be put before the Pope, that he might eat of it and die.   The carver at first was horrified at the suggestion, but on the Cardinal offering him 10,000 ducats in gold as a reward he relented and agreed that the box of poisoned sweetmeats should be placed before the Pope.

" In the evening of the same day the Pope accompanied by the Duke arrived at the palace of his Eminence, who as soon as his Holiness had seated himself, flung himself on the ground before him and kissed his feet.   Then with most affectionate words he begged his Holiness would grant him a favour, saying he would never rise from his knees should his Holiness refuse to oblige him.   Surprised at the extreme earnestness of the Cardinal, the Pope asked him to rise from his knees and explain his request.   The Cardinal however persisting, the Pope was surprised at the perseverance of his Eminence and promised to grant him any request he might make.   The Cardinal then rose from his knees and said : ' It is not respectful that when the lord honours his servant with a visit his servant should eat at the same table with his lord and the favour I ask of you is just and honest.   It is that you will allow me during your repast to wait on you as your servant.'   His Holiness to please the Cardinal granted his request.   After the supper was over, the Cardinal placed on the table the boxes of sweetmeats, having first received information from the carver which was the one containing the poison, and *that* the Cardinal placed before the Pope, who under the impression that the one before him did not contain the poisoned sweetmeats ate one of them gaily, and of the other which he believed contained the poison, the Pope pressed the Cardinal to eat, who obeyed him without hesitation. Shortly after His Holiness had departed he fell ill and the next morning died ; while the Cardinal, who still having some fear that the sweetmeats he had eaten might have been poisoned, took an emetic and thus escaped the danger with which he had been threatened."

Lecontour agrees with the account given by Apollinaire in the following words :

" It should be called to your notice that this death has been the subject of many discussions and that the documents transmitted differ very much. Here are some opinions on the subject, and first of all there is the description of the corpse of the Pope by the Marquis of Mantua, in a letter written to his wife Isabella, and then the testimony of those who approached the body and which is made to disquiet us. Here is one :

" Immediately after his death, the Pope became black and so deformed, so prodigiously swollen that it was hardly possible to recognize him, putrefied matter flowed from his nose, his mouth was open and in so terrifying an attitude that one could not look at it without horror, nor suffer the stench without fear of being infected."

In a letter written by the Marquis of Mantua at the time it is stated :

" His body has become putrefied, foam comes from the mouth as from a saucepan on the fire. This has lasted as long as he has remained unburied. He has swelled so enormously that he no longer has the form of a human being, and it is impossible to distinguish between the length and the breadth of the body.

" No one would touch this mass of flesh and putrefaction. No one would put it in the coffin. Those who approached it fell asphyxiated.

" In the end two street porters were found who consented to drag it, by means of cords which were attached to the legs of the death bed, as far as the vault where they let it drop. The flesh detached itself during the transit, leaving a track of putrefying fragments."

Portigliotti, writing of the death of Alexander VI, says :

" There was no religious rapture at his death-bed, no holy prayers beside his corpse. As soon as he had breathed his last, Cesare, who was keeping to his own rooms on pretence of illness, sent his trusted squires to close all doors which gave access to the papal apartment. One of them (says Burckard) drawing a dagger threatened Cardinal Casanova that he would cut his throat and throw him out of the window if he did not give him at once the keys of the pontifical treasury ; the cardinal, terrified, gave them to him. The strong-boxes soon yielded piles of golden ducats, while the servants rifled the wardrobes and rooms, leaving only a few cloth tapestries fastened on the walls.

" The Pope's body, washed and clothed, was placed in a room between two wax candles. None went to recite over it the prayers for the dead, none watched it that night. The next morning it was borne, uncovered according to rite, into St. Peter's Church. The cardinal who presided at the function fearing that some one would gash it out of personal spite, had it brought into a chapel behind a very high and resistent iron grating. 'Vultus erat sicut pannus vel morus nigerrimus,' writes Burckard, 'livori totus plenus, os amplissimum, nasus plenus, lingua deplex in ore, que labia tota implebat, os apertum ed adeo orribile quod nemo videns unquam ad esse talem dixerit.' The orator Costabili mentions that evening in a despatch ' the Pope's body has been all day in St. Peter's, an ugly thing to see, black and swollen . . . and many do not doubt he has been poisoned.' "

To counteract the rumours of poisoning which the rapid decomposition of the body was arousing, it was thought well to keep it covered by day and only to leave it exposed in the evening. But at night, by the yellowish, flickering and smoking light of the candles, Borgia appeared still more horrible and terrifying : a repulsive fetor emanated from that black and putrefying flesh. It was therefore decided to enclose it without more ado in the bier. Two joiners and six porters " ludentes et blasfemantes sive contra papam sive in spretum cadaveris," " had no small difficulty in pushing it into the coffin, which had become too narrow ; and because the stench and the heat were unbearable, they hastened their task without any regard, and forced it in with hand and foot. No priest was present at the funeral operation, not a candle was lit."

In the morning, there was found on the bier these couplets :

" Quis jacet hic. Sextus—Quis funera plangit ? Erymus.
Quis comes in tanto funere obit ? Vitium.
Et quae causa necis ? Virus pro homina, virus,
Humane generi vita salusque fuit."

The Venetian Giustinian who attended him in his last hours wrote the significant words : " Very near the end of the tribulation of Christendom," and a Bolognese priest, noting the date of his death in the margin of a document, says : " To-day he is descended to hell where he was born."

Burckard, whose account is generally favoured, makes no allusion to poisoning but states that " the Pope was attacked by a fever on August 12, 1503, and on the 16th he was bled, the disorder seeming to become a tertian. On the 17th he took medicine, but the following day he became so ill that his life was despaired of. He then received the viaticum during mass which was celebrated in his chamber, at which five cardinals assisted. In the evening extreme unction was administered to him, and a few minutes afterwards he died."

This account is corroborated by Muratori, who quotes many authorities to show that the death of Alexander was not caused by poison, and the balance of evidence certainly seems in favour of the theory that, despite all his crimes, Alexander VI died from natural causes, and that probably a fever of virulent type.

Thus ended Alexander VI, after a pontificate of eleven years, on August 18, 1503.

According to a chronicler of the time :

" Cesare Borgia survived his father, and his life was saved because he had himself plunged into the stomach of a living mule, but on his recovery he lost both his power and his prestige. The Pope Julius II, after the very short pontificate of Pius III, which only lasted twenty-one days, ordered his arrest when he was the master of all Central Italy, after having arrested Varano, Vitelli, the Orsini and the Baglioni. Cesare resisted for a year, sustained by the unimpeachable fidelity of his captains and soldiers. He yielded at last in 1504, was liberated again, but fell into the hands of Gonzalo di Cordova, who sent him to Spain. Having escaped, he took service again in the capacity of commander under his father-in-law, the King of Navarre. He died in 1507 in a fight, pierced by a javelin.

Another historian gives the following account of the end of Cesare :

" At the time of his father's death Cesare Borgia was sick in bed, his illness it is said being caused by swallowing a portion of the poisoned sweetmeats which cost his father his life. Cesare it is related partook of the poisoned sweetmeats in error and omitted to carry out the advice of Macchiavelli always to carry an antidote with him."

It is more probable that he was suffering from an attack of the same fever which his father had contracted.

On hearing of the Pope's death, although unable to leave his room, he at once sent one of his emissaries with several armed attendants to take possession of the palace and allow no one to enter until he had taken away his father's treasure.

As time went on he became more and more unpopular, and public feeling was very strong against him. After some time it was arranged that he should be allowed to quit the Ecclesiastical States. Three days were given him to leave the city, but after the election of Julius II he again returned to Rome. Feeling was still strong against him, and he decided to journey to France to seek the assistance of the King. The King of Navarre gave him command of a troop of horse, and in a small battle under the walls of the castle of Viana, Cesare was killed.

According to Remorsi : " The Duke of Valentinois did not die, because God willed that as a greater scourge this ambitious and cruel spirit should survive fortune and grandeur and see his most down-trodden enemies in power, for the strength of his temperament and of his youth overcame the poison, being aided by good remedies which the doctors gave him. Some of them assert that the most efficacious remedy employed was that of putting him several times into the body of a bull or mule opened for the purpose, like Ladislas, King of Naples, who was delivered in this manner from the poison which was given to him in his youth.

" Others write of having heard the said Cardinal (di Corneto) say in the villa where he took the poison, how he was plunged into a great vessel of cold water, from which he was not taken until his skin had been entirely removed in pieces, because his intestines were completely burned. However his cure was effected, he remained extremely oppressed by the illness for a long time and at a time when he had most need of perfect health in order to remedy the revolution of his affairs. So that he constantly had reason to complain of his reverses of fortune."

Cesare's death was lamented at least by one person, and that was his sister Lucrezia, who at once set out for the Monastery of Corpo di Christo to offer prayers for his soul, where she remained for two nights.

Some of the entries in the book of her household expenses are interesting, and throw a light on the remuneration paid to a Court physician of the time.

In 1507 is an entry :

" To Maestro Ludovico physician to Her Highness 110 lire for the balance of his salary.

" On the 31st December 240 lire as a year's salary for her Highness's physician Maestro Ludovico at the rate of 20 lire a month."

Patroness of poets and painters in her latter days, Lucrezia made herself popular in Ferrara. In the Library of Modeno is a list of her magnificent jewels which she sold to free her husband from the debts he contracted during the wars in defence of his territories. Many of her letters still extant show that during these troublous times the relief of the poor, sick and needy was Lucrezia's constant care. She died during her confinement on June 21, 1519. The accouchement had been long and difficult and the officers and servants of her household were clustered at the foot of the grand staircase leading to her room. Great fears were entertained of her recovery, and they waited in breathless silence for every sound from the apartment. " At length," says the chronicler, " Maestro Alberti, the Court Apothecary, was seen descending the staircase with an ewer in his hand. All pressed forward to ask him where he was going. He replied significantly : ' To get some rose water to wash the body of the duchess.' "

Thus ended Lucrezia Borgia, Duchess of Ferrara, who, to quote a letter written by a cousin of Federico Gonzaga who was present in Ferrara at the time, was " one who appears to have been universally beloved not only for the habitual piety of her life, but for her unbounded charity and kindness of heart."

Lucrezia has been accused of being guilty of the worst possible crimes, including that of poisoning, but there is practically no historic proof of the truth of these stories. It is probable that many of the infamous crimes of her brother Cesare were erroneously attributed to her.

The composition of the so-called " Cantarella," the poison said to have been employed by the Borgias, has long been a subject of dispute. According to Paolo Jovio, it was " a kind of whitish powder, that to a certain extent resembled sugar, and which had been used on a great many poor innocent people who died in a miserable state."

Carelli, physician to Charles VI, gives the following account of how it was prepared. He states : " The abdominal viscera of a sow which had been poisoned with arsenic were powdered with arsenious acid ; they waited until the putrefaction was complete and the liquids which flowed from it were then concentrated by evaporation and constituted a white powder which was called ' La Cantarella.' " Apollinaire's account of its preparation has already been given, from which it may be gathered that it consisted of a mixture of subacetate of copper, arsenic and crude phosphorus.

Several other contemporary writers claim to give the true method of its preparation, and one states that a *bear* was killed, then cut open and saturated with arsenic, and the liquid that dripped from it formed the poison.

It is evident that this method of preparing a venom was employed by some of the Italian poisoners of the period. The combination of the animal poison contained in the products of putrefaction, together with arsenic, would no doubt furnish a poisonous substance of a very powerful nature, but there is no evidence to prove that the Borgias ever used such a preparation.

Sabatini discounts the idea that the Borgias employed a secret poison. He attributes the tradition to the death of Prince Djem who died of dysentery at the Castle of Capua where he had been imprisoned. Rumours that he had been poisoned by the Pope arose almost at once, but as twenty-eight days had elapsed since his parting from Alexander, it is difficult to believe the story of poisoning. Burckard in his Diary says : " On February 25th, died at the Castle of Capua the said Djem through meat or drink that disagreed with him."

Giovo writing in 1561, describes the poison as " a white powder of a faint and not unpleasing flavour." He calls it " cantarella or cantharides," but this it could certainly not have been, as the Spanish fly when reduced to powder is a brownish bronze mixed with the bright green scales of the insect. But the name cantarella may have been taken from the highly poison-ous fungus of that name.

Baron Corvo, in his *Chronicles of the Borgias,* also denies that the family possessed any such secret, and declares that the venom never existed.

The probability is that when the Borgias found it necessary to use a poison for nefarious purposes they employed arsenic, which was so commonly used in Italy at that period. The fact that Cesare Borgia's signet ring contained a secret receptacle which might easily have been used to carry arsenic goes a long way to substantiate this conjecture, and is the strongest evidence we have that he at least used a very powerful poison to carry out his evil designs.

In connexion with the Borgia poison there is an interesting story that the secret of its preparation perished with the Duc Riaro-Sforza, who died in Paris about the middle of the nine-teenth century. Before his death, one evening at the opera, the Duke is said to have confided to a distinguished critic, who occupied the neighbouring stall, that he still possessed the secret of the famous poison, although for centuries it had lain idle in the family archives. Its composition, he added, was simpler than generally supposed, and not long afterwards he told his friends that, feeling age advancing and having no direct heirs, he had thought it best to burn the recipe lest it might fall into bad hands.

CHAPTER XXII

ATTEMPTS TO POISON QUEEN ELIZABETH—THE CASE OF DR. RODERIGO LOPUS—ALLEGED ATTEMPT ON THE LIFE OF THE QUEEN AND THE EARL OF ESSEX BY WILLIAM SQUIRE

THE dread of poisoning by Royal personages in the sixteenth century was not confined to rulers of continental countries, for we find that both King Henry VIII and Queen Elizabeth lived in fear of attempts being made on their lives.

It was commonly reported at the time, that Anne Boleyn had attempted to administer poison to Henry surreptitiously and that the King after hearing this, in an interveiw with young Prince Henry, " burst into tears saying that he and his sister, the Princess Mary, might thank God for having escaped from the hand of that accursed and venomous harlot who had intended to poison them."

In Elizabethan times, according to the Burghley papers, the dread of secret poisoning was constantly in the minds of personages in high places. On June 27th, 1572, Richard Bexley, writing to Burghley advises him " not to take any physic of Dr. Gyfford, recently from Rome, lest he might be ' Italianated ' a significant word apparently coined to express secret poisoning. It is stated that as early as 1561 it became necessary to surround the young Queen with precautions against poisons. Not an untasted dish was allowed to be brought to her table, not a glove or a handkerchief might approach her person which had not been scrutinized and she was dosed every week with precautionary antidotes.

It therefore caused little surprise later when one of Elizabeth's own physicians was seized and lodged in the Tower on the charge of plotting to poison his Royal mistress.

The strange story of this plot shows how poisons were employed as secret weapons by political agents in Tudor times.

The ranks of the medical profession in England at this period appear to have been largely augmented by foreigners, many of whom were Jews, who came to London both to practise and enter the service of wealthy noblemen. Among these was Roderigo Lopus or Lopez, a Portuguese Jew who appears to have settled in England about 1559.

In the census of foreigners living in London in 1571, he is included as resident in the parish of St. Peter-le-Poer and described as "Doctor Lopus, a portingale, householder denizen, who came into this realm 12 years past to get his living by physick."

He was evidently successful in his practice for we find he became a Fellow of the College of Physicians in 1569, and was selected to read the anatomy lecture, which honour, however, he declined. He was the first to be appointed to the office of physician at St. Bartholomew's hospital and was holding this appointment in 1568. It is recorded in the Journal of the hospital that he lived in a house in the precincts which had a hall, parlour, and garden.

He relinquished the post at St. Barts in 1581 and took up his residence first in Wood Street, but afterwards removed to a house in Holborn called Mount Joy's Inn, which a grateful patient is said to have built and given to him.

William Clowes, the surgeon, makes mention of his skill, and records, that he saw with Dr. Lopus, Mr. Andrew Fones, a London merchant whose ship had been set on by Flushingers and who had been wounded by a bullet which lodged under his shoulder-blade. He says : " There was joined with me Maister Doctor Lopus, one of his Majesties Phisitions which afterward showed himself to be both careful and very skilfull not only for his counsell in dyeting, purging and bleeding but also for his direction of Arceus apozema, amongst others it wrought most singularly, the proofe thereof I never had until that time, but since I have used it."

The Arceus or Arcoeus, was a dressing composed of gum elemi, turpentine, oil of St. John's wort and stag's suet, a formula invented by Arcoeus of Amsterdam in 1574, for healing wounds.

The term ' majesties phisition ' meant that he belonged to the Royal College of Physicians founded by the king.

Lopus was called in to attend Sir Francis Walsingham, the Queen's secretary and later is said to have taken service as chief physician in the household of the Earl of Leicester. In " Leicester's Commonwealth " he is described as " Lopez, the Jew " and is credited with being an accomplished poisoner. It is probable he may have been the Dr. Julio previously mentioned in Leicester's service. Through influential friends he had made at Court, he was brought to the notice of the Queen and in 1586 he obtained the appointment of physician to the Queen's Household. Here he became known to the Earl of Essex, Bacon and Dr. Carleton, Bishop of Chichester, who has left us an account of his subsequent career.*

That he became a favourite with the Queen is evident from the fact that in 1589 she granted him a monopoly for the importation of aniseed and sumach into England.

* " A thankful remembrance of God's mercy in an historicall collection of the great and merciful deliverance of the Church and State of England," etc. Collected by Geo. Carleton, D.D., Bishop of Chichester. 1627.

Gabriel Harvey gives the following characteristic sketch of the Jewish physician at the height of his popularity. He describes him as being " none of the learnedest or expertest physitians in the Court, but one that maketh great account of himself as the best and by a kind of Jewish practis hath growen to much wealth and sum reputation as well as with ye Queen herself as with sum of ye greatest Lordes and Ladyes."

At this time owing no doubt to his plausible and ingratiating manners, Lopus became the fashionable physician and the depository of many of the secrets and intrigues of the Court. The Earl of Essex sought to use him as a political agent to gain intelligence from Spain owing to his linguistic attainments, but the wily doctor rejected his offer and instead attached himself as interpreter to Don Antonio, the ex-King of Portugal, a victim of persecution at the hands of Philip of Spain, who had taken refuge in England in 1590 and was living at Eton, with a retinue of servants and other Portuguese refugees. This was his undoing and the story of how Lopus became implicated in an alleged plot to poison the Queen, is told in some detail by Dr. Carleton, the Bishop of Chichester, from which the following account is extracted.

It appears that among the refugees was one Stephen Ferrera de Gama, a Portuguese malcontent, who after plotting against Philip fled with others to England. It was discovered from letters that were intercepted that he was engaged in a plot to kill his own king and Queen Elizabeth by poison and for carrying this out, Dr. Lopus was selected and offered 50,000 crowns. The intercepted letter in which the offer was made was one which Ferrera sent to Dr. Lopus " in a little peece of paper wrapt in a handkerchief."

The neighbourhood of Windsor appears to have been infested with Spanish spies who were trying to bribe Antonio's servants to murder their master as well as Queen Elizabeth. Lopus denied any knowledge of the letter, but on an examination of Ferrera's associates one of them confessed it was true and that the former had promised Lopus 50,000 crowns to be paid out of the King of Spain's coffers to poison Queen Elizabeth. The object was somewhat obscure but it was supposed that Don Antonio finding that his fortunes were without hope of recovery, he and his friends, in order to ingratiate themselves with the King of Spain, sought to kill Queen Elizabeth.

In 1593, the Government became aware of what was going on and the Queen gave instructions to the Earl of Essex to have Ferrera de Gama arrested and his papers examined. This was carried out, but nothing incriminating was discovered. Ferrera was at that time living in the house of Dr. Lopus with whom he was on close terms of friendship. He was taken to Windsor and handed over to Don Antonio at Eton. Essex then sought the Queen's permission to arrest Lopus who he believed was implicated in the plot, but Elizabeth told him, that " he was a rash and temerarious youth to enter into a matter against the poor man which he could not prove."

Nevertheless Essex pursued his investigations and gave strict orders that all letters directed to Portugal should be intercepted and brought to him.

Among these, a letter addressed to one Diego Hernandes was discovered purporting to be written by Francis Torres, in Portuguese, concerning certain merchandise. Ferrera was confronted with this letter and acknowledged that the letter was intended for him and that Hernandes was an assumed name. He said that Francisco Torres was a Portuguese who served Don Antonio and that under the name of Manoel Lowys he was living in Brussels. He confessed that Dr. Lopus was acquainted with Don Emmanuel the eldest son of Don Antonio who had been constrained to submit to the King of Spain.

Essex then informed the Queen of his discoveries and how far Lopus was implicated but she, far from suspecting him, gave instructions that he was to see the intercepted letter and translate it into English.

Meanwhile, a Portuguese named Manoel Pays was apprehended at Dover in the act of carrying a large packet of letters from Ferrera which he was on his way to deliver to Manoel Lowys in Brussels.

Within a few days afterwards, on the arrival of the post from Antwerp at Dover, a Portuguese called Gomez d'Avila was landed by the same vessel. He was carefully searched and a number of letters found on him were forwarded to the Earl of Essex in London. Among them was a letter which Lopus had sent to Ferrera and addressed to his own house in London. From this it appeared that Ferrera was a spy who conveyed intelligence from London to the King of Spain under the guise of a merchant.

In another letter from Manoel Lowys to Ferrera it was requested that " a jewel be sent and reported how the amber and muske was highly esteemed and spoke of Broad cloth, scarlet, threads of pearls, a diamond and sundry kinds of merchandise so sorted and matched, as if it might easily appear these words did serve for cipher to colour greater matters."

From these and other letters it appeared that Ferrera was expecting a reply on some important and secret matter from Spain.

According to Dr. Carleton, as soon as Gomez d'Avila was brought to the Court, " he used all means he could to let Lopus understand of this apprehension. He entreated a honest gentle-man that understood Spanish (being by chance in the chamber of the Earl of Essex at that time) to tell him so much and he

meeting Lopus in the base court at Windsor did give the message
and observed sudden alteration in Lopus's countenance."

Hereupon by the cunning of Lopus other means were devised
of communication and a woman whom d'Avila called his wife
was employed. " She being a cunning peece," says the
chronicler, " did solicit it with great importunity very diligently.
And under colour of her importunity Lopus himself moved her
Majestie for his inlargement." Gomez confessed that there was
a great sum of money certainly to be sent hither and named
50,000 crowns but made out that this money was for Don
Antonio. Later he confessed that the letters he had brought
were in answer to one written by Lopus, offering to take the
Queen's life as soon as he should receive an answer from Spain,
saying how it should be done and how much money was promised
for carrying it out. He further stated he was daily expecting
the reply from Spain and was afraid the letter would fall into the
hands of the Earl of Essex.

Ferrera was kept a close prisoner at Dutton Park and placed
in charge of a young man called Pedro, and being unaware of
what had transpired, greatly wished to warn Lopus of d'Avila's
arrival. He contrived by bribing his keeper to send a message
written on a small piece of paper wrapped up in a handkerchief
to Lopus, but it miscarried and through this the alleged plot
was disclosed. Ferrera was closely examined and declared that
Dr. Lopus had long been a devoted adherent of the King of
Spain.

Essex was determined not to let the doctor escape this time
and at once had him brought to be examined by the Lord
Treasurer and Sir Robert Cecil. Lopus had taken care to burn
all his papers shortly before, and denied with great oaths and
execrations all knowledge of the matter. After further examinations at the end of January 1594, he was committed to the
Tower.

In the meantime Manoel Lowys, another conspirator, fell
into the trap and arrived at Dover from Brussels where he was
apprehended and brought to London. On being questioned
what letters he had brought, he denied carrying any. He was
taken to the Gatehouse at Westminster to have his clothes all
carefully searched and among other papers found concealed
on him were two letters of credit without limitation of
amount.

The Queen appointed Sir Robert Cecil to examine him,
" who asked him what letters he had brought from the King
of Spain, whereupon he produced two, which he had concealed
and denied on oath."

The letters after being shown to the Queen were given to Sir
Robert, who demanded Lowys " to expound the meaninga nd
secret sense of them, but he held his mouth so close and had his

lesson so well cunned, as a man might easier plucke out his teeth than the truth by any persuasion.

"Being further dealt withall," continues the chronicler significantly, "he at last confessed that he verily thought the service required of the doctor was a thing horrible to be named and most detestable to be undertaken, to poyson her Majesty. And for reasons to induce him to conceive the same he did allege that he knew the doctor of a profession (meaning him to be a Jew) and by the credit of her Majesty and reason of access might easily do such villainy."

After further examinations of Lowys and Ferrera and explanation of the letters, it was revealed that the plot was to poison the Queen. Ferrera declared that Lopus had written to Spain offering not only to poison the Queen but Don Antonio also.

Lopus was then re-examined at the Tower but still denied the charge "with oaths and execrations and called down imprecations on himself if ever he intended any evill against Queen Elizabeth.

"I love Queene Elizabeth," he exclaimed, "better than I love Jesus Christ.

"Some believed that therein he said truly for he was a Jew."

On being confronted with his confederates, he was exhorted to confess, but he forswore the whole accusation.

The Queen, having been informed, then sent the Earl of Essex, the Lord High Admiral, and Sir Robert Cecil to the Tower to try again and persuade Lopus. With grave, mild persuasions they exhorted him not to aggravate so foul an offence with impudent and fruitless denials, especially after the testimony of those who were acquainted with the whole course of his treasons. But he still held to them and kneeling down very solemnly lifted up his hands, his eyes and countenance to heaven and besought God to "heape vengence upon him and his, here and in the world to come, if there was any such thing."

"On February 25th, 1593," continues Carleton, "Lopus made a confession for discharge of his conscience, admitting such speeches passed between Ferrera and himself at his house in London and did offer to poison the Queen so he might have 50,000 crowns but that he never meant to do it. But he doth affirm, that Ferrera meant verily that her Majesty should be destroyed with poison in a syrrop, which he said, because he knew that her Majesty did never use to take any syrrop. He confessed also that Ferrera told him there should come over in fashion of a mariner, that should bring the value of 50,000 crowns in rubies and diamonds. But he saith when the money was come, he meant to have brought the same to her Majesty and to have told her that the King of Spain had sent him to poison her Majesty. The pearls and the price mentioned in the letter, was to give him to understand how the news he had sent how that the doctor would kill the Queen."

A special commission was appointed to try Lopus but before it could meet a member of it died and a fresh Commissioner had to be appointed which caused some delay, but he was eventually brought to trial at the Guildhall on February 28th, 1594, Sir Edward Coke as solicitor-general prosecuting.

Bacon, who was present at the trial, in his account entitled " A true report of the Detestable Treason intended by Dr. Roderigo Lopez, a physician, attending upon the person of the Queen's Majesty," throws further light on this extraordinary story. He begins by stating that " This Lopez of a nation Portuguese and suspect to be in sect secretly a Jew (though here he conformed himself to the rites of Christian religion) for a long time professed physick in this land ; by occasion whereof, being a man very observant and officious and of a pleasing and applicable behaviour, in that regard, rather than for any great learning in his faculty, he grew known and favoured at Court and was for some time since sworn physician of her Majesty's household ; by her Majesty's bounty of whom he had received divers gifts of good commodity was grown to good estate of wealth. Lopez had asked 50,000 crowns from the King of Spain for the deed and received a jewel in part payment. His defence was, that he was cozening the King of Spain.

" For the purpose of conveying his intelligence he used one Manuel Andrada, a Portuguese revolted from Don Antonio to the King of Spain.

Antonio Perez, who was known as Don Antonio in England, laid claim to the throne of Portugal and sought favour with the King of Spain by selling him English secrets."

Essex, who appears to have been convinced that there was a spy at work who was using Lopus as a tool, when told by the Queen he was acting as a rash and temerarious youth, was so indignant at her rebuke that he would not come out of his chamber for two days.

" I have discovered a most dangerous and desperate treason," he wrote to Anthony Bacon on January 28th. " The point of conspiracy was her Majesty's death. The executioner should have been Dr. Lopus. The manner, poison ! This I have so followed as I will make it clear as the noonday."

It became apparent from the intercepted letters that some important secret was in hand but it was so carefully wrapped up that nothing could be distinctly made out, until Ferrera himself in his anxiety to avoid detection, furnished a clue in the letter he sent to Lopus.

Bacon states that it was Andrada the intermediatory or messenger, who brought the jewel : " A very good jewel gar-nished with sundry stones of good value," and handed it to

Lopus. He accepted it and then " cunningly cast with himself that he should offer it to her Majesty. First he was assured that she would not take it. Next, that thereby he should lay her asleep and make secure of him for great matters, which accordingly he did with protestations of his fidelity, and her Majesty as a princess of magnanimity, not apt to fear or suspicion, returned it to him with gracious words," and so Lopus retained the jewel.

At the trial, Sir Edward Coke described Lopus as " a perjured and murdering villain and a Jewish doctor worse than Judas himself."

In spite of his fervent protestations of innocence, Lopus was found guilty and sentenced to death.

Sir Robert Cecil writing to Thomas Windebank on the last day of the trial says : " a most substantial jury found him guilty of all the treasons with the applause of the world."

Such however was the Queen's partiality for her doctor, she delayed signing the death warrant for three months. On June 7th however, Lopus was taken from the Tower to the Court of Queen's Bench at Westminster and when asked to declare why execution of the sentence should be further delayed, " made his submission and affirmed he never thought any harm to her Majesty."

A few hours after, he was dragged on a hurdle to Tyburn and hanged, drawn and quartered with the other two Portuguese.

Camden mentions the execution and the derision with which the speech Lopus made on the gallows was received.

In the August following, we find that Sara Lopus, his widow, petitioned Queen Elizabeth for the restoration of some of her late husband's property. She states that she had no notion that her husband was embarking on such affairs as those for which he had been tried and executed. The Queen ordered his personal property to be returned to the widow excepting the jewel, a fine ruby, which she retained for her use and which it is said she wore on her girdle until the time of her death ; a strange fancy indeed, as it was declared to be part of the price paid to Lopus for compassing her death.

Popular feeling about Lopus is evidenced in the literature of the time and Sir Sydney Lee suggests that Shakespeare may have taken the character of Shylock from the notorious doctor, as the *Merchant of Venice* was probably completed about 1596.

His career appears to have also attracted the attention of other dramatists like Henslowe, who in 1594 produced *The Jew* and *The Jew of Malta*, both of which may have been suggested by Lopus.

In Marlowe's *Doctor Faustus*, when the doctor after unhappy reflections has fallen asleep, he is waked by a horse-courser shouting " Alas, alas ! Doctor Fustian, quothe ? Mass, Doctor

Lopus was never such a doctor ; has given me a purgatory, has purged me of forty dollars. I shall never see them more." (Scene XIV.)

In Middleton's play, *A Game of Chess*, the Black Knight, minister of the Black King (the King of Spain), says : " Promised also to Doctor Lopez for poisoning the maiden queen of the white kingdom, ducats twenty thousand," (Act IV., Scene II.) while Dekker makes Lopez himself say : " What physicke can, I dare, only to grow (but as I merit shall) up in your eye."

This was not the only attempt to poison Queen Elizabeth for according to Dr. Carleton, another plot was discovered against her life in 1596. This was also alleged to be due to Spanish influence.

The instrument selected to carry out the crime in this case was one Edward Squire who lived in Greenwich, where he earned his living as a scrivener. He next obtained employment in the Royal stables where he remained for two years, but having a great desire to go to sea, he shipped in one of the vessels under Sir Francis Drake and was taken prisoner by the Spaniards. He was landed in Spain where it is said he became acquainted with Richard Walpole, a Jesuit and a fugitive from England. Walpole seeing in him a tool who was likely to be of use to him, first had him seized by the Inquisition and kept a prisoner, but he was afterwards liberated and told by Walpole that he owed his freedom to his influence and in this way he secured his allegiance and promise to carry out his commands.

After preparing him concerning the tyrannies and persecutions exercised in England over the Roman Catholics, Walpole suggested it would be a good thing to kill the Earl of Essex and the Queen herself.

Learning that Squire had been employed in the Royal stables, he thought he might thus be enabled to carry out his plan, which was to poison the pommel of the Queen's saddle " at such a time as she should ride abroad, her Majestie being like to rest her hand thereupon for a good time together, and not unlike for her hand to come often about her face, mouth and nostrils. This by reason of his former acquaintance and service about the stable, he thought he might easily perform and safely."

To these suggestions, on being given his liberty, Squire agreed, and Walpole further promised him that " if imminent death should issue thereupon he might not accomplish of it, he could be assured that he would have the state of a glorious saint in heaven."

To this end, Squire kneeling before Walpole took a vow to be constant, and receiving his benediction, was despatched on his mission which he was bidden to carry out with " diligence and resolution."

Before departing, Walpole gave him full instructions for placing the poison, which he said he should receive in a " double bladder, and when it was about to be used, he was to prick the bladder full of holes upon the upper part and so carry it within the palm of his hand with a thick glove as a safeguard, and on the instant when it was to be applied, he should turn it in his hand upside down and so press it hard upon the pommel of the saddle." He further told him the nature of the poison, and that it would " lye and tarrie long where it was laid and that it would not be checked by the aire."

Lastly, upon his leaving, he " delivered him the confection itself in such a bladder as described."

Walpole impressed on Squire that the poisoning of the Earl of Essex was urgent, so it might prevent him sailing on a voyage he was expected to take about May, 1597.

Squire was given money, yet we are told, " not so abundantly as might make him love his life too well," and he travelled with two Spaniards as far as Calais.

He arrived in England about a fortnight before the Earl of Essex was due to sail. He soon found an opportunity however, of making the attempt on the life of the Queen which he decided to carry out first.

On the Monday after his arrival in London on making inquiries at the Royal stables, he found that horses were being made ready for her Majesty to ride abroad. " Then," according to the chronicler, " he slipped into the stable yard where the Queen's horse stood ready, and in a familiar and cheerful manner in the hearing of divers that stood thereby, having all things prepared according to his instructions, he laid his hand upon the pommel of the saddle and cried : ' God save the Queen ' and bruised the poison as he had been directed."

The diabolical plan however was foiled as the Queen did not arrive, having meanwhile postponed her journey.

Squire was equally unsuccessful in his attempt on the life of the Earl of Essex, although within five or six days he contrived to get on board the Earl's own ship. He took with him the remains of the same poison in a little pot in his portmanteau, " and when the ship was between Faial and St. Michael, he bestowed it upon the arms of a wooden chair which the Earl was accustomed to use when he supped and dined, but nothing came of it."

On reaching port, Squire decided not to return to Spain and face Walpole, and his attempts would have remained undiscovered but for letters sent from Spain inquiring about him. Upon the plot being thus discovered, he was arrested as a spy and confessed although he declared : " he had not any purpose to perform it."

CHAPTER XXIII

HISTORIC POISON CASES IN FRANCE

IN the latter part of the sixteenth century the mania for criminal poisoning spread from Italy to France. The practice increased with great rapidity, and poisons appear to have been commonly employed by those of the highest to the lowest classes of society, to get rid of enemies and undesirable persons. The epidemic of poisoning was without precedent and L'Estoile says, in referring to the execution of a magician named La Miraille, that in Paris in 1572, the number of sorcerers and vendors of love-philtres was above thirty thousand. It is stated that the Prior of Cluny and his valet Saint-Barthélemi, with grim humour, even poisoned their physicians in order to avoid paying them. It may be said of the many stories of poison mysteries in France that have come down to us from the sixteenth century, that though their truth may be doubtful they are not without romantic interest.

Jeanne d'Albret, mother of Henry IV, who died of a fever after four days' illness, was generally believed to have met her death by wearing poisoned gloves. The most incredible stories were often spread abroad after the sudden death of distinguished persons, and in this case it was stated that the gloves were placed in a box with a double bottom, beneath which was placed a mixture of opium, belladonna, hyoscyamus, and other poisons. These are supposed not only to have impregnated the gloves but to have been administered to the victim while asleep, the box being exposed under her nostrils.

Francis II, the first husband of Mary Queen of Scots, who died in 1560, was supposed to have succumbed to poison, and Beaucaire de Péguillon goes so far as to charge Ambrôise Paré, the great military surgeon, with having been the cause of his death. The Duc d'Albe asserts that Mary Stuart was the cause of his death, but John Knox was nearer the mark when he wrote on hearing of it : " The potent hand of God from above sent unto us a wonderful and most joyful deliverance ; for unhappy Francis, husband to our Sovereign, suddenly perisheth of a rotten ear . . . that deaf ear that never would hear the truth of God." As a matter of fact, it was proved from an investigation by Courladon a few years ago, that Francis, who was born with an obstruction of the nose and mouth probably due to adenoids, died from chronic suppurative otitis.

During the religious wars poison was frequently employed and the following incident which took place at the siege of Châtellerault and Poitiers in 1569 is related by d'Aubigné. " Upon the same day was executed Dominique d'Albe, captured by the people of Monsieur for having killed or poisoned his master, the Admiral ; for the head of whom, likewise of that of Vidame de Chartres, Count de Montgomeri and others there had been made a promise for the sum of fifty thousand escus, for the Admiral, and lesser sums for those of less importance, and in order to ensure the compensation and the justification of the assassins, it was expressed by a decision pronounced in the Court of Parliament in Latin, German, Spanish, English and French."

A curious method of introducing poison is recorded in the story of the Cardinal of Lorraine, uncle of Mary Queen of Scots, who is said to have died after handling some gold coins on which poison had been smeared. There is, however, evidence to show that his death was due to pleurisy caused by a cold caught in walking barefooted at the head of a procession at Avignon. Catherine de' Medici was credited with having poisoned her three sons, Charles IX, the Duc d'Anjou and Francis II, but the story has apparently no foundation.

Towards the end of the sixteenth century a romantic case connected with poison, which aroused great interest in Paris, was that of the death of Gabrielle d'Estrées. The divorce proceedings between Henry IV and Marguerite de Valois were almost complete, when all preparations for the marriage of the King to Madame d'Estrées were brought to a sudden end in Holy Week, 1599, by her mysterious death. A post-mortem examination made by the doctors threw no light on the cause of death, and hints began to be spread abroad that she had been secretly poisoned by the Grand Duke of Tuscany. According to the story, she had arrived in Paris on Tuesday, April 6th, and stayed the night at the palace of Zametti, a wealthy Italian Jew. He presented her with an exquisite scent bottle containing a very powerful perfume. On the following Thursday, while in the Church of Saint-Antoine, she was taken ill with headache and vertigo and had to leave before the end of the service. Severe convulsive attacks followed, which increased in violence and frequency until she lost consciousness and died during the night of April 10th.

There appears little doubt that her death was due to eclampsia and her entire illness presents a true picture of this condition showing its various stages and lastly the end in coma.

For centuries mystery surrounded the death of Princess Henrietta Anne of England who married the Duke of Orleans. It was generally believed that she had been poisoned by accident or design, although every effort was made according to the knowledge of the time, to ascertain the true cause of her death.

She was a woman possessing great charm as well as beauty and was noted at the French Court for her brilliant wit and humour.

In 1670, she came to England on a political mission in connexion with a proposed agreement between England and France and succeeded in getting the Treaty of Dover signed by the minister of her brother Charles II, on June 11th of that year.

She remained at Dover from May 24th to June 12th and then embarked for France delighted with the success of her mission. She arrived at St. Germain on June 18th apparently in her usual health, although somewhat fatigued.

She was twenty-six at the time and, says Madame de la Fayette, " had the attractions bestowed by youth and beauty that won her a kind of homage as a tribute to her personality rather than her rank."

De Boislisle compares her more to the jasmine than the rose and describes her as being " very slender, delicate, slightly round-shouldered but not less pleasing for that. She was exhausted, not only by four accouchements in rapid succession, but also by the fast life then led at Court and was only kept up by that sanguine temperament which is the prerogative of highly strung women."

The Abbé Bourdelot tells us that she had several illnesses and used to complain of a cruel burning pain in her chest. From other accounts she appears to have suffered from a chronic gastritis, as she was frequently sick and at such times could only take milk and remained in bed for days together.

The day after her return from England, she stayed in bed but on the 24th, a week afterwards, she went to St. Cloud where she arrived at six o'clock.

The story of the following five days is thus graphically told by Madame de la Fayette who was with the princess until she died.

" I arrived at St. Cloud on Saturday at six o'clock in the evening and found her in the gardens. She told me that I should think her looking cross and that she was not at all well. She had supped as usual and she walked in the moonlight till midnight.

" On Sunday the 29th, at dinner Madame ate as usual and after dinner she lay down on some cushions, as she often did when she was at liberty. She then fell asleep. When she awoke she rose with a haggard face and went away into the drawing room where she walked up and down for some time with Boisfranc, Monsieur's treasurer, and while talking to him she complained several times of the pain in her side.

" Monsieur went downstairs to return to Paris but he found Madame de Meckelbourg on the steps and came up again with her.

" Madame left Boisfranc and came to Madame de Meckel-bourg and as she was speaking to her, Madame de Gamaches brought to her as well as to me, a glass of chicory water that she had asked for some time before.

" Madame de Gourdon, her tire-woman, gave it to her. She drank it, and then replacing the cup on the salver with one hand, she pressed her side with the other, saying in a tone that be-tokened severe pain, ' Oh ! What a dreadful twinge ! Oh ! what a pain ! I can bear it no longer.' She reddened in uttering these words and next moment turned a livid pallor. She con-tinued to cry out and told us to take her away as she could no longer stand.

" We took her in our arms ; she tottered along half doubled-up and I held her while someone unlaced her. She moaned all the time and I noticed that she had tears in her eyes.

" Kissing the arms I was holding, I said she was evidently in great pain and she told me I could not imagine how great.

" She was put to bed and as soon as she was there she cried out more loudly than she had yet done and threw herself from one side to the other like a person in infinite agony.

" Someone went off to find her chief physician, Monsieur Esprit.

" He came and said it was colic and prescribed the ordinary remedies for such ailments. All the time the pain was dreadful.

" Madame said she was dying and begged someone to go in search of a confessor for her. The young Princess believed that she was poisoned !

" A sort of antidote was brought her in the shape of oil and powdered adder which made her vomit.

"No relief however was obtained and the physicians acknow-ledging their helplessness, advised her to receive the last sacraments of the Church without delay. The Princess on hearing this desired that Bossuet, who had attended her mother, Queen-dowager of England, should be called in, and three messengers were immediately despatched for him, but before he arrived at St. Cloud, between eleven and twelve at night, she had received the sacrament from the hands of the Abbé Feuillet who appears to have treated the suffering woman with some harshness. Between her shrieks, caused by the violent pain, he told her that her sins were not punished as they deserved."

Meanwhile, Bossuet arrived at the bedside and the Princess entreated him not to leave her until she had breathed her last. He fell on his knees holding a crucifix in his hand and in tremu-lous tones invited her to join him in devotion. She recognized the crucifix which he held towards her as the same which he had given to her mother to hold in her agony. She took it in her hand and held it until the end. Before she died, she spoke to Madame de la Fayette in English expressing her gratitude for the assistance she had received from Bossuet and requested that an old emerald ring set with diamonds, of great value, might be presented to him.

She died at three o'clock in the morning and the news being conveyed to the King, he sent for Bossuet and gave him the emerald ring, placing it on his finger and desiring him to wear it for the rest of his life.

The announcement of her death caused consternation in the palace and suspicions that she might have been poisoned were at once aroused, as she had remarked herself after drinking the chicory water. The Duke ordered that some of the water that was left should be given to a dog but it had no effect, and Madame Desbordes the Princess's maid declared that she had made the drink and had some of it herself, while Madame de Meckelbourg drank some also. It was therefore evident that no poison had been added to the chicory water.

Then the cup was suspected, as it was recalled that methods were said to be known by which goblets and silver cups might be prepared in such a way that the person who drank from them would be poisoned.

Francois Belot, who was formerly of the King's bodyguard, was said to have been an adept in the preparation of these cups until his secret was discovered. He was broken on the wheel on June 10th, 1679, notwithstanding that he confessed to the Commissioners of the *Chambre Ardente* that " what he did to the silver cups and trenchers was done solely to get hold of them."

As the physicians were unable to account for her sudden death and rumours of poison soon gained currency, not only at the Court but also in England, Holland and Spain, it was decided that a post-mortem examination should be carried out in the presence of fifteen physicians and surgeons. Dr. Hugh Chamberlain, who was at that time physician-in-ordinary to King Charles II, was commanded to attend as an independent representative of the English Government.

The autopsy was made on June 30th, 1670, and showed that the Princess did not die from the effects of poison.

Dr. Hugh Chamberlain, who made an independent report states : " Being commanded by his Excellency the English Ambassador to attend at the dissecting of Madame's corpse, I observed at the opening of her lower belly an offensive air to breathe forth.

" Her epiploon was tinged with a deep yellow bile and putrefied. All her bowels were more or less of the same tincture, inflated and inclining towards gangrene. The liver was ashen-colour, rotten and without blood. The reins were indifferent, the left the worse. Her spleen was good. Her stomach was lined with that adust bile and so was the oesaphagus up to her throat.

" In the middle venter her heart was well, but her lungs on the left side were adhering, and being opened on that side there issued only an ichorous humidity ; on the right side they were better conditioned but not of the due colour. Both venters were repleted with bilious humours and an oil floating thereon. Her finger ends were livid."

Littré who made a very careful investigation of the matter was of the opinion that the Princess died from acute peritonitis, the immediate result of the perforation of the stomach by an ulcer. Anatole France in commenting on Littré's conclusions says : " he does not hesitate to diagnose a simple ulceration of the stomach which Professor Cruveilhier was the first to describe and which Madame's physicians could not recognize because they knew nothing about it. They found the stomach was pierced with a little hole but thought it had been done by accident during the autopsy." The chicory water, which the Princess was in the habit of taking, was a common domestic remedy included in most of the pharmacopœias of the time, and was prepared from the leaves of the chicory plant infused as a simple tisane and used as a slight stimulant. The powdered viper or adder which was given with oil, was regarded as a veritable panacea for hysteria and colic and an antidote to poison.

Professor Brouardel points out, that if the chicory water had contained the smallest amount of corrosive sublimate, a poison that might have been used, the Princess would have rejected the cup after the first sip and to kill a person at least ten to fifteen centigrammes are necessary. This dose corresponds to a quantity of the solution representing about two hundred grammes of the liquid. The Princess certainly did not drink two hundred grammes of her chicory water, she only took a few sips. Admitting ulceration of the stomach or what is most likely a duodenal ulcer, all the phenomena supervene with classic exactitude.

This then disposes of the conjecture that the Princess Henrietta Anne met her death by poison and proves that the rumours that were spread abroad at the time had no foundation in fact.

Spain also was not without its historic poisoning mysteries about this period. In September, 1689, Marie Louise the wife of King Carlos II of Spain was taken suddenly and seriously ill. After undergoing terrible sufferings, she died at the age of twenty-six years and it was officially announced that she had succumbed to an attack of cholera. Rumours were spread abroad that she had been poisoned and that her nails had fallen off before her death.

Ten years afterwards, when the morbid king visited the tombs of his dead progenitors in the Royal Mausoleum at the Escorial, he had the coffin of Marie Louise opened. As the elaborate grave-clothes were unfolded, the torchlight fell on a face that seemed to be that of a sleeping woman. Her eyes appeared to gleam beneath their thick lashes, and the delicate lips and cheeks appeared tinged with colour. All those present commented on the remarkable preservation of the body that had been interred for ten years, but no one seems to have realised that here was a sinister argument in favour of the rumours that the Queen had died from arsenical poisoning.

CHAPTER XXIV

THE FRENCH POISONERS OF THE XVII CENTURY— THE CASE OF THE MARQUISE DE BRINVILLIERS

CATHERINE DE' MEDICI is said to have been instrumental in introducing the Italian methods of poisoning into France, and after her time deaths in Paris attributed to poisons increased to an alarming extent. Her Florentine perfumers were supposed to have been adepts in mixing poisons with sweetmeats and articles of food.

René Bianchi or Bianco who came to Paris in her train, was both her confidant and accomplice and it is said it was he who furnished the Queen with poisoned substances when she had need, for it was well-known that she passed much time in his shop.

Côsme Ruggieri, another Italian who practised astrology and followed her to France, was also looked upon as a poisoner and was accused of having hastened the death of Charles IX with Môle and Coconnas and was condemned to the galleys.

From the highest to the lowest all seem to have had the dread of meeting death in this way, and it is said that Henry IV, when a guest at the Louvre, ate only eggs which he cooked himself and drank only water which he drew from the Seine.

Towards the end of the seventeenth century the epidemic of poisoning appears to have again broken out and a feeling of alarm and insecurity was felt especially among people of the higher classes. This fear was increased by the disclosures consequent on the arrest and trial of the Marquise de Brinvilliers in 1676. This historic case is one of the most remarkable on record and aroused intense interest throughout the country.

Marie Madeleine d'Aubray who afterwards became Marquise de Brinvilliers, was born on July 22nd, 1630, and was the eldest of the five children of Antoine Dreux d'Aubray, lord of Offemont and Villiers, who was councillor of State and lieutenant-general of the mines of France.

She received a better education than most girls of the period, but her religious instruction appears to have been wholly neglected and of moral principles she was entirely destitute. In 1651, she was married to Antoine Gobelin, Marquise de Brinvilliers, who was a lineal descendant of the founder of the famous tapestry manufactory and held a commission as an officer in a Norman regiment. He is said to have had an income of 30,000 livres a year and his wife brought him another 200,000 livres as a dowry.

At this period she is described as being a charming and spritely girl with large expressive eyes and a frank and vivacious manner. She had thick chestnut hair, rounded features and blue eyes, while her figure was slight and dainty. She lived for pleasure and amusement. Of a passionate temperament, she showed extraordinary energy in anything that might serve for the gratification of her desires. On the other hand, she was at once sensitive to anything that touched her vanity or self-love.

Such is the description left to us of a woman who became one of the most infamous poisoners in history.

The Brinvilliers began their married life with every prospect of happiness and all went well until 1659, when the marquise made the acquaintance of a young man called Godin, a captain of horse who was known as Sainte-Croix. Of good appearance and pleasing manners he became a close friend of the marquise and his wife and was a constant visitor at their house. Owing to his extravagant habits he was constantly in debt but eventually he so ingratiated himself with the Brinvilliers that he took up his residence with them.

It was not long before he fell in love with the young marquise and she, who had already made many conquests, made no secret of their intimacy. There was also living in the house at the time, a young man named Briancourt, who was tutor to the children and who it is said had also fallen a victim to the charms of the marquise.

For some reason, probably with the ultimate idea of getting rid of her husband, the marquise developed an enthusiasm for the study of poisons and this was known to Sainte-Croix. Paris, at this time, swarmed with alchemists, astrologers and practitioners of the occult arts, and among them was Christopher Glaser, a Swiss apothecary who had a shop in the Faubourg Saint Germain.

Glaser was a man well-versed in the scientific knowledge of his time and was demonstrator in chemistry at the Jardin des Plantes, while he also held the appointment of Apothecary to the King. He no doubt kept many poisons in stock and knew methods of preparing them; it is therefore more than probable that the marquise and her lover obtained their knowledge of toxicology from Glaser. Confirmation of this is revealed in their correspondence, where reference is made among the poisons they used to a " recipe of Glaser."

Glaser was the author of a work entitled " A New Treatise on Chymistry " which was translated into English and German.

The marquise is said to have begun her experiments by

visiting the hospitals and under cover of sympathy with the patients, gave them confections and wine which she had previously doctored for the purpose of observing the effects of various poisons.

Even her husband appears to have developed a distrust of her and began to be suspicious that his wife was making attempts to poison him. He was ever on the watch and it is said that when at dinner he always took care Sainte-Croix sat on the lady's right, while he occupied a place near the sideboard. He was always waited on by his own valet whom he instructed never to change his glass and to rinse it out whenever he served him with wine.

To avert any suspicion arising, the marquise would occasionally call in her medical adviser, Dr. Brayerone, one of the most famous physicians in Paris, to see her husband if he complained. According to Madame de Sévigné, Brinvilliers owed his life on these occasions not so much to his wife, as to the fear of her lover who did not relish the idea of marrying her. " While the marquise gave her husband poison, Sainte-Croix gave him antidotes, so that after being tossed like a ball from one to the other in this way five or six times, now poisoned, now restored, he remained alive."

As a result of these experiences the unfortunate man began to suffer from a chronic lung trouble. He always carried about with him a box of therica or treacle of Andromachus which was at that time believed to be an antidote to all poisons and with this he frequently dosed himself and also his servants.

M. Dreux d' Aubray at length incensed by his daughter's conduct in flaunting her lover in public, obtained a letter de cachet against him on March 19th, 1663, and in consequence, Sainte-Croix was arrested while sitting at the side of the marquise in her carriage and lodged in the Bastille.

During his imprisonment, he is said to have met an Italian who called himself Exili but whose real name was Egidi or Gilles, who had been attached as alchemist in the service of Queen Christina of Sweden and who had been arrested on the charge of secret dealing in poisons. He is said to have been the cause of the death of 150 persons in Rome and according to Michelet, was in the employ of Marie Olympia, Queen of Rome, under Innocent X. He settled in Paris and there seems no doubt that he became the instructor of many of the notorious poisoners of that city.

Sainte-Croix showed great interest in this man and there is little doubt he obtained from him further information respecting poisons.

Meanwhile, the marquis died but instead of inheriting a fortune, his wife found that his property had practically all vanished and what was left she speedily dissipated in extravagance. She conceived a deadly hatred against her father for causing the imprisonment of her lover and impatient to gain possession of the money she would inherit on his death, decided to try and hasten his end by poison.

She found subjects for her experiments to this end among her servants, one of whom named Roussel in giving evidence at her trial declared that her mistress had one day given her some gooseberry jam on the point of a knife which made her very ill. She also stated that the marquise had given her some ham, " which gave her great pain and she felt as if she had been pricked in the heart, after which she was ill for three years."

The marquise having satisfied herself that her method of administration was not likely to be easily discovered, turned her attention to its use for her own purposes and determined to make the attempt on the life of her father.

The opportunity occurred after he had been suffering for some little time from a slight ailment and she decided to pay him a visit.

After her arrival he grew worse and eventually died on September 10th, 1666, after being ill for eight months during which he had suffered great agonies.

His daughter subsequently confessed that she had administered poison to her father twenty-eight or thirty times with her own hands or had it given to him by his valet. It was sometimes given in water or in the form of powder mixed with his food and the process lasted eight months. From this statement it seems probable she employed arsenic in small doses in his case. His physicians attributed his death to natural causes but subsequently rumours got abroad that he died from the effects of poison.

After his death and when she had got possession of the money from his estate, she resumed her wild life and extravagant way of living. She contracted heavy debts and soon ran through her fortune and in this she was helped by Sainte-Croix, who, as soon as he was liberated from the Bastille, renewed his intimacy with her.

He took up his residence in a mysterious house in a cul-de-sac off the Place Maubert where he fitted up a laboratory and was said to be engaged in experiments in chemistry.

At this time it is said " the marquise developed a demoniac temper and inhuman cunning such as perhaps no mortal ever exhibited and she seemed to loose all restraint in her debaucheries."

In debt everywhere and pressed for money she next determined to poison her two brothers who lived together, and with this object in view introduced a man named La Chaussée, who was in her pay, into their house as footman.

Acting under the direction of the marquise, who wished to

divert all suspicion from herself, he began a system of administering a poison, with which she supplied him, in small doses in their food.

One eventually died from the effects after suffering for three months from continuous vomiting and burning pains in the stomach.

After the death of the second brother, which occurred a few months later, the physicians who had attended him insisted on holding a post-mortem examination, with the result that they declared that he had died from the effects of poison.

Apparently no suspicion was thrown on La Chaussée who carried out the crime, as his victim left him a legacy for his devoted services.

The marquise was now in the power of La Chaussée as well as Sainte-Croix who had grown intensely jealous, and differences began to arise between him and his unscrupulous mistress. Brooding over the intrigues in which he was involved, he kept locked up in a small box several of her letters, two promissory notes signed by her and a collection of poisons.

The marquise becoming aware of this used every endeavour to gain possession of this box and on his refusing to sell it to her, she threatened to have him assassinated. She wrote him constant letters and in one to which she received no reply, she stated : " I have thought it best to put an end to my life and I have therefore taken this evening what you gave me at so dear a price—the ' recipe of Glaser '—by which you will see that I have willingly sacrificed my life to you ; but I do not promise you before I die that I will not await you somewhere to bid you a last farewell."

She is said to have actually taken the poison but quickly repenting of the act, she swallowed great quantities of warm milk and so saved her life although she suffered from the effects for several months.

Becoming still more reckless she made no secret of her passion for using poisons and even talked about them to her servants. One of them later deposed that meeting her one day going to her room carrying a sort of casket in her hand, she told her she had there the wherewithal to wreak vengeance on her enemies and that there were many " inheritances in that box," a phrase that was repeated at her trial.

Sainte-Croix who was overwhelmed in debt was found dead in his apartment and all that was discovered in his so-called laboratory beyond his papers and a red box, oblong in shape, was a small furnace. Attached to the box was a paper signed and dated by Sainte-Croix, May 25th, 1672, containing a request that after his death it should be delivered to the " Marquise de Brinvilliers who resides at the Rue Neuve Saint Paul."

The authorities decided to retain possession of this box in spite of all the efforts the marquise made, even by trying to bribe the officials, to get possession of it.

On being opened, it was found to contain a number of compromising letters from the marquise, together with bonds for large sums which she had promised Sainte-Croix as hush-money in the matter of her crimes :

The following is a translation of the document directing its delivery in full :

" I humbly entreat those into whose hands this casket shall fall to do me the favour to place it in the very hands of Madame de Brinvilliers who resides in the Rue Neuve Saint Paul, the contents appertaining to her and to her only, and being moreover no use to any one else in the world. In the event of her death taking place before mine, it is my desire that the casket and all its contents be burned unopened and undisturbed ; and that none may plead ignorance, I swear by God whom I adore and by everything that is most sacred that nothing is here said save what is most true ; and if by any chance my request be con-travened, just and proper as they are in this point, I charge such contravention upon their conscience, both in this world and in the next, in discharge of mine own conscience. And this I say and sign as my last will.

" Signed, DE SAINTE-CROIX.

" Done at Paris, this afternoon of the 25th day of May, 1672."

Underneath were added the following words :

" There is one single packet, addressed to M. Pennautier, which must be restored to him."

" Precautions too elaborate frequently produce an effect the opposite of that intended," says the historian. " If in this casket, which was securely locked up, there had been the mere words, ' This casket belongs to Madame de Brinvilliers,' it is probable that it would have been forwarded to her unopened, but the very style of the injunction was calculated to arouse suspicion. The casket was opened, and an inventory made of its contents, and the following is the description of this deposit which was so solemnly placed under the safeguard of God and of all things sacred " :

1. A packet, sealed with eight seals of various armorial bearings, and endorsed : " Papers to be burned in the case of my death, they being of no value to any one. I most humbly entreat that they be burned by whomsoever may find them. I even charge it upon their conscience to do this, and to do it without opening the packet." In this packet was enclosed another, which contained corrosive sublimate.

2. Another packet, secured by six seals of various armorial bearings, similarly endorsed, and enclosing another packet, consisting of a pound and a half of corrosive sublimate.

3. Another packet, secured by six seals of different armorial bearings, in which were three other packets, one containing half an ounce of sublimate, a second containing two ounces of Roman vitriol, and the third calcined and prepared vitriol.

4. A large square phial full of a clear light liquid, the quality of which could not at the moment be ascertained.

5. Another phial of light-coloured liquid, at the bottom of which was a whitish sediment.

6. A small earthenware jar, in which was a quantity of prepared opium.

7. A folded paper, in which were two drachms of corrosive sublimate, in powder.

8. A small box containing " Infernal Stone." (Copper Sulphate.)

9. A paper containing an ounce of opium.

10. A piece of regulus of antimony, weighing three ounces.

11. A packet of powder marked. . . .

12. A packet secured by six seals, superscribed like those already described. This packet contained twenty-seven pieces of paper, on each of which were the words : " several curious secrets."

The first care of the civil authorities was directed to a careful examination of these substances, to have them analysed, and to experiment with them upon animals.

The result of the examination and experiments is very curious, and the following is the report which was made by the chemists and men of science to whom they were entrusted.

" This artful poison " (it runs) " defies the researches attempted to be made into its nature ; it is so disguised that it cannot be detected—so subtle that it defies all the science and ability of the doctors. Upon this poison all experiments blunder, all rules are false, and all aphorisms absurd.

" The most certain and usual experiments are made by means of the elements, or upon the bodies of animals. In water the weight of the poison precipitates ; it is the superior must needs be precipitated. No less sure is the action of fire ; it evaporates, it dissipates, it consumes all that is innocent and all that is impure, with the exception of a sharp and acrid substance which alone can resist its effects. Upon animals the effect of poison is even more obvious ; it carries malignity into every part which it touches, vitiating, burning, and withering up the whole internal economy as with a strange fire.

" The poison of Sainte-Croix has been subjected to all trials ; it defies all the skill and science of the doctors, and mocks and

baffles all experiments. This poison swims in water instead of
sinking, and it escapes from the test of fire, leaving behind
only a mild and innocent substance. In animals it so completely
hides itself that it cannot be detected ; all the parts of the
poisoned animal remain living and sound even while it is
shedding death all around it.

" All sorts of experiments have been tried upon this poison.
In the first instance some drops of a liquor contained in one
of the phials were poured into oil of tartar and water. No
precipitate was formed in the vessel.

" In the second experiment some of the same liquid was
poured into a sanded vessel, the sand retained no acridly tasting
substance. The third experiment was made upon a turkey hen,
a pigeon, and a dog ; they died in a brief space, and on their
being opened on the following day, only some coagulated blood
was found in the ventricles of the heart.

" Another experiment was made with some white powder,
which was given, with some mutton, to a cat. The cat vomited
for half an hour, and on the following day was found dead ; it
was opened, and no interior part showed marks of the action of
the poison. A second trial of the same poison was made upon
a pigeon, which died in a short time. When opened the bird
had only some red liquid in its stomach."

Such was the dying present of Sainte-Croix to his accomplice
of which she was soon to reap the consequences.

Grave suspicions now began to be entertained by the
authorities against the marquise, but there seems to have been
a reluctance to order her arrest on account of her rank and
position.

Madame Antoine d'Aubray her sister-in-law however,
decided to take action, as she was convinced that her husband
had been poisoned and she presented a petition to the Châtelet
and was admitted plaintiff in a civil action for damages against
the marquise and La Chaussée.

The marquise on learning this, at once fled to England leaving
La Chaussée to defend himself. The action was decided against
him and a decree was pronounced sentencing him to preliminary
torture.

On being put to the question he confessed to being the
instrument of several murders and was condemned to be broken
alive on the wheel, while the marquise was sentenced to be
beheaded for contempt of court. This news was conveyed to
her in London where she was living in distress, a prey to constant
fear of being arrested.

After the confessions of La Chaussée, the Secretary of State
through the French Ambassador, requested the English government to extradite the marquise and although Charles II gave
his consent, he refused to allow her arrest to be made by English

officers. While correspondence was being exchanged on this point she fled to the Netherlands, and making her way to Liége, took refuge in a convent where she was eventually arrested.

Her arrest was carried out under somewhat romantic circumstances which seemed befitting with her former career. An officer named Des Grais, was sent from Paris with a warrant for her apprehension but on arrival at Liége, was unable to get access to the convent where she was kept in strict seclusion. At last, finding that he would be unable to remove her by force, he disguised himself in the garb of an abbé and so obtained access to the convent and found the means of making her acquaintance. After making love to her, as she was by no means reluctant to respond to his advances, he induced her to accompany him on a pleasure excursion but once they were outside the building, he officially arrested her and set out to convey her to Paris.

On the journey, while at Maestricht, where he had her locked up in the Hotel de Ville, she attempted to commit suicide by swallowing pins and some fragments of a glass which she had broken with her teeth, but she did not succeed and all her endeavours to escape were frustrated.

Knowing that M. Pennautier's name had been mentioned in the documents discovered and he as Receiver-General of the clergy was a person of importance, she sought to implicate him.

She was first interrogated at Mézières on April 17th, 1676 but denied all the accusations made against her. Nine days afterwards she was taken to Paris and lodged in the Conciergerie. On April 29th she wrote the following letter to Pennautier which was read by the authorities : " I hear from my friend that you are intending to help me in this business " and she recommends him to buy the silence of Sainte-Croix's widow. This letter aroused suspicions against Pennautier and he too was arrested and lodged in the Conciergerie, although there was no evidence of his complicity in the crimes.

The trial of the Marquise de Brinvilliers, which need not be recapitulated, took place before the judges of the High Court in Paris. It lasted from April 29th to July 16th, 1676 and occupied twenty-two sittings. There were some intensely dramatic scenes and even the judges were greatly moved, especially when she was confronted with Briancourt, the tutor to her children and a former lover, to whom it was said she had confided all the secrets of her crimes. In spite of all, she retained her audacity and stoutly denied all the accusations brought against her, declaring that she had no knowledge of poisons or antidotes, but the evidence was overwhelming and she was found guilty, sentence being postponed.

The President of the Court, Lamoignon, appointed the Abbé

Pirot a Jesuit priest, who was also a doctor of the Sorbonne and a man of great intelligence, to attend her, in the hope that he would induce her to reveal the names of her accomplices, the compositions of the poisons she had used and the means of counteracting them.

She accepted his ministrations with graceful courtesy and is said to have convinced him of her penitence. It is stated that shortly before her death she declared the poisonous substances she had employed, but said : " I do not know exactly what they were, I should like to know the composition of the poisons I used and which were used at my direction, but all I know about them is, there was toad's venom and that there were some that consisted of rarified arsenic."

It is quite possible that she may not have known the exact composition of the preparations she had used, especially if they had been compounded by Glaser or Sainte-Croix ; on the other hand there is evidence that she had an intimate knowledge of preparing drugs.

She declared that the only antidote she was aware of was milk and her only accomplices were Sainte-Croix and certain servants.

The judgment of the Court was pronounced on July 16th, 1676 and is recorded as follows :

" The Court has declared and declares the said D'Aubray de Brinvilliers duly attainted and convicted of having procured the poisoning of M. Dreux D'Aubray, her father, and the said Messrs. D'Aubray, Civil Lieutenant and Councillor in the said Court, her two brothers, and attempted the life of the late Teresa D'Aubray, her sister, and by way of reparation has condemned and condemns the said D'Aubray de Brinvilliers to make public apology in front of the principal door of the Church of Paris, whither she will be taken in a cart, with bare feet and a rope round her neck, holding in her hands a lighted torch of two pounds weight, and there on her knees to say and declare that wickedly, and in order to possess their goods, she procured the poisoning of her father and her two brothers, and attempted the life of her deceased sister, of which she repents and asks pardon of God, the King, and the law : this done, taken and conveyed in the same cart to the Place de Grève of this city, to have her head cut off there on a scaffold to be erected for the purpose in the said place ; her body burnt, and the ashes thrown to the winds. She is first to be put to the question, ordinary and extraordinary, in order to obtain a disclosure of her accomplices."

After the sentence had been read she was taken to the torture-chamber and according to the record, " raising her voice, she made a clear and complete avowal of the crimes of her life."
An enormous crowd assembled to see her taken to the scene of

execution and Madame de Sévigné, who witnessed it from the window of one of the houses on the bridge near Notre Dame says : " Never was such a crowd seen or Paris so excited or interested." The marquise drew herself to her feet in the cart and with her eyes flashing, cried out in a loud voice charged with contempt : " You have come to see a fine spectacle."

Such is the story of Marie Madeleine de Brinvilliers, who is described by a contemporary writer at the end of her tragic life, with " a face degraded by excesses and distorted by evil passions, but with features extremely regular, with a rounded face that was once full and beautiful, and a certain look which seemed to breathe goodness."

Much has been written from time to time concerning her career, but stripped of the romantic elements of her life, she was but a murderess of a common type in whom sensuality, cunning and vice were combined, her motives being due to lust and greed of wealth, to obtain which she was ready to risk all.

It seems very probable that she acquired much of her knowledge of poisons from Glaser the apothecary, who states in his treatise on Chemistry that he was " an artist in his profession " and declares that he writes of " nothing he has not done and sets down as preparations but what I have made and well-experienced."

Among the mineral poisons he describes are vitriol of Luna (silver), Lapis Infernalis (copper sulphate), sugar of lead, corrosive sublimate (mercury perchloride), antimony, in the form of tartar emetic and arsenic.

He describes his rarified arsenic as having the same properties as antimony but more violent in action, and another powerful poison called the ' corrosive liquor of arsenic.' This was a combination of arsenic and corrosive sublimate made by mixing equal parts in powder and distilling them with water with slow heat. The result is a gummy liquor, " which hath the same properties as antimony but is more violent." This was probably the " Glaser's recipe " referred to in the marquise's papers.

There is evidence from a document in the autograph of the marquise that was discovered among the archives of the Bastille and which is now preserved in the Bibliotheque de l'Arsenal, that she was conversant with methods of preparing drugs not commonly known.

The following is her recipe for making ' eye drops,' from a manuscript stated to be in her handwriting, (Translation) :—

" Recipe for the eyes

" Take six new laid eggs, harden them in hot ash then shell them and afterwards remove their yolks, cutting them very neatly in half. Then re-fill the said eggs with sugar-candy and white copperas (zinc sulphate) in equal amounts well pulverised. Then join them together and tie them with thread, then attach them to a little stick so that they hang down, putting them thus hanging into the cellar, putting under them a glazed dish.

" Leave them for forty-eight hours in the cellar, then take the water which has distilled from the said eggs and put it in a phial. Then when one wishes to make use of it one must take a thimble full of it with two ounces of plaintain water. Mix together and put two or three drops of it into the eyes in the evening only, three times a week ; and according as one find oneself benefitted by it, one must diminish (the amount) and only apply it twice and so on."

CHAPTER XXV

THE CHAMBER OF POISONS—LA VOISIN—THE EMPEROR NAPOLEON AND POISONS

In 1662 it was thought necessary to devise some more drastic method of dealing with the secret sale of poisons, and a decree was issued by Louis XIV, forbidding apothecaries to sell arsenic, sublimate, or any drug reputed to be a poison except to persons known to them. It further required that the purchaser should sign a register declaring the purpose for which he was buying the poison. A similar condition had been imposed by the local authorities in Montpellier about twenty years previously, but Louis applied it to the whole of France.

The priests of Notre-Dame became appalled at the number of self-accusations of murder by poison made to them in the confessional, and conveyed an intimation of the fact without names to Colbert and Louvois, then Ministers of State. The authorities were placed on the alert, and by means of a clue obtained from an intercepted letter, they arrested the Chevalier de Vanens and the Count de Bachimont, who were found to be secret purveyors of poisons. On private examination, they implicated a large number of persons, insomuch that a judicial commission was appointed by Louis XIV, by which strict justice was to be done, without distinction of person, condition or sex. It sat for three years and was known as the *Chambre Ardente*, or Chamber of Poisons, and was established at the Arsenal near the Bastille.

The stir and mystery made by the examinations of this Court apparently drew more attention to poisons than before, and many began to learn how to employ them, with the object of succeeding to heritages or of ridding themselves of persons they disliked.

Among those arrested and brought before the Court were members of some of the noblest families of France, together with magistrates, priests and a number of women, who had practised as witches, fortune-tellers, *sages-femmes* and poisoners. Confessions, which were extracted from these people by torture showed that systematic poisoning had for some time been carried out by the ladies of the Court of the *Grand Monarque*.

One of the worst of the poison-fiends in human shape was Catherine Deshayes, the wife of Antoine Monvoisin a peddling jeweller, who was popularly known as La Voisin. She practised as a fortune-teller and sorceress and although by no means beautiful, she appears to have had an extraordinary influence over her dupes.

She is said to have amassed in a few years a sum equivalent to £20,000 which she squandered chiefly in revelry. Among her lovers was Guillaume, the executioner of Paris, Viscount de Cousserans and Blessis, the alchemist, to whom she gave large sums of money when she had need of his services.

She claimed to have founded her art and success on face-reading or what we should now call psychology. She received all kinds of secrets and confessions from her fashionable customers and had a regular trade in selling poisons to wives who wished to rid themselves of their husbands. This was proved in the case of Madame Leféron investigated by the *Chambre Ardente*, in which it was found that the necessary poison had been obtained from La Voisin.

Madame de Montespan is said to have been one of her clients and it was La Voisin who provided her with " love-powders " to give Louis XIV which are declared to have been composed of cantharides, dried moles in powder and the blood of bats.

Marguerite Monvoisin, the daughter of La Voisin, is said to have freely confessed the infamous trade carried on by her mother, but it is open to doubt if much of her story is true.

When Madame de Montespan at last lost favour with the King and was superseded by Mademoiselle Fontanges, she resolved to put an end to both of them and sought the aid of La Voisin and three of her accomplices in the Rue Beauregard. Two of these creatures were Romani and Bertrand, who were bold enough to call themselves " artists in poison." They undertook to kill Mademoiselle, while La Voisin and La Trianon, another associate of hers, plotted to poison the King. According to the plan the first attempt was to be made on the life of the King, the price for which they asked being 100,000 crowns.

In accordance with ancient custom the monarch used to receive in person, on certain days, the petitions presented by his subjects of all ranks, and of this easy access to his presence they resolved to take advantage. They proceeded to prepare a petition and impregnated the paper on which it was written with a powerful poison which they hoped might be absorbed as he handled it. However, the project, ridiculous as it was, failed, for owing to the crowd, La Voisin was unable to get near the King and a few days afterwards she was arrested.

Another plot contemplated by this gang was to poison the Duchess de Fontanges by means of a pair of gloves, specially prepared, so that after wearing them they would cause a lingering death.

Romani was to be disguised as a travelling pedler and to present his wares to the Duchess, on the presumption that even if she did not buy his other goods she would be sure to take the gloves which were of the finest quality from Grenoble. He was to prepare them previously according to the recipes of the Italian poisoners.

This plot however did not mature, for the Duchess died a natural death in the Abbey of Port Royal in 1681.

La Voisin and all her accomplices were arrested and were eventually tried, condemned and burnt at the stake.

The papers of one of the Italian adventurers, named Primi Visconti, which were discovered and translated a few years ago, throw some light on the methods of these parasites of society. Visconti, who had obtained entry to the French court by his professed skill in palmistry and chiromancy and had become somewhat popular with the courtiers, relates that " it had come to the King's knowledge that the infamous Sainte-Croix had sought to obtain the position of *maître d'hotel* in the palace of Versailles, and had been recommended to the position by a wealthy and avaricious person named Pennautier, Receiver-General of the Clergy, who was also suspected of being concerned in the recent crimes."

The *Chambre Ardente* during its existence dealt with charges against 442 persons, and ordered the arrest of 367 ; 218 were kept prisoners, 36 were executed, 2 died in prison, 5 were sent to the gallows, and 23 were banished.

In spite of this it is said, that the worst criminals escaped owing to the influence that they brought to bear in their favour. " The chief culprits," says Ravaisson, " belonged to the nobility or the law, and almost all of them had amongst the members of the court friends, clients or relatives." The King had set a bad example by allowing some individuals who were compromised to go free. The judges had not the courage to be more severe, and the weight of the condemnations fell almost entirely on the miserable creatures who sold the poisons and not on those who bought and used them.

La Voisin had kept a list of her clients and when this was discovered they were arrested and brought to private trial before the *Chambre*. The list contained such names as the two nieces of Cardinal Mazarin, the Duchesse de Bouillon and the Comtesse de Soissons.

At the trial of the Duchesse nothing could be proved beyond her statement that she had resorted to Le Sage to consult him as a fortune-teller. He also claimed to be able to show her even the Devil himself. Le Reiné, one of the judges of the court, was indiscreet enough to ask the Duchesse if this had taken place and if she had ever seen the Devil ? The lady quickly replied that she saw him at that very moment, that he was extremely ugly and very hideous, and appeared to her in the guise of her questioner.

The charge brought against the Comtesse de Soissons and the Marshal de Luxembourg was more serious. La Voisin's creatures claimed to know the secret of the particularly poisonous powder known as the *poudre de succession*, so-called from the real or supposed frequency with which it had been used to hasten or change the succession in the families of the rich. According to later writers, the *poudre de succession* consisted of arsenic, sometimes mixed with vegetable poisons such as aconite, belladonna and opium. The names of those who obtained possession of it had been reported to the Government. It is said that the King intimated to the countess that if she was guilty she had better escape by flight. Although she declared her innocence, she said she could not endure the scandal of a public trial and fled to Brussels, where she died in 1708.

With respect to the Marshal, his explanation of his connexion with the infamous trio was that he had consulted them in order to recover some lost papers of value. He had done this through the medium of a man named Bonard ; Le Sage swore, however, that the Marshal had applied to him to poison a woman who had possession of the papers and refused to give them up. His accomplices testified that they had accordingly poisoned her and disposed of the body into the river at the instigation of the Marshal. The Marshal was imprisoned and placed in a dungeon six and a half feet long, where he fell sick and remained five weeks before being brought to trial. His trial was prolonged fourteen months, after which he was released without being condemned or acquitted.

In the eighteenth century, there is evidence that poisons were sometimes secretly administered by means of a clyster, the use of which was very common at the time. Arsenic, corrosive sublimate, cantharides and opium are said to have been given in this way.

Louis XVIII is said to have narrowly escaped death by poison in 1804. At that time he was living under the name of the Comte de Lille near Warsaw, and had in his household a servant named Coulon, a French adventurer, who had been a prisoner of war at Portsmouth and arrived in the Polish city in 1803. He declared that he was approached in July, 1804, by two emissaries " charged to poison Louis XVIII, his wife, and also the Duke and Duchess d'Angoulême," who were living with the royal couple. The emissaries offered him four hundred louis d'or if he would place in the soup served to the King and his family some hollow carrots filled with poison. A postchaise would await Coulon to carry him at once to France, where the regicide would be asked no questions so long as his victim was a Bourbon. Coulon accepted the carrots, but denounced the couple. Part of Poland was then subject to Prussia, and the Prussian police appear to have been singularly averse to taking action in the matter, and allowed the two emissaries to escape. This circumstance, coupled with the fact that Napoleon was all-powerful at the period, and the supposition that the man who ordered the Duc d'Enghien to be shot was capable of compassing the death of other Bourbons, gave rise to the suspicion that the plot was really set on foot by Napoleon's police. Louis XVIII requested that Coulon might be arrested and the carrots officially analysed, but the Prussian authorities refused to act.

" Seeing that it was impossible to rely either upon the law or the Prussian police," the narrator continues, " d'Avray went with Dr. Lefèvre, the King's physician, to call upon Dr. Gazat-kiewick, one of the most celebrated practitioners of Warsaw. Here, in the presence of a second physician, Dr. Bagenzorve, and of M. Guidal, a local pharmacist, the seals placed by the Archbishop on Coulon's packet were broken. The three carrots therein contained were opened and found to be filled with a sort of paste formed of three arsenics,, yellow, white and red."

A report was drawn up and handed to M. de Tilly, head of the city police, but he declined to take any notice, saying the affair was outside his province.

The question of the various poisons used during this period in France for criminal purposes has been investigated by Dr. Lucien Nass, who has had access to the documents relating to the various important trials that took place. He says, that according to police inventories of articles found in the domiciliary visits made by them in the course of their inquiries into these poisoning cases, many substances were employed. If one failed another was tried. The method of administration was varied with considerable ingenuity, and arsenic, opium, cantharides and lead acetate were the substances mostly used.

When Napoleon was driven from Leipzig in defeat and disaster, culminating in his abdication at Fontainebleau, it is said that he attempted to end his life by swallowing opium. During the retreat from Moscow, the Emperor is stated to have requested his physician to provide him with means to prevent his falling into the hands of the enemy alive, and was supplied with a drug which he carried in a small packet suspended round his neck. Either from the poison losing its properties or having become innocuous, it is stated " to have thrown Napoleon, after he took it, into a deep sleep, from which he awoke in spasms."

From these and other accounts he appears to have had a dread of being taken a prisoner alive, and Charles Louis Codet who was his personal pharmacist and accompanied him on his Austrian campaign confirms this. Codet who died in 1821, in his biography states that after his return from Elba, Napoleon consulted him regarding the preparation of an infallible poison in as small a compass as possible, which he might use if the campaign should fail. Codet supplied him with the drug and it is said that the Emperor actually swallowed the poison after the battle of Waterloo, but quickly repenting of his act, he speedily obtained an emetic from Codet and got rid of the dose.

CHAPTER XXVI

POISON PLOTS AND CONSPIRACIES

DURING the Middle Ages a strange dread of wholesale poisoning spread throughout Europe and caused numerous panics. Some of these rumours may probably have been circulated by unscrupulous traders who had articles to sell, or some business interests to forward, but of this disturbing fear, authentic record still exists that it affected whole communities.

England was probably freer from crimes of this kind than almost any other country, but in 1530 a case occurred which aroused great public indignation. Fisher, Bishop of Rochester, was accustomed to feed many poor people daily from his table, and one day a large number of his guests, together with some of the officers of the household, were taken ill and died. After examination of the food had been made, it was declared that the yeast used in the bread had been poisoned. Parliament took up the case and the bishop's cook, one Roose, was found guilty. He was tried and sentenced to be boiled alive as a terrible example to others. This was a common penalty for poisoners during the Middle Ages, a fact which doubtless shows the great abhorrence in which crimes of this kind were held.

During the case of Sir Thomas Overbury, at which Lord Bacon performed the duties of Attorney-General, he emphasized the enormity of the offence of poisoning, although he maintained that poisoning was not a crime to which English people were predisposed. " It is a crime," he stated, " the more to be dreaded because it is so easily committed and so hard to be prevented and discovered."

As a result of the Rochester case a law was passed about 1531 making murder by poison high treason, the punishment being death by boiling. The wording of the act which records the story of the crime is as follows :

22 Henry VIII, c. 9. The Kynges royall majistie callyng to hys moste blessed remembraunce that the makyng of good and holsome laws and due execution of the same agaynste the offendours thereof is the only cause that good obedyence and order hath ben preserved in this Realme, and his highnes havyng moste tender zeale to the same emonge other thynges consyderyng that mannes lyfe above all thynges is chyefly to be favoured, and voluntary murders moste highly to be

detested and abhorred, and specyally of all kyndes of murders, poysonynge, which in this Realme hytherto our Lord be thanked hath ben moste rare and seldome comytted or practysed ; and now in the tyme of this presente parliamente, that is to saye, in the xviij daye of Februarye in the xxijd yere of his moste victorious reygn, one Richard Roose late of Rouchester in the Countie of Kente, Coke, otherwyse called Richard Coke of his moste wyked and damnable dysposicyon dyd caste a certeyne venym or poyson into a vessel replenysshed with yeste or barme standyng in the Kechyn of the Reverende Father in God John Bysshopp of Rochester at his place in Lamehyth Marsshewythe which yeste or Barme and other thynges convenyent, porrage or gruell was forthwyth made for his famylye there beyng wherby not only the nombre of xvij persons of his said famylie which dyd eate of that porrage were mortally enfeebled and poysoned and one of them, that is to say, Bennett Curwen gentylman thereof ys decessed, but also certeyne pore people which resorted to the sayde Bysshops place and were there charytably fedde wyth the remayne of the sayde porrage and other vytayles, were in lyke wise infected, and one pore Woman of them that is to saye Alyce Tryppytt wydowe is also thereof nowe deceassed : our sayde sovereign Lorde the Kynge of hys blessed disposicion inwardly abhorrying all such abhomynable offences, because that in manner no person can lyve in suertye out of daunger of death by that meane, yf practyse thereof shulde not be exchued, hath ordeyned and enacted by auctorytie of thys presente parlyament that the sayd poysonyng be ajuged and demed as high treason, And that the sayde Richarde for the sayde murder and poysonynge of the sayde two persones as is aforesayde by auctoritye of thys presente parlyament, shall stande and be attaynted of high treason : and by cause that detestable offence nowe newly practysed and comytted requyreth condigne punysshmente for the same ; It is ordayned and enacted by auctoritie of this presente parliamente that the said Richard Roose shal be therfore boyled to deathe withoute havynge any advauntage of his clargie."

Under this statute, also according to Lord Coke, in his third institute, Margaret Davy, a young woman, was attainted of high treason, for poisoning her mistress, and some others were boiled to death in Smithfield, the 17th of March, the same year, 1524. " But this act," continues Coke, " was too severe to live long," and was therefore repealed by 1 Ed. VI, c. 12, and 1 Mar., c. 1. It is thought probable that the common expressions, to " keep out of hot water " and to " get into hot water," may have had their origin in the punishment attached to this crime in the XVI century.

Over two hundred years ago, while the island of Malta was still possessed by the Knights of St. John, a Jew waited on the

Grand Master and revealed to him a plot that had been planned for exterminating the whole population at one stroke. The man kept a coffee-house frequented by Turkish slaves, and, understanding their language, the conversation of his customers had aroused his suspicions. The Grand Master, believing the truth of the man's statement, took immediate action. The slaves were at once seized, and put to torture; they confessed a design of poisoning all the wells and fountains on the island, and, to make the result surer, each of the conspirators was to assassinate a Christian. One hundred and twenty-five were found guilty; some were burned, some broken on the wheel, others were ordered to have their arms and legs attached to two galleys, which, being rowed apart, thus dismembered them. Whether these fearful punishments were carried out is not known, but the fact remains that the people of Malta still commemorate their escape from poisoning on the sixth of June.

Wholesale poisoning appears to have been frequent in Eastern countries, especially in India and Persia. The wells or other water sources were usually chosen as the media for disseminating the poison, and in this way whole villages have often been destroyed by some miscreant.

An extraordinary poison plot was discovered in Lima towards the close of the eighteenth century. During the insurrection of 1781 a rich cacique, who professed loyalty, went into a chemist's shop and asked for two hundred pounds of corrosive sublimate. He was willing to pay any price for it. The chemist had nothing like that amount in stock, but, not wishing to send away so good a customer, substituted two hundred pounds of alum. On the following day all the water in the town was found to be impregnated with alum, and on examination being made, the fence round the reservoir was found to have been broken down, the banks strewn with alum and the water rendered undrinkable.

Although the use of poison for taking life was, according to Bacon, abhorrent to the English character, in some of the Latin countries the feeling was just the opposite, as evidenced by the following story:

The Duc de Guise in his memoirs relates, in a most matter-of-fact way, how he requested the captain of his guard to poniard a troublesome demagogue at Naples. The captain was shocked. He would poison anyone at his grace's command with pleasure, but the dagger was a vulgar instrument. So the Duke bought some strong poison, the composition of which he describes at length, and it was duly administered. But Gennaro, the intended victim, had just eaten cabbage dressed in oil, which is said to have acted as an antidote, and so he escaped the effects of the dose.

Coming to more recent times, in the early part of 1917, a plot to murder two of His Majesty's Ministers of State was brought to light, which suggests some of the subtle methods employed in the Middle Ages. Three women named Alice Wheeldon, Hetty Wheeldon and Winnie Mason—mother and daughters and a man named Alfred George Mason, husband of the latter, were charged with conspiring to kill the then Prime Minister, Mr. Lloyd George, and Mr. Arthur Henderson, his colleague on the War Council, by means of strychnine or curare.

The plot was discovered by two secret agents of the Government who were employed for the purpose of obtaining information of the schemes of persons desirous of evading military service or otherwise conspiring against the country, and who had been directed to keep a watch upon this particular family. They obtained an introduction to the Wheeldons, who lived in Derby, by representing themselves as sympathizers and so won their confidence. They succeeded so well in ingratiating themselves with the family, that not only was the plot revealed to them but they were actually entrusted by Mrs. Wheeldon with the task of carrying out the deed.

The suspicions of the two men became aroused when they found that a letter had been sent to Mason with the object of procuring some poisons. The woman had previously shown one of the agents a stuffed skin of a snake shaped in the form of a bracelet, stating that it was poisonous, and remarked that she wished she had a hundred of them. The Wheeldons always showed the greatest animosity to the Prime Minister and Mr. Henderson, expressing the wish that they hoped they would soon be dead. Mrs. Wheeldon also told him that the Suffragettes had spent £300 in trying to poison Lloyd George, the plot being to get into an hotel where he was staying and drive a nail which had been dipped in poison through his boot; this, however, was frustrated by his going to France. She also declared her intention of killing another Minister by inserting a poisoned needle into his skull, and other schemes of an extraordinary character were discussed.

Before handing over the poison to one of the agents, Mrs. Wheeldon was stated to have said : " You know what you are doing ! You will rid the world of a bloody murderer and be a saviour of the country." Asked how the poison was used, she replied : " It is a crystal, and you drop two drops of water on it, dip your article in, and when the water evaporates it leaves the poison." As the men were about to leave, Mrs. Wheeldon shook hands with them, and said that when she handed the poison over to them she washed her hands of it, and would deny on her word of honour that she ever gave it to them. She assured them that the phial contained enough to kill five hundred people. Walton Heath had been selected as being the most likely spot to offer a suitable opportunity, and an air-gun was to be used as a medium.

The agents at once informed their superior officer, who had the prisoners arrested and the house searched. Among the objects found was a small stuffed snake skin which was said to contain four glass phials embedded in cottonwool.

The accused were charged at Derby on February 4th, 1917, and they were tried in London at the Old Bailey on March 7th, of that year.

The prisoners were described by the Attorney-General as a very dangerous and desperate type of people, who were habitually hostile to this country. They were shelterers of refugees from the army and persons who did their best to injure Great Britain in the war then proceeding. Mrs. Wheeldon's son William was himself a conscientious objector.

At the trial a two-ounce tin tobacco box was produced containing four phials sealed. Instructions were enclosed which had been copied by both the agents and were as follows :

" Powder in tube ' A ' is sufficient for two or even three doses to be given by the mouth or in solution.

" Powder ' C ' to be injected either in solution or by a dart, which will penetrate into the body and stop for a while. Rusted in solution or fired from an air-gun, or a rusty needle if driven well in with powder will do, but don't advise unless in urgent dilemma.

" Solution ' B '—either by mouth or injection.

" Solution ' D '—injection only.

" All are certain.

" All four will probably leave a trace, but if the bloke wanted dies suspect, it will be a job to prove it so long as you have a chance to get at the dog, dead in twenty seconds. Powder ' A ' on meal or bread is O.K. If you care for microbe can supply needle thirty-six hours in strong solution and allow to dry in air, dip again for ten seconds and allow again to dry. Cover with ' C ' powder."

Upon analysis the phials were found to contain :—

" A," 7½ grammes strychnine hydrochloride in crystals.

" B," 1½ drachms strychnine hydrochloride in solution.

" C," curare in powder.

" D," 1 drachm of curare in solution.

The box containing the poison was sent to Mrs. Wheeldon by her son-in-law, Alfred Mason, who was a lecturer on pharmacy at Southampton University College and who was said to have made a special study of curare. Only a few weeks before the preceding Christmas, he had shown a student in the college a specimen of it and described its properties. The tobacco box containing the phials and instructions are said to have been despatched by him from Southampton to Derby at the request of Mrs. Wheeldon.

Mrs. Wheeldon volunteered to give evidence, in which she acknowledged she had been active in helping men to escape from their military duties ever since conscription had been introduced. There was no form of help that she could give them that she had withheld. Her own son was a conscientious objector. She was quite prepared in the circumstances to violate what she knew to be the law and had no regard to consequences. She expressed her bitter hatred of Mr. Lloyd George and was ready to do him a mischief.

Alfred Mason on being examined said he had devoted some time to the study of criminology in relation to poisons, but *he did not know that strychnine was used for poisoning*. If poison was to have been used for a human being he would have definitely stated in his instructions that it should be mixed with food. He said he had had experience in destroying two thousand dogs, and that when his mother-in-law had written she had said she wanted some poison for a dog, and that it was a dangerous dog, and the impression left on his mind was that it was difficult to get it. He treated the allusion to the microbe as a joke.

Counsel on behalf of the prisoners denied the charges as a vindictive prosecution of the worst of its kind that had ever taken place in England. He submitted the curious suggestion that the proper trial of this case would be by ordeal, on which the judge remarked : " I am afraid that it has been abolished." Counsel said he submitted it to the jury. The judge asked him if he proposed that the prisoners should walk over hot ploughshares or something of that kind, to which counsel replied : " I do, in order to prove their innocence." He threw ridicule on the idea that Mr. Lloyd George could have been killed by poisoned darts or arrows.

Mr. Justice Low, in summing up, said that of all forms of murder, poisoning was the most dastardly and the most dangerous, and conspiracy to murder by poisoning was the worst of all. It was almost incredible that these prisoners had by their own admission behaved as these people had done. The jury having found the prisoners guilty, the elder woman, Mrs. Wheeldon, was sentenced to ten years' penal servitude, the man Mason to seven years and his wife to five years ; the girl Harriet Wheeldon was found not guilty and discharged.

In December, 1909, a sensation was caused throughout Austria owing to the arrest of a young officer named Lieutenant Hofrichter of Linz, who was charged with being concerned in a plot to poison a captain of the Imperial General Staff and other highly-placed Imperial officers by sending them poisoned samples of a new patent medicine.

The alleged motive was said to be a desire to clear a path

for promotion by the removal of officers of higher rank. Suspicion was first directed towards him by the statement of a brother officer at Linz where he was stationed, who mentioned that he had received from the lieutenant a box exactly similar to that in which the fatal powder had been sent.

About a week before this, a Captain Mader, together with several officers of the General Staff, had received by post a sample of a supposed patent medicine, and on taking some of it he died shortly afterwards. It was found that the medicine contained a large proportion of potassium cyanide.

On suspicion falling on Hofrichter, his quarters were searched and a copying apparatus which apparently had been used for the circulars accompanying the poisoned medicine was found. He was also identified as the purchaser of capsules, boxes and envelopes, similar to those which had been sent to the officers. Hofrichter was brought to Vienna for trial by the military tribunal, from which the public were excluded.

The first hearing of the case lasted seven hours, and in the course of the investigation it was stated that four officers had fallen victims to the effects of poison, the first being Captain Mader. In consequence of the order of the military court, the dwellings of eighty officers were searched in Vienna and the provinces and a series of extraordinary tragedies followed. One of the officers who was engaged at the War Office felt the indignity to such an extent that he shot himself immediately afterwards. Another victim was a brother-in-law of the accused, who after devoting himself to collecting evidence and examining possible witnesses hoping to prove the innocence of Hofrichter, died suddenly. The cause of his death was said to have been hastened by his anxiety and excitement over the case. A Lieutenant Schmidt, who had been summoned to appear before the military court in Vienna, also committed suicide.

The tribunal then proceeded to inquire into Hofrichter's previous career, which brought to light the fact that, some years before, he was engaged to be married to the daughter of a pastor in Bohemia, but the engagement was broken off after he entered the Vienna Military Academy. The girl, in despair, is stated to have poisoned herself with potassium cyanide, and a letter from Hofrichter which arrived after her death, was buried unopened with her.

It was rumoured that Hofrichter had sent the girl the poison and the tribunal decided to have the body exhumed. This was carried out, and the unopened letter that had been sent five years previously was found. The remains of the body were subjected to analysis, but no trace of poison was discovered.

Meanwhile, the case was postponed for further investigation. This finally revealed the fact that Hofrichter had been leading a double life for a considerable time and had done so with

extraordinary cunning. In the army he had been generally liked
and esteemed as a hard worker and a good officer, while under
the name of Dr. Haller he carried on a criminal career.

Letters to his wife which were intercepted from the prison,
revealed that he intended to commit suicide, and in one of
these he asked her to conceal various poisons including atropine
and hyoscyamine in a bunch of flowers, which he had asked
for to lay on an altar he had made in his cell. At his house
in Linz a considerable quantity of poisons and drugs were
discovered.

The long delays between the meetings of the military tribunal
were very trying to the accused man. For months he faced the
ordeal of a severe cross-examination. He feigned insanity with
great ability, and the methods of the police inclined the public
in his favour. At length, after a trial lasting for four months, his
defence broke down, and he confessed. He was found guilty
and sentenced to death by hanging.

During the year 1921 several attempts were made on the
lives of well-known people, which appear to have been carried
out by weak-minded persons or those on the border line of
insanity. Such cases are not infrequent in the history of criminal
poisoning, where attempts have been made by homicidal maniacs
to take life without any apparent motive.

Early in the year it was reported that the Vice-Chancellor
of Oxford had received a box of chocolate creams by post,
and being suspicious at the receipt of such an anonymous gift,
he submitted them for examination to one of his colleagues, a
professor of science. This gave rise to rumours that they
contained something of a deleterious nature, but the result of
an analysis showed that the sweets were innocuous. An under-
graduate was reported to have confessed, and the presumed plot
against the Vice-Chancellor was declared to be a hoax.

In November, 1922, a sensation was caused in London by
an attempt to poison the Chief Commissioner of the Metro-
politan Police at Scotland Yard. On November 9th it was
reported in the newspapers that the Chief Commissioner had
been seized with an apparent heart attack in his office at Scotland
Yard, which came on while he was dressing before proceeding
to the Lord Mayor's banquet. It was not till nine o'clock that
night that the doctors summoned to attend him definitely
concluded that it was a case of poisoning by arsenic.

It appeared that on November 3rd, six days previously, a
package addressed to the Assistant Commissioner, New Scotland
Yard, Westminster, had been delivered by parcel post. On
being opened it was found to contain four chocolate éclairs,
wrapped in grease-proof paper. Enclosed with the éclairs was
a small white card three inches long by one and a half wide,
bearing upon it the following : " A good lunch and a hearty

appetite.—Molly." The box had been posted in the Balham district. The éclairs were sent to an analyst for investigation, but before the result had been received, a second parcel arrived on November 9th, addressed to Brigadier-General Horwood, New Scotland Yard, Westminster, S.W., and was opened by the Chief Commissioner himself. The box is described as being of cardboard, $7\frac{1}{2}$ by $1\frac{3}{4}$ inches, and was wrapped in a piece of stiff white paper addressed in block letters and contained whipped cream walnuts. The box was tied with string and was also posted in the Balham district about 4 p.m., November 8th.

The morning that the box arrived Sir William had received a letter from a relative who said that she was sending him some chocolates for his birthday, and he accordingly opened the box unsuspectingly. He took one of the chocolates and offered them to his secretary who was in the room. She, however, only bit off a small piece of the outer covering of hers, and remarking that it tasted bitter, threw it away and told the Commissioner. He, still believing the package to have come from his friend, suspected nothing, and though he noticed it burned his throat a little, he ate more later in the day. While dressing for dinner that evening the Commissioner was seized with severe pain and showed symptoms of having swallowed an irritant poison, and was removed to St. Thomas's Hospital next day.

On the chocolates being carefully examined it was found that there was a small square mark at the bottom of each, as if a portion of the chocolate coating had been removed, a poison mixed with the cream inside and the square of chocolate afterwards replaced. On investigation it was found that the poison employed was undoubtedly arsenic, which was plainly to be seen and took the form of dark greenish-tinted matter.

On November 10th another box was received at Scotland Yard. This was a small cardboard box $2\frac{1}{4}$ by $1\frac{3}{4}$ inches by $\frac{3}{4}$ of an inch, greyish tint with plain card pasted on lid, wrapped in light brown tissue paper, addressed in block letters to The Commissioner of the Police, New Scotland Yard, Westminster. This box contained two small tablets of Bournville chocolate wrapped in white paper. The box was sealed with black sealing-wax, and was posted in the Balham district about 3 p.m., on November 9th.

The Chief Commissioner, though for some days in a very critical condition, got better and made a complete recovery.

A few weeks afterwards a small cardboard box was received at the Home Office addressed to " The Secretary for Home Affairs, Whitehall, S.W." It was taken to the registry and opened, and was found to contain cream fondants. The parcel was obviously sent by the same person who sent the poisoned chocolates to the Commissioner of Police. The sweets had apparently been tampered with and were sent for analysis, but no arsenic was found in them. The writing on the address was similar in each case and the box had been posted in the same district of Balham.

Previously to this, the police authorities had issued a warning to well-known people, putting them on their guard against similar attempts.

Early in February, 1923, a man living at Balham was arrested by the police at his residence, and was charged with attempting to murder the Chief Commissioner and the two Assistant Commissioners of Police. He made the following statement : " I sent the Commissioner chocolates. I sent them for analytical purposes. I have had no real rest since then ; I would not harm him for anything."

In the house where he lived, a quantity of weed-killer was found, coloured in a similar manner to that found in the chocolates.

The analyst to the Home Office, who examined the chocolate éclairs sent to the Commissioner, found that they each contained arsenic, the amount estimated in one being $3\frac{1}{4}$ grains. The three whipped cream walnut chocolates which were addressed to the Assistant Commissioners also contained a considerable quantity of arsenic, the amount in one of them alone being six grains.

He also examined the two Bournville chocolates which had been drilled with holes and filled with arsenic. The quantity of arsenic in one of these was $\frac{1}{5}$ of a grain. In two Dairy Milk chocolates he examined, similar holes had been drilled, which had been filled up with the same kind of arsenic as that used in the weed-killer and was in the form of a greenish powder which was strongly alkaline.

The prisoner was committed for trial, was found to be insane, and ordered to be detained during the King's pleasure.

CHAPTER XXVII

POISONS IN FOOD

POISON IN BEER—POISON IN FOOD—POISON IN HONEY—POISON IN COCOA, CHOCOLATE, FRUIT AND SWEETS

In the latter part of the year 1900, a fairly widespread epidemic of peripheral neuritis of the extremities and its attendant symptoms was noted by medical men in certain districts of Manchester. In addition, many of the sufferers complained of swelling of the legs, weak circulation, vomiting and pigmentation of the skin. It was noticed by the medical officers of the various hospitals who examined these patients, that in every case they were heavy beer drinkers, and patronized public-houses supplied from certain breweries.

The mysterious epidemic spread and cases were reported from different parts of the north of England. In Manchester and Salford there were five hundred and twenty-two cases, in Liverpool seventy-one, fifty at Birkenhead and fifty at Stourbridge ; at Darlaston, Staffordshire, there were upwards of fifty cases, forty were reported from Chester, thirty-two in Birmingham and thirty in Leeds and district.

Many deaths ensued, and the whole train of symptoms and circumstances were such, that had they happened two or three hundred years ago, they would have created widespread consternation.

The beer was the clue, and scores of samples were purchased at public-houses miles apart, and the ingredients used in the manufacture of the beer in breweries spread over the North of England were carefully examined. Dr. Hitchin, the Medical Officer of Health for Heywood, Lancs, stated that two or three hundred persons were attacked, and he had discovered arsenic in stout as well as beer.

The result of the analysis was startling, as in the majority of the cases it led to the discovery of arsenic in the beer. This was first detected by Dr. Reynolds, of Manchester, and at his instance the public were warned against drinking cheap beer.

Meanwhile, research into the whole mystery went on. That large quantities of the beer were contaminated was certain, but how the poisonous substance got into it was the question which had to be determined.

A clue was found when certain experts who were engaged in investigating the materials used in the brewing of certain kinds of cheap beer, discovered that in every instance glucose had been used in the preparation, and on analysis of the glucose it was found to be impregnated with arsenious acid. This was followed by still further examination of the materials employed in making the glucose, and it was found that the sulphuric acid used for this purpose was brown in colour and contaminated with arsenic, showing that it had been made from iron pyrites containing arsenic as an impurity, and thus the ring of evidence was complete and successful.

The result opened up possibilities of even more widespread poisoning. Samples of jams and golden syrup were obtained for analysis, but all gave negative results when tested for arsenic. It appears that there are only about a dozen manufacturers of glucose in England, a great deal of it being imported from America. It was therefore concluded that the makers of the contaminated glucose must be some particular firm who sold their product to brewers only, and that within a certain area. Some samples of glucose that were subjected to test showed in one instance a proportion of arsenic that was absolutely deadly, and this was located to one firm. They instantly sent out telegrams to their customers stopping the use of this ingredient. Everything was done to prevent further mischief, and the output of the poison-impregnated material was stopped. Heroic measures were taken by one brewery, which placed an embargo on all beer in the cellars of their customers, until it was certified as pure by analysts deputed to visit them in turn. Some brews were recalled wholesale, and the loss to the firm amounted to several thousand pounds.

The manufacturers of the glucose had, of course, not the faintest idea that the mysterious poison which had caused so many deaths emanated from them. Although it was said that the sulphuric acid had been tested, curiously enough it was admitted it had never been tested for arsenic, and the explanation was put forward that the pyrites sent from a copper mine in Spain had been obtained from a new lode which was charged with an undue proportion of arsenic. After a full investigation had been made, special precautions were laid upon brewers to examine all ingredients used in making beer, and since then no recurrence of the trouble has occurred.

The epidemic caused almost a panic in and around Manchester, and several cases of ordinary illness were put down to arsenical poisoning. The hospital wards were filled, but the prompt measures taken had their effect. It was said by the Manchester coroner at one inquest, that the only pleasant feature of the epidemic was for the temperance people. " The consumption of fourpenny ale was not a fraction so great as it had been a fortnight previously. Arsenic had proved a temperance argument."

Within the last few years many cases of food-poisoning of one kind or another with fatal results have been reported. It is probable that in spite of every precaution such cases will occasionally occur. Some may have been due to the fact that bacteria were actually living in the food at the time it was consumed, or as probably in the case of the Loch Maree fatalities, it may have resulted from toxins left by bacteria which once lived in the food. The former type of food-poisoning which is most common in this country, results from the eating of food which has become contaminated by certain bacteria, whose presence may be due to disease in the animal before it has been slaughtered, or if they have gained access to the food in course of its preparation.

The heat used in cooking is generally sufficient to kill such organisms, and no doubt often does so. Again, it may be introduced from the outside, as in a recent case, when the medium of infection was found to be a contaminated knife used in cutting ham for sandwiches.

In cases of food-poisoning due to a toxin formed by organisms, these probably being dead, the organism concerned is what is known as *Bacillus botulinus*, so called from its having first been discovered in German sausages. The bacteria thrive, especially in a medium in the absence of oxygen, and so breed with rapidity in air-tight tins or inside sausage skins, and are to be found even in vegetable matter. They form a very powerful poison, acting upon the nerve centres in the brain, causing paralysis of the muscles which move the eye and eyelids and those concerned in speaking and swallowing. The resulting disease known as botulism has fortunately been rare in England, where there is not a very large consumption of tinned meat or vegetables, but it is frequently met with in America and Germany.

Botulism and food-poisoning, therefore, must not be confused, as the former is a poisoning by a specific toxin and the latter may be called an infection.

A curious case of poisoning was brought to light some years ago at an inquest held on a woman who had died with symptoms of poisoning after attending a wedding breakfast. The guests, after regaling themselves with wedding cake, had finished up with kippered herrings, and shortly afterward one of them was taken ill with severe pain and died.

During the inquest it was pointed out that it was possible that some of the ingredients used in curing the kippers, when brought into contact with almond paste on the wedding cake, would possibly liberate prussic acid. This was possible if the almond paste had been made with bitter almonds.

The poisonous effects produced by honey gathered in certain districts has been known for centuries, and the story of some of Xenophon's soldiers having been poisoned by this means more than two thousand years ago is well known. This poisonous property was formerly attributed to the bees having gathered the honey from the flowers of henbane and hemlock but it has now been proved that poisonous principles may be extracted by bees from other plants, according to the locality in which the honey is found. Thus, American honey has been found to contain poisonous ingredients derived from gelsemium or golden seal.

A serious case in which fourteen persons were poisoned after eating honey, one of whom died, is reported from Princetown, N.S. The honey was found to contain andromedotoxin, a poisonous principle obtained from certain ericaceous flowers.

Another mysterious case was reported in 1924, where two persons were seized with persistent vomiting, pain and diarrhœa after partaking of honey in their tea. An examination of the honey revealed the presence of arsenic in considerable quantity but the means by which it had got into the honey was never discovered.

There are other instances on record of honey which has been contaminated by bees through carrying poison from certain flowers, but cases in which poison has been introduced into honey for criminal purposes are rare.

Some years ago, a young man was arrested at Coire, in Switzerland on his own confession, of having murdered two young women to whom he had been engaged to be married, by introducing strychnine into the cells of some honeycomb which he presented to his victims. In each case the girls died in great agony on their wedding eve, after a visit from the man. One victim had been buried two years and the other some months, before suspicion was aroused and the bodies exhumed for examination, and the man was convicted of the crime.

Within recent years the contamination of food products with arsenic has again come into some prominence. Towards the end of November, 1922, the Public Analyst acting for the Reigate Town Council, reported on seven samples of cocoa that had been taken under "The Sale of Foods and Drugs Act," in one of which he found arsenic (arsenious oxide) to the extent of 1/75th grain to the pound of cocoa. It was obvious that such a report could not be allowed to remain unnoticed, as, according to the Royal Commission on Arsenical Poisoning, it is illegal for an article of food to contain 1/100th of a grain or more of arsenic per pound.

The matter was reported to the Minister of Health who

took a serious view of the matter, and it culminated in summonses being issued by the Surrey County Council against the vendor and the manufacturer, the charge being that the cocoa was " adulterated with arsenic (arsenious oxide) to the extent of 1/40th of a grain per pound."

The cocoa had been purchased at a shop in Richmond and was labelled " Pure Cocoa Essence. Guaranteed absolutely pure Cocoa." On analysis this sample was found to contain 1/40th of a grain per pound, but on inquiry from the manufacturers it appeared to be a mystery how the arsenic had got into the cocoa. The investigation was rendered more difficult when it was found that the actual sample purchased was a blend of seven different cocoas. However, samples of these were taken, and one was found to contain arsenic to the extent of 1/10th of a grain per pound.

On tracing back the source of contamination it appeared that an alkali such as potassium carbonate is mixed with cocoa to render it more soluble, and in this case the impurity was discovered in the potassium carbonate, which was found to contain a substantial quantity of arsenic. The manufacturers, on finding this out, sacrificed three hundred and fifty tons of cocoa and did everything they could in the interests of the public to stop the sale. The retail firm, directly they heard of the impurity, also withdrew sixty-five tons from their shops and twenty-five tons from their warehouses and had them destroyed.

Although potassium carbonate is not used in the making of chocolate, several cases have been reported of illness caused through eating sweets in this form.

About the same time a London lady was taken seriously ill after eating some marzipan sweets which she purchased at a Church bazaar. It appears she ate about half a dozen of them and became ill shortly afterwards, the symptoms pointing to arsenical poisoning.

In the early part of September, 1930, public interest was aroused by an outbreak of poisoning in certain districts in Cheshire and Staffordshire, after eating sweets contaminated with arsenic, the victims being chiefly children.

Attention was first directed to the matter by a doctor in the Norton district of Stoke-on-Trent, who had been called in to attend twelve children who had been taken ill after eating certain sweets.

From inquiries, it was found that all the sweets had been purchased at one shop. The particular sweets were cough-drops. The symptoms in every case were the same and came on from one to two hours after eating one or more of them. The suspected sweets were at once submitted to analysis with the result that large quantities of arsenic were found.

Almost at the same time, the Medical Officer of Health for

Congleton reported that he had had similar cases in his district. Here, thirteen children in a local school had been taken ill with internal pains and sickness, and the origin was traced to a penny-worth of cough-drops which a child had bought and distributed among twelve of her friends.

Samples of the sweets when analysed at the Ministry of Health were found to contain arsenic in the proportion of 150 grains to one pound of sweets.

The source of the sweets was traced to a small factory in Stoke-on-Trent and the police succeeded in recovering 49 bottles which had been distributed to various dealers in the district, including shops in Burslem, Tunstall, Hanley, Stoke, Fenton, Longton, Crewe, Leek and Congleton. By means of the tele-phone and car, the retailers were at once stopped from selling any more of these sweets.

The proprietor of the factory on being questioned, stated that the cough-drops contained white sugar, brown sugar and glucose, the flavouring consisting of paregoric, oils of peppermint, aniseed and cloves, horehound essence, and eucalyptus oil. The cough-drops made at the end of August had not been made by him, but had been manufactured by another sweet-boiler, and that this same man had brought to the works a bag of dusting powder which he had purchased a week previously.

On analysis this dusting powder proved to be *pure white arsenic*.

The origin of the dusting powder was next traced to a work-shop in Tunstall where, buried under a heap of rubbish under the staircase, the police found a large wooden box containing about half a hundredweight of a whitish powder which proved to be arsenious oxide.

The sugar-boiler used this powder believing it to be French chalk, the box having originally belonged to a man who had carried on business in Hanley as a manufacturer of iron enamels. He had left his stock and gone to America and thus the box had remained in the Tunstall works for three years.

Other sweets suspected included treacle toffee, honey and lemon drops and " humbugs," and on these being analysed a sample of treacle toffee was found to contain arsenic equivalent to one-fifth of a grain to the pound, while the " humbugs " were found to contain nine grains of arsenic to the pound. Seventy other bottles were then seized.

The manufacturer of the sweets and his son were found to have suffered severely from the effects of arsenic, no doubt due to eating food with hands contaminated during the making of the sweets.

In all, about forty children and adults suffered from the effects of eating the poisoned sweets.

" The extraordinary thing about the whole case," says Dr.

Wotherspoon the Medical Officer of Health for Stoke-on-Trent in his report, " is the fact that there have been no deaths ; possibly because the large quantities of arsenic caused vomiting and so were expelled from the system before further absorption had taken place.

" The quantities of arsenic varied in the several analyses carried out from 77 to 150 grains in every pound of sweets. Some of the sweets contained as much as two-thirds of a grain in each and there were about five sweets to an ounce which could be purchased for a halfpenny."

The enormous quantities of arsenic which had been used as dusting powder in the process of manufacture, were found to have permeated almost all the ingredients in the works, and arsenic was found in quite large quantities in treacle and several other substances.

The whole of the arsenic found was destroyed immediately.

Glass vessels, bottles and containers are generally supposed to be innocuous and entirely free from deleterious matter, but this idea was shattered by a case which came before the Birmingham magistrates on April 7th, 1923, when a firm was summoned for selling potassium carbonate containing eighty parts of lead per million and about ten parts of arsenic per million.

On investigation of the case it appeared that the potassium carbonate was pure when placed in the clean bottle, so that the presence of lead and arsenic could only be attributed to the glass.

The bottle was broken up and when tested revealed the presence of arsenic and lead in the glass, and from an experiment made, it was found that by placing potassium carbonate in a similar clean bottle at the end of a fortnight, less than five parts per million of arsenic had increased to fifteen parts per million which had been absorbed from the glass.

In these days when glass containers are so largely employed for holding preserved foods, this danger must not be overlooked, also the possible presence of minute particles of glass in the product.

Bubbles of air in the wall of a glass container, especially if close to the internal surface of the jar, may burst, causing flakes of glass to become detached and pass into the product when it is poured whilst hot.

The danger in careless packing and handling of arsenic imported to this country has recently been commented on by the Medical Officer of Health for the Port of London. He states in a report that " a ship from Oporto had aboard about fifty bags of shelled almonds. On the same deck were twenty-two cases of white arsenic.

" When examined by the inspector two of these cases of arsenic were standing on end with their heads open, and one was leaking at its bilge on to the deck.

" Two of the bags of almonds which had become displaced showed arsenic on their surfaces. Minute quantities of arsenic were found on almonds taken from one of the bags."

In another case, a ship had landed 160 cases of arsenic at the King George V Dock.

" The cases containing the arsenic were composed of old, dry wood, and from some of them the poison was leaking on to the floor of the shed. The possibility that some of it might find its way into any food handled in the same shed cannot be overlooked."

That such carelessness might lead to very serious consequences is obvious.

Thus the danger of the presence of arsenic in food and drink is a very real one and there have been many instances of this in recent years. The minute amount necessary to destroy life, even its accidental presence calls for the most careful investigation. A person might even be suspected of causing the death of another by means of arsenic and yet be innocent.

At an inquest held on the body of a woman at Llanelly on August 30th, 1928, Sir William Willcox who was called to give evidence said, that although one seventy-fourth of a grain of arsenic was found in the body it might possibly arise from natural food-stuffs.

Towards the end of 1925 public interest and some alarm was aroused by the discovery of the presence of arsenic on certain apples imported to this country from the United States.

The matter was brought to light when in November several fruiterers in the Hampstead district were summoned for selling " Jonathan " and " Newtown " American apples which contained arsenic varying from one thirtieth to one thirty-fifth of a grain. In one instance where a specific case of illness followed the eating of apples, five samples of imported " Jonathans " were found to contain one-hundredth of a grain of arsenic to the pound.

It was stated by the analyst, that although he subjected the apples to washing he could not get rid of the arsenic. One-thirtieth of a grain per pound he considered to be absolutely dangerous.

The presence of the arsenic was found to be due to a lead arsenate solution sprayed on the trees three times a year to combat an insect pest known as the Codlin moth, a pest unknown in this country. The spray forms a deposit on the apples and the leaves, which after a time becomes soluble.

From experiments made at the instance of the Ministry of Health, with a view to showing whether the arsenic got into the body of the fruit, it was stated that the trouble was due to exceptionally dry weather on the west coast of America where there had been insufficient rain to wash off all the spray. Dr.

Caldwell found arsenic in some cases had penetrated to the core, and he noted how the arsenic in the apple acted as a preservative, and the extraordinary freshness of the cut surface of an apple after the lapse of some time in arsenic-preserved apples.

Washing removed the visible traces of arsenic from the skin but it did not remove it from the inside of the fruit, consequently neither peeling nor washing was sufficient to eliminate the arsenic in the fruit.

The general alarm caused the National Federation of Fruit and Potato Trades Association to issue a notice urging all retailers to brush and wash all foreign apples before selling them.

Since that time nothing further has been heard on the subject and no doubt the growers have taken steps to prevent a recurrence of the danger.

CHAPTER XXVIII

CRIMINAL POISONING WITH BACTERIA

THE REMARKABLE CASE OF O'BRIEN DE LACY AND PANCHENKO

THE exploitation of pathogenic bacteria for criminal purposes has not been neglected by the poisoner, but owing to ignorance on the one hand, and the difficulty of obtaining the material on the other, it has led to failure even when used under the most cunning circumstances. The person with sufficient scientific knowledge to prepare cultures is not as a rule one with criminal instincts, and the clumsy handling of such deadly material would lead to certain detection if used by one who did not understand it.

One of the most remarkable cases of its kind on record occurred in Petrograd in 1911, when a man named Patrick O'Brien de Lacy, who claimed to have been a lineal descendant of the Irish kings, was accused of having procured the death of his brother-in-law an official in the Ministry of the Interior, his father-in-law General Buturlin, and his mother-in-law, in order to inherit a large amount of money of which rumour said they were possessed.

From his youth upwards, O'Brien de Lacy is said to have been a ne'er-do-well. Having left a Russian school without finishing his education, he frequented the London Polytechnic, and also studied naval architecture, but all the plans he founded upon his technical knowledge were nullified by the defeat of the Russian navy at Tsushima and other events. He first married a lady of excellent family, who, being herself married, agreed to divorce her husband in order to espouse him. He then entangled her in all his own financial difficulties, spent her money, and obtained power of attorney to transact her business. Finally, making the acquaintance of a Mdlle Buturlin, he divorced his first wife as she divorced her first husband. Then he sought out a doctor and conspired with him to poison the lady before pledging his troth to her at the altar. After his second marriage, O'Brien is said to have laid his plans with extraordinary cunning in order to remove every human obstacle that stood between him and his father-in-law's wealth. He endeavoured to carry these out by inoculating them with the germs of deadly diseases which included cholera and diphtheria. He arranged his scheme even to the smallest detail, and if there is such a thing as a genius in crime, this most extraordinary man was typical of it.

Having to employ a medical man to carry out his designs, like Romeo, he selected a needy practitioner, one Dr. Panchenko, before whose eyes he dangled a dazzling reward. Money was the magnet to attract Panchenko, and O'Brien de Lacy offered him, it is said, 10,000 roubles to compass the death of his brother-in-law, 50,000 roubles to dispose of his father-in-law, and 500,000 roubles if he put a speedy end to his mother-in-law, who was the richest of the family.

In 1910, the younger Buturlin died at Petrograd after a week's illness. He was an employee of the Ministry of the Interior, and symptoms during his illness or signs after death suggested foul play. Old General Buturlin, who arrived from Vilna before the funeral, stopped the interment of his son's body and demanded a post-mortem.

His widow endorsed this demand, both surmising neglect on the part of the physician, but on investigation it was concluded that blood-poisoning was the cause of death.

By a curious coincidence, on the same day, a man named Bobroff called on the Chief of the Secret Police. He told him he was a book-keeper and that a comrade of his named Petropavlovski, possessed proofs that young Buturlin's death was caused by Dr. Panchenko, who also had designs on the life of the General with a view to inheriting property. Petropavlovski's story is a very curious one and may be given in his own words :

" A conscience is the only possession I can call my own, and it has driven me here to denounce my unique benefactress. She is my landlady, Madame Muraviova, who allows me a room in her flat, and has been very kind to me. She is the mistress of Dr. Panchenko, with whom she has been hugger-muggering of late in suspicious ways. The door and walls being thin, I have heard snatches of conversation, which I have pieced together, and I find they point to Dr. Panchenko as the instrument of young Buturlin's death and O'Brien de Lacy as the employer of that instrument. The penniless Dr. Panchenko often journeyed to Vilna, where O'Brien de Lacy resides, and always returned with a fat purse and high hopes. Madame Muraviova, too, babbled about her improving prospects, saying she was shortly coming into 300,000 roubles.

" One day in April, Dr. Panchenko left for Kronstadt, where plague-stricken dogs are studied, and after his return he talked of little else. Soon afterwards young Buturlin, Panchenko, and O'Brien de Lacy went on the spree together. The next thing I noticed was that Panchenko was weeping and sobbing. I entered the common sitting-room, and found him beside himself with excitement while his paramour was burning heaps of papers. She spoke first, saying that she had been scolding him for visiting a diphtheria patient without disinfecting himself. In an aside to Dr. Panchenko she asked : ' Did you do it properly ? ' He answered : ' Well, I squirted two full doses, although one would have been enough.' "

After this revelation, Dr. Panchenko was interrogated by the police, and he stated that he treated the deceased for loss of energy and injected a certain remedy, but knew nothing of the cause of death. He had made O'Brien de Lacy's acquaintance in the train, and subsequently had business dealings with him. De Lacy was then asked for an explanation by the police, and he stated that his relations with the doctor were purely commercial, and affirmed that he could not possibly benefit by young Buturlin's death. The police, however, attached so much importance to the story of the informer that they arrested Panchenko and O'Brien de Lacy.

It was while in prison awaiting trial that Panchenko broke down and revealed the full story in the following words :

" Patients were brought to me occasionally by a friend named Raffoff, who acted as a tout, receiving a share of the profits. One day he introduced me to O'Brien de Lacy. We adjourned to a private room in a restaurant, where, in Raffoff's presence, he asked me if I would perform a certain illegal operation for 1,700 roubles. I assented. O'Brien de Lacy seemed pleased, and gave me 100 roubles. I asked him to visit me in my own study. I was a physician of the Petrograd district of the Northern Railway.

" Subsequently O'Brien intimated that he would prefer to talk with me without a witness. I acquiesced. He told me he had just become a bridegroom, and the operation he really wanted was to have his future brother-in-law made away with. For this service he would pay 10,000 roubles. After that it would be necessary to remove the father-in-law. For that riddance I would be paid 50,000 roubles, and lastly, the old man's divorced wife must be launched into eternity. For this job he would not grudge 500,000 roubles. He impressed upon me the necessity of extreme circumspection, and advised me to begin with young Buturlin, to whom he proposed I should administer cholera germs on bread, buttered and covered with caviare. Death by cholera, he explained, would evoke no surprise at a moment when that epidemic was making havoc in Petrograd. Therefore he had much to say in favour of cholera germs, and informed me that young Buturlin was using anti-cholera subcutaneous injections.

" By this time I had extracted 2,000 roubles from O'Brien de Lacy. At last he introduced me to Buturlin, on the ground that we were interested in founding a sanatorium, but I was to whet his curiosity about a certain drug and get him as a patient. Then, instead of the drug, I was to inject some poison or other, and having done the job, to abstain sedulously from writing or telegraphing, as a kinsman of his, Count Roniker, who had been charged with murder in Warsaw, had been tripped up by a telegram. The plan was successful ; I treated young Buturlin, substituting diphtheria toxin for the other drug.

" I received the germs from a chemist, who believed my story that it was required for experiments on rabbits. I injected two large doses into the victim's thigh. Later, I learned he was very ill, and, being conscience smitten, I wired for O'Brien de Lacy, who was furious that the telegram should have been sent. He exclaimed : ' You may as well give yourself up now.' I visited young Buturlin after this, and learned from his own lips that he had had high fever and sharp pains, but was now much better. The other physician who was called in did not diagnose the malady. Then I read of Buturlin's death in the papers. It occurred exactly as had been calculated, seven days after the injection. When I read that the day of the burial would be announced later, I knew it boded evil.

" Meanwhile, General Buturlin arrived and demanded a post-mortem. O'Brien de Lacy supported the demand, convinced that the examination would be fruitless. I, too, was of the same opinion, because throats are never analysed during such investigations, and few symptoms of diphtheria infection would be visible in the throat."

Such was Panchenko's story, to which he added that Muraviova was innocent, having had no inkling of his crime. Muraviova herself asseverated her innocence, affirming that her relations with Panchenko were pure. She accepted material help from him, but deprecated the luxury in which he maintained her. He, however, assured her that he would soon inherit a large sum.

The trial of the prisoners began in Petrograd at the end of January, 1911, and excited intense public interest. Bobroff, the book-keeper, who gave away the secret to the Chief of Police, was first examined and adhered to his original story. A servant of the Buturlins related how Dr. Panchenko visited Buturlin for the first time, saying : " Let's get the treatment over before your wife returns." After that he came twice daily until the fourth day, when the patient fell ill. When his condition grew serious, Buturlin sent for the doctor, but Panchenko was not to be found. A chance physician had to be summoned, but produced no improvement. Nose-bleeding, vomiting, and sharp pains ushered in the agony, during which the dying man said : " Three months long they were at me to have the injections, but I refused as though I had a presentiment of what was coming."

The Court asked the experts to answer the question : " What caused Buturlin's death ? " and asked them to bear in mind Panchenko's admission that he had injected diphtheria toxin. He then made the following statement :

" On May 16th I visited Buturlin, and injected a pure drug from a phial. I repeated the injection on the following day. Before my evening visit to Buturlin on the same day, I broke the necks of the two drug-phials in my own lodging that nobody should notice it. Having emptied the contents, I filled the phials with diphtheria poison by means of a paper funnel, plugged them with wadding, and, putting them into my waist-coat-pocket, set out for Buturlin's. Before starting I gulped down vodka for courage.

" I got to Buturlin's about eight or nine in the evening, with trembling in my legs and throbbing waves of darkness filling my eyes and fitfully blotting out my sight. I had been wont to break off the necks of the phials in Buturlin's presence, first putting them in a handkerchief to avoid cutting my fingers. That is why he could not notice that this time the necks were already snapped off. I made two incisions in Buturlin's body, injecting each time the contents of one phial of the diphtheria poison. Each vessel held about two cubic centimetres, but as the effects of the diphtheria poison had not been tested on human beings, I injected two phials full in order to be quite sure of a deadly issue. As soon as I had finished the business my face was ghastly, and I quivered in every limb. I was in dread that Buturlin might discern my state. Pulling myself together, and mastering my failing voice, I asked him whether it hurt. He answered, ' Not at all.' I then left for home, and threw the phials into the street. The livelong night I could not close an eye. Conscience-ache racked me ruthlessly."

Panchenko's extraordinary career, as revealed at the trial, shows him to be one of the most diabolical characters ever connected with the practice of medicine.

He was sent by the Red Cross Society to Harbin during the Russo-Japanese War and was dismissed for irregularities, after which he introduced himself to the then Premier as a schoolmate of the Premier's brother, and received an appointment as physician to a railway company.

One witness recounted how a certain banker resolved to poison his own uncle, and had recourse to Panchenko, who initiated his friend Dreyden into the scheme. The latter used the information as a lever to extort blackmail, but the police, being hand in glove with the banker, sent Dreyden away.

Panchenko next edited a periodical entitled *Life's Mysteries*, which was suppressed. Despatched to Paris for the purpose of advertising a certain drug, Panchenko met a Russian officer bound for Abyssinia who asked him for a potent poison for suicidal purposes in case he should be taken prisoner. For forty francs Panchenko furnished him with prussic acid, and the officer swallowed it and died. Panchenko declared that what he supplied was not poison, but only magnesia, and that in any case he had confessed since to a Russian priest in Paris, who comforted him by saying: " The officer would have committed suicide anyhow, my son."

At the trial, another witness stated that Panchenko propounded a plan for coming into a heritage of two million roubles by " removing " two persons who stood in the way.

Circumstantial evidence was next offered by experts in the culture of various toxins. Dr. Heinrich, assistant director of the laboratory of plague cultures, spoke of Dr. Panchenko visiting the laboratories, requesting cholera endotoxin, and excusing himself from the obligation of writing his name in the visitors' book on the ground of haste. Dr. Panchenko received two tubes of endotoxin. One had a label that a dose is mortal for certain animals. Some months later Dr. Panchenko revisited the laboratory, and asked for more cholera endotoxin. Dr. Heinrich gave it, but warned him of its deadly effects.

Dr. Panchenko informed the Court that he gave this liquid to O'Brien de Lacy for twenty-five roubles.

Professor Zabolotny explained the nature of the effects of various cultures, and deposed that he gave diphtheria toxin to Dr. Panchenko, whose object was stated to be the study of its action on the nervous system.

A professor, named Zdrjekoffski, of the Institute of Experimental Medicine, deposed that Dr. Panchenko had asked him for diphtheria toxin.

" I gave him, I forget whether one or two phials of diphtheria toxin, each containing thirty or forty cubic centimetres. I explained to Dr. Panchenko the action of this toxin and the minimum dose tht would cause death."

A criminal called Logatcheff, with whom Panchenko had shared a cell, and who was escorted to court by two soldiers, deposed that Panchenko had repeated to him in gaol the whole story of how he had poisoned Captain Buturlin. He said De Lacy had offered him 550,000 roubles to poison Captain Buturlin and his father, General Buturlin, and mother, and told him he went to Kronstadt, to the Zabolotny Institute of Experimental Medicine to obtain toxins. Panchenko had described experiments which he had made on a guinea-pig at an hotel, adding that he afterwards threw the body into the street.

De Lacy, while denying that he married for money, stated : " It is true that at one time I was afraid that the General would dispose of his fortune in his will in such a manner that my wife would receive only a fourteenth part. I certainly thought this unjust, but I reasoned as follows : the General is sure to live for a long time, and three years will suffice for me to induce him to enter into all my undertakings, including that of the steamboats.   Then his whole capital will be at my disposal."

Continuing, he said that he was not aware of the total amount, but he knew that a sum of £300,000 was deposited in foreign banks.

At the end of this remarkable case, after a trial which lasted nearly three weeks, O'Brien de Lacy and Dr. Panchenko were found guilty, the latter with extenuating circumstances.   The woman Muraviova was acquitted.   De Lacy was sentenced to penal servitude for life and Panchenko to fifteen years' penal servitude.

Another case of attempted murder with pathogenic organisms occurred about ten years ago, when a Hungarian artist was tried for attempting to murder his wife by means of typhoid and cholera germs.   The cholera medium in his possession was found to have lost all activity through having been kept too long, while the typhoid culture, though quite a virulent one, failed to kill the victim.   The discovery of the crime was made through his attempts to obtain cultures from a private laboratory and demanding virulent strains.   So far, cases of this kind have been extremely rare, and the risk of failure is so great that criminals so inclined are likely to think twice before venturing to attempt life by this diabolical method.

CHAPTER XXIX

POISON HABITS

THERE is a peculiar property attached to certain poisons, especially those possessing narcotic properties—which renders them capable of forming the most enslaving habits known to mankind. Thousands of people to-day are enchained in the slavery of the poison habit in one form or another, and very few are ever successful in wresting themselves free, when once it has been contracted. The habit is often formed in a most insidious manner. It is usually begun by taking some narcotic drug to relieve pain or induce sleep. In a short time the original dose fails to produce the desired effect; it has to be increased, and afterwards still further increased, until the victim finds he cannot do without it, and an intense craving for the drug is thus created. After a while, the stupefying action affects the brain; the moral character is sapped, and the unfortunate being is at last ready to do anything to obtain a supply of the drug that is now his master.

This is not an overdrawn picture, but one of which instances are constantly to be met with. The enslaving habit of alcohol, when once contracted, is too well known to need description. Opium probably comes next in the point of influence it exerts over its victims, and only a very small percentage ever free themselves from the habit when it is once contracted. In most instances, as stated, it is taken in the first place to relieve severe pain, as evidenced in De Quincey's case. He says, in his *Confessions of an Opium-Eater*: "It was not for the purpose of creating pleasure, but of mitigating pain in the severest degree, that I first began to use opium as an article of daily diet." Like others, he was compelled to increase the dose gradually, until at last he consumed the enormous quantity of 320 grains of the drug a day. He graphically describes the struggle he first had to reduce the daily dose, and found that to a certain point it could be reduced with ease, but after that point, further reduction caused intense suffering. However, a crisis arrived, and he writes: "I saw that I must die if I continued the opium. I determined, therefore, if that should be required, to die in throwing it off. I apprehend at this time I was taking from 50 or 60 grains to 150 grains a day. My first task was to reduce it to 40, to 30, and as fast as I could to 12 grains. I triumphed; but think not my sufferings were ended. Think of me, as one, even when four months had passed, still agitated, writhing, throbbing, palpitating, shattered ; and much perhaps in the situation of him who has been racked."

Other cases are commonly met with in this country, where opium-eaters take on an average from 60 to 80 grains of the drug a day. The smallest quantity which has proved fatal in the adult is 4½ grains ; in other cases much larger quantities have been taken with impunity. Guy states that recovery once took place, after no less than eight ounces of solid opium had been swallowed.

Morphine, the chief alkaloid of opium, is also abused by many, and is swallowed as well as used by hypodermic injection. Its action is very similar to that of opium. It has been recently stated on good authority, that in Chicago—that city of hurrying men and restless women—over thirty-five thousand persons habitually take subcutaneous injections of morphine to save themselves from the pains and terrors of neuralgia, insomnia, and nervousness. Dr. Van Dyke has recently stated that " no country suffers more from the narcotic drug evil than the United States. It is estimated that there are more than 1,500,000 addicts, many of them boys and girls."

To a delicate woman one grain of this drug has proved fatal, yet, under the influence of habit, a young woman has been known to take from 15 to 20 grains daily. A man in a good position, and head of a large commercial house, contracted the habit of taking morphine from a prescription that had been given to him containing four grains of the drug. As the habit grew, he would have the medicine prepared by four different chemists daily, and swallow the contents of each bottle for a dose, until he took on an average over 24 grains a day. This being prevented by his friends, he commenced to take chloroform, which he would purchase in small quantities until he had collected a bottleful. He drank it, usually mixed with whisky. He eventually had to be placed under restraint.

A remarkable account of the sensations experienced when under the influence of morphine, was recently recorded by a New York doctor who, after taking six grains of the drug, seated himself at his desk and wrote notes of his sensations as death approached.

" This morphine," he wrote, " has put me in a condition of absolute mental painlessness. It is now 7.17 p.m. and if I did not know that I had taken sufficient poison to warrant results, I could not notice it from my condition.

" Aside from fluttering heart action and contracted eye-pupils, and moderate drowsiness, I feel no results.

" Still, I cannot make up my mind to swallow the cyanide. and have lit a cigar, awaiting further increase of drowsiness, and hope to be soon able to coax myself into the inevitable.

" 7.42 p.m.—I am here yet, hesitating to take this cyanide. My thoughts become blurred from the morphine, and a sensation of supreme quietude reigns in me. If it was not for my beloved wife, who has just 'phoned, I would go on waiting, but I am afraid of too long a delay because a lapsing into unconsciousness might result in my being saved by medical assistance. Ten more minutes, and then the end by cyanide.

" I am in no manner kept in suspense—just pleasantly and curiously watching developments. Queerly enough, my only wish is that I had an additional handkerchief, so that I could dispose of the surplus perspiration, it being close and my skin clammy from the morphine effects."

Since 1913, when it was first introduced, heroin (diacetyl-morphine) has been frequently used as a substitute for morphine but it has been proved to have no advantages medicinally over morphine or codeine. At first it was easily obtained and actually exported to the East as a cure for opium smoking, but now in common with other dangerous drugs its sale has been properly restricted.

Chloroform when swallowed is very similar in its effects to alcohol, from which it is in fact prepared. It first excites and then causes a condition of stupefaction, and although it does not injure the stomach tissues and the liver to the same extent as alcohol, the taking of it almost invariably ends in death. Some of its victims drink the liquid diluted, and others inhale it.

A case of a well-educated man is recorded who acquired the habit of drinking chloroform. It was known to his friends, and he did not deny it, but no one saw him take it, until it was eventually discovered that he first secretly added it to his whisky bottle, then diluted this mixture with a small quantity of water and swallowed it at a draught. Its property seemed to accentuate the intoxicating power of the alcohol. Every effort was made to break him of the habit, without avail, and he eventually poisoned himself.

Another case of chloroform-drinking occurred in the East End of London. The victim was a young chemist's assistant, who had been in the habit of taking the drug since he was four-teen years of age. According to his own admission, he did not at first take it to alleviate pain, but began it as an experiment before he had been in his first situation a month. He got beyond the control of his parents, who notified the chemists in the district, and when unable to obtain it there, he called on various medical men and endeavoured to obtain chloroform by false pretences. He was able to swallow considerable quantities, and it was stated that he took enough in an hour to kill six people.

One who was addicted to this terrible habit, states that he began by " inhaling a small quantity, which was followed by a perfectly delicious state of semi-unconsciousness in which one lost sight of all discomfort and all things external. But this state was very transient and passed rapidly. The quantity had to be increased and increased until existence became a perfect misery. The whole moral fibre and character was swiftly ruined. Nausea was constant, dyspepsia and kindred troubles followed ; and the victim became haggard and thin. For the two hours of semi-unconsciousness induced in this way, twenty-two hours were spent in unimaginable misery."

The quantity of chloroform used by those accustomed to it in this way is said to be astonishing. One victim, a woman, is known to have bought sixteen ounces a day, and inhaled it from a blanket. Persons have recovered after swallowing from two to six ounces, although much smaller doses have proved fatal.

Sudden insensibility from inhaling chloroform is impossible and much nonsense has been written concerning the " chloroformed handkerchief " and its immediate effect. False charges have also been made owing to this misconception.

If a person is asleep, the application of the vapour might intensify it, but when swallowed it produces a species of intoxication.

Some years ago the habit of taking ether became common, especially in Ireland, Scotland and the eastern parts of England. Its action is similar to chloroform, but it is slower in its effect. It first produces exhilaration, and, as with chloroform, when swallowed mixed with whisky, produces intense excitement, amounting almost to mania. The habit, when formed, is even more terrible than chloroform, and the victim has to resort to several doses a day.

Some years ago, in the North of Ireland, it was stated on good authority, that the population of one large district were almost entirely ether drunkards. Its consumption has now greatly diminished, probably owing to the increase in price which occurred at the time of the war, which would put it out of the reach of many of its victims.

Chlorodyne, which formerly contained both morphine and prussic acid in its composition, is also much abused, especially by women. Some women have been known to consume as much as two ounces a week of this preparation.

During the past few years the increase in the taking of cocaine has probably surpassed all other poison habits. Cocaine is an important alkaloid, prepared from the dried leaves of the *Erythroxylon Coca* and other varieties of the coca plant that grow in the northern parts of Peru and Bolivia. For a considerable period before the active principle was discovered, the leaves of the plant were much used by natives of these countries and travellers, who chewed them on account of their stimulating effect. It was not until 1860 that the active principle cocaine was discovered by Niemann.

Its chief use in medicine is as a local anæsthetic, especially for the eye. The discovery of this valuable property was due to Eckstein, who, in 1870, pointed out that the most delicate operations could be performed painlessly on the eye after its injection.

The effect of cocaine taken by inhalation, injection or by the mouth unfortunately became too well known. At one time it was largely used as an ingredient in the preparations used like snuff, commonly recommended and sold for influenza colds. The habit, once induced, led to the use of stronger preparations, until the victim found he had become enchained by a habit that enslaved him to such an extent it seemed impossible to break it. More subtle than other poisons, cocaine appears to sap completely the moral strength of its victims. Slowly and surely it deadens the sensibilities until death is sought as a relief in the end.

During the past few years, and since the beginning of the war, the consumption of cocaine in one form or another has enormously increased in both the Eastern and Western hemispheres. Recent cases that have been brought to light in the police courts, show only too plainly the terrible condition to which the victims of this habit are reduced. The cocaine habit may be compared to a human being gradually enclosed in the coils of a serpent, that slowly winds itself round the body with increasing pressure, to the terror of its victim, until it reaches a vital part, which ends in death.

Rarely is there any permanent breaking of the coil when once it starts. In most cases the simple inhalation is the beginning, and in the case of this poison, it is not used as much to relieve pain, as for the passing pleasurable sensation that is produced. From inhalation, the victim of the habit, finding the effects weaken, passes to the hypodermic injection, which is more rapid and more powerful in its action. As the coils of the serpent tighten, all moral sense and character seem gradually blotted out, and the whole individual physiologically is altered.

Fatalities have resulted from inhaling cocaine through the nose as well as by injecting it under the skin, and when it is stated that three-quarters of a grain has been known to cause death it can readily be imagined how easily a lethal dose can be taken.

The subtlety of the habit lies in its very simplicity. Exhilaration follows much more rapidly than after alcohol and is followed just as speedily by the deepest depression.

As a drug, cocaine was found to powerfully excite the central nervous system, inducing a feeling of energy and restlessness. It fascinates by the rapidity with which it relieves exhaustion and dispels depression.

Tolerance can be acquired, as in the case of morphine, and there are cases on record in which 100 grains were taken daily, but as a habit, its evil influences are worse than morphine and its demoralising effects more serious.

Nearly all the cocaine sold in London is smuggled into this country either by Chinese or foreigners, and it is stated that before it gets into the hands of the actual victim, quite a number of persons have made substantial profits out of it. In most cases it has been traced to Limehouse and the region of the London Docks or other seaports, where Continental steamers land, on the East Coast, and latterly to some of the big seaports like Cardiff and Newcastle.

These narcotics are rarely alluded to by those who traffic in them by their proper names. As is well known, cocaine is generally alluded to as " snow " or " C " ; heroin as " H " ; and opium is designated " Chandoo " or " Pop."

A great amount of smuggling and illicit traffic in the drug is also carried on in the underworld of Paris and New York, and though the drug is costly, a ready market is found for it. This traffic has been found rife in certain clubs of a low class, conducted by unscrupulous people whose precautions as to secrecy have been ingeniously conceived. The greatest cunning has been exercised in bringing it to England from the Continent. A hollow cane containing a glass phial, which, when concealed by a screwed silver top looked like an ordinary walking-stick, was one method discovered some time ago. Another and still more artful device was discovered by the Custom-House authorities on the landing of a passenger at an East Coast port. As his appearance aroused suspicion a search was made, and he was found to be wearing a *truss*, the bulb end of which was hollow and filled with cocaine.

In another case, where a man was arrested in the West End and charged with being in possession of nearly five ounces of cocaine, it was found that he had brought the drug from Germany, and concealed it in cavities he had skilfully cut out in the heels of his shoes, which he had afterwards covered with leather.

During the War, which increased the nervous tension of the individual to a hitherto unknown degree, thousands of Canadian and American troops passed through London on their way to and from the fighting fronts, and many of the men provided potential victims for the trafficker in poisons. Many of these men who fell into bad hands were drugged with opium in the form of cigarettes and then robbed.

In proof of this statement, on July 19th, 1916, seven men were charged at Marlborough Street Police Court with being concerned in selling cocaine to soldiers. The prosecuting solicitor for the Commissioner of Police said that the evil had grown to such dimensions in London that it was necessary for steps to be taken to check it. "The use of cocaine in this country had increased enormously, and the habit appeared to have been brought here with soldiers from across the seas. Since the War began it had been sold in the streets in small boxes each containing a grain ; it was offered to soldiers in particular, who were told to use it like ordinary snuff on account of its exhilarating effect. The habit grew and grew till it produced symptoms of intoxication, the moral and physical senses were clouded, and insanity and death resulted. The number of persons engaged in this abominable traffic was very large." The case having been proved against the men by several members of the Military Police, they were sentenced to various terms of imprisonment.

The efforts of the police to stop the traffic revealed the existence of what is practically an organization for the sale of the drug. The chief agents are men, mostly of foreign nationality and the worst possible type. They sell it, often adulterated with boric acid in small quantities, at enormous profit. Women sell it to other women, one acting as a carrier, being in the possession of a number of boxes of the drug, and the other undertaking actually to sell it in single boxes. The price of cocaine sold illegally in the West End of London a few years ago was at the rate of £10 an ounce, and as it became more difficult to get, owing to the restrictions, the price increased. A bottle containing two and a half ounces was said to have been sold for £100.

In the autumn of 1922 there arrived at Hong-Kong a Japanese steamer, which was boarded by Revenue officers. A passenger who was a Japanese subject was arrested, and a quantity of his belongings, which included four cases of furniture, were seized. On examining the furniture, consisting of two sofas and four arm-chairs, which were cut open, there was found hidden in the upholstery 2,400 ounces of morphine and 2,500 ounces of cocaine. The quantity of morphine concealed in the furniture would provide 2,100,000 maximum doses, according to the *British Pharmacopœia*, and the quantity of cocaine was equal to 4,375,000 doses.

The Commission of the Treasury of the United States in 1921 estimated that the country contained at least one million addicts to the drug and no laws appear to have put a stop to its use.

Like other prohibited articles, everything can be obtained if the price offered is high enough and appropriate to the risk, with the result, that smuggling is rampant on the Pacific and Atlantic coasts from Canada to Mexico. But drastic laws may duly increase the vice they aim at arresting. Distribution is organized by underground channels by means of the dope pedlars. It is stated that the difficulty in getting alcohol in the

United States leads people to try any substance which may have a stimulating effect.

There is little doubt that the cause of the great increase in addicts to drugs during the last few years has been the nervous sensibility which appears to be a product of civilization, wealth, luxury and probably the excessive indulgence in the satisfaction of desires in fast living.

It is such people, usually termed neurotics, who form the class peculiarly prone to succumb to habit forming narcotics. Weary of the strain and anxiety involved in the fight for existence, anything that gives them any relief from their cares and worries is seized with avidity.

This type of drug addict is a product of modern civilization all over the world and is in reality a symptom of a diseased mind. But independent of this class we have those who take drugs for their effects. Some young women conceive the idea that drug-taking renders them more mysterious and fascinating ; indeed, vanity plays a considerable part with many at the beginning, and human curiosity impels the victim to go on. The beginner cannot conceive the after-effect. The entire moral character appears to be sapped and rendered inert, the victims sink down unknown to themselves to the lowest depths of depravity and degradation, all restraint is lost, and they become a prey to those who may use them for any evil purpose at will.

Confirmed drug-takers cannot be cured by persuasion, argument or attempted coercion. They will have the drug or they will die, and the only way of dealing with them and preventing the drug habit, is to prevent its importation into the country.

Insomnia is a frequent cause of the formation of a poison habit, and for this purpose chloral hydrate is capable of producing more serious results than any other drug of its class. The fact that it accumulates in the system, and that the dose needs constantly to be increased, always renders its use dangerous in unskilled hands. Many gifted men have fallen victims to the habit, among others Dante Rossetti, who seldom was without a bottle of the narcotic near him. Latterly, sulphonal, veronal, and other drugs derived from coal tar possessing hypnotic properties, have been largely used, while antipyrine, a popular remedy for headache, is also capable of forming a pernicious and dangerous habit. The practice of self-dosing with drugs of this description cannot be too strongly deprecated. In all cases they should only be taken when prescribed by a medical man.

In Egypt where the consumption of hashish so readily procured from India is very large, the traffic in morphine, cocaine and other narcotic drugs has alarmingly increased.

In 1927, no less than 700 soldiers under 40 officers were employed in rounding-up gangs in Cairo alone, which led to 500 arrests and the seizure of large quantities of drugs.

A large quantity of hashish was found in the house of a police official and a quarantine employee was caught carrying cocaine from Alexandria to Cairo, where several persons openly engaged in the traffic are stated to have amassed fortunes.

In Great Britain, an effort to control the sale of poisonous products which includes many drugs such as veronal, barbatone and others synthetically manufactured, was made in 1920 by the " Dangerous Drugs Act," which prohibits their sale, except on the prescription of a qualified medical practitioner, which may not be repeated without a fresh order from him. The Act also renders the possession of such drugs without a licence an offence, even to medical men and dentists, and limits their supply, but there is considerable doubt if it has been effective in lessening the traffic. Smuggling, by the most artful methods is still practised throughout the continent of Europe.

The League of Nations has also endeavoured to stop the traffic by endeavouring to control the manufacture of dangerous drugs, but so far it has been unable to obtain the support of all the nations signatory to the League. Many of the civilized Powers have however, undertaken to control the manufacture and distribution of opium, cocaine, heroin and morphine in conformity with the International Convention.

The issue of a report for the year 1929 by the British Government shows how far the Dangerous Drugs Act of 1920-25 has brought the illicit traffic under control. Three-fourths of the raw opium imported for medicinal purposes to this country comes from India, and only about one fourth from Turkey. Prepared opium for smoking is absolutely prohibited in Great Britain and all quantities seized are destroyed.

Cocaine was manufactured for the first time in this country in 1928, and in 1929, 9,326 ounces were so manufactured against 4,934 ounces the previous year, but the imports of the alkaloid showed a corresponding decline.

There is still a widespread and dangerous illicit traffic in opium, morphine, heroin and cocaine, and no machinery which can be contrived to grapple with this complex problem will be effective until the nations which have solemnly pledged themselves to effectuate treaties, enact and enforce the legislature which such treaties imply.

At the 59th Council of the League of Nations held in May, 1930, the British representative cited the case of a steamer that had recently left a port of a certain producing country, carrying 2,000 cases of opium entirely destined for illicit traffic. The Council endorsed the desire that steps should at last be taken to limit the production of dangerous drugs to medical and legitimate requirements.

CHAPTER XXX

POISONS USED IN WARFARE

THE use of poison as a weapon in warfare is by no means a modern practice. It may be traced back to the use of poisoned arrows and spears, and from the time of the discovery of gunpowder, when surgeons believed that a bullet formed a septic wound.

François Bernier, who served in the capacity of physician to Aurungzebe, the Grand Mogul, and died in Paris in 1688, in describing a battle fought at Agra against the Mogul, states that the Rajputa, a hereditary race of warriors, were great opium-eaters and consumed it in large quantities, and when going into battle they always doubled the dose to their soldiers, which had the effect of rendering them insensible to danger. " They threw themselves," he states, " into combat like wild beasts, knowing no retreat, and died at their Rajah's feet if he would keep his post."

It was on April 22nd, 1915, that the French and Canadian troops in the front line in the neighbourhood of Langemarck saw what appeared to be a wave of curious green mist approaching them. It soon caused them to choke and gasp and seemed to seize them in a deadly grip from which they could not escape. A gap was made in the line in that sector, but the results of this first use of poison gas in the Great War, although serious, were not disastrous.

A thrill of horror went up from the Allied nations against this fiendish manœuvre, which was regarded as a crime against humanity and will never be forgotten. The gas first used was chlorine, the effects of which are well known, and it was liberated by the enemy from cylinders concentrated on a front of six hundred yards. The first attack was evidently made as an experiment, and in the interval, owing to the activity of British chemists, our men were supplied with a temporary respirator as a defence from this new peril.

During the following months of May and June, several other gas attacks were made by the Germans, but not on a very large scale, as for some time the prevailing winds had been in favour of the Allies, which would be likely to blow the deadly cloud back into the enemy's lines.

On December 19th, 1915, a more important attack with poison gas was made on the British front in the Ypres salient, on a front of three and a half miles. Gas was released continuously for an hour, but thanks to the protective measures which had been adopted by this time, although 25,000 troops are stated to have been in the area of attack, the casualties were small.

Disappointed in the effects of their first essay with this diabolical weapon, the Germans next introduced phosgene, a very deadly vapour, and one against which the respirators then used were no protection. A new type of respirator, however, was speedily devised, and proved effective against the danger. The effective gas helmet with its special filter, invented by Lieut.-Colonel Harrison, came into use, and our men became very quick in placing it in position.

In August, 1916 the Germans launched a highly concentrated phosgene attack against the Allied lines, on a hot and stifling day, the effects of which were felt as far as nine miles behind the lines.

The uncertainty of the atmospheric conditions led the Germans to adopt another vile method of disseminating poisonous vapours, and later they introduced the gas-shell, of which numerous varieties were eventually made. The contents of these shells were distinguished by the Germans by special marks in the form of coloured bands on the shell cases ; the so-called " blue cross " contained diphenyl chlorasine, a substance which when scattered as a fine powder caused intense sneezing to those in the neighbourhood of it. Two-thirds of the shell were filled with high explosive, and the intention was to produce uncontrollable sneezing, so that the wearing of a respirator was made impossible.

Other gas shells were filled with di-phosgene (trichlor methyl chlorformate), which formed a vapour of a very deadly character immediately the shell burst and produced most serious consequences. Another type contained, in addition to di-phosgene, a quantity of chlorpicrin, which was not only deadly, but produced severe running at the eyes and nose.

These vapours, however, were succeeded in July, 1917, in the neighbourhood of Ypres, by the use of di-chlorethyl sulphide, called " mustard gas." Mustard gas was undoubtedly one of the most terrible and deadly of the gas poisons used. It not only blistered the skin and turned it brown, but caused intense inflammation of the eyes and lids, the throat and nose, often causing permanent blindness and loss of voice, and eventually producing septic broncho-pneumonia, frequently ending in death.

In the autumn of that year it was used on a large scale against the Italians, and largely assisted the Austro-German armies in the break-through at Caporetto.

Clothing, boots, soil or other things which came in contact with it were liable to affect seriously those brought near them, days after the articles had been contaminated, but even against this terrible weapon our gas masks were made effective if put on with sufficient quickness and the men could be warned in time.

The use of poison as a lethal weapon in the Great War was by no means confined to deadly gases. Numerous instances, many of which are authenticated, were recorded from 1914 to the time of the Armistice, of poisoned sweetmeats and disease organisms that were dropped from enemy aeroplanes in France and other countries.

On November 4th, 1916, it was reported by cable that Prince Mercier, the youngest child of King Ferdinand of Rumania, who was only five years old, had died of typhoid.

According to Helen Vacarescu, the Rumanian poetess, the Prince was the victim of poisoned sweets which were dropped by German airmen into the streets of Bucharest and other cities of Rumania. Some of these sweets are said to have fallen into the garden of the Royal Palace, and the little Prince while playing there picked some up and ate them. According to Miss Vacarescu, he fell sick almost immediately, and when he told about the sweets he had eaten, a search was instituted, and some of them were found in the garden. On a scientific investigation being made of these, they were found to be impregnated with typhoid bacilli. According to *Le Temps* it is said that all the families who ate the sweets died.

According to *The Times* of October 31st, 1916, an aeroplane coming from Transylvania scattered boxes of poisoned sweetmeats for the purpose of murdering children, an act which excited the greatest indignation in the district. According to further reports, several of the sweets contained the micro-organisms of various infectious diseases.

On October 12th, 1916, a report was received from Petrograd of an enemy air squadron which dropped bombs on Constanza, the Rumanian Black Sea port, as well as darts and poisoned sweets saturated with cholera bacilli.

According to an official report, on October 9th, 1916, a squadron of eight German aeroplanes flew over Bucharest at eleven o'clock one morning and dropped bombs in the neighbourhood of some linen warehouses. The damage done was insignificant, but an investigation of the German Legation led to the discovery of numerous cases of high explosives buried in the garden, as well as phials labelled Virus Morbi Glanders, which are supposed to have been sent to propagate an epidemic against cattle and horses in the country. The discovery is

vouched for by a representative of the United States Legation.

In May, 1917, it was reported from Rome that during an
Austrian air-raid over Codigaro, near Ferrara, sweets were
thrown out which were found to contain cholera bacilli. The
local authorities issued an order directing that all wells thereafter
should be kept covered.

On December 17th, 1917, an account is reported of an air-raid
on Calais, where the Germans dropped a number of small
boxes bearing instructions in English to the effect that they
contained soup-powder. Directions were given to dissolve the
powder in water and to add to it a pint of boiling liquid.
Several deaths resulted from using these packets, and an
analysis proved that they contained an extremely virulent
poison.

On February 20th, 1918, it was reported from Southend that
when a raiding Gotha passed over the town the previous Monday
night, a curious patter was heard on the roofs of some houses in
the district. In the morning, a number of sweets about the size
of small eggs were found in the roadway and gardens, believed
to have been dropped from the enemy aeroplane. They were
handed to the Medical Officer of Health for Southend, who
reported that he had discovered traces of arsenic in the sweets
found on the public footpath.

A sensation was caused in America on July 29th, 1917, by an
announcement made by the Attorney-General, that expert
examination had disclosed the presence of tetanus germs in
court plaster which was believed to have been distributed by
German agents, and he essayed to warn the public to avoid
using plaster of that description. The New York State Health
Department published a statement that specimens of such plaster
sold by pedlars had been sent to the State laboratory for examin-
ination. Despatches had been received from Western and
Southern areas of the United States, reporting epidemics of
anthrax in herds in the same region, after the use of such plaster
recommended for cuts and other injuries to cattle.

Poison was used extensively in various ways by the German
forces, although frequently where wells were said to have been
poisoned, our men drank from them freely without any bad
results. On the other hand it was not uncommon sometimes
to find, left behind in trenches, large tins of cocoa and other
tempting commodities which on analysis proved to be
contaminated.

The use of bacteriological methods was also not neglected
by the enemy, and it was stated in a despatch from Washington
on July 9th, 1917, that the Germans, before evacuating the
territory west of St. Quentin, inoculated the French inhabitants,
men, women and children, with tuberculosis bacilli. The *New*

York World commissioned Dr. Theodore C. Beebe, a pathologist, of Boston, in charge of the American Ambulance Hospital at Neuilly, to make an independent investigation of this matter. Dr. Beebe, in his report, states that while there was no way to obtain indubitable proof of the allegation, the evidence pointed to the belief that the Germans made a deliberate attempt to spread tuberculosis throughout France under the pretence of vaccinating the inhabitants to protect them from smallpox which they said was sweeping over the country. Dr. Beebe pointed out that only those persons vaccinated developed tuberculosis, while unvaccinated children and older persons, although suffering from pneumonia and other diseases, showed no trace of it. He found these inoculations were never made until a month or six weeks before the Germans were evacuating the place ; in other words, when it became apparent to the Germans that they were forced to retreat. Of course only an examination of the serum at the time of the inoculation would determine whether it contained tuberculosis bacilli or not, and that was impossible ; but the investigator concluded that the facts he had ascertained led him to the belief that the charge brought against Germany of having committed this most horrible crime was true.

On March 30th, 1917, it was reported that a discovery had been made of a plot to kill the cavalry horses within the British lines. This was to have been carried out by bacteriological cultures introduced into the food, or by making a wound inside the horse's nostril with a contaminated wire. This plot, which was discovered in time, was part of the German plan of retirement, but was fortunately found out and frustrated before any casualties occurred.

Probably the only case on record of the use of poison gas in an attempt to murder, was reported from Germany in November 1922, when two men were charged at Leipzig with attempting to kill a man called Scheidemann at Cassel on Whit-Sunday. They carefully charged glass syringes with cyanogen gas, and secreting them in their pockets, they awaited the coming of their victim and discharged the poison gas in his face. Scheidemann eventually recovered, and the two men were convicted of an attempt to murder him.

During the Napoleonic Wars, the curious suggestion was made by Perceval that the Allies could bring the French to their knees by prohibiting the importation to the Continent of cinchona bark and other valuable drugs. " The suggestion," says a writer of the time, " is well worthy of the statesman. To bring the French to reason by keeping them without rhubarb, and exhibiting to mankind the awful spectacle of a nation deprived of natural salts ! Without castor oil they might for some months be able to carry on a lingering war, but could they do without

bark ? Will the people live under a Government where antimony cannot be procured ? Will they bear the loss of mercury ?
Depend upon it they will soon be brought to their senses, and
the cry of ' Bourbon and Bolus ' be raised from the Baltic to
the Mediterranean ! "

CHAPTER XXXI

SOME CURIOUS POISON STORIES

SOME curious stories associated with poisons appear in the newspapers from time to time, and although many of them may be assigned to the realms of fiction or the lively imagination of the descriptive writer, there are others which have features that render them worthy of record.

The story of the ' poisoned kiss ', which emanates from America, is improbable but not impossible.

In 1923, a man while awaiting trial on charges of stealing a large quantity of jewellery was one day allowed to receive a visit from a female relative.

Tall and smartly dressed, this woman drove up to the prison in a motor car and presented a permit to see the prisoner. She was so closely veiled that her features could not be distinguished. Placed in charge of a warder, she was conducted to a corridor where she could talk to the prisoner through the bars of his cell. What words passed between the couple, the warder who stood but a few yards distant could not hear, but just on leaving, she suddenly raised her veil and putting her face close to the bars, imprinted a long and ardent kiss on the lips of the man in the cell.

In a few moments he was seen to stagger to his bench where he collapsed with his face buried in his arms. Meanwhile, the woman veiling her face walked away sobbing, accompanied by the warder who saw her to the gate, whence she quickly drove away.

On returning to the cell he saw the man still in the same position and on examining him found that he was dead. Between his lips was a cigarette paper crushed and discoloured.

The medical officer was at once summoned and on examining the piece of paper found it to be strongly impregnated with cyanide of potassium.

From the warder's evidence it was concluded that the woman had transferred the poisoned cigarette paper which she secreted between her lips to those of the prisoner in the course of the lingering kiss. The rapid effect proved he had swallowed cyanide. No clue was found to the woman's identity and she was never traced.

A pathetic and unusual case in which a young German

scientist took his life with a poison that could not be determined, and of which he was said to have been the discoverer, came to light in an inquest that was held on the body of Dr. Joseph Born by the Kensington coroner in January, 1925.

He was a man of high scientific attainments and had formerly had considerable means, but determined to devote his fortune to science he had spent over £50,000 on his research work.

Before coming to England, he had a laboratory in Utrecht and claimed to have discovered processes for making several of the vegetable alkaloids such as atropine, cocaine and nicotine, synthetically, thereby reducing the cost of their manufacture by three or four hundred per cent.

He came to London in August, 1924, with the object of selling his inventions, but the negotiations were so protracted that all his funds were exhausted and he was unable to provide for his wife and children. This evidently preyed on his mind and he was found lying dead in one of the rooms of his flat.

" I must die by my own invention. Is it not funny ? " was the sardonic farewell message that was found on his body.

At the inquest, Dr. Weir who made the post mortem examination said he could not determine the nature of the poison used. It was not one of the ordinary commercial poisons. It was evident that he had killed himself with some poison of his own invention which could not be detected.

The Coroner stated it was clear that Dr. Born's scientific claims were not figments of the imagination by the fact that the poison with which he had committed suicide had baffled detection.

The value of broadcasting in case of urgent emergency was proved in September, 1926, when a chemist in the Midlands discovered that he had made an error in dispensing a box of a dozen pills. According to the prescription, each pill should have contained one-fortieth of a grain of strychnine but instead of this medicinal dose of the powerful poison, a quarter of a grain had been placed in each. It was not until after the pills had been called for, that this serious error was discovered, and only the name of the person they were intended for was known. Telegrams were immediately despatched to all persons of that name in the district and the British Broadcasting Corporation being communicated with, the following message was at once sent out :

" At 4 p.m. yesterday, a gentleman called at a chemist's shop in a Midland town and requested twelve pills containing one-fortieth of a grain of strychnine. By some misunderstanding these pills were made up containing one-quarter of a grain. The prescription was for a Mrs. P——. Will anyone communicate with her or the police to avoid a serious accident."

The following day a telephone message was received by the

police from a man in London, stating that he was the customer.
He described the box and contents but said he had posted the
pills to his wife in Shrewsbury.

A police officer was rushed off in a motor-car to the address
given and he arrived a few minutes before the postman. He
took charge of the box of pills as soon as it was delivered which
was found to be intact, so what might have resulted in a tragedy
was thus averted.

There was a strange story current in 1917 respecting the then
notorious Rasputin, which on the authority of the " *Russkoye
Slovó* " of March 23rd of that year, was the real reason of his
extraordinary influence at the Russian Court. It stated that
Rasputin owed his power, to his influence upon the health of
the Tsarevich who suffered from an unaccountable hæmorrhage
which none of the Court physicians could diagnose or cure.
The monk who was supposed to possess some occult power of
healing was sent for, and as soon as he had laid hands on the
young patient and made some passes, the illness disappeared in
a short time.

The Tsarevich had long suffered from a strong tendency to a
flow of blood and this is said to have been purposely aggravated
by a Madame Vyrubova by means of certain drugs, which she
obtained from a man called Badmayev who was a student of
Tibetan medicine. Thus, when Vyrubova wished to increase
Rasputin's influence she cunningly mixed the powders she
received from Badmayev in the Tsarevich's food or drink. His
illness then developed and these means were continued until
Rasputin was summoned. When he was in attendance, Madame
Vyrubova stopped giving the powders and the Tsarevich got
better.

The drugs prepared by Badmayev are said to have consisted
of ginseng root and young stag's horns. Both of these are well
known remedies and highly valued by the Chinese. The ginseng root, which like the mandrake, often resembles the human
form in shape, is highly esteemed as a powerful tonic and
rejuvenator and is used as an ingredient in their love-philtres.
In large doses it is said to rapidly increase the blood pressure,
especially in those who have any abnormal tendency in that way.
Stag's horn powder, also greatly valued in China, is prepared in
the early spring when the stags shed their horns. The small
knobs that appear in the place where the new horns are develop-
ing, are removed and then powdered, and when taken mixed
with ginseng are said to increase the action of the heart.

The story of how Rasputin met his end is dramatically told
by Prince Youssoupoff in his book entitled " *Rasputin : His
Malignant Influence and Assassination.*" *

The Prince and his friends having planned to deliver Russia

* " Rasputin : His Malignant Influence and Assassination "—Jonathan Cape.

from " her most dangerous internal enemy," at last invited him to visit his house—Rasputin agreed to come at midnight on December 16th, 1916.

" By eleven o'clock," the narrative continues, " everything was ready. The samovar stood on the table, with various cakes and sweetmeats for which Rasputin had a great liking. On one of the sideboards was a tray with wines and glasses. . . . I drew from the cupboard a box containing poison, and took from the table a plate of cakes ; there were six, three with chocolate and three with almond icing. Dr. Lazovert put on rubber gloves and took out the crystals of cyanide of potassium. He crushed them, and having removed the upper layers from the chocolate cakes, sprinkled each of them with a strong dose of poison, afterwards replacing the tops. All that now remained to be done was to shake some powdered crystals into the wine glasses. . . . The total amount of poison applied was enormous : the doctor assured us that the dose was many times stronger than would be required to cause death."

Rasputin arrived. The Prince took him into a dining-room which he had improvised in the cellar of his house.

" He exhausted his ordinary topics after a time," the Prince continues, " and asked for some tea. I poured him out a cup, and pushed a plate of biscuits towards him. Why I offered him the biscuits which were not poisoned, I cannot explain. It was only some time afterwards that I took the plate of poisoned cakes and passed them to him. He declined them at first. However, he soon took one, then a second. Without moving a muscle, I watched him take them and eat them, one after another. The cyanide should have taken immediate effect ; but to my utter amazement he continued to converse with me as if he were none the worse for them."

Then Rasputin had some of the poisoned wine. " I stood in front of him and followed each movement he made, expecting every moment to be his last. But he drank slowly, taking small sips at a time just as if he had been a connoisseur. He got up, and moved about the room. . . . Time passed. The hands of the clock pointed to half past two. This nightmare had lasted over two hours.

" He swallowed glass after glass without being any the worse. It seemed impossible to poison him."

Finally the Prince resolved to shoot him.

According to a story published in the newspapers in July, 1926, Dzerjinsky, the friend of Zinoviev author of the notorious "Red Letter " of secret instructions to Communists in Great Britain which had such important political repercussions, met his death from poison which had been placed in a glass of water on the table of a platform from which he had been speaking. Drinking the water after his speech, he is reported to have left the meeting in the best of health but on arrival at his house he complained of feeling sick and was seized with vomiting. He is said to have died in great agony but before he finally collapsed he was heard to murmur : " So, it is the end. They have done their business."

A strange tragedy in which poison played a part occurred in September, 1926, when a motor-car was discovered in a Bedfordshire lane completely burnt. To add to the mystery of how the car came to burst into flames, to which it was evident its occupants had fallen victims, a revolver was discovered on the riverbank close by.

It subsequently transpired, that the charred remains found were those of a Mr. and Mrs. Lindsay H. Marshall of South Mill Farm, Blunham, Bedfordshire, who had driven out in their car on the night of September 9th and never returned.

On investigation, it was at first thought that Mr. Marshall had shot his wife, staged a collision, poured petrol over the car and his wife's body, then set the car alight but how he met his death seemed likely to remain a mystery. The finding, however, of some fragments of amber glass among the debris, led to the discovery, that on the same day that he and his wife were thus found, he had purchased an ounce of prussic acid from a chemist in Bedford.

The chemist who sold it said it was Scheele's acid and was supplied in an amber glass bottle.

At the inquest, the Coroner said that what had happened had obviously been very carefully thought out. If Mr. Marshall did not shoot his wife, there was no reason that they knew of why he should have thrown the revolver into the river. Had he thrown it on the other side of the river it would have gone into deep water and they would have known nothing about it. No medical man could have found a bullet or poison in the charred remains. It would appear that he had afterwards poisoned himself and a verdict of murder and suicide was returned.

SOME FAMOUS POISON TRIALS AND MYSTERIES

CHAPTER XXXII

THE ROMANTIC CASE OF MARY BLANDY

WOMEN poisoners have rarely been either beautiful or charming but Mary Blandy, whose trial for murdering her father excited great interest in 1752, must have been an exception, as she is described as having been a most attractive and accomplished girl.

Her father, who was a man of some means was a retired solicitor who lived with his wife and their one daughter at Henley-on-Thames.

Mary's beauty and accomplishments attracted many admirers in the little riverside town but the attentions of local swains were outrivalled when a young Scottish officer named Captain Cranstoun arrived at Henley on recruiting service.

He soon became friendly with the Blandys and was a frequent visitor to their house. Although some years her senior, he began to pay marked attention to Mary, who no doubt attracted by his bearing and uniform, favoured his advances. As the affair progressed, Mr. Blandy began to make inquiries into Cranstoun's antecedents and found that he was already married and had a wife and children living in Scotland. The Captain had, however, already prepared Mary for this discovery but told her the marriage was not a real one.

Her father disbelieved this statement and informed Captain Cranstoun that he must cease his attentions to his daughter and eventually forbade him the house.

Mary found an ally in her mother who was attracted by the young officer and later on, when she was taken ill, Mrs. Blandy would not be satisfied until Cranstoun was allowed to return and he again became a frequent visitor.

Mrs. Blandy got gradually worse and shortly afterwards died.

After her death, Cranstoun returned to Scotland but before leaving, seeing that Mr. Blandy's opposition to a marriage was likely to be revived, he persuaded Mary that her father must be got out of the way, and told her that he would send her the means to accomplish it in the shape of a powder he used " to clean Scotch pebbles."

There appears to be little doubt that at this time, the pair deliberately plotted to poison Mr. Blandy on account of his opposition to their union and Mary was urged by her lover to carry out the deed.

When Cranstoun returned to Henley, he at once endeavoured to prepare the way to carry out the scheme. He claimed to have the power of second-sight and first gave out that music had been heard in the house, which was a warning that Mr. Blandy would die within twelve months. He further declared that an apparition of Mr. Blandy had appeared to him in Scotland. Mary even mentioned these warnings to the servants and told them that she was sure that her father would not live long.

In the autumn following, Mr. Blandy was taken ill with severe intestinal pains. It transpired that on one occasion he complained to his daughter that his tea had a bitter taste and did not drink it; it was however, afterwards drunk by one of the servants who was suddenly seized with violent internal pains. Mary appears to have given her father several doses in tea.

In the July of the following year Mr. Blandy was still alive and Cranstoun who was again in Scotland kept up a correspondence with Mary in which he urged her to renew her efforts to get rid of her father. In the same month he wrote to her saying : " Do not spare the powder in order to keep the rust off the pebbles." Thus egged on by her lover, she insisted on preparing his food herself and openly warned the servants not to taste it.

In the meantime, Cranstoun had been endeavouring to get his Scottish marriage dissolved but it was held to be good in law and he was unsuccessful.

He continued his letters to Mary urging her to renew her efforts to kill her father and she, finding her efforts to place sufficient of the poison in his tea unavailing, began to mix it with the water gruel which she made for him.

Mr. Blandy now lived in continual pain and torture, until at length touched by his terrible sufferings of which she was the cause, Mary, one day, confessed the whole plot to the sick man, placing all the blame on Cranstoun, whom she promised never to see again if her father would forgive her. The old man who was then in a sinking condition and beyond recovery, gave her his blessing and prayed her to amend her life. He died shortly afterwards.

Mary little thought that retribution was to follow so swiftly, but the servants had been suspicious of their mistress for some time, and directly after Mr. Blandy's death when one of the maids was about to throw away a basin of untasted gruel, she noticed a glistening white powder at the bottom of the bowl. She showed it to a neighbour who kept it and sent it to an apothecary to be tested and it proved to be arsenic.

On another occasion Mary was noticed endeavouring to burn a packet of letters which turned out to have been written by Cranstoun. One of them but partly burnt, was afterwards picked out of the grate by a maid who noticed the words " Powder to clean the pebbles " and this was afterwards brought in evidence against her.

It transpired later that shortly before her father's death Mary had given a visitor a letter addressed to Cranstoun to post and he, being suspicious, opened it. He took a copy of it and gave the original to her father just before he died. The sick man read it and afterwards murmured : " Poor love-sick girl. What will not a woman do for the man she loves."

The rumours and suspicions that were rife in the town aroused the Coroner to action and he stopped the funeral, until a post-mortem examination had been made on the body of Mr. Blandy.

At the inquest, the apothecary who had examined the sediment found in the basin said that he had burnt some of the dried powder on a hot poker and judged from the smell, it was arsenic. The local doctor who made the post-mortem confirmed this and said he had used white arsenic in the same way and got the same smell and results. He believed that the " powder for pebbles " consisted of white arsenic.

On the conclusion of the inquest, Mary Blandy was arrested and charged with the wilful murder of her father. She was removed to Oxford Gaol and was brought to trial at the Assizes held in that city.

She was found guilty and sentenced to death, and was hanged at Oxford on April 5th, 1752.

On the day that her father died, Mary tried to get away to London and is said to have offered a man-servant £500 to drive her there, but he refused and her escape was cut off.

Cranstoun who was undoubtedly the instigator of the crime, fled to France immediately he heard that Mary Blandy had been arrested. Changing his name to Dunbar, he afterwards took refuge in Flanders and ended his days in a monastery.

CHAPTER XXXIII

THE MYSTERY OF LAWFORD HALL

In the summer of the year 1780, the quiet hamlet of Little Lawford in Warwickshire, situated about three miles from Rugby, was the scene of a tragedy which aroused great interest not only in the immediate locality, but throughout the country.

At that time there lived at Lawford Hall, Sir Theodosius Boughton, a young baronet who had not yet attained his majority, together with his mother, his only sister and her husband, Captain Donellan, a half-pay officer.

The career of the latter gentleman, who plays an important part in the story, had been an eventful one. In 1757 he was gazetted as a subaltern in the 39th Regiment, then stationed in Madras on foreign service. There he entered the East India Company's service and joined in an expedition against Masulipatam in 1758 and was wounded in action after the taking of that place. Trouble, however, arose over the question of certain loot that had been taken from the merchants ; Donellan was court-martialled, sentenced to be discharged from the service, and returned to England.

On his return, his great ambition was to shine as a beau in fashionable society. Dress and gaming are said to have occupied his whole attention, and he eventually became Master of the Ceremonies at the Pantheon, in Oxford Street, London, then a much frequented and smart resort for dancing.

Here, it is probable, he met and wooed Miss Boughton, whom he married, and a year afterwards the couple came to live at Lawford Hall with Lady Boughton. At this time, young Sir Theodosius was finishing his education. After leaving Eton he had lived for a couple of years with a tutor, and then came home to Lawford to settle down with his family.

He was a young fellow of high spirits and fond of outdoor sports, but like other young men of his class he was inclined to live a fast life, and this had told more or less upon his health.

From the time of his residence at home, for some reason or other, he did not get on well with his brother-in-law, Captain Donellan, and the latter appears to have adopted a patronizing attitude towards the young man while living in his house. According to his father's will Sir Theodosius did not come into his property, which was worth about £2,000 a year, until

he was twenty-one, and meanwhile he was under the guardian-
ship of Sir Edmund Wheeler, an old friend who lived eight
miles away from Lawford.   According to the will, should he
die before attaining his majority, his sister, Mrs. Donellan, was
to benefit largely from the estate.

Matters thus went on for nearly two years when Sir Theodosius, as the result of his former gay life, became unwell and
placed himself under the care of an apothecary in Rugby.

Donellan, who became aware of this, talked a good deal to
various friends, remarking that the young man was ruining
his health, that his life was not worth a year's purchase, and
that he could not possibly live if he did not take more care of
himself.

The young baronet, however, appeared in good spirits, but
the conditions of life became so unpleasant at the Hall that he
at length decided to go and stay with a friend in Northampton
until he came of age.

About five o'clock on a Tuesday afternoon, August 29th,
1780, Sir Theodosius, accompanied by several of his men-
servants, set off down to the river on a fishing expedition.
During his absence a dose of medicine in the form of a draught
was delivered at the Hall from Mr. Powell, the apothecary,
which was to be taken by the young man the first thing on the
following morning.   The bottle was taken upstairs and placed
on a shelf in his bedroom.   Soon after Sir Theodosius had set
out, his mother Lady Boughton, and Mrs. Donellan went into
the grounds to take the air and remained in the garden some
hours.   About seven o'clock they were joined in their walk by
Captain Donellan, who remarked that he had been fishing with
Sir Theodosius, and that he was afraid if he stayed out so long
in the damp he would take cold.   Sir Theodosius, however,
returned home all right somewhat later and, after having supper,
retired to bed.

At six in the morning a servant called him, and he got out
of bed and spoke to him.   An hour later his mother went into
his bedroom to remind him about taking his medicine.   He
asked her to give it to him, and she, taking it from the shelf,
poured the contents into a cup and gave it to him.   He swallowed
about half and complained that it tasted so nauseous he would
be unable to retain it.   He handed the cup back to his mother
who smelt it and was struck with the powerful smell of bitter
almonds, but gave it back to him again.   Sir Theodosius then
swallowed the remainder and lay down, but in a few minutes he
was taken very ill with vomiting.   On his becoming more composed, Lady Boughton left him for about ten minutes, thinking
he would sleep.   On returning to his room she found him
collapsed and foaming at the mouth.   Struck with alarm at his
condition she sent a servant for the apothecary and to call

Captain Donellan. The latter came in a few minutes, and on his entering the room Lady Boughton exclaimed : " Here is a terrible affair, I have given my son something that was wrong instead of what the apothecary sent. I am sure it would have killed a dog." Donellan replied : " Why the devil did Mr. Powell send such a medicine ? Where is the bottle ? " Lady Boughton pointed to it on the mantelpiece and Donellan at once took it up, poured some water into it, shook and rinsed it and emptied the contents into a basin of dirty water standing near.

Astonished at his action Lady Boughton said : " Good God, what are you doing ? Let everything remain just in the same place until Mr. Powell the apothecary arrives." Donellan made no reply, but took an empty phial which had contained a previous draught which was also standing on the same shelf and rinsed that out in the same way, then, calling a servant, ordered her to take the basin away, in spite of Lady Boughton's remonstrance.

Meanwhile Sir Theodosius became worse, and died in about thirty minutes.

Some time elapsed before the apothecary arrived, and he was taken up to the room by Donellan, who explained to him that Sir Theodosius had been out fishing late the previous night, and had no doubt taken cold, which had caused his death. He made no mention of the effect of the draught, but told him the young man had died in convulsions. The apothecary apparently offered no solution as to the cause of death and left the house.

On the same morning that Sir Theodosius died, Donellan wrote to Sir William Wheeler, his guardian, informing him of his death, stating also that he had been under the care of Mr. Powell, of Rugby, for a similar complaint to that which he had had when at Eton. Within a day or two, however, rumours of foul play became current and Sir William Wheeler communicated these to Donellan and insisted that to allay public suspicion a post-mortem examination should be made. He named a Dr. Rattray and two surgeons, Messrs. Wilmer and Snow, whom he desired to conduct the examination. These gentlemen were accordingly sent for and arrived at Lawford Hall on Monday evening, September 4th. They were received by Captain Donellan, who, after some conversation, showed them to the room. The body of the unfortunate young man being in an advanced state of decomposition, the doctors showed reluctance to proceed with the autopsy. After a cursory examination, they left the Hall without coming to any satisfactory conclusion, nothing having been said to them by Donellan of any suspicion of foul play.

Donellan then wrote to Sir William Wheeler stating that the

doctors had fully satisfied the family, but Sir William was still dissatisfied, and on hearing that no actual post-mortem had been made, insisted that two other surgeons, viz. Messrs. Bucknell and Snow, should examine the remains. On their arrival, however, Donellan again circumvented their intentions and the body was duly interred. This increased the rumours instead of dispelling them, and eventually the coroner of the district was informed of the case and he decided to hold an inquiry.

The inquest lasted three days, and on the third day Donellan addressed a letter to the Coroner in which he stated that Sir Theodosius used to procure arsenic to kill rats, and frequently bought as much as a pound at a time, also that he used to make large quantities of Goulard Water.

This was to account for the suspicion of poisoning which was now rife. After hearing the evidence, the Coroner ordered that the body should be exhumed. On Saturday morning, September 9th, the body was removed from the vault and placed in the churchyard. About five hundred people had collected to witness the gruesome sight, which in those days was conducted in public. When all was ready Mr. Bucknell, a young surgeon, put on a wagoner's smock frock that had been dipped in vinegar, and with a napkin that had been soaked in vinegar tied over his mouth and nose, opened the body, which was duly inspected by the doctors present and re-interred.

As a result of the inquest Captain Donellan was arrested and charged with the wilful murder of his brother-in-law by poisoning him with arsenic.

The trial, which excited intense interest throughout the country on account of the social position of the persons involved, took place at the Warwick Assizes on March 30th, 1781, before Mr. Justice Buller.

Six counsel, led by Mr. Howarth, appeared for the Crown, and the prisoner was represented by Mr. Newnham and two juniors. The case mainly depended on the medical evidence, a review of which forms an interesting picture of the state of medicine and toxicology of the time.

The first witness was Mr. Powell, the apothecary, of Rugby, who was treating Sir Theodosius at the time of his death. He swore that the draught he sent the baronet was quite harmless and consisted of rhubarb, jalap, spirit of lavender, nutmeg water and simple syrup.

Dr. Rattray, of Coventry, the next medical witness, described the visit he paid to Lawford Hall at the wish of Sir William Wheeler with the other surgeons. The reason they did not proceed with the post-mortem, he stated, was that they thought it too late, and that so long after death nothing could be discovered. He was present when the body was opened in the churchyard, and from its appearance he was now of the opinion that poison was the cause of death.

Mr. Wilmer, a surgeon, described some experiments he had made with laurel water. He gave an ounce to a young greyhound and to his great surprise it died immediately. He next gave a pint and a half to a mare and in a few moments she went into convulsions and died in fifteen minutes. He believed that an ounce of laurel water was enough to kill a strong man. Dr. Ash, a physician of Birmingham, next gave his opinion that the young man had died from the effects of poison.

Further medical evidence was given by Dr. Parsons, Professor of Anatomy at Oxford University. He stated he believed that Sir Theodosius had been poisoned by laurel water which had been given to him instead of the purgative draught.

Important evidence was then given by a female servant named Mary Lines, who stated that Captain Donellan had a still, which he kept in his own room and which he used for distilling rose water.

A gardener at the Hall, named Amos, who was next called, said Captain Donellan brought the still to him two or three days after Sir Theodosius died. It was full of wet lime at the time and he asked him to clean it for him. He mentioned that the lime was used for killing fleas.

For the defence Mr. John Hunter, the famous surgeon, of London, was called to give evidence and said he had dissected some thousands of subjects. The symptoms he had heard described were not conclusive that the baronet had taken poison. He had never known in his practice of laurel water being given to a human being. From the description he had heard of the appearance of the body, he should not have drawn the inference that death had resulted rrom poison. Apoplexy or epilepsy would produce similar symptoms to those he had heard described, but he would not swear that the deceased man died a natural death.

The judge in summing up commented on the doubt Mr. Hunter seemed to have in giving evidence, and the failure of counsel to get from him a conclusive opinion. On the other hand five medical men were agreed that death had been due to the draught, and that the draught had been laurel water. How did the poison get into the medicine bottle ? Why also did the prisoner rinse out the empty bottles and see they were taken away and destroyed in the face of the suspicious circumstances attending the death ? The evidence concerning the still was also important, as it proved the prisoner had a knowledge of its use and he often used it for distilling rose and lavender waters. The deceptive way in which the prisoner had acted was also likely to arouse suspicions as well as his endeavour to prevent an examination of the body.

The jury after a few minutes' consideration found the prisoner " Guilty," and the judge pronounced sentence of death. The prisoner's body afterwards to be delivered to the surgeons and be dissected and anatomized. " The prisoner," says a contemporary writer, " neatly dressed in black, was driven in a coach to the gallows and was hanged."

Thus ended the brilliant Captain Donellan, the much envied beau of London Society in the time of George the Third.

CHAPTER XXXIV

THE STRANGE CASE OF ELIZABETH FENNING

THE case of Elizabeth Fenning, which excited intense interest in London early in the nineteenth century, is noteworthy as showing how an innocent girl was tried, convicted and executed for a crime she never committed.

On April 11th, 1815, this girl, who was engaged as cook to a law stationer in Chancery Lane, was tried at the Old Bailey before the Recorder on a charge of having poisoned her employer, Mr. Olebar Turner, his wife and his father, Robert Gregson Turner. The girl, who was only twenty years of age, had been employed as cook in Mr. Turner's house for six weeks, and on March 21st had made some yeast dumplings for dinner.

The dumplings were brought to the table and partaken of by the three persons. A few minutes after eating a portion of one, Mrs. Turner was taken ill with violent pains and vomiting, and shortly afterwards the two men, who had also eaten of the dumplings, were attacked in the same manner. Mr. Marshall, a surgeon, was sent for several hours afterwards, but all three persons had by this time recovered. The girl herself and a young apprentice in the house had also eaten of the dumplings and were affected in the same way.

Mr. Turner said he suspected arsenic had been put in the food and made a search next morning. In the kitchen he found a brown dish in which the dumplings had been mixed, with what appeared to be some remnants of the food still adhering to it. He put some water into the dish and stirred it, and found in a few minutes a white powder or sediment fell to the bottom, which he kept and handed to the surgeon.

He knew that arsenic was kept in a drawer in his office in two wrappers labelled " Arsenick, Deadly Poison " and was used for killing mice. The drawer was always unlocked. He had last seen the packet of arsenic in the drawer on March 7th, and it was now missing. He had noticed that the knives they had used to cut the dumplings had turned black.

He had charged the girl with putting something in the dumplings, and she had replied it was not in the dumplings but in the milk that was used to make them, which had been brought to her by Sarah Peer, a fellow-servant.

Mr. John Marshall, the surgeon who was called in, said he

found the family suffering from symptoms that would be produced by arsenic, and the prisoner was also ill in the same way. He had examined the remnants found in the dish by Mr. Turner and washed them with a tea-kettle of warm water and then decanted it. He found half a teaspoonful of white powder left. After washing it a second time he found it was arsenic. Arsenic would turn the knives black. He had examined the remains of the yeast used and the flour employed in making the dumplings, but found no trace of arsenic.

The girl, in her defence, swore she was quite innocent of the whole charge.

The jury found her guilty and she was sentenced to death.

The result of the trial aroused public interest in London, and caused an outburst of popular feeling, the general opinion being that the evidence was insufficient to prove the girl guilty. The Prince Regent was petitioned, also the Lord Chancellor and the Secretary of State, and several meetings of influential persons were held, agitating for a remission of the sentence. The girl, however, was executed at Newgate on July 26th, 1815, exclaiming : " I die innocent, but God will convince you by a circumstance this day." In 1834, her employer, Olebar Turner who had accused her, died in the workhouse, but confessed before his death that he had put the arsenic into the dumplings and falsely sworn away the girl's life.

CHAPTER XXXV

THE CASE OF JOHN TAWELL, THE QUAKER

THE case of John Tawell, a Quaker, who was charged with the murder of Sarah Hart at Salthill in 1845, by administering prussic acid to her, is interesting on account of the ingenious theory advanced by counsel in his defence, that the poison detected on analysis in the organs of the body of the deceased woman was due to apple-pips. The strange career of the accused man was disclosed at his trial.

Born at Aledby in Norfolk, he came to London as a young man and obtained a situation as traveller to a wholesale druggist in Queen Street, Cheapside. He soon became known to his fellow commercials on the road as the " Quaker traveller " and was trusted by his customers and valued by his employers for his business ability.

Unknown to them, he became involved in a case of forgery on the Uxbridge Bank, a capital offence at the time, and having been found with a forged Bank of England note in his possession, he was tried, convicted and transported to Sydney, in 1814.

Here his knowledge of drugs stood him in good stead and in place of being assigned to a settler up country, he was retained as one of the assistants in the Convict Hospital.

Owing to his intelligence and assiduity, after serving in this capacity for three years, he was granted leave and an emancipation ticket, and was thus enabled to start business as a chemist and druggist in Hunter Street, Sydney.

Success attended his venture and he not only rapidly made money in his shop, but also added to his wealth by speculations in the oil and shipping trade.

Having amassed over £30,000 he returned to London where he rejoined his wife and family and settled down to live in Bridge Street, Southwark. Here after a time, his wife was taken seriously ill and he engaged a young woman named Sarah Hart to nurse her.

An intimacy sprang up between Tawell and this girl, which continued after the death of his wife, and by her he had two children.

Through the Society of Friends, of which he remained a member, Tawell became acquainted with a Mrs. Cutforth, a widow, who carried on a prosperous drapery business at Berkhampstead.

This lady lived in comfortable circumstances and after their friendship had ripened, Tawell married her in February, 1844.

Meanwhile, he had placed Sarah Hart in a cottage at Salthill, a village near Slough, where he continued to visit her, but eventually fearing that his wife might discover the illicit connexion, he resolved to remove her from his path altogether.

On January 1st, 1845 he went to Salthill to see Sarah and after he had spent a short time with her, he sent her to an inn close by to get a bottle of porter. She was then in good health and spirits and returned with the bottle to the cottage and gave it to Tawell.

In an adjoining cottage lived a Mrs. Ashley who was sitting at work at the time, when she heard a noise like a moan or stifled scream and as the sound continued, she became alarmed and went to the door. As she stood for a moment, she saw Tawell, who appeared in an agitated state, come out of the next cottage and go down the path. While he fumbled at the gate, Mrs. Ashley asked him if anything was the matter with her neighbour. He made no reply but hurried along the lane and she, thinking something was wrong, went into Sarah Hart's cottage. Pushing open the door she was amazed to see the woman lying on the floor with her cap off, her hair dishevelled and one shoe off. She was still moaning but was unable to speak and apparently in a dying condition. On a table in the room, she noticed a bottle of porter opened and two glasses, in one of which was a little froth and in the other some porter or porter and water. Rendering what aid she could, she sent at once for a local doctor, but before he arrived Sarah Hart had died.

Meanwhile, Tawell had hurried towards the railway station and jumped on a bus which was however going away from it. Finding this out, he alighted and made his way back to the station to wait for a train. While on the platform he was recognised by a clergyman, who noticing something was seriously wrong with him communicated with the police, and they sent a telegram from the new telegraph station at Slough to Paddington to the effect that a person dressed as a Quaker who would arrive by the next train was to be watched.

On the arrival of the train, a policeman in plain clothes was waiting on the platform who recognised Tawell and saw him take an omnibus to the city.

The next day, the police having been informed of the happenings at Salthill, visited the Jerusalem Coffee house which Tawell was known to frequent and there arrested him.

On being questioned at the police station he stated that Sarah Hart who had lived in his service for five years, had pestered him with letters demanding money and that she had sent to him to say she would make away with herself. He went to

Salthill to see her and she again asked him for money which he refused. She then asked him for beer for which he sent her and on her return, both of them had a glass. She then exclaimed : " I will, I will," and from a small phial, no bigger than a thimble, she poured something into the beer, drank part of it and threw the rest into the fire. She then lay down on the hearthrug and he walked out.

As there was no evidence to show that she had died either from natural causes or external injuries, a post-mortem examination was made by Mr. Champneys, a local surgeon and the stomach was submitted to chemical examination, with the result, that death was attributed to prussic acid.

Tawell was then charged with the murder of Sarah Hart and committed for trial.

The case caused considerable interest at the time, especially in Berkhampstead and neighbourhood, where both Tawell and his wife had become well known for their philanthropic work. They lived in a large double-fronted old brick house in the High Street almost opposite the church, and he was fond of driving himself about in a pony carriage.

At the trial, which took place at Aylesbury on March 12th, 1845, Mr. Champneys who made the post-mortem, stated that he found nothing to account for the woman's death but he removed the contents of the stomach and sent them for analysis.

Mr. Cooper, a practical and consulting chemist of Blackfriars deposed that he examined the contents of the deceased's stomach, a piece of cake and a piece of bun. He found nothing in the two latter, but in the stomach contents by boiling and by tests he produced Prussian blue. He also obtained cyanide of silver from a sample after treating it with nitrate of silver. He found some portions of apple in the stomach but no pips. The quantity of prussic acid he had obtained from apple-pips experimentally was inappreciable. He calculated that as nearly as possible, the bottle which held the contents of the stomach contained a grain of real prussic acid equivalent to twenty grains of Scheele's acid and about fifty grains of the acid of the London Pharmacopœia.

In cross-examination, Mr. Cooper said he had never tested the contents of a human stomach containing prussic acid until this case. He had no personal experience of the quantity it would take to kill a human being and he could not say if all apple-pips contained the same quantity of prussic acid. In reply to a question put by the judge he said he had no doubt of the presence of prussic acid in the stomach.

Mr. Norblad, a surgeon of Slough said he knew of no other poison likely to produce so sudden an effect. He was present when Mr. Cooper made the analysis and was satisfied of the presence of prussic acid. He afterwards experimented on two dogs five hours after feeding them. To one he gave four drachms of Scheele's prussic acid and to the other one drachm mixed with Guinness's stout. In fifty seconds the dog which had received the smaller dose fell and in ten minutes he was dead. The other fell about the same time and died in five minutes.

On opening the bodies eighteen hours afterwards, there was no smell of prussic acid either in the stomach or in the stout.

Mr. Pickering, a surgeon who was present at the post-mortem made by Mr. Champneys, declared that he perceived the odour of prussic acid directly after the first incision was made in the body.

Henry Thomas, an assistant, with Mr. Hughes a chemist of Bishopsgate deposed that on January 1st, Tawell came to the shop and asked for two drachms of Scheele's prussic acid. He brought with him a small phial labelled " Scheele's Prussic Acid ". As he could not remove the stopper, he gave him a bottle of his own.

He came again next day and asked for two drachms more saying he had broken the bottle with the other. Tawell told him that he had been a chemist and apothecary abroad and suffered from varicose veins for which he used the acid.

He was examined by counsel for the defence with reference to some experiments he had made with apple-pips and stated that he had produced prussic acid from them.

Mr. Kelly who defended Tawell, in addressing the Court said, the first question was, had the deceased woman really died from poisoning by prussic acid ? He contended that the evidence was not such as ought to induce a jury to condemn a fellow-creature to death. None of the medical men who had been called had any personal experience of the character of prussic acid or its effects upon the human frame. None of them had ever before examined the body of a person supposed to have died from the effects of that poison.

The case for the Crown was, that the woman had died by the administration of one grain of prussic acid. They must therefore be satisfied that one grain of prussic acid would destroy life, but nothing of the kind had been proved. He called attention to the fact that some of the surgeons had said that no smell of prussic acid had been detected in the body, and he denied that it was possible that a grain of the acid could have been taken without the smell of it being perceptible immediately after death.

He contended that the prussic acid detected in the stomach might have been educed from several causes. It existed in a latent state in innumerable substances, in apple-pips to a greater extent than in any other substance in nature except bitter almonds.

It was quite possible therefore, that the quantity of poison actually found had been produced from apple-pips eaten by the deceased. Mr. Cooper had indeed said that from the pips of fifteen apples he had obtained only an inappreciable quantity of the poison, but Mr. Thomas had actually obtained from the same quantity, two-thirds of a grain of pure acid, which was more than the whole quantity found in the woman's stomach.

He pointed out that Mr. Cooper had not actually obtained a grain of the acid, but only inferred that such a quantity existed in the whole contents of the stomach.

The whole case he declared was involved in mystery.

Tawell's purchase of the poison told in his favour, as he was known to have suffered from varicose veins, for which he had been in the habit of using prussic acid. If he had wanted it for any other purpose, would he have gone to a shop where he was perfectly well known even by name ?

Several witnesses were then called who gave evidence of the especially kind and benevolent disposition of the prisoner.

After the judge had summed-up, the jury, after rather more than thirty minutes deliberation returned with a verdict of guilty and Tawell was sentenced to death.

He was hanged in the balcony of the window of the County Hall at Aylesbury facing the Market Place.

On April 10th, 1845, Mr. Sherriff the Governor of Aylesbury gaol communicated to the magistrates at Buckinghamshire Quarter Sessions, that Tawell had made a confession of the crime.

He stated that he sat up with him the whole of the night before his execution, and about five o'clock in the morning Tawell handed him a written statement which contained an admission of his guilt. Leaning his head against the fireplace in the cell, he said : " Yes, I am guilty of the crime. I put the prussic acid into the porter and I also attempted the crime in September last, not by prussic acid but by morphia."

He requested that the statement might not be copied or allowed to appear in the newspapers.

Although the kernels of stone-fruits such as the peach, damson and cherry contain principles that by contact with water on mastication yield prussic acid, the ingenious suggestion put forward in Tawell's defence was discounted by the fact that only portions of apple and no pips were found in the stomach.

This case is also historic as probably being the first in which the electric telegraph, then but recently installed in the railway stations, was employed in the arrest of a suspected criminal.

CHAPTER XXXVI

THE CASE OF MADELINE SMITH

In the spring of 1857, great excitement was aroused in Glasgow by the arrest of a young and charming girl who was well-known in the best social circles of the city, on the charge of poisoning Pierre Emile L'Angelier, a clerk who was employed in a business house in the great Scottish seaport.

Madeline Smith was as beautiful as she was attractive and a favourite with all who knew her. She is described as having " a graceful figure with a charming face and a complexion clear and fresh, soft and fair, but with features that indicated that she had character and a strong will."

At the age of eighteen she met Pierre Emile L'Angelier a young Jerseyman and fell in love with him. Knowing that her parents would disapprove of the attachment she kept the matter secret, but it did not prevent her meeting him clandestinely and she even did not scruple about admitting him to her bedroom through a window at night. She was of an impulsive and passionate nature and between their meetings she constantly wrote letters to her lover expressing in extravagant terms her attachment to him. One of these produced at her trial ran : " Our intimacy has not been criminal as I am your wife before God. You are my very dear little husband."

After a time the flame of love began to burn low, and as L'Angelier was becoming troublesome and pressing her to make their engagement known, she began to avoid meeting him. Meanwhile, her parents encouraged another suitor to pay Madeline attentions and to him, with the consent of her family, she became engaged to be married. L'Angelier was furious when he heard of her engagement and threatened, that unless she broke it off, he would send the letters she had written to him, to her father.

To prevent him from carrying out this threat and with the object of pacifying him, she continued to see him.

About the end of February 1857, L'Angelier was taken suddenly ill in an inaccountable manner, with vomiting and violent pain. Although he recovered for a time, it was noticed, that these attacks usually seized him after he had been visited by Madeline Smith. On March 22nd, he was taken with another attack of the same kind and from this he never recovered but died on the following morning.

Suspicion as to the cause of his death was almost immediately aroused and five days after he had been buried, the body was exhumed and an analysis of the organs showed that he had died from the effects of arsenical poisoning.

Madeline Smith, who was known to have been frequently in his company was then arrested and charged with the crime.

At the trial, counsel for the Crown contended that she poisoned her lover so that she might be betrothed to a personage of high social position. That L'Angelier died on March 23rd from the effects of arsenic was amply proved, but while suspicious acts were alleged against the accused girl, no direct evidence was adduced to show that she administered the drug. The worst point against her was the fact of her having possession of the poison. Irrespective of two previous purchases of coloured arsenic, for which she had given false reasons, it was proved that she had purchased one ounce, as she said " to kill rats," on March 18th, only five days before the death of L'Angelier. The arsenic sold was coloured with indigo, according to the regulations.

When charged with the crime, and required to account for the poison, she replied that she had used the whole of it to apply to her face, arms, and neck, diluted with water, and that a school companion had told her that arsenic was good for the complexion.

From the post-mortem examination and subsequent analysis *eighty-eight* grains of arsenic were found in the stomach and its contents. Dr. Christison, the greatest toxicological expert of the time was called, and stated he knew of no case in which so much as eighty-eight grains of arsenic had been found in the stomach after death.

This was made a turning point of the defence, and it was contended that so large a dose of arsenic could not have been swallowed unknowingly, and, therefore, suicide was indicated. The jury accepting this view of the case, returned a verdict of " not proven," and Madeline Smith was liberated, after a trial which lasted ten days.

Some interesting particulars concerning the subsequent life of this lady were published some time ago. After the trial she decided to go abroad ; but before starting she is said to have married a certain mysterious individual named Dr. Tudor Hora. With him she lived for many years in Perth, but few people ever saw her, and the doctor always declined to divulge his wife's maiden name. He kept a small surgery, and is said to have been in receipt of about £400 a year from an unnamed source. Some years after, believing that his wife had been recognized, he bought a practice at Hotham, near Melbourne, and they sailed for Australia. Shortly after their arrival, Mrs. Hora left her husband and remained absent from Melbourne until his death.

Soon afterwards she married again, but it is said her second marriage was not by any means a happy one. She remained unknown, and sought no society. She was an excellent musician, and spent most of her time reading and playing. She had no children, and died at the age of fifty-five.

Six years after the trial of Madeline Smith a case was tried at the Chester Assizes, in which a woman named Hewitt or Holt was charged with poisoning her mother. Although the symptoms of irritant poisoning were very clearly marked, the country practitioner who attended the woman at the time certified that the cause of her death was due to gastro-enteritis. Eleven weeks after she had been buried, the body was exhumed and examined. An analysis revealed the presence of *one hundred and fifty-four grains* of arsenic in the stomach alone. The possession of a considerable quantity of arsenic was brought home to the accused and also direct evidence of its administration, and she was found guilty. This case is interesting from the fact of proof being obtained of the administration of so large a dose of arsenic, and if it had occurred before the trial of Madeline Smith it might have demolished her counsel's main line of defence.

CHAPTER XXXVII

THE CASE OF CATHERINE WILSON

A SERIES of cold-blooded crimes carried out by a woman whose sole object was to obtain the money possessed by her victims, was brought to light almost by accident in 1862.

In April of that year, a woman named Catherine Wilson was charged at the Marylebone Police Court with having administered oil of vitriol with intent to kill a Mrs. Connell who lived in Crawford Street, Marylebone.

Mrs. Connell had been living separated from her husband and had sought Wilson's good offices to effect a reconciliation.

With that object in view, she invited Catherine Wilson one afternoon in February to have tea with her. After tea, Mrs. Connell was seized with a sudden illness and Wilson ran out to the nearest chemist's shop and brought back a bottle supposed to have contained " Black Draught," from which she gave Mrs. Connell a dose. She complained at once that it was very hot and burnt her mouth, but Wilson reassured her by telling her she had warmed it and begged her to take it all. It made her very sick and she complained that her mouth was blistered. She also noticed that even the bedclothes were burnt where a few drops of the liquid had been spilt.

Suspecting Wilson, she informed the police, but meanwhile she had disappeared, and it was not until some time afterwards that she was met accidentally by a policeman in the street who recognized and arrested her on the charge of administering poison to Mrs. Connell.

Catherine Wilson was committed for trial at the Central Criminal Court, but as the evidence of intent was deemed insufficient by the jury she was discharged.

While she had been awaiting her trial however, the police had been inquiring into her previous history and discovered, that wherever she had lived, there had been several mysterious deaths ; she was therefore immediately re-arrested and was charged with the murder of a Mrs. Soames with whom she had formerly lived.

It transpired that in 1853-4, she had been living as housekeeper to a Captain Peter Mawer, a master mariner of Boston, Lincolnshire who was a sufferer from chronic gout, for which he had been in the habit of taking colchicum. He died suddenly in October 1854 and left a will bequeathing all his property to Catherine Wilson.

About two years later it was found that she had been living with a man called Dixon in the house of Mrs. Soames in Alfred Street, Bedford Square. Dixon died suddenly under mysterious circumstances, but Wilson remained on in the room in Alfred Street being on very friendly terms with Mrs. Soames the landlady.

About Christmas 1855, Mrs. Soames had inherited some money from a half-brother, a fact that was well known to Wilson, who was determined to obtain possession of it when a suitable opportunity occurred. At length Mrs. Soames was taken ill with constant attacks of vomiting and became so weak that a doctor was called in. She was devotedly nursed by Wilson, who always kept the bottle of medicine which the doctor had ordered in her possession and administered it herself. She grew rapidly worse and died a few days afterwards in great agony. The doctor refused to give a certificate of death until a post-mortem had been made, but afterwards at the inquest, he testified that death was due to natural causes.

At the trial of Wilson, Dr. Taylor deposed that all Mrs. Soames' symptoms pointed to colchicum having been administered in large and repeated doses. These symptoms were now also recognized by the doctor who had attended Dixon at the house of Mrs. Soames in Alfred Street before he died, from which it appeared that both he and Mrs. Soames had succumbed to poisonous doses of colchicum, the deadly properties of which Wilson was well aware.

In spite of there being no proof that Wilson had administered the drug or had been in possession of it, the jury found her guilty of the murder of Mrs. Soames and she was sentenced to death.

Soon afterwards it was discovered that a Mrs. Jackson with whom Wilson had also lived at Boston in 1859, had died very suddenly. She was known to have been on very friendly terms with her and that she had a hundred and twenty pounds in her possession before her death.

She succumbed after four days illness, exhibiting the same symptoms as shown by Dixon and Mrs. Soames and her money was found to have disappeared. Her body was exhumed in January 1860 but no trace of poison was detected in the stomach.

It further transpired that Mrs. Atkinson, a milliner of Kirkby Lonsdale, who stayed with Wilson when she visited London in order to purchase goods for her business, had died under mysterious circumstances in 1860. She was known to carry about a hundred pounds in notes which she kept sewn up in her clothes to pay for her purchases, and on her last visit, after staying four days with Wilson, she suddenly died. On the arrival of her husband, who was summoned by a telegram, he found the money had disappeared and on asking Wilson what had become of it, she explained that Mrs. Atkinson had told her that she had been robbed at Rugby on her way to London.

Although a post-mortem examination was recommended at the time none was made as Mr. Atkinson had no suspicion of foul play. Her body was also exhumed in May 1862 but no trace of poison was found in the organs.

There is little doubt that Catherine Wilson was responsible for the deaths of all these persons. They all died while in a state of health, with similar symptoms and without any apparent natural cause to account for death and the motive was obvious in each case. In the case of Mrs. Soames it was pointed out, that the symptoms always appeared in the evenings after she had taken tea made by Wilson.

It is believed that she prepared her poisonous draughts from colchicum seeds which she could easily procure and either infused them in wine or brandy, or added the infusion to tea. In most of the cases she appears to have administered it in divided doses over a period of a few days.

It is difficult to conceive the fiendish cunning of this woman, who, while pretending to nurse her victims and give them every comfort, watched them die in agonies. In keeping with her character she remained absolutely callous to the last. She made no confession and exhibited no compunction for her crimes. At her execution, at which twenty thousand people are said to have been present, she faced the immense crowd without a sign of emotion.

CHAPTER XXXVIII

" THE BRAVO MYSTERY "

PROBABLY no trial in which antimony has figured caused more interest than that concerning the mysterious death of Mr. Bravo in 1876.

The story begins with the marriage of Mr. Bravo, a young barrister of about thirty years of age, to Mrs. Ricardo, who was then a wealthy widow and a lady of considerable personal attractions. After the marriage, which followed a very short acquaintance, the couple went to reside at Balham. According to a statement made by Mrs. Bravo, she informed her husband before the marriage of a former lover, and there is little doubt that it rankled in Mr. Bravo's mind and he frequently taunted his wife with the fact. He was a strong, healthy, and temperate man, but appears to have been both weak and vain in character.

On Tuesday, April 18th, 1876, after breakfast at his own house at Balham, he drove with his wife into town. On their way, a very unpleasant discussion took place. Arriving in town he had a Turkish bath, lunched with a relative of his wife's at St. James's Restaurant, and walked on his way home to Victoria Station with a friend and fellow-barrister, whom he asked out for the following day. He arrived home about half-past four. Shortly after his return, Mr. Bravo went out for a ride, in the course of which his horse bolted and carried him a long distance, and he got back to his home very tired and exhausted. At half-past six he was noticed leaning forward on his chair, looking ill, and with his head hanging down. He ordered a hot bath, and when getting into it he cried out aloud with pain, putting his hand to his side. The bath did not seem to relieve him much, and he appeared to be suffering pain all through dinner, but appeared to avoid attracting the attention of his wife and Mrs. Cox, her companion, who dined with them.

The food provided during the dinner was partaken of more or less in common by all three, but this was not the case as regards the wine. Mr. Bravo drank Burgundy only, while Mrs. Bravo and Mrs. Cox drank sherry and Marsala. The wine drunk by Mr. Bravo had been decanted by the butler some time before dinner ; how long he could not say, but he had noticed nothing unusual with it.

The wine was of good quality, and Mr. Bravo, who was

something of a connoisseur, remarked nothing peculiar in its taste, but drank it as usual. When he had Burgundy for luncheon he usually finished the bottle at dinner ; but if not, as on the day in question, the remains of the bottle were put away in an unlocked cellaret in the dining-room. The butler could not remember whether any Burgundy was left on this day or not ; but none, however, was discovered.

This cellaret was opened at least twice subsequently to this, and prior to Mr. Bravo's illness, once by Mrs. Cox and once by the maid.

Mr. Bravo seems to have eaten a good dinner, although he was evidently not himself from some cause or other. It was said he was suffering from toothache or neuralgia, and had just received a letter that had given him some annoyance.

The dinner lasted till past eight o'clock, after which the party adjourned to the morning-room where conversation continued up to about nine o'clock.

Mrs. Bravo and Mrs. Cox then retired upstairs, leaving Mr. Bravo alone, until Mrs. Cox went to fetch Mrs. Bravo some wine and water from the dining-room.

Mrs. Bravo remained in her room and prepared for bed and drank the wine and water brought to her by Mrs. Cox, who remained with her.

The housemaid, on taking some hot water to the ladies' room as was her usual custom at half-past nine, was asked by Mrs. Bravo to bring her some more Marsala in the glass that had contained the wine and water. On her way downstairs to the dining-room, the girl met her master at the foot of the stairs. She noticed that he looked " queer " and very strange in the face, but did not appear to be in pain. He looked twice at her, yet did not speak, though it was his custom, but passed on.

Mr. Bravo was alone after the departure of his wife and Mrs. Cox until the time when he passed the housemaid at the foot of the stairs. He entered his wife's dressing-room, and the maid Mrs. Bravo's bedroom. In the dressing-room, according to Mrs. Cox's statement, Mr. Bravo spoke to his wife in French, with reference to the wine. This had frequently been the subject of unpleasant remarks before ; but Mrs. Bravo had no recollection of the conversation on this occasion.

After leaving his wife in her room, Mr. Bravo went to his own bedroom and closed the door. The maid left Mrs. Bravo's bedroom and met her mistress in the passage partially undressed and on her way to bed. Mrs. Bravo and Mrs. Cox entered their bedrooms and the former drank her Marsala and went to bed.

In about quarter of an hour, Mr. Bravo's bedroom door was heard to open, and he shouted out, " Florence ! Florence ! Hot water." The maid ran into Mrs. Bravo's room, calling out that Mr. Bravo was ill. Mrs. Cox, who had not yet undressed, ran at once to his room. She found him standing in his night-gown at the open window, apparently vomiting, and this the maid also saw. Mrs. Cox further stated that Mr. Bravo said to her, " I have taken poison. Don't tell Florence " (alluding to his wife) ; and to this confession on the part of Mr. Bravo, Mrs. Cox adhered. After this, Mr. Bravo was again very sick, and some hot water was brought by the maid. After the vomiting he sank to the floor insensible, and remained unconscious for some hours. Mrs. Cox tried to raise him, and got some mustard and water, but he could not swallow it. She then applied mustard to his feet, and coffee was procured, but he was also unable to swallow that. Meanwhile a doctor, who had attended Mrs. Bravo, and who lived at some distance, was sent for. Mrs. Bravo, who was aroused from sleep by the maid, and who seems to have been greatly excited, insisted on a nearer practitioner being sent for, and in a short time a medical man, living close by, arrived on the scene. The doctor found Mr. Bravo sitting or lying on a chair, completely unconscious, and the heart's action almost suspended. He had him laid on the bed, and then administered some hot brandy and water, but was unable to get him to swallow it. In about half an hour another medical man arrived, and was met by Mrs. Cox, who said she was sure Mr. Bravo had taken chloroform. Both doctors came to the conclusion that the patient was in a dangerous state, and endeavoured to administer restoratives. Realising the critical nature of the case, Dr. George Johnson, of King's College Hospital, was sent for. Meanwhile, Mr. Bravo was again seized with vomiting, mostly blood, and the doctors came to the conclusion he was suffering from some irritant poison. About three o'clock he became conscious and able to be questioned. He was at once asked, " What have you taken ? " But from first to last he persisted in declaring, in the most solemn manner, that he had taken nothing except some laudanum for toothache. In reply to other questions, asking him if there were any poisons about the house, he replied, there was only the laudanum and chloroform for toothache, some Condy's Fluid, and " rat poison in the stable." Mr. Bravo did not lose consciousness again until the time of his death, which occurred fifty-five and a half hours after he was first taken ill.

Immediately after, his bedroom was searched, but nothing was found but the laudanum bottle, and a little chloroform and camphor liniment which had been brought from another room. There were no remains of any solid poison in paper, glass, or tumbler, and nothing to indicate any poison had been taken.

The post-mortem examination showed evidence of great gastric irritation, extending downwards, but there was no appearance of any disease in the body, or inflammation, congestion or ulceration. It was left therefore to the chemical analysis to show what was the irritating substance which had been introduced into the body, and supply a key to part of the mystery. The matters which had been vomited in the early stage of Mr. Bravo's illness had been thrown away ; but on examination of the leads of the house beneath the bedroom window, some portion of the matter was found undisturbed, although much rain had fallen and the greater part must have been washed away. This was carefully collected and handed to Professor Redwood for analysis. From this matter he extracted a large amount of antimony. Antimony was also discovered in the liver and other parts of the body, and it was concluded that altogether nearly forty grains of this poison must have been swallowed by the unfortunate man. How he came to swallow this enormous dose, whether the design was homicidal or suicidal, there was not the slightest evidence to show. The possession of the antimony could not be traced to anyone in the house, and there was no evidence to show how the poison had been obtained. The whole affair was shrouded in mystery, and a mystery it remains.

CHAPTER XXXIX

THE CASE OF DR. LAMSON

THE only case on record in which the active principle of aconite has been used for the purpose of criminal poisoning is that of Dr. Lamson, who suffered the extreme penalty of the law for administering the drug to Percy Malcolm John, and thereby causing his death.

The story is remarkable for the cold-blooded way in which the murder was carried out.

George Henry Lamson, a surgeon in impecunious circumstances, had a reversionary interest, through his wife, in a sum of £1,500, which would come to him on the death of his brother-in-law, Percy Malcolm John. The latter, a sickly youth of eighteen years of age, was paralysed in his lower limbs from old-standing spinal disease.

At the beginning of December, 1881, Lamson went down to the school where John had been placed as a boarder, and had an interview with him in the presence of the headmaster, professing at the same time a kindly interest in the youth and his health. During the interview he produced some gelatine capsules, one of which he offered to the headmaster in order that he might see how easily it dissolved in the mouth, and another he filled with a white powder presumed to be sugar and gave to his brother-in-law. Directly after seeing him swallow it he took his departure. Within a quarter of an hour, the boy became unwell, saying he felt the same as when Lamson had given him a quinine pill on a former occasion, also adding : " My skin feels all drawn up and my throat burning."

Violent vomiting soon set in, and he became unable to swallow. This was rapidly followed by delirium, and in three hours and three quarters, death ensued.

A post-mortem examination was ordered, and the organs of the body, together with the remainder of the capsules and various pills and powders found in the boy's room which had been sent to him at different times by Dr. Lamson, were sent for analysis. Meanwhile, from information received by the police from another quarter, Lamson was arrested and charged with the murder of his brother-in-law.

The trial began on March 9th, 1882, before Mr. Justice Hawkins, the Solicitor-General, Mr. Poland, appearing for the prosecution and Mr. Montagu Williams and others for the defence.

The Solicitor-General in his opening speech stated that the post-mortem on the body revealed the fact that the only sign of disease was the old-standing curvature of the spine and evidence of paralysis in the lower extremities. There was much, however, that called for remark in the condition of the stomach and other organs. The conclusion that the medical men came to was, that there was no natural cause to account for death, but that the state of the stomach indicated that death had resulted from poison—not what was called a local irritant poison, but some vegetable poison which had acted upon the nerves and other centres.

Dr. Stevenson, who, together with Dr. Dupré, had conducted the analysis, gave evidence, and began by stating that he had received besides the organs of the body, certain packets of pills, powders and sugar. Working in collaboration with Dr. Dupré, he applied a modification of Stas's process to the liver, spleen and kidneys, and the result obtained was an alkaloidal extract which contained a trace of morphine, and when placed on the tongue gave a faint sensation like that produced by aconitine. The contents of the stomach, treated by the same process, also revealed an alkaloidal extract which when tasted produced the same faint sensation as that of aconitine. " When placed on the tongue," he continued, " the contact caused a burning sensation which extended to the lip, although the extract did not touch the lip. The character of the sensation was a burning and a tingling, a kind of numbness. It is difficult to describe. It produced a salivation, a desire to expectorate and a sensation at the back of the throat as if it were swelling up, and this was followed by a peculiar seared feeling as if a hot iron had been drawn over the tongue, or some strong caustic placed upon it.

" The effect of aconitine is a burning feeling extending down towards the stomach. It is a sickening feeling peculiar to this substance. I have never found it in any other alkaloid, and I have tasted a great number.

" With a portion of the alkaloidal extract," Dr. Stevenson continued, " I made an experiment. I dissolved it and injected it beneath the skin of a mouse. The animal was obviously affected in two minutes. From that time onward it exhibited symptoms of poisoning and died in thirty minutes from the time of the injection of the substance. I then made a similar experiment with Morson's preparation of aconitine, procured specially for this purpose. I dissolved it in the same solution that I had used for the extract and operated with it on the mouse in the same manner. The effect was indistinguishable from that of the extract."

This same experiment was repeated with extracts made from the different organs, and each time the same result was obtained. On analysis of the vomit, an alkaloidal extract was again obtained. Dr. Stevenson applied this to his tongue and found it had a very powerful result, the effect lasting markedly for six and a half hours. On an injection being made into the back of a mouse, it was severely affected in two and a half minutes and death resulted in fifteen minutes. " Parallel results," he stated, " were obtained with aconitine. In my judgment the vomit contained a considerable quantity of aconitine. Approximately, it was not less than one-seventh and not more than one-fourth of a grain. There has only been one fatal case that I know of in which aconitine has caused the death of a human being, and the quantity that proved fatal—the quantity that actually caused death—was known not to be less than one-thirteenth of a grain."

Dr. Stevenson then described the results of the analysis of the various powders, pills and other substances, that had been handed to him. In the sweetmeats, cake and sugar he found no trace of poison at all. He then turned to the quinine powders, of which there were fourteen. " My attention," he said, " was called to one by Dr. Dupré. That it was a little different in colour, as also were two others, was obvious to the trained eye. An analysis of one revealed 0.83 gr. of aconitine and 0.93 gr. of quinine." On testing one of the pills, he came to the conclusion that it contained 0.45, or nearly half a grain of aconitine.

The capsules were handed to the judge, who remarked that the half grain took up barely one-tenth of the space in the capsule.

In the course of the trial it transpired that the prisoner had become possessed of aconitine a few days before the crime was committed. On the 11th of November he had been to a chemist in Oxford Street, and had a prescription made up consisting of atropine and morphine. On the 16th he called again and asked for a grain of digitalin, saying it was for external use. The liquid in the bottle was found to be discoloured and the assistant, fearing it might be impure, refused to supply it. A few days later Dr. Lamson called again and asked for some aconitine. The assistant, knowing this was a poison of a very dangerous character, declined to supply it and advised him to go where he was better known.

On November 24th, Dr. Lamson went to a firm of chemists in the city and asked for two grains of aconitine. When requested to sign his name, he wrote George H. Lamson, Bournemouth, and the name being in the Medical Directory, he was duly supplied with the required amount.

When the name of Dr. Lamson appeared in the newspapers in connexion with the death of Percy John, the assistant who had supplied the poison drew the attention of his employers to the circumstance, and the police were communicated with.

Mr. Montagu Williams, for the defence, urged that the results of Dr. Stevenson's and Dr. Dupré's experiments were consistent with other causes and suggested that the extracts which were so fatal to the mice might contain certain animal poisons, the result of decomposition. He contended that it had been admitted that very little was known of aconitine, and that therefore these tests were not to be relied upon. The proper verdict, he submitted, would be the Scottish one of " Non Proven," and as that was not possible in England, the prisoner was entitled to an acquittal. He reminded the jury of the weak state of the boy's health, and the general expectation that he would not live long.

The judge, in summing up, said the question for the jury to decide was whether they were satisfied the deceased came to his death by poison, and if so, whether the poison was administered by the prisoner. It was for the prosecution to prove the guilt of the prisoner, and if they failed to do so the case was at an end. The trial lasted for six days, and after the summing-up, the jury retired, returning after an absence of twenty-five minutes, with a verdict of " Guilty." The judge then pronounced sentence of death on Lamson, which was duly carried out on August 28th, 1882.

According to evidence at the trial, it is probable that Lamson had made several previous attempts on the boy's life with aconitine in the form of pills and powders, which he had given him under the pretence of prescribing for his ailments. The money to which he was entitled on the death of John doubtless supplied the motive for the crime.

Lamson, as a medical man, no doubt knew that there was no chemical test for aconitine, and that it would not be likely to be detected during the post-mortem. In fact, there was nothing to show after the autopsy that the cause of death was not natural, and it was only the few words uttered by the dying boy, alluding to his sensations, which gave the clue to the scientific investigators.

The difficulty of proving the presence of a rare vegetable alkaloid in the body after death was, no doubt, duly considered by Lamson when he selected aconitine as the medium for his evil design, but science proved the master of the criminal, and the evidence of the instrument by which the crime was committed was indisputably proved.

CHAPTER XL

" THE PIMLICO MYSTERY "

CHLOROFORM belongs to the class of neurotic poisons which act on the brain, and produce loss of sensation. It is a colourless, heavy and volatile liquid, having a peculiar ethereal odour which cannot be easily mistaken, and a sweet pungent taste when diluted. For producing insensibility it requires both careful and experienced administration, and more lives have been lost by carelessness in using than from the noxious character of the drug.

The stories that appear from time to time, of persons who have been rendered unconscious by simply waving a chloro-formed handkerchief before the face, usually emanate from the fertile brain of some imaginative fictionist. As an internal poison chloroform has rarely been used, although there are many cases on record where persons have accustomed themselves to drinking chloroform, until they have been able to swallow it in very large quantities. The one recorded instance in which it was alleged to have been used internally for the criminal destruc-tion of life was in the remarkable case which came to be known as the " Pimlico Mystery."

The trial of Adelaide Bartlett, for the wilful murder of her husband by administering chloroform to him, was held before Mr. Justice Wills at the Central Criminal Court on April 12th, 1886, and lasted for six days. The case attracted considerable attention and interest throughout, which culminated in a dramatic scene at the close, and the acquittal of the accused woman. The strange relations which existed between Mrs. Bartlett and her husband, the yet more strange relations between her and the man who in the first instance was included in the accusation, together with the exceptional circumstances of his acquittal and his immediate appearance in the witness-box, formed a case of peculiar dramatic interest.

Thomas Edwin Bartlett, the husband of the accused, was a grocer, having several shops in the suburbs of London, and at the time of his death was forty years of age. In 1875, he married a young French girl named Adelaide Blanche de la Tremoille, a native of Orléans, whom he met at the house of his brother. After the marriage he sent her to a boarding-school at Stoke Newington, and she lived with her husband only during the vacation. At a later period she went to a convent school in Belgium, where she remained for about eighteen months, after which she rejoined her husband, and settled down to live in London.

During Christmas of 1881, she gave birth to a stillborn child which so affected her, that she came to the resolution that she would have no more children. Some four years later, Mr. Bartlett and his wife made the acquaintance of the Rev. George Dyson, a young Wesleyan minister, who soon became on terms of great social intimacy, visiting and dining with them frequently. The admiration for their friend seems to have been common to both husband and wife. In 1885, Bartlett made a will, leaving all he possessed to his wife, and making Mr. Dyson and his solicitors his executors. Shortly afterwards, the Bartletts removed to furnished apartments in Claverton Street, Pimlico, where they apparently lived on good terms and were still frequently visited by their friend Mr. Dyson.

On December 10th in the same year, Mr. Bartlett became seriously ill. Peculiar symptoms developed, which excited the curiosity and surprise of the medical man called in to attend him. The state of his gums suggested to the doctor that the illness was due to mercury, which in some way was being administered to him, and he complained of nervous depression and sleeplessness. He appeared to be gradually recovering from this, but on December 19th Mr. Bartlett himself suggested that a second doctor should be called in, lest, as he put it, " his friends should suspect, if anything happened to him, that his wife was poisoning him." The cause for this was put down to some ill-feeling which had formerly existed between Mrs. Bartlett and her husband's father. A second practitioner, was therefore called in and the patient, on December 26th, though still weak, was apparently well and went out for a drive.

The next day, Mrs. Bartlett asked Mr. Dyson, who was constantly calling at the house, to procure for her a considerable quantity of chloroform, which she told him she had previously used on her husband for some internal ailment of long standing, and that this internal affection had upon previous occasions given him paroxysms. She further expressed a belief that he might die suddenly in one of these attacks. Dyson seems to have yielded to her request without question and obtained three different lots of chloroform, in all six ounces, from various chemists, giving the reason that he required it for taking out grease spots. He then placed it all together in one bottle. Two days after he met Mrs. Bartlett on the Embankment and handed her the chloroform.

During his illness, Mr. Bartlett had slept on a camp bedstead in the front drawing-room, his wife occupying a sofa close by. On December 31st he was apparently in good health, and about half-past ten o'clock in the evening, Mrs. Bartlett told the servant she required nothing else and retired with her husband for the night. At four o'clock in the morning the house was aroused by Mrs. Bartlett, and it was discovered that her husband was dead in bed.

The statement made by the lady was, that when her husband had settled for the night she sat down at the foot of the bed with her hand resting upon his feet. She dozed off in her chair, but awoke with a sensation of cramp, and was horrified to find her husband's feet were deathly cold. She tried to pour some brandy down his throat, but found he was dead. She then aroused the household.

The first person who entered the room was the landlord, who noticed a peculiar smell that reminded him of chloric ether. The doctor was promptly sent for but from external examination he could find nothing to account for death. The only bottle found was one that contained a drop or two of chlorodyne. A post-mortem examination was held, and the stomach showed evidence of having contained a considerable quantity of chloroform. There was no internal disease or growth, the organs being quite healthy, and nothing to account for death beyond the chloroform, which the medical men concluded must have been the cause of death.

The coroner's inquiry resulted in a verdict of wilful murder against Adelaide Bartlett and George Dyson, and they were both arrested.

At the trial, the Crown decided to offer no evidence against Dyson, and, after being indicted and pleading "Not guilty," he was discharged by the judge to be called as a witness.

A brilliant array of counsel were engaged on the case. Sir Charles Russell had charge of the prosecution, while the defence of Mrs. Bartlett was entrusted to Sir Edward Clarke, and that of Mr. Dyson to Mr. Lockwood.

Dyson's examination occupied nearly the whole of the second day of the trial, during which he detailed the form of the curious intimacy between Mrs. Bartlett and himself. He related how he procured the chloroform and disposed of the bottles after hearing the result of the post-mortem, by throwing them away on Wandsworth Common while on his way to preach at Tooting. He was in the habit of kissing Mrs. Bartlett, and usually called her Adelaide. He had had conversations with Mr. Bartlett on the subject of marriage, and had heard him express the opinion that a man should have two wives, one to look after the household duties, and another to be a companion and confidante. He had told Mr. Bartlett he was becoming attached to his wife, but the latter seemed to encourage it, and asked him to continue the intimacy. He did not mention the matter of having procured the chloroform for Mrs. Bartlett until he had heard the result of the post-mortem.

The medical man called in to attend Mr. Bartlett during his

illness described the condition in which he found him, and his recovery. He also gave an account of a very extraordinary statement, which was made to him by Mrs. Bartlett after the death of her husband. She said at the age of sixteen years she was selected by Mr. Bartlett as a wife for companionship only and for whom no carnal feeling should be entertained. The marriage compact was that they should live together simply as loving friends. This rule was faithfully observed for about six years of their married life, and then only broken at her earnest and repeated entreaty that she should be permitted to become really a wife and a mother. The child was stillborn, and from that time the two lived together, but their relations were not those of matrimony. Her husband showed great affection for her of an ultra-platonic kind and encouraged her to pursue various studies, which she did to please him. He affected to admire her and liked to surround her with male acquaintances, and seemed to enjoy their attentions to her. Then they became acquainted with Dyson. Her husband conceived a great liking for him, and threw them together. He requested them to kiss in his presence and seemed to enjoy it and gave her to understand that he had " given her " to Mr. Dyson. As her husband gradually recovered from his illness he expressed a wish that they should resume the ordinary relations of man and wife, but she resented it. She therefore sought for some means to prevent his desire and for this purpose she asked Dyson to procure the chloroform.

On the night of his death, some conversation of this kind had taken place between them and when he was in bed she brought the bottle of chloroform. She gave it to him, informing him of her intention to sprinkle some upon a handkerchief and wave it in his face, thinking that thereby he would go peacefully to sleep. He looked at the bottle and placed it by the side of the low bed, then turning over on his side, apparently went to sleep. She fell asleep also, sitting at the foot of the bed, with her arm round his feet ; she heard him snoring, then woke again, and found he was dead.

Dr. Stevenson, who made the analysis, gave evidence as to finding eleven and a quarter grains of pure chloroform in the stomach of the deceased, but judging from the time that had elapsed and the very volatile nature of the liquid, he concluded that a large quantity must have been swallowed. No other poisons were found. The jury, after deliberating nearly two hours, returned a verdict of " Not guilty," and Mrs. Bartlett was acquitted.

There was no evidence to prove that chloroform had been administered to Mr. Bartlett, and it was suggested that he had awakened and by mistake swallowed some of the contents of the bottle which was standing by his bedside.

CHAPTER XLI

THE MAYBRICK CASE

THE trial of Mrs. Florence Maybrick on the charge of causing the death of her husband by the administration of arsenic, was one of the most memorable poisoning cases of the nineteenth century.

The case excited the keenest interest both in this country and in the United States, where the principal actors in the tragedy were well-known.

Mr. James Maybrick, a cotton broker, who lived at Grassendale, a suburb of Liverpool, was about fifty years of age at the time of his death and was some twenty-five years older than his wife, who was but eighteen when they were married.

For some years they lived a quiet domestic life but in the Spring of 1889 they had a serious quarrel apparently arising out of Mrs. Maybrick's relations with another man. Immediately after this disagreement, she consulted a solicitor with a view to a separation but a reconciliation took place, although her husband apparently continued to distrust her.

Mr. Maybrick had been a sufferer from chronic dyspepsia and for some years had been medically treated by physicians both in Liverpool and in London. He was also in the habit of dosing himself and a considerable number of medicine bottles were found at his office and in the house after his death.

On April 14th, 1889, he consulted a physician in London who prescribed a tonic containing nux vomica, which he appeared to have been taking.

About the 21st of that month, Mrs. Maybrick purchased a packet of fly-papers at a local chemist's shop where she was well-known and on the 29th she bought a further packet at another shop together with some tincture of benzoin and elderflowers with the object, she subsequently stated, of making an arsenical face-wash which she wished to use before going to a ball. To do this she steeped the papers in water in the bedroom where three of her servants saw it, and she attended the ball with her brother-in-law on the 30th, after which nothing more was seen of the fly-papers.

On April 27th Mr. Maybrick had attended the Wirral races and dined at a friend's house although he complained of having felt unwell all day. On the following morning he was still feeling ill, and his wife gave him an emetic of mustard and water and sent for the local doctor.

He got sufficiently well to go to his business and did so until May 3rd. He told one of the maids he thought that the medicine he had had made up in London had disagreed with him. On that night he was taken seriously ill and his local doctor who had been treating him for extreme irritability of the stomach, becoming puzzled by the persistent vomiting and the rapidly increasing weakness of his patient, decided to call a physician from Liverpool in consultation.

Up to this time, Mrs. Maybrick had nursed her husband, and no suspicion of poisoning was aroused, until a letter she had written and addressed to her lover and given to a nursemaid to post, was opened by the girl who handed it to Mr. Maybrick's brother. This intercepted letter which conveyed the intelligence to her lover that her husband was " sick unto death," revealed the connexion between them and proved one of the strongest pieces of evidence against Mrs. Maybrick at the trial. From this time suspicions were aroused and trained nurses were called in and placed in sole charge of the sick man, with instructions to watch and see that his wife administered nothing to him.

On the night of the 8th, Mr. Maybrick's brother who was in the house, gave one of the nurses a bottle of meat-juice which was left on the landing-table till the following evening when she opened it and gave her patient one or two spoonfuls, after which he fell asleep. While he was sleeping, according to her statement, Mrs. Maybrick took the bottle of meat-juice into the adjoining dressing-room where she slept, and returning in two or three minutes, replaced it on the table. She spoke to the nurse and asked her to go for some ice which the latter refused to do, on which Mrs. Maybrick retired to her room requesting the nurse to call her when her husband awoke.

Shortly afterwards Mr. Maybrick awoke with a choking sensation and was sick. The nurse called Mrs. Maybrick, who on coming into the bedroom at once removed the bottle of meat-juice from the table, where it stood among the medicine bottles, to the wash-stand. There it remained for twelve hours until Mr. Maybrick's brother removed it and handed it to Dr. Carter who took it away for analysis. The contents of the bottle which was about half-full was found to contain half a grain of arsenic.

How the arsenic got into the meat-juice was revealed by Mrs. Maybrick herself later. According to her statement, her husband asked her to put a certain " white powder " into it and told her where to find it. As she did so, she spilled some of the meat-juice and added water to make up the amount. She declared that she did not know what this powder was at the time, but concluded it was arsenic when she heard that arsenic had been found in the bottle when analysed. She said afterwards that she had removed the meat-juice bottle at the earliest opportunity, to the wash-stand where it was out of his sight and reach.

Shortly afterwards, Mr. Maybrick grew rapidly worse and died on the evening of May 11th.

Soon after his death, a search was instituted in the house and a packet containing seventy-one grains of arsenic mixed with charcoal, labelled " poison for cats," was found in a trunk in the linen room. A number of bottles and a tumbler containing arsenic in solution were found in Mr. Maybrick's hat-boxes which were lying on the floor of the room and with them a bottle of meat-juice, some of which Mrs. Maybrick was known to have given to her husband, also a handkerchief. More than one of the bottles discovered in the dressing-room contained arsenic in solution, apparently made from the charcoal mixture in the packet, but none of them were labelled poison.

A post-mortem examination of the body was made on May 13th and certain portions were removed for analysis but at first only traces of arsenic were found in the intestines and spleen. It was afterwards decided to exhume the body for a further analysis, which was carried out by Dr. Stevenson, analyst to the Home Office, who found 0.049 of a grain of arsenic in the liver.

Mrs. Maybrick was then arrested and charged with the wilful murder of her husband.

The trial took place at the Liverpool Assizes before Mr. Justice Stephen on July 31st, 1889, Mr. Addison Q.C. leading for the Crown while Sir Charles Russell appeared for the defence.

The scene in court when the trial opened on a bright, warm summer morning was a memorable one. The court was crowded long before the Judge arrived and every available space was occupied. The galleries were filled with women in light summer costumes who came provided with fans and smelling bottles. Many of them were friends and had been entertained by the unfortunate woman who was to be placed in the dock. The well of the court was thronged with barristers, prominent among whom was Sir Charles Russell, whose pale intellectual face and clear-cut features rendered him especially noticeable. In striking contrast was the portly figure of Mr. Addison, whose jovial face suggested more the country farmer than one learned in the law.

A fanfare of trumpets heralded the approach of the Judge, Sir James Fitzjames Stephens, who aged and bent with years, slowly walked to his chair followed by the Earl of Sefton, High Sheriff for the County.

Meanwhile, the prisoner, a short, slender figure, dressed in black, wearing a widow's bonnet and a thin black veil which partly concealed her face, ascended the steps from the cells below and almost unnoticed took her place in the dock. At a motion from the wardress who accompanied her, she stepped forward and stood facing the Judge with her hands clasped in front of her.

Mr. Addison opened the case for the Crown and dispassionately unfolded the story of the tragedy. Evidence was given by the servants of fly-papers having been seen in process of maceration in Mrs. Maybrick's bedroom. The pert nursemaid told how she intercepted her mistress's letter which led to the arousing of suspicion. The trained nurses who had charge of Mr. Maybrick during the last days of his illness gave evidence as to Mrs. Maybrick's suspicious conduct after she was banished from the sick-room and her suspected tampering with the bottle of meat-juice.

Dr. Stevenson, the Home Office analyst, gave evidence how he found arsenic in various medicine bottles, on handkerchiefs, in bottles of glycerine and in the pocket of a dressing-gown belonging to Mrs. Maybrick. He told how he had obtained 0.049 of a grain of arsenic from the liver and how he discovered traces in other organs of the body. In his opinion the body of the deceased man at the time of death probably contained a fatal dose of arsenic.

The medical evidence was very conflicting and while the doctors who had attended Mr. Maybrick during his illness and other experts stated that they believed death had been caused from the effects of arsenical poisoning, Dr. Tidy, a well-known toxicologist of the time stated in his opinion, the quantity of arsenic found in the body did not point to the fact that an overdose had been administered.

He believed that death had been due to gastro-enteritis and that the symptoms and post-mortem appearances distinctly pointed away from arsenic as the cause of death.

Dr. Macnamara, ex-President of the Royal College of Surgeons of Ireland stated that in his opinion Mr. Maybrick's death had not been caused by arsenical poisoning and he agreed with Dr. Tidy that Mr. Maybrick's death was due to gastro-enteritis unconnected with arsenical poisoning.

Witnesses were called to prove that Mr. Maybrick had been in the habit of taking arsenic in considerable quantities for some years, and that while he was in America he frequently purchased arsenic from chemists who knew he was in the habit of taking it.

A negro who had been in the service of Mr. Maybrick in America stated that he had seen his Master taking this " white powder " in beef tea.

Sir Charles Russell in his speech for the defence said it had been proved that Mr. Maybrick had been in the habit of taking arsenic for many years and that he was a man who prided himself on his knowledge of medicine. What was more likely than that he should have had a supply of that poison in the house and that he had ultimately dosed himself to death with it ?

After the last witness for the defence had left the box, Sir Charles Russell held a rapid consultation with Mrs. Maybrick. A glance of dissatisfaction crossed his face as he turned to the judge and asked if the prisoner might make a statement. The judge replied in the affirmative and the accused woman rose to her feet, and in a low voice broken by emotion, amid the breathless silence of those in court, read the following plea from a written paper she held in her hand :

" My Lord, I wish to make a statement, as well as I can, about a few facts in connexion with the dreadful and crushing charge against me—the charge of poisoning my husband and father of my dear children. I wish principally to refer to the fly-paper solution. The fly-papers I bought with the intention of using the solution as a cosmetic. Before my marriage, and since for many years, I have been in the habit of using this wash for the face prescribed for me by Dr. Graves, of Brooklyn. It consisted, I believe, principally, of arsenic, tincture of benzoin, elderflower water, and some other ingredients. This prescription I lost or mislaid last April, and as at the time I was suffering from an eruption on the face, I thought I should like to try and make a substitute myself. I was anxious to get rid of this eruption before I went to a ball on the 30th of that month. When I had been in Germany among my young friends there, I had seen used a solution derived from fly-papers soaked in elderflower water, and then applied to the face with a handkerchief well soaked in the solution. I procured the fly-papers and used them in the same manner, and to avoid evaporation I put the solution into a bottle so as to avoid as much as possible the admission of the air. For this purpose I put a plate over the fly-papers, then a folded towel over that, and then another towel over that. My mother has been aware for a great many years that I have used arsenic in solution. I now wish to speak of his illness. On Thursday night, May 9th, after the nurse had given my husband medicine I went and sat on the bed beside him. He complained to me of feeling very sick, very weak and very restless. He implored me then again to give him a powder which he had referred to earlier in the evening, and which I declined to give him. I was over-wrought, terribly anxious, miserably unhappy, and his evident distress utterly unnerved me. As he told me the powder would not harm him, and that I could put it in his food, I then consented. My Lord, I had not one true or honest friend in the house. I had no one to consult, no one to advise me. I was deposed from my position as mistress of my own house, and from the position of attending on my husband, and notwithstanding that he was so ill, and notwithstanding the evidence of the nurses and the servants, I may say that he missed me whenever I was not with him ; whenever I was out of the room he asked for me, and four days before he died I was not allowed to give him a piece of ice without its being taken out of my hand. I took the meat-juice into the inner room. On going through the door I spilled some of the liquid from the bottle, and in order to make up the quantity spilled I put in a considerable quantity of water. On returning into the room I found my husband asleep. I placed the bottle on the table near the window. As he did not ask for anything then, and as I was not anxious to give him anything, I removed it from the small table where it attracted his attention and put it on the wash-stand where he could not see it. There I left it. Until Tuesday, May 14th, the Tuesday after my husband's death, till a few moments before the terrible charge was made against me, no one in that house had informed me of the fact that a death certificate had been refused—or that there was any reason to suppose that my husband had died from any other than natural causes. It was only when a witness alluded to the presence of arsenic in the meat-juice that I was made aware of the nature of the powder my husband had been taking. In conclusion, I only wish to say that for the love of our children, and for the sake of their future, a perfect reconciliation had taken place between us, and on the day before his death I made a full and free confession to him."

It was evident from Sir Charles Russell's manner when he rose to make his final appeal, that Mrs. Maybrick had made her statement against his wish, but he still fought valiantly in her cause. He urged that if it had not been for the act of infidelity on her part there could be no motive assigned in the case and surely, he declared, there was a wide difference between the grave moral guilt of unfaithfulness and the criminal act involved in the deliberate plotting, by such wicked means, the felonious death of her husband. He closed his eloquent and brilliant appeal by putting two questions to the jury :

1. Was there clear, safe and satisfactory unequivocal proof that death was in fact caused by arsenical poisoning ?

2. Had the accused woman administered that poison, if to the poison the death of her husband was due ?

On the eighth day of the trial the judge in summing up the evidence, pointed to Mrs. Maybrick's relations with her lover as affording the best guide to a decision between the conflicting opinions of the doctors with regard to the cause of death. The

jury retired at 3.15, and had barely been absent thirty-eight
minutes when they returned to the court with the verdict of
" Guilty."

On being asked by the clerk if she had anything to say, Mrs.
Maybrick replied : " I have been found guilty, but excepting
my moral fault I am not guilty." The judge then passed
sentence of death.

The sentence aroused considerable feeling and the public
was divided into two parties, one protesting that Mrs. Maybrick
was innocent and the other that she was guilty. An agitation
was at once raised throughout the country for a reprieve, which
ended in a respite being granted, the sentence being afterwards
commuted to penal servitude for life.

For some years afterwards efforts were continually made to
secure the release of Mrs. Maybrick and successive Home
Secretaries investigated the circumstances of the case, but the
conviction was allowed to stand.

Sir Charles Russell frequently affirmed his belief in Mrs.
Maybricks' innocence and attributed the jury's verdict to the
judge's remarks upon the moral aspect of the case and even
after he became Lord Chief Justice of England, he stated his
personal belief that she had not been proved guilty.

The late Lord Moulton, who was eminent as a scientist as
well as a lawyer, took a deep interest in the case and in a letter
to the writer dated 1899, states :

" The point of interest was one of evidence as to the cause of
death. I have always been of opinion that—taking into consideration the fact that the deceased was an arsenic-eater—there
was no evidence that he was poisoned. The weight of the
medical testimony was in favour of that view, but that was not
the main point. In my opinion, the testimony for the prosecution entirely failed to support the onus which lay upon it.
The witnesses could not point out anything inconsistent with
non-poisoning."

Sir William Willcox, commenting on the case observes " it
is interesting from the fact that the proof of fatal poisoning
rested on the presence of 0.049 grain of arsenic in the liver, the
minimum fatal dose being about two grains."

After serving fourteen years imprisonment, Mrs. Maybrick
was released in January 1904 and went to live with her mother in
America.

The mystery of how and where the large quantity of arsenic
found in the house was obtained, was not solved during the trial.
It was obvious that arsenic obtained from fly-papers had little
to do with the case with the copious supply at hand, and the fly-
paper theory as to the origin of the poison employed may be
disregarded.

Since the trial, several interesting statements have been

published regarding fresh evidence on this point. One of these was a sworn statement made by Mr. Valentine Charles Blake, who was sent to Liverpool from America to see Mr. James Maybrick in 1888 and 1889, with a view to obtaining his assistance in placing a substitute for cotton on the market, in the process of making which arsenic was employed. He stated that in the course of conversation, Mr. Maybrick told him that he took arsenic when he could get it, and asked him if he could obtain some for him. In February, 1889, he called at Mr. Maybrick's office in Liverpool and gave him all the arsenic he had at his command, amounting to about 150 grains, some of the " white " and some of the two kinds of " black " arsenic, in three separate packets. " When we separated, James Maybrick took away the arsenic with him saying he was going to his house in Aigburth."

Interest in the matter was again aroused in 1926 on the publication of a book entitled *Fifty-two Years a Policeman*, by Sir William Nott-Bower, who was Chief Constable of Liverpool at the time of Mrs. Maybrick's trial. In it he states :

" Some time after the Home Secretary had announced Mrs. Maybrick's reprieve, a highly-respectable Liverpool chemist, carrying on business in the centre of the town, came to the police and stated he wished to make a voluntary confession.

" He said that in the Spring of 1889 Mrs. Maybrick drove up to his shop in her dog-cart and asked for powdered arsenic to kill rats (or cats), and he supplied her with a large quantity, which she took away with her.

" A week or two later she again drove up to his shop and told him she had lost the arsenic she had from him and asked for more, with which he supplied her. He said he was afraid to tell the police of this at the time, as he feared that being mixed up with such a case would injure him in his business, and also that he had made no entry of the transaction in his books. I reported the statement to the Home Office, but of course it was then useless for any practical purpose. If it had been given as evidence at the trial it is clear it would have been of supreme importance."

The one missing link in the chain of evidence at the trial was how arsenic was obtained in such large quantities.

Was this the solution of the mystery as to the source of the arsenic ?

The assertion in Sir William Nott-Bower's book called forth further statements in the press, including one giving the name of the chemist and another from Dr. Paul the pathologist who was engaged in the case. In a letter dated January 19th, 1926 the latter states :

" The source of the ' arsenic for cats ' was only a mystery to the prosecution. It was quite well-known to the defence some time before the trial. I was engaged to examine certain articles and give evidence respecting them and was consequently present at all the consultations. I remember the name of the chemist and where his shop was situated, and I was under the impression that his reason for some personal anxiety was that he sold the arsenic without added pigment which was illegal.

The information certainly came from the chemist and not from the accused, and it may be therefore, that Sir William Nott-Bower's memory was not at fault after all. A man whose confession had apparently been ignored by the defence might very well later on offer it to the prosecution."

To these statements Mrs. Maybrick herself made a reply on January 31st, 1926 to a newspaper representative in America. She said : " The chemist's story (of two packets of arsenic) was gone into at the time. The Crown lawyers had it investigated.

" It was so obvious that I could not have been in that part of Liverpool or indeed in the city at all on one of the occasions sworn to, that the evidence could not be relied upon.

" On the contrary it was part of the Crown case, that on this particular date I was at a London hotel with my lover. They had to choose between these two conflicting stories ; and much as it was to their interest to prove the purchase of the arsenic, they could only rely on the hotel story. That is why this alleged confession was never of any use."

Mrs. Maybrick again visited England a few years ago hoping to find fresh evidence in this new aspect of the case. During an interview she said : " The charge against me was that I had administered arsenic taken from fly-papers to my husband and much was made of the fact that this was the only way in which the poison could have come into the house. At the same time my mind was in such a torment that I could not think clearly, but thinking over the case since, I have recalled facts that suggest my husband was in the habit of taking arsenic in fairly strong doses.

" There is also the evidence of a Liverpool chemist, who remembers having sold the poison to my husband some time before his death.

" I believe this evidence was brought forward after the trial and had weight with the Home Secretary in advising a reprieve for me."

With reference to Mrs. Maybrick's liberation, Mr. Henry Seymour, formerly hon. secretary of the Maybrick Committee made the following interesting statement in a letter to the *Sunday Times*, on January 31st, 1926 :

" It was on the direct intervention of King Edward that Mrs. Maybrick was released on licence in 1904. Mr. Choate, the

American Ambassador at the time, had prevailed upon his Majesty to examine the case personally and he did so."

It is interesting to add that the late Lord Birkenhead in commenting on the case in his *Famous Trials*, states : " I cannot myself resist the conclusion that there was evidence upon which she could have been found guilty."

CHAPTER XLII

THE LAMBETH POISON MYSTERIES

TOWARDS the close of the year 1891 and the early part of 1892, public interest was excited by the mysterious deaths of several young women of the unfortunate class residing in the neighbourhood of Lambeth. The first case was that of a girl named Matilda Clover, who lived in Lambeth Road. On the night of October 20th, 1891, she spent the evening at a music-hall in company with a man, who returned with her to her lodgings about nine o'clock. Shortly afterwards she was seen to go out alone and purchased some bottled beer, which she carried to her rooms. After a little time the man left the house.

At three o'clock in the morning the inmates of the house were aroused by the screams of a woman, and on the landlady entering Matilda Clover's room, she found the unfortunate girl lying across the bed in the greatest agony. Medical aid was sent for, and the assistant of a neighbouring doctor saw the girl, and judged she was suffering from the effects of drink. He prescribed a sedative mixture, but she became worse, and, after a further convulsion, died on the following morning. The medical man, whose assistant had seen her on the previous night, gave a certificate that death was due to delirium tremens and syncope and Matilda Clover was buried at Tooting.

A few weeks afterwards, a woman called Ellen Donworth, who resided in Duke Street, Westminster Bridge Road, is stated to have received a letter, in consequence of which she went out between six and seven in the evening. About eight o'clock she was found in Waterloo Road in great agony and died while she was being conveyed to St. Thomas's Hospital. Before her death she made a statement, that a man with a dark beard and wearing a high hat had given her " two drops of white stuff " to drink. In this case a post-mortem examination was made and on analysis, both strychnine and morphine were found in the stomach, proving that the woman had been poisoned.

These cases had almost been forgotten, when some six months afterwards, public attention was again aroused by the mysterious deaths of two girls named Alice Marsh and Emma Shrivell, who lodged in Stamford Street.

On the evening of April 11th, 1892, a man, who one of the

girls in her dying testimony called " Fred " and whom she described as a doctor, called to see them, and together they partook of tea. The man stayed till 2 a.m., and during the evening gave them both " three long pills."

Half an hour after the man left the house, both girls were found in a dying condition. While they were being removed to the hospital, Alice Marsh died in the cab, and Emma Shrivell lived only for six hours afterwards. The result of an analysis of the stomachs and organs revealed the fact that death in each case had been caused by strychnine.

There was absolutely no evidence beyond the vague description of the man for the police to work upon and this case, like the others, seemed likely to remain among the unsolved mysteries of London. The perpetrator of these cold-blooded crimes however, was at last brought to justice by the following curious chain of circumstances.

Some time after the deaths of the two girls Marsh and Shrivell, a Dr. Harper of Barnstaple received a letter, in which the writer stated that he had indisputable evidence that the doctor's son, who had recently qualified as a medical practitioner in London, had poisoned two girls—Marsh and Shrivell—and that he, the writer, required £1,500 to suppress it. Dr. Harper placed this letter in the hands of the police, with the result that on June 3rd, 1892, a man named Thomas Neill, or Neill Cream, was arrested on the charge of sending a threatening letter. He was brought up at Bow Street on this charge several times, during which it transpired that in the preceding November a well-known London physician had also received a letter, in which the writer declared that he had evidence to show that the physician had poisoned a Miss Clover with strychnine, which evidence he could purchase for £2,500, and so save himself from ruin.

Neill Cream was remanded, and in the meantime the body of Matilda Clover was exhumed, and the contents of the stomach sent to Dr. Stevenson, one of the Government analysts, for examination. He discovered the presence of strychnine, and came to the conclusion that some one had administered a fatal dose to her.

An inquest was then held on the body of Matilda Clover, with the result that Thomas Neill, or Neill Cream, was committed on the charge of wilful murder.

The man's lodgings were searched after his arrest and a curious piece of paper was discovered, on which, written in pencil in his handwriting, were the initials " M. C." and opposite to them two dates, and then a third date, viz. October 20th, which was the date of Matilda Clover's death. On the same paper, in connexion with the initials " E. S.," there was also found two dates, one being April 11th, which was the date of Emma Shrivell's death. There was also found in his possession a paper bearing the address of Marsh and Shrivell and it was afterwards proved that he had said on more than one occasion that he knew them well.

In his room, a number of small pills were also discovered, each containing from one-sixteenth to one-twenty-second of a grain of strychnine, also fifty-four other bottles of pills, seven of which contained strychnine, a pocket medicine-case, and a bottle containing one hundred and sixty-eight pills, each containing one-twenty-second of a grain of strychnine. These, it is supposed, he obtained while acting as an agent for the Harvey Drug Co., of America. It was found he had purchased a quantity of empty gelatine capsules from a chemist in Parliament Street, which there is little doubt he had used to administer a number of the small pills in a poisonous dose.

Thomas Neill, or Neill Cream, was tried for the wilful murder of Matilda Clover at the Central Criminal Court before Mr. Justice Hawkins, on October 18th, 1892, the trial lasting five days.

It transpired that Cream, who had received some medical education and styled himself a doctor, came to this country from America on October 1st, 1891, and on arriving in London first stayed at Anderton's Hotel, in Fleet Street. Shortly afterwards he took apartments in Lambeth and became engaged to a lady living at Berkhampstead.

He was identified as having been seen in the company of Matilda Clover, and also by a policeman as the man who left the house in Stamford Street on the night that Marsh and Shrivell were murdered.

Dr. Stevenson, who made the analysis of the body of Matilda Clover on May 6th, 1892, stated in his evidence that he found strychnine in the stomach, liver, and brain, and that quantitatively he obtained one-sixteenth of a grain of strychnine from two pounds of animal matter. He also examined the organs from the bodies of Alice Marsh and Emma Shrivell. He found 6.39 grains of strychnine in the stomach and its contents of Alice Marsh, and 1.6 grain of strychnine in the stomach and its contents, also 1.46 grain in the vomit and 0.2 grain in a small portion of the liver of Emma Shrivell.

The jury, after deliberating for ten minutes, returned a verdict of guilty, and Thomas Neill, or Neill Cream as he was otherwise known, was sentenced to death. He was executed on November 15th, 1892.

CHAPTER XLIII

THE KIDWELLY MYSTERY

IN 1919, there was living at Rumsey House in the little town of Kidwelly in South Wales, Mr. Harold Greenwood a solicitor who practised at Llanelly, with his wife and family and a sister of Mrs. Greenwood who shared the house with them. He had been married about twenty-three years, his eldest daughter being twenty-two at the time when a tragic event happened in their home.

Mrs. Greenwood, who was forty-seven years of age, had for some time been in delicate health and under medical treatment. She was liable to fainting attacks and suffered from heart-trouble for which she had been treated by a local medical practitioner for some fifteen years. During this period he had prescribed various tonics for her but she gradually grew worse. At this time, her sister was away from Rumsey House and Mrs. Greenwood, although weak and feeling ill, still carried on the household duties and did not call in her doctor until two or three days before her death.

On June 14th, 1919, she attended a tennis club meeting at Ferry Side in company with the vicar of the parish. She came back with him, and was apparently fairly cheerful and took part in the business transactions of the club. On the Sunday morning she was not so well but invited a Miss Phillips to come and take supper with the family that night.

On Sunday she had luncheon about 1.30 with her husband, her eldest daughter and son. The luncheon consisted of roast beef and gooseberry tart with custard. The table was laid by a maid called Maggie Williams, and whilst so doing she had occasion to go to the cupboard for china, where she saw Mr. Greenwood, who, according to her account, remained there for a quarter of an hour. She waited until he left the cupboard; she then placed on the table as was her custom, wine and whisky which she took from the cupboard in the dining-room. Mrs. Greenwood usually drank Burgundy, and on the previous Saturday she had bought a bottle in Kidwelly. When the maid went to the cupboard to get the wine, she found what she believed to be a bottle of port, which she said had a red label with the words " Port Wine " on it. She noticed also that it was not a full bottle, but she put it on the table before Mrs. Greenwood's place. She saw Mr. Greenwood in the dining-room during luncheon, and Mrs. Greenwood drank some of the wine while he had whisky and soda. According to her account, Miss Greenwood drank water.

The same maid laid the table for supper and again put the whisky on the table as at lunch. By supper-time the wine bottle had gone and she looked for it again on the following Monday morning in the cupboard, but it was missing.

In the afternoon Mrs. Greenwood had complained of suffering from diarrhœa which her husband told her was probably due to her having eaten gooseberry tart at lunch. At 5.30 she took a walk slowly up the garden and sat on the lawn, but complaining to her husband of considerable pain about the heart, he went into the house and brought her some brandy. This she was unable to retain, and within an hour became very faint. She was taken by her husband and her daughter to her bedroom and the doctor was sent for. At 6.45 p.m. Mr. Greenwood went across the road to fetch the doctor, who lived only about ten yards away. The doctor found that Mrs. Greenwood had been very sick and she told him that the gooseberry tart had upset her. The doctor and Mr. Greenwood then went into the garden where they played a game of clock golf, the latter remarking that he was anxious about his wife's condition and had detained the doctor for that reason. As a result of this detention, it was stated, no medicine was sent to Mrs. Greenwood until 7.30 that evening.

About 6.45 p.m. Miss Phillips, the lady Mrs. Greenwood had invited to supper, arrived and went up to Mrs. Greenwood's room and saw her. Being alarmed at her condition, of her own accord she sent for the district nurse who, on her arrival, found Mrs. Greenwood in a state of collapse. She was vomiting and was very cold. At nine o'clock the nurse went home and returned again at ten, when she became seriously alarmed at Mrs. Greenwood's condition. She asked Mr. Greenwood to go for the doctor and he went. At the doctor's house he saw his sister, and told her his wife was very ill and that he thought she might not get over it as the attack was worse than one of her usual fainting fits.

Between one and three a.m. Mrs. Greenwood was much worse and she died at 3.20 in the morning. The doctor certified that her death was due to valvular disease of the heart and Mrs. Greenwood was buried at Kidwelly.

So far we have a very ordinary, commonplace story, which to all appearance might have happened in any family, and probably has done, but in small towns and villages among little communities there is always a considerable amount of gossip, and so rumours are spread and enlarged as they are passed on from one to another. Possibly there was an undercurrent of gossip not untinged with malice going on in the small town, but matters did not come to a head until April 1920. Nearly twelve months had elapsed, since Mrs. Greenwood's death, when an application was made by the Coroner to the Home Office for the exhumation of her body. This was carried out and a post-mortem examination was made, and an analysis disclosed the presence of a considerable quantity of arsenic in the remains. From the evidence that came before the Coroner, Mr. Greenwood was detained by the police while the jury were deliberating on their verdict. He was afterwards arrested and committed for trial on the charge of murdering his wife by poison and was tried before Mr. Justice Sharman at the Carmarthenshire Assizes on November 2nd, 1920.

At the trial the prosecution sought to show some motive that would point to their interpretation of Mr. Greenwood's actions. It transpired that in the middle of 1919 he was often visited by a young lady to whom he made some valuable presents and on October 21st he married her at the Registrar's office in Llanelly.

On inquiries being made, it was found that on March 30th, 1919, Mr. Greenwood had ordered from an Edinburgh firm a quantity of " Eureka " weed-killer and they had supplied him with ten gallons on April 22nd. This weed-killer was composed of arsenic with a solvent, so that three grains would approximately contain two grains of arsenic.

On October 24th, 1919, Mr. Greenwood was invited to make a statement to the superintendent of police in reference to his wife's death. In this he suggested that the morphine pills given by the doctor to his wife were too strong. He mentioned this in conversation with the vicar of the parish who was a friend of the family, and wondered if she had taken something herself.

Miss Phillips, the friend of Mrs. Greenwood, described how she found her on the Sunday evening, and said that on the table at supper she noticed a small flask of wine at the seat where Mrs. Greenwood sat ; she saw no bottle of wine and she had never seen the flask before. She related an incident how one day Mrs. Greenwood had said to her she thought her wine had been tampered with ; she said it was nasty and she could not drink it. This was the burgundy which she was in the habit of drinking.

The nurse who was called in to Mrs. Greenwood on the night of her death said she had sent for the doctor who prescribed some pills. She became very drowsy afterwards, then comatose and in about twenty minutes afterwards she died. She said Mr. Greenwood had told her when she went to pour out the second dose of the medicine that his wife had complained that the first dose had caught her at the back of the throat. She took some herself, and then she gave her the second dose, but she did not make any remark.

She was well enough to take the pills and she herself put them on her tongue, and within five or ten minutes she was asleep. She declared that if she had known they contained one grain of morphine she would not have given them. She stated that the two morphine pills which she gave to Mrs. Greenwood were given to her by Mr. Greenwood who told her to give them to the patient.

The doctor, who attended Mrs. Greenwood to the end, said he gave a certificate stating that death was due to valvular disease of the heart and that four or five weeks before her death he had noticed a marked change in her, due to a tumour and heart trouble. None of the medicine he prescribed for her contained arsenic. The two pills which were ordered to be given, one immediately and one in half an hour, contained half a grain of powdered opium, which would be equivalent to one-fortieth of a grain of morphine in each pill.

While making this statement the doctor was interrupted by Sir Edward Marshall Hall, who defended Mr. Greenwood, with the remark that he had previously sworn that each pill had contained half a grain of morphine. " One grain of morphine " said counsel, " is a fatal dose."

The judge asked the doctor how he came to say that there was half a grain of morphine in each pill when it was opium, and his reply was that it was a mistake which he had made that day. He further said that he had attended Mrs. Greenwood for about sixteen years and she suffered from hæmorrhage and catarrh of the throat, and he suspected internal trouble, the cause of which he found at the post-mortem examination was a tumour. He thought when he saw her that she was suffering from acute indigestion, but did not hear about the diarrhœa. It was after ten o'clock when he prescribed the pills. He agreed that there was an enormous difference between morphine and opium, and said that opium pills were sometimes called morphine pills. The judge then asked the doctor if he had given a whole grain of morphine and not of opium, would it not then have been very dangerous, and he replied : " I have no doubt at all."

Sir Marshall Hall, counsel for the defence, repeated the doctor's evidence before the magistrate in which he said in each pill there was half a grain of morphine, and had stated that in her condition at 10.30 it would have been perfectly safe to have given a grain of morphia. " Do you mean to say," continued Sir Edward, turning to the doctor, " you understood then they were talking about opium ? " The doctor replied : " It was opium I gave."

The doctor further stated that he knew that Mr. Greenwood had told the police it was the pills that did it, and that after taking them his wife went to sleep and never woke. The pills he sent to Mrs. Greenwood contained not half a grain of morphine but half a grain of powdered opium.

Margaret Morris, who was cook to the Greenwood family, said she prepared the luncheon on June 15th, the day her mistress was taken ill. The servants had part of the same food and felt no ill effect.

The parlourmaid, who laid the table, said she put whisky upon it for Mr. Greenwood and a bottle of port at the side of Mrs. Greenwood. The bottle bore a label and was three parts full. She gave some wine to Mrs. Greenwood and no one else had any of the wine. On laying the table for supper she placed the bottles in the same way, taking them from the cupboard in the room. She did not clear away the supper and had not seen the bottle since. On the Sunday morning she noticed that Mr. Greenwood was in the china cupboard a quarter of an hour. She told the police, when questioned, that the bottle of wine she put on the table had a red label printed in black letters and she read on the label the word " Port." She was emphatic on this point and remarked that the burgundy was in a bottle which had a white label. She placed a tumbler of water on the table for Miss Greenwood and had never seen her drink burgundy.

The chemist in Kidwelly said that Mr. Greenwood bought two quart tins of " Weedicide " from him on June 7th, and 8th, for which he signed his poison register, and Messrs. Dobbie of Edinburgh produced an order from Mr. Greenwood in February, 1919, for " Eureka " weed-killer which was delivered after April. The amount supplied on April 23rd, 1919, in the form of powder, was enough to make a hundred gallons, and the chemist to the firm said the weed-killer contained 60 per cent of arsenic, three grains of the powder containing two grains of arsenic, and it was pink in colour and was very soluble.

Mr. Webster, who carried out the analysis for the Home Office, said he found arsenic present in all the organs removed from the body of Mrs. Greenwood, the total amount being .278 of a grain, or a little over one quarter of a grain. He found no trace of morphine or other poison. He described the tests that he had made, and produced the mirrors obtained from the analyses of the various organs and compared them with standard mirrors in which a certain quantity of arsenic was contained. By means of these he found the following amounts of arsenic in the various organs : in the stomach, .009 gr. ; in the small intestine, .067 gr. ; in the large intestine, .008 gr. ; in the liver, .131 gr. ; in the spleen, .006 gr. ; in the kidneys, .019 gr. ; in the uterus, .012 gr. ; in the rectum, .006 gr. ; in the heart, .004 gr. ; in the lungs, .012 gr. ; in the œsaphagus, .003 gr. and in the brain, .001 gr. ; making in all a total of 0.278 of a grain.

He had examined " Eureka " weed-killer and found that four

grains would correspond to two and a quarter grains of arsenic and that amount could be dissolved in about ten drops of water. The addition of two grains of arsenic in this way could be made to a wineglass full of port wine without notice in colour or flavour. He produced two small bottles, one containing port wine, and the other, port with four grains of weed-killer dissolved in it. The same quantity in tea made practically no difference to the taste. The colour in the case of the tea would be slightly darker, but it would not be noticeable unless carefully compared with the original tea. There was a very slight darkening also in the case of the port.

Sir Edward Marshall Hall asked Mr. Webster if he would not expect in his experience to find arsenic in almost every human body. The reply was, a very minute quantity in some cases, in others none. He had got absolutely negative results in dozens of cases. Sir Edward here made reference to the cases of arsenical beer poisoning in Manchester and the North of England which formed the subject of a Royal Commission, and Mr. Webster agreed that glucose was made up by a sulphuric acid process, and that the Royal Commission in the case referred to attributed to the glucose used in the beer the arsenic that the beer contained. He would expect to find arsenic in glucose unless the ingredients used in its manufacture were carefully controlled. He agreed that there was a wide distribution of glucose in a considerable number of things in daily use. He would agree that if one grain of morphine had been given the day before Mrs. Greenwood's death, he would expect to find traces in the body ten months after. Mr. Webster made the statement that of a hundred bodies, about ten per cent might be found to contain minute traces of arsenic which he would reckon out at about one-thousandth part of a grain.

Dr. Willcox, who gave evidence for the Home Office, stated that he examined the body after exhumation and found it was well-preserved considering the time which had elapsed since death. On examination he found no trace of valvular disease of the heart, but he found a small tumour, though not a malignant one, and one not dangerous to life. He found no traces of natural disease which would account for death, and in his opinion the cause of Mrs. Greenwood's death was arsenical poisoning. The minimum fatal dose of arsenic would be about two grains. He believed that the poison was taken in solution, probably by the mouth, because a certain amount of the poison was found in the alimentary tract. The fact that there was very little in the stomach indicated that several hours must have elapsed between death and the time the poison was taken. He would suggest about nine hours before, assuming that it was taken in one dose. As a medical man he had never heard the

terms " opium pill " and " morphine pill " used interchange-
ably.

Counsel asked whether a person sitting in an evening sun on
ground that had been dressed with weed-killer might possibly
absorb arsenic. Dr. Willcox said he thought it would not be
possible. Arsenic could be absorbed from a wallpaper in a
closed room in a gaseous form. In the ordinary use of weed-
killer by watering paths, there would be no risk of arsenical
poisoning to anyone walking on those paths or sitting in the
garden. Counsel then asked Dr. Willcox if he agreed that if
arsenic had been given to Mrs. Greenwood by means of wine
on the table at one o'clock—if her daughter had taken a wine-
glass of the same wine would she have escaped the symptoms ?
Dr. Willcox replied : " Not if it came from the same wine as
that which provided the fatal dose to Mrs. Greenwood." He
did not believe that gooseberry skins would produce gastro-
enteritis so severely as to simulate arsenical poisoning. He had
considered the possibility that the gooseberries might have been
sprayed with arsenical solution, either accidentally or in order
to kill the weeds underneath them. If they had been sprayed
immediately before picking, obviously there would be some
arsenic in them, and if they had not been washed before being
cooked there would have been some arsenic in the gooseberry
tart. In that case it is probable that the other people who partook
of the tart would be affected by the poison.

" Assuming one quarter of a grain of arsenic was found,"
asked Counsel, " is that inconsistent with the amount that
might be absorbed by food ? "

Dr. Willcox replied : " I think it would be inconsistent with
any amount of arsenic that could get into foodstuffs accidentally."
He should think approximately the minimum fatal dose had
been administered.

Sir Edward Marshall Hall introduced a dramatic interlude
into the case by producing two bottles which he handed to
Dr. Willcox. " Look at these two bottles," said the Counsel,
" both of which contain a red liquid." One contained bismuth
and the other contained a standard arsenical preparation in
solution. " If by some unfortunate mistake," slowly proceeded
Counsel, " the doctor gave Mrs. Greenwood four teaspoonfuls
of that solution and not bismuth, would that be sufficient to
account for the arsenic found in the viscera ? "

" Yes," said Dr. Willcox.

The doctor was then recalled and asked by Counsel in a voice
hushed almost to a whisper : " Is it possible on that night you
might have dispensed Fowler's solution of arsenic instead of
bismuth ? "

" Quite impossible," was the reply.

Mr. Greenwood gave evidence on his own behalf. He

declared that he did not give his wife arsenic, and he had nothing whatever to do with her death, and was cross-examined for the period of two hours. He stated it was pure invention of the maid's that he was in the china cupboard for a quarter of an hour. He did not realise his wife was so seriously ill. It was he who took the pills over, after the doctor gave them to him wrapped up in a piece of paper. He said : " Here are two morphine pills. Give them to the nurse. The directions are inside." When the police came to him first he thought the only rumours had reference to his wife's dying of the morphine pills, because the nurse had asked him to say nothing about them.

Sir Edward Marshall Hall in his speech for the defence made an important point in saying that had the police taken a statement down from Miss Greenwood they would have found that she drank from the bottle from which the alleged poison was taken. It had first been denied there were two wine glasses on the table, but now this was admitted. Two expert witnesses had come to prove two sets of facts by which inferences were to be drawn by examination of mirrors and chemical processes so fine, that they could detect 1–32,000th part of arsenic in the solution they examined, and who actually said they found 1–5,000th part of a grain of arsenic in the brain. Counsel said he intended to call doctors to express the view that death was due to gastric disturbance caused by gooseberries.

" Further, it was admitted that two doses of a mixture sent over by Dr. Griffiths were given some time after eight o'clock. Knowing that the two solutions were almost of the same colour, that they were both stock solutions, that they were both in the surgery, was it so widely impossible, was it beyond reasonable supposition, that this unfortunate mistake was made ? In such a case, he contended, all the arsenic that was found was accounted for."

Dr. Toogood for the defence expressed the view that death was due to gastro-enteritis. Had two opium pills been given, Mrs. Greenwood would have been alive now. Asked by the judge what he considered the cause of her death he replied : " Morphine."

Dr. Griffiths of Swansea expressed the view that Mrs. Greenwood's death was due either to morphine poisoning or gastro-enteritis. He also said that under certain circumstances it was possible to have two and half grains of arsenic in the body without suffering any evil effects.

Miss Irene Greenwood said in evidence she remembered the last Sunday her mother was alive. She could remember everything about what the family drank for luncheon. Her father had whisky and soda, her brother, soda water ; and her mother and herself had burgundy (Beaune). The burgundy was in a straight down bottle something like a champagne bottle. She drank the burgundy in a little red tumbler which was used as a wine glass. She always had burgundy on Sunday and three or four times during the week. She had supper with her father and Miss Phillips that night, and again drank burgundy from the same bottle that they had for luncheon.

The police had never asked her to make any statement. She thought her mother had died of disease of the heart, and she was not aware of any rumours to the contrary until just before the inquest.

Sir Edward Marshall Hall in his final speech said the case for the prosecution was that Mr. Greenwood poisoned the bottle of red wine with arsenic, and that in consequence of taking a glassful of it his wife died. They had seen a young woman standing in the witness-box while her father was on trial for his life. Her evidence destroyed the case for the Crown. He submitted that if the jury believed Miss Greenwood, the case was at an end. She swore that having taxed her memory on the Tuesday as to what she drank on the Sunday, she testified that she drank burgundy with her mother and drank it again at supper. This evidence was tested by the most searching cross-examination but had not been shaken one iota. It would be idle to suggest that Mr. Greenwood had not the opportunity of administering arsenic. The sole evidence was that of the maid, Maggie Williams. " Have you ever " asked counsel " seen a label on a bottle with the words ' Port Wine ' or ' Sherry Wine ' ? The words Port, or Sherry, Yes. No, it is just a touch of the domestic servant. The maid had declared that she only put one wine glass on the table at luncheon, then she said she put two, but that Miss Greenwood's glass was not used. These discrepancies were of supreme importance. Would Mr. Greenwood put a bottle of wine on the table where his son and daughter were sitting ? Would he place such a bottle containing twelve doses of such a poison, with the knowledge that his wife might say to his daughter : " You are looking a little pale, have a glass of wine ? "

Coming to the question of arsenic in the body, Sir Edward said this poison was to be found in sulphuric acid, bismuth, glucose, magnesia and face powder. " The doctor had told the coroner and the magistrates that he prescribed bismuth mixture for her. He had a pink bismuth mixture in a stock bottle and also Fowler's solution of arsenic. He said it was impossible to have made a mistake. But supposing he made a perfectly honest mistake, then instead of two teaspoonsfuls of bismuth mixture at eight o'clock there were given to this unfortunate lady two teaspoonsfuls of Fowler's solution, which would contain one grain of arsenic.

" The colour of the two solutions was practically the same, and detection would have been practically impossible. It is admitted that if the bismuth mixture was administered it would have caused no discomfort, but if arsenic were administered it would cause a burning sensation. It is proved by the nurse that when Mrs. Greenwood took it she complained that it caught her throat."

Sir Edward addressing the jury with dramatic effect, concluded his speech with the words : " I demand at your hands the liberty of Harold Greenwood."

The judge in summing up said the question the jury had to decide was, had this man administered intentionally a dangerous dose of arsenic. If he had, it was attempted murder even if he did not succeed in causing her death. If he did succeed it was murder. Dealing step by step with the evidence the judge asked was there a dangerous quantity of arsenic in the body ? Had the prisoner put it there ? This, he maintained, was the real difficulty in the case. Motive was no proof of the act of a crime at all ; if the jury thought the symptoms were consistent with arsenic, was it administered in the wine. They could not accept as conclusive in any sense the evidence of the maid. But how had the arsenic got into the body if it was not administered in the wine ? He referred to the suggestion made by the counsel for the defence, that the doctor had by mistake sent a solution of arsenic instead of a bismuth mixture. It was only one factor in the case. They had no proof how he could have made such a mistake. It was not for the accused to prove his innocence, but for the prosecution to prove his guilt.

The jury retired at 1.30 to consider their verdict and did not return to Court till 3.45 p.m. The foreman said they had agreed upon their verdict which was " Not Guilty " and in it they were unanimous. It subsequently transpired that when the jury returned their verdict of " Not Guilty " they added the following rider, which was handed to the judge but not made public at the time.

" We are satisfied on the evidence of this case that a dangerous dose of arsenic was administered to Mabel Greenwood on Sunday, 15th of June, 1919, but we are not satisfied that this was the immediate cause of death. The evidence before us is insufficient and does not conclusively satisfy us as to how and by whom the arsenic was administered." Mr. Greenwood was thereupon acquitted.

He left Kidwelly and on giving up practice went to live near Ross-on-Wye where he died on January 17th, 1929.

CHAPTER XLIV

THE SOUTHWARK POISON MYSTERY

In the last week of July, 1902, a girl named Maude Marsh, about twenty years of age, was admitted as a patient into Guy's Hospital suffering from internal inflammation and vomiting. She was placed under treatment, and in a few weeks' time her condition so improved that she was discharged from the institution. She was employed as a barmaid at The Crown, a licensed house in the Borough High Street. There she passed as the wife of the proprietor, with whom she lived. About a month after her return to The Crown she was again seized with a similar illness, and was attended by a local medical practitioner and also seen by a medical man from Croydon who visited her at her father's request. The former was told by the sick girl that the doctor at Guy's Hospital thought she was suffering from peritonitis, but after visiting her several times he came to the conclusion she was suffering from inflammation of the stomach and bowels. On calling to see his patient on the afternoon of October 22nd, the doctor was told she had died two or three hours earlier. He refused to give a certificate and insisted on a post-mortem examination. The examination failed to reveal the cause of death, and the doctor removed certain internal organs and submitted them for analysis. In consequence of the report he received, he then communicated with the police.

On October 25th, South London was gaily decorated in honour of the State procession of the King and Queen, and the streets were thronged with people. Shortly before the royal procession was due to pass through the Borough High Street, two detectives entered The Crown public-house which was festooned with flags, and passed into the bar. A notice on the wall announced seats ' to let ' to view the pageant, and the windows were already filled with sightseers, who took no notice of the two men who had entered so quietly.

Behind the bar was the landlord, a small, dark-complexioned man with prominent cheek-bones and sallow skin.

" Are you George Chapman ? " asked one of the detectives.

" Yes," was the reply.

" I am an Inspector of police and wish to speak to you quietly."

Chapman motioned the detectives towards the billiard-room at the rear and the three men entered together.

" Maude Marsh, who has been living with you as your wife, has been poisoned with arsenic," said Detective-Inspector Godley at once.

"I know nothing about it; I do not know how she got the poison. She has been in Guy's Hospital for the same sort of sickness," replied Chapman.

Chapman was asked to accompany the inspector to the police station, where he was detained pending inquiries, and at 10.15 that night he was formally charged with the wilful murder of Maude Marsh.

When the accused man quietly took his place in the dock at the police court the following morning, no one could have imagined that the curtain was about to be withdrawn from a series of murders which for sheer heartlessness are almost unprecedented in the annals of crime.

The only witness was Inspector Godley, who gave but sufficient evidence to obtain a remand pending the inquest. He stated that from inquiries he had made, he had found that Chapman was the only person who had fed the girl, and that he would not allow anyone else to give her food or to go into the kitchen when it was being prepared. He found five books, all dealing with medicine, in the possession of the accused, and also some white powders which had not yet been analysed. Arsenic, however, had been discovered in a portion of the viscera which had been removed from the body of Maude Marsh at the time of the post-mortem. The doctor who had attended Chapman's former wife during her fatal illness had been called in to attend Maude Marsh, and he had noticed that both women had displayed the same symptoms. Chapman was then remanded.

Meanwhile, a further examination of the body was made by Dr. Stevenson, the official analyst to the Home Office, the result of which was given at the next hearing before the magistrate. He stated that he found no evidence of natural disease to account for death.

"Was arsenic suggested to you as the cause of death?" asked the solicitor who prosecuted on behalf of the Treasury.

"Yes, but I suggested to the other doctors present I did not think arsenic had been the cause," replied Dr. Stevenson. "I attributed it to another metallic poison, antimony, which I found in the stomach and its contents, the liver, the spleen, the kidneys, the brain and elsewhere in the following quantities:—

Metallic Antimony.

In the stomach	—	—	—	—	0.23 grains.
,, ,, abdomen	—	—	⁓	—	5.99 ,,
,, ,, liver	—	—	—	—	0.71 ,,
,, ,, kidneys	—	—	—	—	0.14 ,,
,, ,, brain	—	—	—	—	0.17 ,,

Total 7.24 grains.

Tartar Emetic.

In the stomach	–	–	–	–	0.64 grains.
„ „ abdomen	–	–	–	–	16.64 „
„ „ liver	–	–	–	–	1.98 „
„ „ kidneys	–	–	–	–	0.39 „
„ „ brain	–	–	–	–	0.47 „

Total 20.12 grains.

" In every organ and tissue that I examined I found some antimony," added Dr. Stevenson.

He further stated that two grains of antimony had been known to produce fatal results in a very weak person, but in the case of an ordinary person, fifteen grains would kill. In the case of repeated doses, three grains taken at a time might be expected to result in death. From the position of some of the antimony he thought a dose was taken within a few hours of death. Dr. Stevenson said he received from the police over thirty articles, including pills and ordinary medicines, and analysed them, but found neither arsenic nor antimony in any but one. This bottle was apparently empty when he received it, but he found there were a few drops of a liquid still remaining and looking into it he saw a little bit of white powder sticking to the side. He rinsed the bottle out with water and then analysed it and found the water contained both bismuth and antimony.

At this stage the case was adjourned. Meanwhile the coroner's inquest on the body of Maude Marsh was concluded, which resulted in a verdict of wilful murder against Chapman.

When he was brought before the magistrate for the tenth time on December 31st, 1902, the Counsel for the Treasury had the sensational announcement to make that Chapman had since his last appearance been further charged with the murder of two other women, viz. Mary Isabella Spink (or Chapman) on Christmas Day, 1897, and Bessie Taylor (or Chapman) on February 13th, 1901.

These two women, said the counsel, had lived with him for some time prior to their deaths. It had also been discovered that the prisoner's real name was Severino Klosowski, and that he had assumed the name of George Chapman since coming to live in England. He was a Polish Jew and had studied medicine and surgery in Warsaw.

The story of Klosowski's life is an extraordinary one. He was born in 1865 and educated at a military school in Poland. Afterwards he became a male nurse in a hospital at Warsaw and learned something of medicine. In 1888 he emigrated to England and obtained work in a small barber's shop in White-chapel Road, London. After he had been in London about twelve months, he married a woman named Lucy Baderski. At one time they went to America, but she returned alone, and does not appear to have lived with him again.

In 1895 he left Whitechapel and was next heard of in a barber's shop at Tottenham, where he was recognised by a hairdresser's traveller who had known him in Warsaw. He next started a small shop on his own account, and at this time was living with a girl called Annie Chapman, whose name he afterwards adopted. His business failing, he again took a situation in Church Lane, Leystonstone, where he earned thirty shillings a week. While living at Leytonstone in 1895, he became acquainted with a Mrs. Spink, whose husband had deserted her. Klosowski, or Chapman as he now called himself, became on intimate terms with Mrs. Spink, and after a time he informed a Mr. Ward with whom he lodged, that he and Mrs. Spink were going to be married. One day in October, 1895, they went out and on their return stated that the wedding had taken place, and afterwards lived together as husband and wife.

Mrs. Spink had about £560, which was vested in a trust deed, and while she lived with Chapman some £250 had been advanced to her by the trustee. In 1897 the balance was handed over to the couple and they left London for Hastings, where Chapman purchased a barber's business in George Street.

About February, 1897, Chapman's affection for his wife seemed to wane, as he is said to have treated her cruelly and she complained of his treatment to people they knew. Then she became ill, suffering from irritation of the stomach, which resulted in great weakness and depression. In April of that year, Chapman is known to have purchased an ounce of tartar emetic (tartarated antimony) from a chemist in Hastings. In August they left Hastings and took a beerhouse called The Prince of Wales in Bartholomew Square, St. Luke's, London. Mrs. Chapman, who had been better for a time, again became ill with the same symptoms, and her husband is said to have recommenced his ill-treatment of her. As she grew worse, a Dr. Rogers was called in to see her. Here a Mrs. Doubleday came upon the scene, and she noticed that Chapman frequently felt his wife's pulse, and was much occupied in consulting medical books. He prepared her food and also her medicine, sending every one out of the room while he did it. She suffered terrible pain with vomiting and diarrhœa and finally died on Christmas Day, 1897. The doctor appears to have had no suspicion of poison and gave a certificate that the cause of death was phthisis.

After her death, Chapman advertised for a barmaid and eventually engaged a woman named Bessie Taylor in that capacity. She came from Cheshire and had been in a situation as housekeeper at Peckham before coming to Chapman at Easter in 1898. She told a friend she was going to be married before going to live with Chapman at The Prince of Wales. In August, 1898, they left London and went to live at Bishop Stortford, where Chapman took an inn called The Grapes. In March, 1899, the couple again returned to London, Chapman first becoming tenant of The Monument, a public-house in Union Street Borough, and afterwards removing to The Crown in High Street. A Miss Painter, a friend of Bessie Taylor's, who called to see her at The Crown, noticed that Chapman treated her with indifference and once even threatened her with a revolver. Calling to see her on another occasion some time later, Miss Painter found she was very ill and was troubled with persistent vomiting. Chapman attended to her, cooking her food and feeling her pulse.

In January, Dr. Stoker, a local practitioner was called in to see the sick woman, and he attended her until her death in February, 1901. The doctor had no suspicion she had been poisoned and certified the cause of death as intestinal obstruction, vomiting and exhaustion. The bodies of both women were exhumed under an order from the Home Secretary, and an analysis was made in each case by Dr. Stevenson.

The analysis of various organs removed from the body of Mary Isabella Spink revealed the presence of antimony in all the viscera examined :—

In the stomach	–	–	– 0.08 grains
„ „ intestines	–	–	– 1.15 „
„ „ liver	–	–	– 2.42 „
„ „ kidneys	–	–	– 0.18 „

Total   3.83 grains of tartarated antimony

Dr. Stevenson remarked on the amazing preservation of Spink's body after being interred for five years. He found the head and features were so well preserved that they were as little altered as though only buried a day. This he attributed to the preservative properties of antimony, which in sufficient quantity practically mummified the body. He could find no case like this on record, and he regarded it as unique. There was no indication of phthisis, the cause of death being gastroenteritis caused by the administration of antimony.

The analysis of the remains of Bessie Taylor also revealed the presence of antimony in the following quantities :—

In the stomach and its contents			0.32 grains
„ „ intestines	–	–	– 23.43 „
„ „ liver –	–	–	– 4.55 „
„ „ kidneys	–	–	– 0.82 „

Total   29.12 grains of tartarated antimony

Taylor's body was also in a remarkably good state of preservation after being buried twenty-one months, and showed no appearance of recent disease, but signs of acute non-ulcerative gastro-enteritis set up by antimony were evident.

It was about eighteen months after Bessie Taylor's death that Chapman engaged Maude Marsh as a barmaid at The Monument public-house, and her illness and death closely resembled that of the other women with whom Chapman had consorted.

He was committed for trial on December 19th, 1902, and was arraigned before Mr. Justice Grantham at the Old Bailey on March 16th, 1903.

For the defence the counsel for the prisoner urged the absence of motive for the crimes, and although he admitted that antimony had been found in the bodies of the three women, he asked if the methods of science were absolutely conclusive ?   There was, he contended, room for mistake, unless such evidence was accompanied by corroborative evidence of the most powerful kind. There was no proof that Chapman had antimony in his possession since 1897, and his behaviour had been that of an innocent man.

The Solicitor-General, Sir Edward Carson, in his reply, said that although the prisoner was indicted only with regard to Maude Marsh's death, the cumulative evidence of the two earlier murders was perhaps the most fatal testimony.   One woman after another was betrayed and abandoned, and all poisoned in the same way and with the same poison.   Each received the same " attention " on Klosowski's part during their fatal illnesses.   As to motive, the history of the man was one of unbridled, heartless, cruel lust.   If a man was proved a murderer, one need not look for motive, but if motive were wanted in this case, it was easily to be found.

The judge, in summing up, said the case was unique from three points of view, viz. legally, chemically and medically. Chemically, it was unique by reason of the discovery which it enabled Dr. Stevenson to make of the power of antimony to preserve the tissues of the body in almost a perfect state of embalmment ; from the legal point of view, because it was the first time the antecedents of a prisoner had been investigated in the way they had been in this case.

Medically, it was a sad reflection that a man who had only been a hairdresser's assistant should be able to defy the doctors of this country, and for years carry on a practice of this kind without the slightest fear of being found out.   The only question for the jury to determine was by whom the antimony was administered.

After a consultation of ten minutes, the jury returned a verdict of guilty, the foreman adding " We are all agreed."   Klosowski, or Chapman, was then sentenced to death, and paid the penalty of his crimes at Wandsworth Gaol on April 7th, 1903.

CHAPTER XLV

THE CRIPPEN CASE

In 1883, an American named Hawley Harvey Crippen came to England to attend various hospitals for the purpose of seeing operations. He was born at Coldwater, Michigan, U.S.A., in 1862, where he was educated at the Homœopathic College at Cleveland, and took a degree as Doctor of Medicine. After being in England some months, he returned to the States as an assistant to a Dr. Porter of Detroit, but later he specialized in the eye and ear, and after his marriage went to live in New York.

It was here in 1893, after the death of his wife, he first me. Cora Turner, whom he eventually married, and removed to Saint Louis, where he started practice as a physician and optician. Cora Turner was the daughter of a Russian Pole and a German woman, and her real name was Makamotsky. A woman of extravagant tastes who delighted in jewellery and dress, she seems to have been fascinated by Crippen. Possessing a fine voice, it was her ambition to go on the operatic stage and Crippen, at this time having been offered a post as physician to Munyon's Remedies Company, removed to New York, where he paid for the training of his wife's voice. When it was completed, however, it was found she had no chance of singing in opera.

Crippen was transferred by his employers first to Philadelphia and then to Toronto, where he managed Munyon's business. About 1900, he was sent to England in charge of the Company's branch, but leaving them he became physician to what was known as the Drouet Institute. He left the Institute to become medical adviser to a company known as " The Aural Treatment and Sovereign Remedy Company." This also appears to have failed, and he went back to Munyon's Remedies Co., where he acted as manager till he took on the business as agent. At the same time he was running a business called the " Gayle Teeth Specialists Company," in which he had a partner named Rylands, but the headquarters of his " Aural Remedies " was at Craven House, Kingsway, London. Here a Miss Ethel Le Neve was employed as a typist and clerk, and to her Crippen seems to have confided his domestic trials and found in her a sympathizer.

When the Crippens came to London they took a house at

39 Hilldrop Crescent, Kentish Town, where Mrs. Crippen had the assistance of a charwoman to help her in the housework. After they had settled down, Mrs. Crippen wanted to go on the music-hall stage, and her husband paid a fee on several occasions so that she might have a trial turn at minor music halls. In spite of an attractive personality, elaborate dresses, and a pleasant, clear voice, she could not get a sympathetic hearing, proving that she had no stage talent whatever. She was known on the stage as Belle Elmore, and being bitterly disappointed at her inability to get engagements, she became nervous and irritable and subject to fits of violent temper.

Crippen's domestic infelicities were commonly known to his friends, before whom his wife would openly abuse him, often for the most trivial occurrences. His home affairs went from bad to worse, and his wife gave him continual uneasiness and trouble. On several occasions she threatened to leave him and go off with another man with whom she had become intimate.

On January 31st, 1910, in the afternoon, Crippen called upon two friends and invited them to his house for the evening to have a game of cards. They agreed, and came to dinner, Mrs. Crippen preparing the meal and helping to serve it, there being no servant present. Apparently husband and wife were on quite good terms and their guests departed about one o'clock in the morning, leaving Crippen and his wife alone in the house.

This was the last time Mrs. Crippen was seen alive.

On February 2nd there was a meeting of the Committee of the Music Hall Ladies' Guild, of which Mrs. Crippen was the honorary treasurer and a regular attendant, but this time she did not put in an appearance. To explain her absence, Miss Le Neve came to the meeting, bringing with her two letters. One was addressed to Miss May, the secretary of the Guild and stated that the illness of a near relative had called Mrs. Crippen to America at a few hours' notice, and tendered her resignation. This was signed " Belle Elmore, per pro H. H. C."

The other letter, which was addressed to the Committee of the Music Hall Ladies' Guild, was similar in purport and repeated her resignation of the honorary treasurership, and enclosed a cheque-book and deposit-book for the immediate use of her successor. The letter concluded by saying, " I hope some months later to be with you, and in the meantime wish the Guild every success." This was also signed " Belle Elmore," although the letter was obviously in her husband's writing.

The reading of the letters took the members of the Committee by surprise. A few days afterwards a friend of Mrs. Crippen, who was very fond of her, met Dr. Crippen and asked him more particularly about his wife's journey but could gain nothing very definite in reply. Shortly afterwards this lady again saw Crippen, who informed her that he had that morning heard from his wife who stated she had been rather ill having something the matter with her lungs.

About the last week in February, there was a dinner given by the Music Hall Artists' Benevolent Fund. Dr. Crippen attended it, accompanied by Miss Le Neve, and it was noticed that she was wearing a brooch that several of those present recognized as one they had often seen Mrs. Crippen wearing. During dinner, a lady member of the Guild asked Crippen some details of his wife's whereabouts, and he told her that she was then up in the mountains in the wilds of California.

As time went on her friends still continued to make inquiries about her mysterious disappearance, and on March 21st a letter was received by Mr. and Mrs. Martinetti from Crippen, in which he said he had been upset by serious news about his wife, having received a cable that she was dangerously ill with double pneumonia. A day or two later, meeting Mrs. Martinetti, he said he was expecting a cable at any time saying his wife was dead. On March 23rd he sent a telegram to Mrs. Martinetti saying he had heard his wife was dead. Three days later he inserted an announcement of her death in the *Era* and gave notice to his landlord that he would be leaving the house in Hilldrop Crescent on June 24th.

Mrs. Crippen's friends still continued puzzled about her mysterious disappearance and a Mr. Nash, who was connected with the music-hall profession, on returning from America where he had been on a visit, interviewed Crippen. He was evidently dissatisfied with Crippen's replies to his questions respecting the disappearance of his wife, and he went to Scotland Yard, placing his suspicions before Inspector Dew.

After exhaustive inquiries with a view if possible of finding Mrs. Crippen or some trace of her, the Inspector decided to see Crippen himself and to find out if he could obtain some information from him. He called at Hilldrop Crescent on July 18th, about ten in the morning, and saw Miss Le Neve, who was there with a young French maid. The Inspector asked where he could find Crippen, and Miss Le Neve seemed unable to give him any information, but she gave him his business address at Albion House, Oxford Street. Inspector Dew went there and saw Crippen and asked him what light he could throw on the death of his wife. Crippen replied : " Well, I suppose I had better tell the truth. All my stories about her illness and death are untrue ; so far as I know she is not dead at all."

He then made a long detailed statement to the Inspector, which was committed to writing and signed.

In this statement, which began with an account of his career from the time he was born, he said that his wife had often threatened to leave him, saying she would go out of his life and he would never hear from her again. On the night that their friends came to dinner they had a quarrel afterwards, and she said : " I shall leave you to-morrow and you will not hear from me again."

" She told me," he stated, " that I was to arrange to cover up any scandal from our mutual friends. I went to business next morning and on returning home between five and six o'clock I found she had gone. I then wrote the letters to the Guild secretary, and realising this would not be sufficient to explain her not coming back, I added she was ill with pneumonia, and afterwards, that she had died in California.

" When my wife went away I cannot say whether she took anything with her. She took some of her jewellery, I know, but she left her rings behind. I do not know what clothes she took away. It is true that I was at the Benevolent Fund dinner at the Criterion with Miss Le Neve, and she wore the brooch left behind. She also wore my wife's furs. After I told them my wife was dead, Miss Le Neve and I went to Dieppe for five days. My belief is that my wife has gone to Chicago to join Bruce Miller, a man whom she knew and who, I believe, had speculated and made money."

Crippen signed this statement and Inspector Dew said : " That is all very well, but your wife has got to be found," and suggested an advertisement in the newspapers and discussed with Crippen the form of it. They drew up an advertisement between them, as follows :

" Makamotsky. Will Belle Elmore communicate with H. H. C. or authorities at once. Serious trouble from your absence. Twenty-five dollars for communicating her where-abouts to——."

The address was left open for Crippen to decide upon.

On Crippen's invitation, Inspector Dew made a search of the house in Hilldrop Crescent, but found nothing of a sus-picious nature. The next morning, Crippen arrived at his place of business a little earlier than usual, and his clerk remarked on his worried appearance. Crippen said that he had been bothered, as there was a little scandal. He told him that he was going away, and that if anything happened to him the clerk must deal with the letters. He then sent him out to purchase a suit of boy's clothes, and about 11.30 Miss Le Neve came to the office, where she changed her clothes for the boy's suit purchased by the clerk and left the office disguised as a boy without anyone noticing her. Crippen then saw the manageress of Munyon's Company and asked her to change him a cheque for £37, showing his pass-book at the Charing Cross Bank, where he had a balance to that amount. He produced a cheque signed Belle Elmore, the account being in their joint names, and the manageress gave him cash in exchange.

This occurred on July 9th, and from that date Crippen and Miss Le Neve disappeared. On July 11th Inspector Dew again went to Hilldrop Crescent to have a further interview with Crippen and Miss Le Neve, but found they had gone. He then began a systematic search of the premises, and on the 13th, his suspicions were aroused by something he saw on the floor leading to the cellar. He decided to examine it more carefully, and finding some bricks which appeared to be loose, he decided to take up the floor. Beneath it he discovered what were obviously human remains, and sent for the divisional sergeant of police. The remains were as far as possible uncovered, but not removed, and on July 14th they were examined by Mr. Pepper, at whose request they were removed to the mortuary for closer examination. The remains having been buried in quicklime were found to be in a fairly good state of preservation, most of the internal organs, such as the heart, the spleen, intestines and stomach being intact. The extraordinary part of the matter was that no bones were discovered, and the head, hands and feet were missing. It was apparent that the individual who had carried out the evisceration, had done everything possible to prevent identification as regards the body. Some things, however, had been forgotten, such as portions of articles of clothing, and some hair done up in curling pins, some strands of which were fully eight inches long, proving they had belonged to a female.

Another point noticed was that the hair had been bleached. The articles of clothing proved to be the arm-piece of a suit of pyjamas, and separately, the right back portion of the jacket of a similar suit, with the maker's name on it. The woman's clothing consisted of a camisole. The name on the pyjamas was discovered to be the same as on those which Crippen wore that were found in his box.

Following this discovery, a warrant was issued on July 16th for the arrest of Crippen and Miss Le Neve.

The scene now changes to the Atlantic. On July 20th the steamship *Montrose* sailed from Antwerp bound for Quebec, and among the passengers who embarked at that port were a Mr. Robinson and his son. They mixed freely with the passengers on the ship, but circumstances arose when they were a few days out, to cause the captain to make particular observation of the son, and from certain characteristics, he began to doubt his sex. Communicating his suspicions to two of the passengers, they soon confirmed his belief that Mr. Robinson junior was, in fact, a girl.

Suspecting something was wrong, on July 22nd the captain sent a wireless message asking the police to follow and board his ship, as he was convinced that Mr. Robinson and his son were the Dr. Crippen and Ethel Le Neve, who were being sought for by the police. This was the first time that wireless telegraphy had been used in connexion with suspected criminals.

The day after the receipt of the message, Inspector Dew and Sergeant Mitchell sailed from Liverpool in the s.s. *Laurentic*, which overtook the *Montrose* at sea. During the voyage, Crippen had become very friendly with the quartermaster of the ship, and a couple of days before the vessel was due at Quebec the quartermaster gave him a hint that the Canadian police were on his track. It is said, that in order to avoid the police on landing, an arrangement had been made between them, that Crippen should be concealed among the cargo, and at an appointed hour there should be a splash in the water as if some one had fallen or jumped overboard, while in the cabin a tell-tale message was to be found. It was thought that no one would think of searching the cargo for the missing man and thus the fugitive was to get clear away. Miss Le Neve in the meanwhile was to be advised of an address where she might join him afterwards, if all went well.

All Crippen's arrangements, however, were upset by Inspector Dew boarding the s.s. *Montrose* at Farther Point, Quebec.

The Inspector saw Crippen pacing the deck near the captain's cabin. " Good morning, Dr. Crippen," he remarked. " Good morning, Mr. Dew," calmly replied Crippen. Dew then told him he would be arrested for the murder and mutilation of his wife, Cora Crippen, in London, on February 2nd. Miss Le Neve, who was still dressed in her suit of boy's clothes, was also arrested. A written card, evidently intended for Miss Le Neve, was found on Crippen. It was in his handwriting and said that he could not stand the horrors he had gone through. There was nothing bright ahead and he had made up his mind to jump overboard that night.

Crippen and Miss Le Neve were brought back to England by Inspector Dew on the s.s *Megantic*, and on landing at Liverpool on August 27th, were taken to London. On their arrival, a great crowd had assembled at Euston Station where the prisoners had a hostile reception, being greeted with groans and hisses. On August 29th they were charged at Bow Street, and committed for trial at the Central Criminal Court, one on the charge of murder, and the other as being accessory after the fact.

At the trial of Crippen it transpired that on January 19th he had purchased at a pharmacy in New Oxford Street five grains of hyoscine hydrobromide, for which he signed the poison register, stating it was required for making homœopathic preparations. At this shop Crippen had previously purchased a number of drugs such as cocaine, morphine, and mercury, and he was well known there. He had also written prescriptions which had been prepared for him.

Mr. Augustus Pepper, surgeon to St. Mary's Hospital, gave

the result of his examination, and said in his opinion, the remains were undoubtedly those of a woman, adding, that the person who removed the various organs showed considerable dexterity. They had been buried very soon after death, and approximately had been in the ground from four to eight months. On a portion of the body found there was a scar, the result of an operation which it was discovered Mrs. Crippen had undergone some time previously. This proved important as evidence of identification. He had examined the hair which was found in the curler, and said that the longest was eight inches and the shortest two and a half inches. It showed signs of having been artificially dealt with and was partially bleached, but the natural colour of the hair was probably a dark brown. The very lightest portion was a pale yellow.

Dr. Marshall, who assisted Mr. Pepper, stated that there was no evidence at all that suggested the remains were those of a male. What little evidence there was pointed to their being those of a female. He was of the opinion that the scar was the result of an operation, and his impression was there were also marks of stitches.

Dr. B. H. Spilsbury, pathologist of St. Mary's Hospital, who was called for the prosecution, stated he had made a microscopical examination of this piece of skin, and confirmed the opinion that it was undoubtedly an old scar, which had been stretched.

Dr. W. H. Willcox, senior analyst to the Home Office, gave evidence as to his examination of the organs of the body found. He stated that he had tested the extracts he had made from the organs physiologically, and in each case got complete paralysis of the pupil of the eye. He also made chemical tests in the case of the liver and intestine, and he concluded that hyoscine was present, corresponding approximately to one-thirtieth of a grain in the whole stomach. He also found an amount of alkaloid corresponding to one-fortieth of a grain in the whole of the kidney, and an amount corresponding approximately to one-seventh of a grain in the intestines, and in the liver, approximately an amount of one-twelfth of a grain. He believed the alkaloid found to be hyoscine, and the total amount to be two-sevenths of a grain approximately. In his opinion there must have been present in the whole body more than half a grain, and the probable fatal dose of hyoscine hydrobromide would be from one-quarter to one-half a grain. It was not commonly prescribed and was chiefly used in sedatives in such conditions as mania and meningitis, in doses from one two-hundredth to one hundredth of a grain. He was of the opinion it had been administered by the mouth and not as an injection, because of the large amount found in the intestines. He believed the cause of death was poison by hyoscine or a salt of hyoscine.

The counsel for the prisoner suggested that alkaloidal substances resembling atropine or hyoscyamine had been met with in decomposed meat, but Dr. Willcox negatived the suggestion.

Dr. Luff, scientific adviser to the Home Office, said he had followed Dr. Willcox's tests in evidence, and he agreed that the poison found was undoubtedly hyoscine. During seventeen years' experience he had always tested for animal alkaloids in toxicological cases, and before that he had conducted a long series of investigations for animal alkaloids, but only on one occasion had he come across them, and that was in some putrefied meat. It was quite impossible that hyoscine could be mistaken for an animal mydriadic alkaloid under Vitali's test.

Mr. Tobin, who defended Crippen, contended that the alkaloid found by Dr. Willcox in the remains, might have been traced to an animal alkaloid produced after death as the result of putrefaction. He dwelt on the fact of the lack of motive Crippen had for the suggested crime ; and that although he had purchased five grains of hyoscine hydrobromide, he had signed his name in the poison register, although there was no need for him to have done so. He bought the drug in January when he was still agent for Munyon's Remedies, for the purpose of making it into a liquid and using it in the form of the tiny homœopathic tablets which he sold in bottles of three hundred each, to patients. He said that although no obligation rested upon Dr. Crippen to go into the witness box, he chose to go of his own accord, and he would call him.

Crippen was taken through the story of his life by the examining counsel, and coming to the question of his purchase of drugs he said he always made up the preparations he sold, and had bought considerable quantities of different poisons, such as aconite, belladonna and *Rhus tox*. He had frequently used hyoscine in making his homœopathic preparations in extremely minute doses. He admitted purchasing the hyoscine and explained how he used it, by first dissolving it in alcohol, then saturating a certain amount of small disks or tablets, two of which would equal 1/3600th part of a grain. He used it in nervous diseases.

Crippen, examined by the Lord Chief Justice, said he took no steps to find out where his wife had gone to, up to July 8th. For three hours he stood the fire of cross-examination by Mr. Muir, the leading counsel for the Crown, and from beginning to end appeared to be utterly devoid of emotion or anything in the least approaching it. He never lost his self-possession or showed the slightest sign of being ruffled throughout the hearing of the case.

During the trial, Mr. Bruce Miller, whose name had been mentioned by Crippen in connexion with his wife, was called, and swore that he had not seen Mrs. Crippen since she left America in 1904.

The Lord Chief Justice, in his summing up of the case, impressed upon the jury that they must be satisfied by the whole of the evidence that the Crown had made out their case, and if not, the prisoner was entitled to the benefit of the doubt. The crime of murder charged against Crippen was that he wilfully and intentionally killed his wife by poison, and then mutilated the body and buried the remains in the cellar at 39 Hilldrop Crescent, in order to conceal his crime. There was no question here of suggesting that it was by some other means or by some other method or agency that Crippen had caused the death of his wife, and it involved two questions : first, whether the remains found in the house were those of the body of Cora Crippen ; if they were not, there was an end of the case ; if they were the remains of this woman then it was a question, was her death occasioned by the wilful act of her husband ? These were the two issues upon which the jury must concentrate their attention.

After exactly half an hour's absence the jury returned and declared they unanimously found the prisoner guilty of wilful murder, and Crippen was sentenced to death.

The following morning the trial of Miss Le Neve took place, she being indicted upon the charge of being accessory after the fact of the wilful murder of Cora Crippen. No witnesses were called, and after some formal proceedings the jury found a verdict of acquittal.

Crippen's case was brought before the Court of Criminal Appeal but the appeal was dismissed, and he was executed at Pentonville Prison on November 23rd, 1910. It is said he made no confession of the crime.

Thus ended the trial of one who was described by Lord Alverstone as " an extraordinary man." Throughout the trial he never showed a symptom of concern or trace of emotion or fear ; he appeared to be never at a loss for a word or explanation, and showed remarkable self-possession all through, the only argument his counsel could adduce in his defence. But after all, this is one of the salient characteristics of poisoners. In Crippen's case, we have a man possessing some medical knowledge who had deliberately chosen a little-known poison to carry out his evil design. He had probably prepared and planned the deed at least a fortnight before it was committed, and then eviscerated the remains of his victim to try and baffle the ablest investigators. He evidently thought his escape from justice sure. But the Nemesis which dogs the footsteps of all poisoners followed those of Crippen, cunning as he was, and he made three fatal mistakes. First in burying a portion of the suit of pyjamas belonging to himself with the remains ; second, although he destroyed the major parts of the body to prevent identification, he left the very remains which contained traces of the poison by which he murdered his victim ; and third, and most remarkable of all, he forgot to remove the portion of the body containing the scar, which ultimately established beyond all doubt the identity of the remains as those of Cora Crippen, his wife.

This case is noteworthy as being the first on record in which hyoscine was used for criminal poisoning in this country. The presence of the alkaloid was clearly demonstrated by Dr. Willcox although the remains had been buried for six months.

CHAPTER XLVI

THE MYSTERY OF THE SEDDONS

THERE have been few cases in the history of poisoning where a man and his wife have been arraigned on the capital charge, therefore the trial of Frederick Henry Seddon and Mary Anne, his wife, on the charge of murdering Elizabeth Barrow at 63 Tollington Park, N., on September 14th, 1911, is one of some interest. The mysterious circumstances connected with the case are also somewhat out of the ordinary, as the evidence was largely of a circumstantial character.

In 1901, Seddon, who was a superintendent of canvassers for an industrial insurance company, was living with his wife and three children at 63 Tollington Park, and on July 26th, 1910, a Miss Eliza Mary Barrow, a woman of 49 years of age, came to lodge with them. She appears to have been a person of a somewhat strange temperament. She was very deaf, and had in her charge a small boy named Ernest Grant, an orphan and the son of some people with whom she formerly lived. Miss Barrow was the possessor of a considerable sum of money, amounting to about £4,000, part of which was invested in stocks, and she was also the owner of some leasehold property. She had a curious, but not unusual, characteristic of hoarding gold and notes to a large amount in a cash-box, which she kept in a box in her room. There was probably £400 in gold and a considerable number of five-pound notes, said to be at least thirty-three, kept in this cash-box.

All this property had disappeared by September 14th, 1911, and on that date there appeared to be little cash left in her possession. All her property had found its way into the hands of the Seddons. This included £600 of India stock, the leasehold property and some £200 in cash as well. During the October following, both Seddon and his wife were dealing with five-pound notes which had undoubtedly belonged to Miss Barrow and had been in her cash-box. On the day when the India stock and leasehold property were transferred, Mrs. Seddon changed two five-pound notes, endorsing them with a false name and address. Six other notes were also paid into Seddon's banking account.

According to Seddon, the money had been transferred to him by agreement with Miss Barrow, and he was to give her an annuity of a pound a week in exchange for the interest on it. He said that he had a verbal agreement with her, by which he was bound to pay her an annuity of £72 a year in addition to the rooms in the house, in return for the property of the India stock.

On September 1st Miss Barrow became ill, from what her medical adviser diagnosed as epidemic diarrhœa, and this continued for at least eight or nine days, after which she began to improve and seemed to be getting better. While she was ill, Mrs. Seddon was the only one who attended to her, with the exception of Seddon, who was known to have gone into her room on September 11th, when she made a will, appointing him as her sole executor and trustee. Mrs. Seddon saw after the cooking of Miss Barrow's food and did everything necessary for her, and no servant went near the apartment.

On the night of the 13th she became rapidly worse, but the doctor was not called in until about six o'clock in the morning of the 14th, when she died. Seddon saw the doctor and obtained a certificate to the effect that death was due to epidemic diarrhœa, and two days afterwards the funeral took place. There were some significant facts with regard to what happened after her death. No relatives were present at the funeral, nor were they informed of her death until September 20th.

After the funeral, there was some inquiry made by one of the relatives, a Mr. Wonderahe, who was not satisfied and had an interview with Seddon. His suspicions being aroused that all was not well, he communicated with the authorities, and inquiries were instituted, which resulted in an order being given for the exhumation of the body on November 15th. A post-mortem examination was made and it was found that Miss Barrow died from the effects of arsenic, the poison being widely distributed throughout her body. The doctor declared that he had not prescribed arsenic in his treatment during her illness, and as Seddon and his wife were the only two people who had come near her during that period, they were arrested and charged with the murder of Miss Barrow.

How the poison was obtained and who administered it were the paramount questions at the trial.

During Miss Barrow's illness no one else appeared to have entered her bedroom but the man and his wife, and yet the quantity of arsenic found in the body was so large, that it was found even in the hair and nails. Shortly after Miss Barrow's death, Seddon was seen by two of his colleagues to be in possession of considerable sums of money, including £200 in gold and also jewellery. He bought shares in a Building Society, which he paid for in cash, and made several payments amounting to £150 in gold.

A chemist at Crouch Hill stated that a girl he had since identified as Seddon's daughter, purchased from him a packet of six arsenical fly-papers ; she had asked for arsenical papers and not the " sticky " ones.

A doctor who treated Miss Barrow in August, 1911, said she was then suffering from congestion of the liver, and at the end of the month had an attack of asthma, but the symptoms were not severe, and she made no complaint of pain or sickness. The doctor who was called in to attend her on September 2nd had attended the Seddons for some years. He found her suffering from sickness and prescribed for her. On the 13th the symptoms of the illness had returned, but he did not consider her condition critical. The following day Seddon came to see him and said Miss Barrow was dead, and he gave a certificate that death was due to epidemic diarrhœa, but he never prescribed arsenic in any form for her during her illness.

Dr. Spilsbury, who conducted the post-mortem examination, stated that the body was in an abnormal state of preservation, and after witnessing tests made by Dr. Willcox, he was of the opinion that death was due to acute arsenical poisoning, which meant poisoning by one or more large doses of arsenic. He had found no sign of internal disease, and in this particular case he could find no external or internal indication of chronic arsenical poisoning.

Dr. Willcox, who made the analysis for the Home Office said he found arsenic in all the remains and tissues, the largest proportion being in the stomach, intestines, liver and muscles. There was arsenic also in the skin, heart and nails and it was distributed throughout the body. He agreed with Dr. Spilsbury as to the cause of death. He estimated that there was in the remains 2.01 grains of arsenic and that would indicate to him that more than that amount had been taken. There might have been an amount of five grains taken within three days of death. In his opinion the fatal dose was given within two or three days of death, probably two days. Two grains of arsenic would be a poisonous dose and might be enough to kill an adult person, and two or three such doses within a short period of time would be fatal.

Dr. Willcox said he had heard a suggestion in this case that carbonate of bismuth contained arsenic. He had made an analysis of some and found a very faint trace of about one in a million, so at least two hundredweight of bismuth carbonate would be required to give two grains of arsenic.

He made an analysis of the arsenical fly-papers and found arsenic in a quantity varying from 3.8 to 6 grains per paper. If the paper was actually boiled in water for some minutes, practically all the arsenic would be got out, and he had obtained 6.6 grs. by boiling one, 6 grs. from another and 3 grs. from another. In his opinion the 2.01 grs. he found in Miss Barrow's body would be sufficient to kill an adult person.

A considerable point was made by the counsel for the prosecution in the cross-examination of Dr. Willcox with respect to the finding of arsenic in the tips of the hair. Counsel remarked that one of the most important subjects of investigation before the Royal Commission inquiry into arsenical poisoning was the presence of arsenic in the hair and the length of time it must have taken before it reached the hair tips. Counsel said that the fact that arsenic was found in the tips of Miss Barrow's hair proved that it must have been given for a period extending over two or three months. Dr. Willcox said that it need not mean that arsenic was being taken continuously, but some might have been taken a year or more previously, and in the present case he was inclined to the opinion that there had been one fatal dose given in the last three days before death.

Dr. Willcox explained how the arsenic had got into the tips of the hair. The hair of Miss Barrow was lying in the coffin in fluid which had exuded from the body. This fluid contained arsenic in appreciable amount and the hair had absorbed the arsenic in this way.

He proved this by the following experiment. Some hair from a woman who had *no arsenic* and whose hair contained *no arsenic*, was allowed to lie for 24 hours in the blood-stained fluid from the coffin, some of which had been reserved at the post-mortem examination. The hair absorbed the arsenic. It was thoroughly washed in water, alcohol, and ether, to remove external contamination. It was then submitted to the Marsh-Berzelius electrolytic test and was found to contain the same amount of arsenic as the hair of Miss Barrow. This experiment proved that the arsenic in Miss Barrow's hair had got into it by absorption after death, from the arsenic present in the blood-stained fluid with which it was in contact.

Mr. Marshall Hall, who defended Seddon, submitted that there was not sufficient evidence to give to the jury and suggested the case was absolutely a unique one. In all other cases of poisoning there was some direct tracing of the poison. In the cases of some men who had been tried previously, such as Lamson and Cream, there had been medical knowledge in the possession of the prisoners, but in this case there were two people charged on circumstantial evidence and it could not be said which of them did it. Beyond the evidence of the chemist, who said he had sold Margaret Seddon certain fly-papers, there was no proof of any poison being in the possession of either party. Mrs. Seddon said that she herself bought some fly-papers in consequence of the request from Miss Barrow that something should be done to mitigate the nuisance of flies in the room. She remembered that on one occasion, the contents of four saucers were emptied into one which was placed on the wash-stand in the room.

Seddon was then called to give evidence and stated that Miss Barrow had asked him about reinvesting her money as she was losing capital. He suggested an annuity, which she agreed to, in exchange for her India stock and the lease of her property. He denied ever handling the fly-papers which came to his house and beyond giving her a little brandy the last night when she was very ill, he had never given her anything to eat or drink. He had not the smallest suspicion at that time that she was fatally or dangerously ill. He declared he had never purchased arsenic in his life in any shape or form, and swore that he had never either administered or instructed the administration of it.

Mrs. Seddon, who also went into the box, said there were a great many flies in Miss Barrow's room and she had asked her to get some fly-papers, " Not the sticky ones, but those you wet." She herself bought them at the shop of a neighbouring chemist and took four, on being told she could get them at a reduced price. The papers were shown to Miss Barrow and placed in a saucer in her room with water on them. During Miss Barrow's illness, she waited upon her and on one occasion only did Mr. Seddon give Miss Barrow any medicine. She had never bought a fly-paper until she bought these, and she had never sent her daughter for anything of the kind. She began by putting them in saucers singly, two on the mantelpiece and two on the chest of drawers. Then there was an accident she remembered, and she emptied them into a soup-plate and repeatedly moistened them if they were going dry.

Mr. Justice Bucknill, in summing up, said if the prisoners were guilty, it was a crime which had been carefully thought out and carefully committed in secret. The history of great poisoning cases showed that the poisoner did not poison in open daylight, in the presence of other persons. It was a secret crime, done in the dark, and if this particular crime was proved against these people, there could be no doubt as to its being an abominable one, and that the love of gold led to it.

The question to answer was, what was the cause of Miss Barrow's death ? A considerable amount of arsenic had been found in the body ; how did it get there ? There was no direct evidence that Seddon had ever been seen to handle a fly-paper or the water in which one had been soaking. In view of the medical evidence it ought not to be difficult to decide that Miss Barrow died from arsenical poisoning, and it was for the jury to decide whether that arsenic was administered by the prisoners, or either of them.

After considering for an hour and five minutes, the jury found Seddon guilty and his wife " Not guilty." Before sentence was passed upon the man, he read a long statement in which he again denied that he was guilty of the crime. Seddon was condemned to death and his wife was acquitted, and he suffered the extreme penalty of the law on April 18th, 1912.

The verdict was much discussed in the Press and some ten thousand persons, including Mrs. Seddon, assembled in Hyde Park and presented a petition at the Home Office to get the verdict set aside. The Court of Criminal Appeal was asked to quash the conviction, but the judges said they saw no reason to say the verdict was wrong or unreasonable.

In November, 1912, Mrs. Seddon made a remarkable statement in the Press which was published in the *Weekly Dispatch* of November 17th. In it she stated that Seddon had committed the crime, that she saw him give the poison to Miss Barrow, and that on the fatal night he deliberately substituted for the medicine the water from the fly-papers and white precipitate powder and gave it to Miss Barrow. She continued :

" Soon afterwards she breathed her last and I threatened to call the police, but he pointed his revolver at my head and told me if I informed on him he would blow my brains out. He had always slept with a loaded revolver under his pillow. It was Seddon who told me about the flies in Miss Barrow's bedroom and asked me to buy the fly-papers. He would not let me arrange them in the room but took them himself. Late that night Miss Barrow complained to me about the medicine tasting funny. Something made me look round. I found a saucer that I had not put there. It was damp, and I put my finger to it and then on my tongue. It tasted very queer. On the night of her death, Seddon went out to a theatre ; several times during that evening Miss Barrow had called out ' I am dying,' and I told my husband this when he came in, but he laughed. Later on he went to the bedroom and I followed him. Miss Barrow begged him to send for the doctor, but he refused ; I left the room for a few minutes. On coming back Seddon did not notice me standing near the doorway. I saw that the doctor's medicine had been put on one side, and my husband was mixing water from fly-papers and white precipitate powder which was to make the mixture look like that sent by the doctor. Then I saw him approach the bed and give Miss Barrow several doses."

Sir William Willcox, commenting on this case, observed it was of interest because arsenic was found in all the organs of the victim, Miss Barrow, and a computation of the total amount of arsenic in the body was made by a determination of the arsenic present in each organ. The corpse was actually weighed for this purpose, as well as the individual organs. A fatal poisonous dose of 2 grains was proved to be present in the body. For the purpose of this analysis the Marsh-Berzelius electrolytic test was used for the first time in determining quantitatively the amount of arsenic in each organ.

CHAPTER XLVII

A CORNISH POISON MYSTERY

TOWARDS the close of the year 1921 a man named Edward Black was living with his wife and stepdaughter Marian, a girl of seventeen, at the village of Tregonissey, near St. Austell in Cornwall. Mr. and Mrs. Black were married in 1914, the latter being her husband's senior by twenty years and they had lived together happily, though quarrels about money matters were frequent. Black carried on business as an insurance agent, and his affairs at this time were the reverse of prosperous.

Mrs. Black had for some time been suffering from gastritis, for which her husband had often given her medicine and was very insistent on her taking it. She complained more than once to a neighbour that the medicine given to her by her husband always upset her and burned her throat.

On October 31st, 1921, Black, as was his custom, prepared the breakfast which consisted that morning of cake and bread-and-butter and tea. Within an hour after partaking of the meal, Mrs. Black was seized with vomiting and pain and was obliged to be taken to bed. As her condition did not improve, a doctor was called in, but in spite of his efforts she died after an illness of eleven days.

Before this happened, Black's money troubles had come to a crisis, and following on discoveries made by the company for which he acted as agent, a warrant was issued for his arrest on a charge of issuing non-existent insurance policies.

Three days before his wife died, Black disappeared, and after a search by the police he was finally traced to Liverpool. When arrested in that city he attempted to commit suicide by cutting his throat and had to be taken to a hospital.

Meanwhile, the circumstances under which Mrs. Black had died appeared so suspicious, that a post-mortem examination was ordered, followed by an analysis of the organs of the body. As a result of the investigation Black was charged at the inquest (which was deferred until he was sufficiently recovered to be brought from Liverpool) with the murder of his wife by the administration of arsenic.

The trial took place at Bodmin Assizes on February 2nd, 1922, before Mr. Justice Rowlatt, Mr. Homan Gregory appearing for the prosecution and Mr. Pratt for the defence.

Evidence was given by an assistant in a chemist's shop in St. Austell, that on October 29th, 1921, Black purchased two ounces of white arsenic, saying he wanted it to kill rats, and that although he was offered other preparations for this purpose, he insisted upon having the arsenic, and duly signed the poison register. Asked by the judge how much two ounces of arsenic would make, the witness replied : " About a heaped teaspoonful ; it would be 960 grains," upon which the judge observed that would amount to nearly five hundred fatal doses.

Counsel for the prosecution said that the fatal dose of arsenic, which was about two grains, would just cover a threepenny bit. The effect upon a person who had swallowed arsenic would depend upon whether it was taken in a dry or liquid state ; in liquid form on a empty stomach its effect would be very rapid.

The doctor who attended Mrs. Black during her last illness stated that at the post-mortem examination, it was found that the heart was normal and that there was nothing to account for the rapid action he had noticed during her illness. Questioned as to the presence of arsenic in some empty medicine bottles which had been found in the house, he replied that it was a common thing to find arsenic in bismuth in spite of every precaution against impurity. The amount found in the bottle, however, was 1/20th of a milligram, a milligram being 1/65th of a grain.

Mr. Webster, analyst to the Home Office, said he examined the stomach, intestines, liver, and one kidney of the deceased woman, together with six and three-quarter fluid ounces of blood. He found arsenic in all the organs, the total amount being 1/17th of a grain, equivalent to 1/6th of a grain in the whole body. Slight traces of arsenic were found in the bottles and other articles found in the house brought to him by the police, but that could not possibly account for the amount of arsenic found by him in the organs of the deceased woman. The traces of arsenic in these things were so small that they would not affect the system at all ; to get a fatal dose from medicine containing that proportion it would require 1,300 bottles.

The amounts found were consistent with the taking of a poisonous dose, or a series of small doses which might produce poisonous symptoms. If such doses had been taken they had probably been well diluted. There was no direct evidence of an irritant poison to be seen in the walls of the stomach or the intestines. It was possible, however, for all the arsenic to have disappeared, even if a fatal dose had been taken. It would depend upon the time the patient lived, and a considerable quantity might have been vomited. He did not agree with the counsel for the defence, who urged that arsenic remained in the body indefinitely. In his opinion that was not the case ; it was got rid of very quickly. Arsenic would remain in the hair and nails, for a considerable period, but after a comparatively short time it could not be detected in the organs.

Sir William Willcox, Consulting Medical Expert to the Home Office, described the symptoms of arsenical poisoning. He said that when a big dose was taken, death usually occurred in three days, but in some cases the arsenic damaged the organs of the body, and death might occur several days after the taking of the last dose. He had known cases in which some months had ensued before death. In his opinion the cause of death in this case was arsenical poisoning. He based his opinion not only on symptoms but on the analysis. He believed that no arsenic had been administered to Mrs. Black within five days of her death. She had not died from the direct effects of arsenical poisoning, but the cause of death was exhaustion coupled with poisoning of the vital organs.

At the suggestion of the judge, Mr. Webster made three cups of tea, one with two grains of arsenic in it, one with one grain, and one with none, and these cups were handed to the judge and jury for their inspection.

Evidence was given by Mrs. Black's daughter Marian and by the neighbours, showing that Black had on different occasions administered medicine to his wife, and that she had frequently complained of it being " peppery " and of her dislike to taking it.

Counsel for the defence urged the lack of motive for the crime and suggested that death was due to gastritis, from which disease Mrs. Black was known to have suffered.

On the second and last day of the trial, Black himself went into the witness-box, and denied, as he had previously done at the inquest, that he had ever had arsenic in his possession, or that he had purchased it at St. Austell on October 29th. He also added that on October 31st his wife was not present at breakfast, but that it was taken up to her by her daughter Marian.

The judge, in summing up the case, said that it was one of circumstantial evidence. As a rule in such cases one found motives included, but in this case there was none. There was no doubt that Black's behaviour all through his wife's illness was that of attention to her, and not either neglectful of her or hostile to her.

The jury, after an absence of forty minutes, returned with a verdict of " Guilty." Black was sentenced to death, and was executed at Exeter Gaol on March 24th, 1922.

In commenting on this case, in an address before the Harveian Society, Sir William Willcox stated : " it is interesting from the fact that although arsenic was present in appreciable amount in all the organs, the total amount found in them was considerably less than a possible fatal dose. The explanation of the small amount of poison in the body was clearly shown by the clinical history. The case was one of delayed arsenical poisoning, a considerable proportion of the arsenic having been got rid of by excretion in the few days which elapsed between the administration of the poison and the time of death."

CHAPTER XLVIII

THE ARMSTRONG CASE

IN 1921, the little town of Hay in Breconshire became the centre of one of the most remarkable poison dramas of modern times. There were practising in the town two firms of solicitors, the head of one being Mr. Robert Rowse Armstrong, M.A., who had held a temporary commission as major during the war and was Clerk to the Bench. The principal of the other was a Mr. Oswald Norman Martin who after demobilization had entered into partnership with Mr. Robert T. Griffith who died in November 1920, leaving Mr. Martin to carry on the practice.

Mr. Martin was married on June 14th 1921, to Miss Davies the daughter of a local chemist, and Major Armstrong was invited to the wedding reception and sent a present. Towards the end of September a parcel arrived at Mr. Martin's house addressed to him in block letters apparently to disguise the handwriting. It contained a box of Fuller's chocolates that had come apparently direct from the makers. It was noticed however, that the ribbon securing the box had been untied and retied in a different way and anything that could lead to the identification of the shop where it had been bought had been taken away. The box was put on one side until October 8th when after a dinner-party given by Mr. and Mrs. Martin it was handed round the table, but only one person Mrs. Gilbert Martin, a sister-in-law of the Martins, took anything from it. Later that evening she was taken ill with vomiting and suffered from palpitation of the heart. After dinner, the box of chocolates was again put away and nothing more thought about it until they were suspected of being the cause of the lady's sudden seizure. The chocolates were then handed over to Dr. Hincks, of Hay, who sent them to London to be analysed. According to the report returned to him it was found that in two of the chocolates in the upper row some holes had been drilled about half an inch long into each of which several grains of white arsenic had been placed, and an attempt had then been made to fill up the ends of the holes with pieces of chocolate.

About this time it appears Major Armstrong began to press Mr. Martin very frequently to come and have tea with him, and at length Mr. Martin agreed and went to Armstrong's

house about five o'clock on Wednesday afternoon October 26th.
When he entered the drawing-room he noticed a three-tier
cake-stand on which was a plate of buttered scones. Major
Armstrong called for a cup of tea for him and handed to his
visitor one of the buttered scones from the plate. He also
had a piece of currant bread and butter which was on another
plate and left the house at half-past six. Shortly after arriving
home he began to feel unwell. Towards evening he got
worse and about nine o'clock violent vomiting set in, which
continued at frequent intervals throughout the night. He also
had attacks of palpitation and diarrhœa. On Thursday morning
a doctor was called in and he gradually got better but was not
well enough to return to business until November 1st. The
following day he met Armstrong, who asked him if he was
feeling better, and remarked : " It may seem a curious thing to
say, but you will have another attack," to which Mr. Martin
replied, " I hope not."

During the three or four weeks following, Armstrong again
repeatedly asked Mr. Martin to come to his house to tea and
extended the invitation also to his office, and seemed particularly
anxious that he should accept. About this time, there was some
business between the two solicitors about a sale of land, Mr.
Martin acting for the purchaser and Mr. Armstrong for the
vendor. There had been very considerable delay in completing
the purchase and Mr. Martin had written that unless the
completion took place, his clients would have to rescind their
contracts and demand the return of their deposits in each case.

The completion had not taken place on October 20th, and
Mr. Martin wrote formally giving notice to rescind the contracts
and demanding the return of the money paid on deposit and
expenses, which amounted to about £456. Armstrong asked as
a personal favour if this could not be postponed. Mr. Martin's
clients decided not to consider the suggestion, and thus the
matter stood at the time.

On December 5th, Mr. Martin wrote on behalf of his clients
to Armstrong's firm, threatening that, unless he received a
cheque for his clients' deposit by December 12th, he would
have to take proceedings.

During Mr. Martin's illness the doctor attending him took
certain samples for analysis which were sent up to Dr. Willcox,
who found in the specimens one-thirty-third of a grain of
arsenic. Mrs. Martin, having mentioned to her mother about
her sister-in-law's illness after eating one of the chocolates,
gave the remainder of the box to her, and she showed it to
her husband, Mr. Davies the chemist. In examining them he
noticed that one had a little white powder scattered over one
end, and that two of them certainly had been tampered with.
He thought that they looked very suspicious and so he took

328 FAMOUS POISON TRIALS AND MYSTERIES

them to Dr. Hincks, who sent the box with the remainder of the chocolates to London to be analysed, with the result that arsenic was discovered.

The police were then informed and commenced to make inquiries, with the result that detectives were called in from Scotland Yard and Armstrong was arrested.

It was then found that Mr. Davies, the chemist in Hay, had sold Armstrong arsenic in considerable quantities in 1913 and 1921, which he said he required for making weed-killer. Following on what the police discovered, they were led to investigate the cause of the death of Armstrong's wife, which had occurred about twelve months previously.

An order for exhumation of the body was given by the Home Office and the internal organs were sent to London for analysis. They were found to contain arsenic to the extent of three and one-fifth grains.

While the charge of attempting to poison Mr. Martin was in process of being heard before the magistrates, Armstrong was charged with the murder of his wife.

Mrs. Armstrong was forty-seven years of age when she died and had been married for about fifteen years. She had consulted Dr. Hincks in 1919, being troubled with neuritis in her left arm. After treating her for this complaint the doctor did not see her again for nearly twelve months, when he received a message from Armstrong to the effect that his wife was suffering from pneumonia. A day or two later he found she was suffering from delusions and that her mental condition was apparently bad. He called in a colleague and it became apparent to them that there was something additional to the mental trouble, as Mrs. Armstrong had been taken ill with vomiting and complained of severe pains and heart trouble. The doctors concluded she had better be removed to an asylum and she was taken to Barnwood, near Gloucester. She was there confined to bed and developed a type of paralysis. She was treated with tonics, and one of these contained a small amount of solution of arsenic. Her condition gradually improved and the doctor told Armstrong that she would be able to go home on January 11th. Consequently Armstrong went to the asylum and brought his wife back to Hay. On that day it was found that Armstrong had purchased a quarter of a pound of arsenic, and at one time in conversation with the doctor had asked him how much arsenic constituted a fatal dose. He also asked Dr. Hincks to visit his wife occasionally and a nurse was engaged to look after her.

For about a month she seemed to be getting better, then in February the sickness and vomiting commenced again. The doctor thought it was a case of severe biliousness, but towards the end of February she got worse and died on the 22nd of that month. The doctor certified that she died from gastritis

and heart disease as at that time he had not the slightest suspicion of foul play.

In 1919 Mrs. Armstrong made a will which was drawn up by
her husband and witnessed by two servants in the house.
She had property of the value of about £2,419.

In a previous will made in 1917, Armstrong was to receive
an annuity of fifty pounds a year, while the property was to
be divided equally between his children, but two years later
in the fresh will drawn up by her husband, she left all her
property to him. It transpired afterwards, that the second will
was drawn up in Armstrong's own writing and purported to be
signed by two witnesses. Mrs. Armstrong was not present and
the two servants who signed it at the request of Armstrong
stated that they did not know it was a will they were witnessing.

To all appearances and in the opinion of her medical adviser
Mrs. Armstrong had died a natural death, but on exhumation
some ten months afterwards, a sufficient amount of arsenic was
found in the remains to poison her. Almost directly after his
wife was buried and he had got the property in his possession,
Armstrong went to the Continent, and immediately on his
return at the end of April was talking about marriage to another
lady. A packet containing white arsenic, without being mixed
with colouring matter, which chemists are bound by law to do
before selling it, was carried by Armstrong in his pocket on the
day on which he was arrested. It was also notable that Mr.
Martin was nearly fatally poisoned after taking tea with Armstrong, and that the amount of arsenic, one thirty-third of a
grain, which was found in the specimen submitted for analysis
pointed to the fact that the amount he had taken a few days
before was a little over three grains. It was further remarked
that after Armstrong had asked Dr. Hincks " What is sufficient
arsenic to cause death ? " and was told three grains, that he
was carrying that exact amount in a packet in his pocket.

Chief Inspector Crutchett, of Scotland Yard, saw Armstrong
at his office on December 31st, and told him that he was investigating the sudden illness of Mr. Martin after taking tea with
him on October 26th. He also told him about the chocolates
which were found to contain arsenic, and it was known that he
had purchased arsenic on January 11th, 1921. He asked him if
he could account for his movements on October 26th, and what
became of the arsenic that was in his possession. Armstrong
then made a statement that was taken down in writing and which
he signed. In it he stated that he also partook of the buttered
currant loaf and scones which he handed to Mr. Martin, who
he knew had not been well before he paid the visit to his house.
He acknowledged that he purchased arsenic in 1914, which he
used for making a weed-killer consisting of caustic soda and
arsenic which he found to be cheaper than any he could purchase.

He was unable to throw any light on the finding of arsenic in Mr. Martin's tests or on the cause of his illness after visiting his house. After signing the statement, Armstrong was arrested and was asked to empty the contents of his pockets on to a desk. Among the articles found in his possession was a small packet containing a white powder and two or three little pellets, rather heavy, in a small envelope, which also had the remains of some white powder. The small packet was found to contain three and three-quarter grains of white arsenic.

At the magisterial inquiry, Mrs. Armstrong's sister said that her sister was a believer in homœopathic medicines, and among them were arsenicum, nux vomica and liquorice, which she not only used for herself, but for the household generally. The doctors who saw Mrs. Armstrong at the asylum and prescribed for her, had ordered her a mixture containing solution of arsenic, iron and ammonia citrate and nux vomica, the solution of arsenic being in five-minim doses. She had taken that medicine as a tonic up to October 4th, but after that date had taken nothing containing arsenic.

Dr. Hincks, who had attended Mrs. Armstrong from 1919, described her complaint and condition. It was owing to her mental trouble that he advised her removal to the asylum, and at Armstrong's request he consented to her return home. He saw her several times afterwards, but her physical condition grew worse and she became weaker every day. On February 16th he told her husband that her case was quite hopeless and later he heard she was dead. He gave a certificate that death was due to gastritis and heart disease. His opinion now was, that all these conditions were due to the presence of chronic arsenical poisoning, and he thought the cause of death was due to the administration of arsenic.

Dr. B. H. Spilsbury, who made the post-mortem on the body of Mrs. Armstrong after exhumation, said he found it in an unusually good state of preservation, allowing for the time which had elapsed since her death. It was a condition which was found in certain cases of arsenical poisoning, to which in his opinion, her death was due. With reference to the mixture which was prescribed for her at the asylum and taken as a tonic for a period of some months, he stated that in that small quantity he would not expect to find any traces of arsenic in the body, with the possible exception of traces in the nails and hair.

The official analyst to the Home Office, who had analysed the chocolates sent to Mr. Martin, said that he found the box contained thirty-two chocolates, two of which had the appearance of having been tampered with. A cylindrical hole nearly half an inch long had apparently been bored and filled with a white powder, and attempts had been made to seal it up with a covering of chocolate. The white powder was found on analysis to be arsenious oxide. He estimated that the amount in one chocolate was slightly more than two grains. The rest of the chocolates showed no trace of having been tampered with. He found arsenic in all the organs of Mrs. Armstrong's body, the total being equivalent to 3.2 grains, which led him to believe that she must have had a considerable amount of arsenic during the last few days of her life, and that her death was due to acute arsenical poisoning. A quantity amounting to a fatal dose must have been taken within twenty-four hours of her death.

The analyst also made an examination of a number of bottles and packets found in Armstrong's house, most of which contained arsenic either in solution or powder.

Sir William H. Willcox, medical adviser to the Home Office, said the mixture that contained arsenic prescribed for Mrs. Armstrong at the asylum, could not have accounted for the arsenic in her body. Arsenic taken thus for a month would be entirely eliminated within about ten days. The symptoms described in the illness of Mrs. Gilbert Martin after eating one of the chocolates, and those of Mr. Oswald Martin, were all consistent with acute arsenical poisoning. He was of the opinion that Mrs. Armstrong was suffering from the effects of an irritant poison when she was taken to the asylum in August, 1920 and on her return home, the reappearance of these symptoms showed she was again suffering from arsenical poisoning. With respect to the distribution of the arsenic in the organs taken from the exhumed body, he had no doubt that a possibly fatal dose of two grains or more must have been taken within twenty-four hours of death. He had known instances of suicide where a large dose or possibly two had been taken, but in this case there were obviously successive doses, giving rise to very painful symptoms, which were not in the least indicative of suicide. He did not believe it possible that she could have taken the doses herself within twenty-four hours of death, and he was confident that she was suffering from acute arsenical poisoning when she died.

On this evidence, Armstrong was committed to the Assizes on the charge of murdering his wife and of the attempt to murder Mr. Oswald Martin.

Armstrong's trial took place at the Hereford Assizes before Mr. Justice Darling, on April 31st. The case for the Crown was conducted by Sir Ernest Pollock, K.C., and others, and Armstrong was defended by Sir Henry Curtis Bennett, K.C.

The nurse attending Mrs. Armstrong said that her husband frequently came into the bedroom the last few days of her illness when she was confined to bed. He was alone with her on several occasions and sat in the room when she went to get her meals. She noticed that sickness occurred about twenty minutes after her patient had taken food. Mrs. Armstrong kept a chest of homœopathic medicines in the bedroom, but up to the Sunday before she died she was unable to get out of bed. She said she did not think it was possible that Mrs. Armstrong on February 13th could have got out of bed and got a packet or bottle out of the cupboard in the room. She had been told by the nurse who was previously in attendance on Mrs. Armstrong, that she was afraid that she might attempt to commit suicide, as she was certainly suffering from delusions.

Chief Inspector Crutchett, who was present at the arrest of Armstrong said he had no opportunity after December 31st of going back to the house, but the house had been searched and he was aware of a little drawer in the cupboard in the study. Sir Henry Curtis Bennett then told him that a small paper packet of white arsenic was found in that drawer by Mr. Matthews, Armstrong's solicitor, his managing clerk and Dr. Chivers. The Inspector declared there was no packet of white arsenic there when he searched the drawer. Counsel remarked that there were actual traces of arsenic in the drawer itself. In reply to the judge the Inspector said, that had the packet been in the drawer when he searched he would have seen it.

A feature of the scientific evidence given by Mr. Webster was the statement, that he had never, in his experience of making analyses of organs taken from three to four hundred bodies, discovered such a quantity of arsenic as he did in the case of Mrs. Armstrong.

Superintendent Weaver, who searched Armstrong's study at his house, said that he had examined the little drawer of the bureau in which it was stated a packet of white arsenic was found after the police search. He distinctly remembered pulling out the drawer and placing it on the desk, and was positive that there was no packet of white powder there then.

The counsel for the prisoner in addressing the jury, asserted that the suggestion that Mrs. Armstrong took arsenic herself, was infinitely stronger than the case made out against the prisoner, and he called Armstrong as a witness to give evidence in his own defence.

Armstrong gave a detailed account of his career and war service. He took his degree as Master of Arts at Cambridge University, and had held important and responsible positions, including that of Justices' Clerk of Hay. He was a partner in the firm of Cheese & Armstrong until 1914, when Mr. Cheese died. He married in June 1907 and had three children. He held a commission in the Volunteer Forces of the R.E. until 1914 and was then gazetted captain. In June, 1918, he went to France, where he remained until October of that year and was demobilized in the Spring of 1919.

Questioned about the second will in his own handwriting,

he said the reason for his wife's deciding to make a second will was, that she had come into some further property since the first will owing to the death of her mother, and she wished to make a shorter and simpler one. He drew up the document at her request and with her full knowledge. He stated that he first became aware that there was something wrong with his wife on August 9th, but he left her apparently in normal health when he went out in the morning. On coming back for lunch she surprised him by saying before the children, that she expected that he would have been arrested ; she had done something to cause his arrest and had told the children they might never expect to see him again. This was the first time he had ever noticed any active delusions, and as they did not diminish, he saw Dr. Hincks and told him what had occurred. Discussing the matter with a friend, he had made the suggestion, that it would not be safe to leave razors about near his wife, and as a matter of fact, he had removed them from the room and also his service revolver. He denied emphatically that there was any truth in the suggestion, that he had ever administered arsenic to his wife prior to her removal to Barnwood Asylum.

Sir Henry Curtis Bennett, K.C., in his speech for the defence said : " This case is a most extraordinary one, because the prosecution set out to prove that in August, 1920, Armstrong started to administer arsenic to his wife ; that in January, 1921, he continued, on her return from Barnwood Asylum, to administer poison to her ; and that finally she died as the result of poison administered by him. They set out to prove that and in doing so, they had not been able to make any suggestion as to how Major Armstrong administered the poison, the time he administered it, or in what it was administered."

Dealing with the purchase of arsenic, counsel said Major Armstrong bought half a pound of arsenic coloured with charcoal in June, 1919. Six out of these eight ounces he had used for weed-killer, and the remainder was discovered in the cupboard in the library. He bought some in 1921, having forgotten that he still had a little left from 1919. He returned from abroad in May and went to the cupboard and found the packet with no string upon it, looking as though it had been opened. He divided it into two parts. One he used by dividing it again into a number of tiny packets like the one found upon him. These little packets he used in a way advised by a chemical company, and he carried them in his garden coat. It so happened that on December 31st, he had on that same garden coat and in one of the pockets he had, together with his business and private letters, that little packet of arsenic.

What happened to the other half of that arsenic ? Having separated those packets for safety, he put that other little packet,

with the blue paper round it, in a little bottom drawer in his
bureau which was not a key-drawer at all.
On December 31st he was arrested. The next day he remembered this little packet and told Mr. Matthews his solicitor
about it. Mr. Matthews went to the house and in the presence
of the housekeeper Miss Penn, opened the drawer, but there
was no packet to be seen. They believed the police had found
and taken it. Mr. Matthews then pressed the police for a
list of things found in the house, and when he had got it, he
found that the packet of arsenic was not mentioned. On
February 9th, therefore, he again went to the house, and going
to the bureau pulled the drawer out bodily, and in putting his
hand in to see if there might be a secret drawer, he found the
packet of arsenic, which had been caught up at the back.
" Thus," said counsel, " the last quarter of a pound of arsenic
bought by Armstrong was accounted for."

Armstrong, questioned as to what he did with the small
packets of arsenic he was said to have made up, declared that
he made these little packets simply by portioning out a small
quantity with his penknife. He had used them all for killing
weeds with the exception of the one that was found in his
pocket with his letters when he was arrested. It was his custom
to drive an old file into the ground over the root and then drop
in the contents of a small packet of arsenic, so that it fell to
the bottom or stuck to the side, and he did this to any dandelion
root he wished to kill. He could not think how he used nineteen
packets instead of twenty, as he was under the impression that he
had used them all. When he was arrested and placed the contents
of his pockets on the table, he did not know the remaining small
packet of arsenic was there until he saw it and recognized
it. When he saw it, he then remembered about the two ounces
that he had left in the drawer of the bureau. He did not tell
the police that they would find white arsenic in the bureau, but
he realised that the finding of the packet had placed him in an
awkward situation.

Mr. Justice Darling questioned Armstrong very closely about
the purchase, use and discovery of the white arsenic. He replied
that previous to buying this quantity which he used for killing
dandelions, he had never had white arsenic in his possession.
He had used nineteen of the little packets on nineteen dandelion
roots.

" Did you notice what became of the dandelions, did they
die ? " asked the judge.

" They did," replied Armstrong.

" That was very interesting, was it not ? " remarked Mr.
Justice Darling. " It was an interesting experiment to you who
wanted to get rid of the weeds ? "

" When you saw the little packet and realised you had arsenic in your pocket, did you realise it was a fatal dose of arsenic, not for a dandelion but for a human being ? "

" No," replied Armstrong, " I did not realise that at all."

" But you had been making rather a study of arsenic ? "

" No."

" It appears now," said the Judge, " that if every one of these little packets was the same as that found in your pocket, it contained a fatal dose of arsenic."

Armstrong replied that he realised that now but did not do so at the time. He had not disclosed to the police that he knew the arsenic was in the drawer, as he thought it was certain they would find it.

Dr. F. S. Toogood, who was called for the defence, said he was of the opinion that Mrs. Armstrong was suffering from chronic indigestion. He thought that up to the time of her removal to the asylum, she was not suffering from arsenical poisoning, and up to February 16th there was no evidence of anything consistent with it. In his opinion death was caused by arsenic taken about February 16th, and if a dose was taken on that date it would account for the amount found in the body.

Dr. Ainslie, of Hereford, who was present at the post-mortem, said that judging from the evidence of her last illness and that of the post-mortem, he was perfectly satisfied that Mrs. Armstrong had died after a large dose of arsenic which was taken about February 16th or 17th. He expressed dissatisfaction over the preliminaries in the case of the test for Mr. Martin, and said that there might have been arsenic in the glass of which the bottle was made, as well as in the medicines with which Mr. Martin had been treated by Dr. Hincks. He was questioned on the subject of arsenic being found in bismuth, and agreed that two parts in one million was the amount allowed. He referred to the possibility of impurity in the supplies of bismuth from America available during the war.

Dr. J. Steed, the last witness for the defence, said he believed that up to the time she was taken to the asylum, Mrs. Armstrong's condition was undoubtedly due to some internal trouble, such as indigestion or a form of neuritis. He believed the cause of her death was the taking of one large dose of arsenic on February 16th.

Sir Henry Curtis Bennett, in his final address, alluded to the important point that had been made of the finding of the white arsenic in the bureau after Armstrong's arrest. The evidence for the prosecution had been that Armstrong had always purchased coloured arsenic, and this discovery of white arsenic was of the highest importance. Supposing that packet of white arsenic, which undoubtedly was bought from Mr. Davies, the chemist in Hay, had not been found, the case would to a very large extent have been made to turn upon how Armstrong

came to be in possession of white arsenic. He would have said :
" I purchased it from Mr. Davies." And the Attorney-General
would have said : " That cannot be true, produce some of it.
Davies has sworn that all the arsenic you purchased was coloured,
and all we have found was coloured." It would have been said :
" It is all very well for you, Armstrong, to say that you were
buying your arsenic openly in your own town. You must have
gone outside to make a secret purchase of arsenic." " And this
is the important part of the discovery of the white arsenic,"
concluded Sir Henry.

The Attorney-General, replying on behalf of the Crown,
admitted that the case for the prosecution had changed. This,
he affirmed, was a poisoning case, and he doubted if in the
history of the world the poisoned cup had been seen to be
poisoned, and when administered had been known to have been
poisoned. In the case of poisoners they would always find
subtlety and an endeavour to cover up things that were sinister.
He claimed that this case depended upon circumstantial evidence;
the prosecution had endeavoured to be fair to the prisoner.
The changes in the case were due to the fact that they now
knew, as they did not know at the start, the defence would admit
that Mrs. Armstrong died of arsenical poisoning ; and they
knew now, as they did not know before, that the defence was
placing no reliance upon her having taken homœopathic
medicines. He did not know before, as he now knew, that in
August, 1920, Armstrong was possessed of two ounces of white
arsenic, the balance of what he had bought in 1919. He was
also unaware before, that in addition to the small packet that
was found, he had some arsenic, approximately two ounces,
which he had bought in 1920.

The central feature of the case was the defence of suicide
raised by Armstrong himself. One person, and one person
alone, was constantly about Mrs. Armstrong in August, 1920,
and again in January and February, 1921. " Let me," said the
Attorney-General, " note a remarkable piece of evidence. When
Armstrong was asked if he was alone with his wife, he replied :
' Yes, I was alone with her. There was milk and soda in the
room,' and when asked ' Did you ever put a cup to her lips,
did you ever minister to her, you the devoted, loyal, faithful,
loving husband ? ' his reply was ' No.' Can this be believed ? "

With regard to the Martin case, the Attorney-General scouted
the suggestion that the arsenic taken from Martin came from a
dirty bottle or cork or from impure chemicals in his medicine.
He believed that the story of the twenty little packets made up
to kill dandelions on the lawn was a falsehood.

The Judge, in summing up, carefully sifted the whole of the
evidence that had been given. He stated that the question
to be decided was, had the prosecution proved that Armstrong

gave his wife the poison. " The case was a deeply interesting one, and he doubted if anyone had any recollection of so remarkable a case in its incidents. It had been said that this case depended upon circumstantial evidence, but circumstantial evidence was as good as any other, provided it was relevant and true. Circumstantial evidence going to prove the guilt of a person was this : ' One witness proves one thing and another witness proves another thing, and all these things prove to conviction beyond all reasonable doubt, but neither of them separately proves the guilt of the person.' It should be remembered that Armstrong was arrested not on the charge of murdering his wife, but of attempting to murder Mr. Martin. Having been arrested for an attempt to murder Mr. Martin on December 31st, only then was some one or other led to think ' What about Mrs. Armstrong, what did she die of ? ' The symptoms were very similar, so an order was obtained and the body was exhumed on January 2nd, and it was then found that there was still in that body a large dose of arsenic, more arsenic than those who were accustomed to dealing with these things had known in any exhumed body before. There was no proof that there was any arsenic in the cupboard in the bedroom, and there was evidence there was arsenic in the cupboard in the room downstairs. It was incredible, therefore, that a woman who was anxious to get better, committed suicide, and had taken a large dose of arsenic two days previously. It was incredible that a woman in the condition in which she was, could get up with the intention of taking a dose of arsenic. Where had she got it from ? She could not have taken the arsenic herself within twenty-four hours of death. If Dr. Spilsbury's evidence was true that was practically impossible."

The jury after retiring for forty-eight minutes found Armstrong guilty on the charge of wilfully murdering his wife, and he was sentenced to death.

The trial lasted ten days, and the dramatic production by Armstrong's counsel of the packet of two ounces of white arsenic found by Armstrong's solicitor, wedged at the back of the drawer of the bureau in his study, six weeks after the police had searched and found nothing in that drawer, was very unexpected. This packet of arsenic became one of the outstanding features of the trial, and by the judge's order the bureau was brought to a room adjoining the Court, where a test was made. Armstrong was instructed to place the packet of arsenic in the drawer where he stated it had been, and afterwards Mr. Matthews, the solicitor, demonstrated where he declared he had found it.

An appeal was made to the Court of Criminal Appeal, when Sir Henry Curtis Bennett said that both Mr. Justice Darling and the Attorney-General had ridiculed the statement that

Armstrong had made of his method of destroying dandelions. He would produce five witnesses to prove that, far from being incredible, it was not an uncommon custom to give dandelions arsenic in small doses in the same manner as Armstrong had described, when asked to account for the packet containing three and three-quarter grains that was found in his pocket. The court, however, ruled out any further evidence.

The Lord Chief Justice remarked that a packet containing three and three-quarter grains of white arsenic was a very unusual thing to find in a solicitor's pocket. Counsel observed that arsenic sufficient to kill three thousand persons could be bought for 2s. 6d.

Sir Henry Curtis Bennett's speech in support of the appeal lasted twelve hours, and in the course of his argument he said : " Mrs. Armstrong went downstairs to get the arsenic ; she knew where it was kept, and on February 16th she had gone downstairs and was teaching her little boy." Both packets were in the cupboard in the room in which the boy was being taught. Armstrong stated that in May he went to the cupboard and found the packet in such a condition that it appeared to have been tampered with. He suggested that on the day and in the room where she was with the little boy, she took a fatal dose of arsenic from the cupboard. From the point of view of the defence, he argued, the finding of the arsenic in the bureau was extraordinarily lucky, for there was till then no evidence that Armstrong had any white arsenic at all. The purchase on January 11th was believed to be coloured arsenic, and if this had not been found with the chemist's label, there would have been a stronger case, that in addition to the quarter-pound of coloured arsenic in January, Armstrong, from an unknown source and for an unknown purpose, had got white arsenic as well.

The Lord Chief Justice consulted with his colleagues and said they were unanimously of the opinion that the appeal must be dismissed. Armstrong therefore suffered the extreme penalty of the law.

CHAPTER XLIX

THE BYFLEET MYSTERY

In the Spring of 1924, Mr. Alfred Poynter Jones purchased the " Blue Anchor Hotel " at Byfleet, Surrey, and shortly afterwards took up his residence there with his wife. Mrs. Jones who had had some financial trouble owing to the failure of a catering business she had formerly carried on at Kingston-on-Thames, early in the following year became unwell and on January 7th she travelled alone to France and stayed at Biarritz.

At the hotel where she stayed, she became acquainted with a man named Jean Pierre Vaquier who was about forty-five years of age, and was employed there as wireless operator.

Their acquaintance rapidly ripened into a warm friendship, although he was unable to speak English and Mrs. Jones could not converse in French. When Mrs. Jones left Biarritz, their intimacy continued and she corresponded with Vaquier and he eventually joined her at Bordeaux.

When Mrs. Jones returned to England, Vaquier soon followed and they met again at an hotel in London. In February, Mrs. Jones arrived back at Byfleet and on her return, her husband went to Margate where he developed influenza which laid him up for a time.

Before he was fit to return, Vaquier arrived at the Blue Anchor Hotel where he asked to be allowed to stay for about a month, until some money he said he was expecting, arrived.

On February 17th, Mr. Jones came back from Margate, still unwell and was suffering from a slight congestion of the lungs, but after some days in bed he gradually recovered his health.

Vaquier's attentions to Mrs. Jones became noticeable to the hotel staff and he was continually seeking her company. Meanwhile, the relations between Mr. Jones and his wife were normal, although he was a heavy drinker and would drink with most of the customers who frequented the house. He was in the habit of taking a dose of Bromo-salts as a corrective, the bottle containing which he kept on the mantelshelf in the bar-parlour.

On the morning of March 29th, at 7.15, when the cook came downstairs, she found Vaquier in the kitchen drinking some coffee which he had made himself. Later on in the morning, the housekeeper, when dusting the bar-parlour noticed two strange bottles on the mantelshelf. One of these bottles seemed to be different to the one she had usually seen there containing Mr. Jones's salts, and she remarked that the other bottle contained iodine. While she was in the parlour, she saw Vaquier move the iodine bottle from one side of the shelf to the other. A few minutes later, Mr. Jones came downstairs and called for a glass of water which he took away with him. About half an hour afterwards, he came downstairs again fully dressed, and after staying about thirty minutes, he went into the bar-parlour where Mrs. Jones was talking to Vaquier. He passed through into a bar adjoining and returned with a glass of water in his hand, then going to the mantelshelf he took the bottle of Bromo-salts and measured out a teaspoonful which he placed in the glass and stirred it.

" This thing won't fizz this morning," he remarked, as he put the glass to his lips and swallowed the contents.

" Oh God ! they were bitter," he exclaimed as he put the glass down.

Mrs. Jones, who was standing near, at once took the bottle and poured some of the contents on to her hand and putting it to her mouth found they tasted very bitter. In pouring the salts into her hand, she spilt a few of the crystals on the floor.

" Yes," she cried to her husband, " they have been tampered with. I will go and get you some salt and water."

Vaquier at once got up from his chair and followed Mrs. Jones into the kitchen and asked the cook for a glass of water. Mrs. Jones, who still held the bottle of salts in her hand, then put it in a drawer in the dresser saying to the cook : " We will put this away and have it analysed."

Mrs. Jones having mixed some salt and water in a glass, took it at once to her husband who swallowed it. A few minutes later he became very ill and with the assistance of Vaquier was carried upstairs.

Mrs. Jones then telephoned for a doctor who came immediately and was shown upstairs.

Meanwhile, Vaquier went into the kitchen and said to the cook excitedly : " Doctor, medicine, quick ! " The cook thinking that the doctor wanted the bottle of Bromo-salts, which she had seen Mrs. Jones place in the drawer, let Vaquier take the bottle from the dresser-drawer and he left the kitchen with it in his hand.

Later on, when Mrs. Jones came to look for the bottle to show the doctor, she found it again in the drawer where she had put it, but she noticed it was not in the same place. She took it to the doctor who remarked there were no salts in it and that it had recently been rinsed out with water, a little of which remained in it.

In spite of medical aid, Mr. Jones died in great agony shortly afterwards.

On coming downstairs from the bedroom, Mrs. Jones encountered Vaquier who asked :

" How is master ? Is he well ? "

" No, he is dead," replied Mrs. Jones. " You know it and you have done it."

Vaquier then burst into tears and falling on his knees, took her hand and cried : " Madame ! Oh God ! Do you accuse me ? "

" Yes," she replied, as she left Vaquier weeping.

On March 30th, Vaquier made a statement to the police and three days afterwards Mrs. Jones on meeting him, directly accused him of murdering her husband. To which he replied : " Yes, Mabs ; for you."

The following day he left Byfleet leaving a note for Mrs. Jones in which he bade her " Adieu for ever."

At the inquest held on the body of Mr. Jones it transpired that while Vaquier was staying at an hotel in London, he had been in the habit of making purchases at a chemist's shop in Southampton Row and on March 1st, he had bought two grains of strychnine for which he had signed the poison register in the name of " J. Vanker."

Mrs. Jones, in the course of her evidence said that while some of the contents of the bottle from which her husband had taken the salts were in her hand, she noticed that there were many transparent crystals among them. She must have dropped some on the floor and after her husband's death she saw the doctor pick them up, put them in an envelope and hand them to a policeman.

Mr. John Webster, senior official analyst to the Home Office, stated that he found in the stomach one-fifth of a grain of strychnine, one third of a grain in the liver and one-thirteenth of a grain in the smaller intestine. In the bottle which had contained the Bromo-salts, there were a few drops of liquid which showed traces of strychnine and in the tumbler and spoon used the contents gave definite reaction for strychnine. The full amount of strychnine he estimated would be a little over half a grain or seventeen-thirtieths of a grain.

The doctor who was called in to Mr. Jones said he was fully conscious when he arrived but in a state of extreme terror. When the bottle which had contained the Bromo-salts was handed to him, it only contained a few drops of a clear, colourless liquid, which was slightly bitter to the taste. The post-mortem examination showed that the cause of death was asphyxia, following poisoning by something active like strychnine.

Sir Bernard Spilsbury, honorary pathologist to the Home Office, in his evidence stated that he found no natural disease to account for death and the conditions pointed to it being caused by asphyxia consequent upon strychnine poisoning.

The minimum fatal dose was half a grain. His approximate opinion was that Jones must certainly have taken not less than one or two grains of strychnine.

Vaquier was committed for trial on the capital charge and was tried at the Guildford Assizes before Mr. Justice Avory on July 3rd, 1924.

Sir Patrick Hastings, K.C., the Attorney-General, in opening the case for the Crown said, the prisoner had, within the preceding few months, developed an infatuation or passion for the dead man's wife, which was probably the motive or one of the motives which actuated the crime.

Mrs. Jones, in the course of her evidence, stated that she had noticed among the salts she poured from the bottle into her hand some long crystals which tasted exceedingly bitter. Before Vaquier left the Blue Anchor she accused him of murdering her husband, to which he replied in English : " Yes, Mabs ; for you." To which she retorted : " I would have killed you had I known you would have done a thing like that."

A chemist carrying on business in Southampton Row said that on March 1st, Vaquier bought some strychnine and perchloride of mercury from him. The quantity of strychnine was .12 gramme. He said he required the chemicals for wireless experiments.

Sir Henry Curtis Bennett, K.C., who defended Vaquier, called him as a witness and he told the story of his acquaintance with Mrs. Jones and their subsequent intimacy. Questioned as to the purchase of the poisons, he declared that on March 1st he gave the chemist a list, ordering five or six different chemicals including 25 grammes of strychnine, 100 grammes of pure iodine, 100 grammes of chloroform. When asked what the strychnine was to be used for, he replied for experiments in wireless.

He then stated that he had bought the strychnine for Mrs. Jones's solicitor, who said he had a dog he wished to destroy. He gave him a pound to procure it, and said that he handed the strychnine to him at the Blue Anchor on the evening of the day he bought it. He said the gentleman who asked him to buy the poison had told him to sign for it in a false name. He denied having anything to do with the death of Mr. Jones.

The solicitor alluded to was called and denied the statements made by Vaquier and declared that they were absolutely untrue.

Sir Henry Curtis Bennett, K.C., for the defence, suggested there was no motive for Vaquier to want to murder Mr. Jones. Sir Bernard Spilsbury had said that Mr. Jones had taken two grains and possibly more of strychnine. If that be correct, Vaquier could not be the murderer because that was more than he had purchased.

The strychnine found in the body was not all the strychnine that was in the bottle. They also knew that some was picked

up from the floor. Mrs. Jones had told them that the quantity
of poison found was about half a teaspoonful. He would put it
lower than that and make it a quarter-of-a-teaspoonful, therefore
there must have been more strychnine in the bottle on March
29th than Vaquier ever bought. He contended that there was
not a scrap of evidence as to whether Vaquier had washed the
bottle out or when he washed it out.

Mr. Justice Avory in summing up said that of all forms of
death by which human nature can be overcome the most detestable was that of poisoning, because it could of all others, be
the least prevented, either by manhood or by forethought.
Therefore, in all cases where a man wilfully administered poison
to another or laid poison for him, and either he or another took
it and was killed by it, the law implies malice, although no
particular enmity could be proved.

The strychnine might have been introduced into the bottle
during the night or early on the morning of the tragedy.

One of the crucial questions of the prosecution was that the
poisoner had the opportunity of introducing that poison into
the bottle during that time. They say that he had poison in his
possession after March 1st. His movements in the bar-parlour
on March 28th were of an unusual character and indicated that
he was watching for the opportunity of tampering with that
bottle and watching particularly to see that the deceased man
should be present to take it.

Vaquier admitted that he had the bottle in his hand from the
drawer. He said he put it back again. But why did he have it
in his hand at all ?

He saw no reason to doubt the evidence of the chemist who
said that Vaquier came with a list requiring twenty grammes of
perchloride of mercury and also including .12 of a gramme of
strychnine. Assuming .12 of a gramme is something less than
two grains—two grains are equal to .13 : that is to say thirteen-
hundredths—what he had was twelve-hundredths instead of
thirteen-hundredths. If he had thirteen-hundredths, he would
have had two grains. Therefore, it was only something very
small—less than two grains.

Assuming he never had any more, counsel invites you to say,
from the evidence of Sir Bernard Spilsbury, there must have
been more than two grains used by the person who committed
this crime. In order to explain that, you are asked to assume
that the man spat out some of the poison.

A man who drank a dose of those salts would not sip it, he
would probably swallow it almost in one gulp, and although he
may have been seen to spit on that occasion, the spitting may
have been a spasmodic action such as is not uncommon of
anybody with a nasty taste in his mouth. You cannot therefore
be sure that the man spat out any of this poison.

If they were satisfied that Vaquier put the poison in the bottle, they need not seriously look for a motive.

How was it, asked Mr. Justice Avory in conclusion, that there was no explanation of the purchase by Vaquier of the perchloride of mercury ? How was it there was nobody at the Blue Anchor who asked him to buy perchloride of mercury in order to kill a cat ? He might just as well have said that, as allege that he bought the strychnine for the purpose of killing a dog.

The jury after an absence of an hour and forty minutes returned with a verdict of Guilty, and the judge then sentenced Vaquier to death.

An appeal was entered against Vaquier's conviction by Sir Henry Curtis Bennett on the grounds that further witnesses might be called for the defence upon two important matters.

On July 9th, it appears that Vaquier made a statement to the Governor of Wandsworth Prison that on a certain day, after the death of Mr. Jones, he had seen a woman go to the tool-shed in the garden of the Blue Anchor Hotel. He also said that on visiting the tool-shed afterwards he found in the wall, behind a loose brick, the bottle he had bought and given to Mrs. Jones's solicitor.

The governor informed the police of this statement and on the 10th, the Deputy-Chief Constable of Surrey and Supt. Boshier went to the hotel. They searched the tool-shed and behind a loose brick at the top of the wall, they found two small glass bottles with metal screw caps. The larger of these contained 23 grains (1.5 grammes) of strychnine and the smaller one strychnine in solution.

The appeal was heard by Lord Hewart, the Lord Chief Justice on July 28th, 1924, who in the course of his remarks, on giving judgment said that the fresh evidence it was sought to offer was that Vaquier was aware of a larger quantity of strychnine concealed in the wall, not far from the place where Mr. Jones took the fatal dose. He desired to say that he knew of that large quantity of strychnine and also that Mrs. Jones knew of it. Vaquier made every kind of attack on Mrs. Jones during the trial and that further evidence would have carried that attack just a little further.

If this evidence had been accepted it would have been apparent that there was a considerable quantity of strychnine to which the prisoner had access, and the argument about the discrepancy in the amount of strychnine that was contained in the bottle of salts would have disappeared for ever. The application was therefore dismissed, and Vaquier suffered the extreme penalty of the law.

CHAPTER L

THE COLEFORD MYSTERY

In July, 1927, Mr. Harry Pace, a sheep-raiser and quarryman, who lived with his wife and young family at Fetter Hill Farm, Coleford, Gloucestershire, was taken ill after dipping some lambs in a tub outside his farm. He complained of violent pains in his stomach, and although he recovered sufficiently to work again he continued to have a recurrence of the trouble.

He was attended by a local doctor but subsequently became worse and especially complained of " burning pains " in his throat.

During his illness his wife nursed and looked after him, and he was visited from time to time by various relatives.

In spite of every attention, the agonising pains in his stomach continued and his sufferings became so acute that on August 19th, he was removed to the Gloucester Royal Infirmary.

Here for a time his health somewhat improved and he recovered to such an extent, that he was discharged at his own request in October and returned to his farm.

In December, he was again seized with a similar attack and in January, when the doctor saw him, he was prostrated with intense abdominal pain and died on the following day.

On January 15th, the funeral was stopped on the Coroner's order and a post-mortem examination was made. An inquest was opened on January 16th, at which Professor Walker Hall stated his belief that Pace's death had been due to arsenical poisoning.

An analysis and minute examination of certain organs led him to conclude, first, that a large dose of arsenic must have been administered sometime between six and forty-eight hours before death. Second. A dose must have been administered any time between fourteen and twenty-one days before death. Third. A dose must have been administered somewhere about January 3rd.

Between Christmas Day and January 10th, the day of his death, he must have had three doses of arsenic. These conclusions were confirmed in almost every detail on the clinical side. The total amount of arsenic he found in the organs was 9.42 grains.

In further evidence Professor Walker Hall deposed that he

had made the examination of certain parts of Pace's body five days after his death. In all the organs he found definite toxic irritation. The liver, heart and kidneys were so damaged that life was impossible. He could find no germs associated with natural disease and he thought the last dose of arsenic must have been taken from six to forty-eight hours before death.

With reference to the absorption of arsenic through the skin he said that a healthy skin would not absorb white arsenic if applied for only a limited period, but it could be absorbed through a cut or abrasion.

Mr. Ellis, the County analyst stated that he had examined a dolly-tub which was used as a rain-tub and contained about eight and a half inches of stagnant water. A sample of water taken from the top contained .012 grains of arsenic per gallon, and the water at the bottom the same. In an empty beer bottle found lying in the bottom of the tub, he found .018 grains of arsenic but no sulphur. If the tub had been used for dipping sheep he would have expected the sulphur in the dip to remain.

Sir William Willcox, medical adviser to the Home Office said that post-mortem findings were consistent with arsenical poisoning.

The dead man was evidently suffering from acute arsenical poisoning from July 24th, and the acute symptoms appear to have lasted seven to ten days, then peripheral neuritis developed.

Besides the dose taken forty-eight hours before death, there must have been a dose taken before the onset of the symptoms on Christmas Day, and it was his opinion that one or more other doses were taken during the intervening period.

The Coroner said there was nothing to support the suggestion that this man died from accident. In July, 1927, he was taken suddenly ill after a meal. He complained that his tea was very sweet. Before that he was mentally and physically sound.

Sir William Willcox had said that in July and December, Pace had suffered from acute arsenical poisoning and the presence of 3.62 grains of arsenic in the liver pointed to the fact that a dose must have been taken some forty-eight hours before death.

After the jury had returned the verdict that the deceased man, Harry Pace, had met his death at Fetter Hill on January 10th, 1928 by arsenical poisoning, his wife Mrs. Pace, was arrested on the Coroner's warrant.

The inquest was a protracted one and lasted for eighteen weeks.

At the magisterial inquiry, Mr. Paling who appeared for the Director of Public prosecutions said that he thought the bench would have no doubt that the arsenic which caused the death of Pace had its origin in sheep-dip. The day before the lamb dipping, two packets of sheep dip had been bought but neither of these packets were used on July 23rd, as two unopened packets were seen in the house in August and when the house was searched two days after the death of Pace, only one was found. The police also discovered a dust-covered bottle containing a dark liquid, which on analysis was found to contain arsenic.

In the course of the hearing, a collier who had called to see Pace to massage him during his last illnesses, stated that Pace told him, that at Gloucester Infirmary he had been told he was suffering from arsenical poisoning and that he would not be able to get about for two years. Mrs. Pace was present at the time.

Pace's son, a boy of nine, in his evidence said that what was left of the sheep-dip was put in the sheep-box which was kept on the top shelf of the kitchen cupboard. When his father came back from the hospital he took the box upstairs and his father put it on the bed. He took something out of it wrapped in paper and then he was told to put the box in a chest of drawers in the bedroom.

The trial of Mrs. Pace took place at the Gloucester Assizes before Mr. Justice Horridge on July 2nd, 1928.

The Solicitor-General, Sir Frank Boyd-Merriman, K.C. led for the prosecution and Mrs. Pace was defended by Mr. Norman Birkett, K.C. and Dr. Earengey.

In opening the case for the Crown, Sir Frank Boyd-Merriman said there could be no doubt about the cause of Pace's death. There was found in his body after death, nine and a half grains of arsenic, two grains being a fatal dose. It was known that large quantities of arsenic were on hand in the house in which Pace and his wife lived, as an ingredient in sheep-dip, which had been bought for a perfectly legitimate purpose.

It almost necessarily follows where poisoning is in question, that it has been done secretly and it also follows that unlike other crimes you cannot overlook the possibility that it may have been self-administered.

Mrs. Pace had made two statements to the police in one of which she stated : " I don't think it possible for any person who has visited him to have given him any poison to take. I don't think anyone would have done it."

In a second statement she says : " It is my view, and I am convinced, that my husband poisoned himself and I don't think anyone else could have done it. If they had, I should have known."

After referring to the symptoms of arsenical poisoning, Sir Boyd-Merriman said that there were 1,400 fatal doses of arsenic in a packet of sheep-dip, and the main characteristics of the dip were—21 per cent of arsenic, about 65 per cent of sulphur, and about 6.75 per cent of soda.

He emphasized that when sheep-dip was mixed with water the arsenic was easily dissolved, whereas the sulphur was not. That meant a colourless fluid could be drawn off.

" If sheep-dip were taken as sheep-dip without the fluid being drawn off and the sulphur left and taken in powder form, you would necessarily find in the body something like three times as much sulphur as arsenic. No sulphur was found in the man's body. Large quantities of arsenic were found, but no sulphur. One can easily understand anyone seeking to poison a victim with arsenic taking care not to put him on his guard by giving something which was indicative of sheep-dip by the presence of quantities of sulphur.

" On the other hand, it is not so clear why a man so minded as to administer sheep-dip to himself in order to put an end to himself, should take the trouble of getting rid of the sulphur before taking the mixture.

" An almost infinitesimal quantity of arsenic was found in the stomach. Over four grains in one way or another were found in the intestines, over three and a half grains in the liver, and over one grain in the kidneys.

" About Christmas-time, Pace asked his young son, Leslie, to bring to the bedroom the box in which sheep-dipping materials were kept. The boy did so, and Pace, after searching in the box, asked the boy to put it away in a chest of drawers in the bedroom.

" What was he looking for," asked Sir Boyd, " and what did he find ? There is a possibility that there was still there the residue of the dip used in July, in which case the inference would be that it might have been used for self-administration. But it may be, he found no sheep-dip there and wondered why. We shall presumably never know what his real motive was, but at that time he knew he had for months been suffering from arsenical poisoning."

The Solicitor-General next related the incident on Christmas Day when Pace got out of bed, went downstairs, struck violently at his wife with a pair of tongs, broke a fender, and, when the irons were taken from him, threatened to get a razor and cut the throats of the whole family.

He emphasized that this violence was displayed by a man who for some months had been suffering from considerable paralysis of the hands and feet.

Reginald J. Martin who gave evidence said he visited Pace every Sunday after he came out of the Infirmary. On Christmas Day, Dorothy Pace, the daughter, asked him if her mother had told him about a little green bottle which she (Dorothy) had found. Mrs. Pace who was present said, " No." She asked Mr. Martin if he thought that her husband had taken anything ? He replied, " No, I should not think he had." Dorothy told him that the bottle contained " foot-rot."

In October, Pace told him that he thought his illness was due to getting into the water when dipping sheep.

Dr. Du Pré who attended Pace stated he never prescribed any medicine for him containing arsenic. He was told that Pace had been for many hours practically immersed in water in the presence of sheep-dipping. He visited him in August and diagnosed peripheral neuritis which got worse, and he was removed to Gloucester Infirmary. When he was taken ill after Christmas, Mrs. Pace trudged to the surgery on Boxing Day, at night, when the snow was higher than her knees, to ask him to come and see her husband. He concluded that the peripheral neuritis was due to arsenical poisoning.

Dr. Never, resident surgeon at the Gloucester Infirmary, said he diagnosed Pace's complaint as peripheral neuritis. He had ordered him no medicine containing arsenic.

A representative of a sheep-dipping firm stated that he had never known a case of arsenical poisoning from absorption through the skin in the case of a human being. Sheep were often known to die from arsenical poisoning after dipping, but eighty per cent of the cases were through swallowing the dip.

Professor Walker Hall repeated the evidence he had given at the inquest and said he would describe the case as one of prolonged arsenical poisoning.

Sir William H. Willcox in further evidence stated that arsenic could find its way through the skin if it was broken but it could not be absorbed through the skin unless it was damaged.

This was a case of protracted poisoning. He agreed that if the most perfect methods of cleanliness were not followed during the process of sheep-dipping, some of the arsenic might be absorbed when taking food if there were rashes on the hand and the person did not wash his hands. A man handling dipped sheep might get arsenic on his hands and in that way it might be possible for arsenic to get into his food. The splashing of the sheep during dipping was another possible source of contamination of the clothing, and there was a possibility that the dip might be splashed into the mouth. It was not possible however, to get the amounts of arsenic found in this case by absorption through a cut.

Mr. Norman Birkett, K.C., for the defence, submitted that there was no case to put before the jury. The scientific evidence he contended was consistent with suicide equally with any other theory. He declared that there was no evidence of administering arsenic.

" On this vital point," he asked, " who did it ? " There was no evidence whatever. The fact that there was arsenic in the body, the quantity found, the effect on the organs, all these are consistent with self-administration. He contended there was no evidence of possession of arsenic by Mrs. Pace and pointed out that there was evidence that only a portion of the first packet of sheep-dip was used and the remainder was screwed up in a piece of paper and put into the box.

The only evidence of possession was that in the sheep-box known to Pace but unknown at the time to Mrs. Pace.

He concluded by submitting that there was not sufficient evidence for the case to proceed further.

Mr. Justice Horridge said : " No case has been more thoroughly investigated and no case could have been conducted with more scrupulous fairness. I am of the opinion it would not be safe to ask the jury to proceed further with it."

He then instructed the jury to return a formal verdict of " Not Guilty," which was done, and Mrs. Pace was acquitted.

In connexion with the use of sheep-dip and the danger to those engaged in using it frequently, Sir Thomas Oliver recently reported a case in the *Lancet*, in which a shepherd developed symptoms of arsenical poisoning which rendered him unfit for work for five months, excretion of arsenic in the urine and hair had continued for more than a year after exposure to the poison.

A suggestion was made after the trial that Pace might have been in the habit of taking arsenic and a lady living at Newport wrote to the Home Secretary, stating that she knew of people living in the Forest of Dean who were addicted to the habit of eating arsenic.

She stated that she knew that the dangerous habit prevailed in the neighbourhood of Coleford and around Tintern. " People get fascinated with the idea that arsenic taken in small quantities at regular intervals will benefit them. They become known as arsenic eaters, and knowing that the habit is condemned by doctors, they try to keep it as quiet as possible."

Another person living in the district corroborated this statement and stated that arsenic eating was a habit well-known in the Forest of Dean. Her aunt, she declared, used to make up a secret preparation of herbs and poison. " In the district arsenic is believed to have wonderful powers and people get gripped with the idea of its potency."

There was, however, no evidence to show that Pace had been addicted to arsenic so the suggestion that he met his death through taking an over-dose can hardly be entertained.

CHAPTER LI

THE CROYDON POISON MYSTERIES

ONE of the most extraordinary poison mysteries of recent times occurred at Croydon in the years 1928 and 1929, when three members of a family died at various periods, from the result of arsenic administered by some person or persons unknown.

The story begins with the case of Mr. Edmund Creighton Duff, a retired Commissioner from Nigeria, who on returning home to Croydon after a holiday in Hampshire on April 26th, 1928, complained of feeling unwell.

A doctor was called in. to see him and at first did not think it was anything serious, but on a second visit later in the day, he realised that Mr. Duff was seriously ill. He was suffering from severe abdominal pains and fits of shivering.

The previous evening, after his arrival, he had partaken of some chicken, potatoes and two bottles of beer and it was thought he was probably suffering from acute ptomaine poisoning. Frequent vomiting set in ; he became rapidly worse and collapsed and died on the night of the 27th.

An inquest was held, but the post-mortem and an analysis of the organs revealed no indication of poison and his death being attributed to natural causes, he was interred at Croydon.

On February 14th, 1929, Miss Vera Sydney, Mr. Duff's sister-in-law, who lived with her mother also in Croydon, was taken suddenly ill.

She had been suffering from a cold and almost immediately after taking lunch with her mother and aunt, she complained of feeling very sick. Both she and her aunt had partaken of some soup, and the cook and a cat, who had also had some of the soup were attacked in a similar manner. Mrs. Sydney who did not have any of the soup was unaffected. It appears that the soup had been made on the previous day, when no ill effects had been observed after taking it, but on the Wednesday, when the three ladies lunched together, some of the soup that had been left over to which some freshly made had been added, was served to them.

Miss Sydney became rapidly worse and in spite of every attention she died on February 15th, her death being attributed to natural causes.

No suspicion of foul play was attached to the deaths of either

Mr. Duff ten months previously, or to Miss Sydney, until three weeks after the death of the latter, when Mrs. Sydney her mother, was taken suddenly ill in a similar manner and died on March 5th. She had been unwell some weeks previously and had been attended by her doctor who had ordered her some medicine. Five hours before she died, her son said she had suggested to him that the medicine she had been taking had a nasty flavour.

An inquest was ordered and the bodies of both Miss and Mrs. Sydney were exhumed on March 22nd and the organs removed for analysis.

Sir Bernard Spilsbury, honorary pathologist to the Home Office in his evidence at the inquest on Miss Vera Sydney said that the cause of death was in his opinion, due to arsenical poisoning as shown by the presence approximately of one and a half grains of arsenic in the body.

The symptoms of her last illness were characteristic of acute arsenical poisoning and he was of opinion that the least possible fatal dose of arsenic was taken not less than twenty-four hours before she died. Dr. Ryffel, the analyst, had stated that the total amount of arsenious oxide he had found in the body amounted to 1.48 grains. She must have taken much more but how much more, depended on the interval of time between taking and death, and how the poison re-acted to it.

The history of Miss Sydney's illness pointed to taking the fatal dose shortly before the attack of vomiting on Wednesday, February 13th. The fact that her aunt (Mrs. Greenwell) was taken ill with similar symptoms about the same time, pointed to the fact that the poison was in some article of food taken at lunch that day.

He was of the opinion that the food containing the poison was probably liquid, and the fact that the cook and the cat were sick after taking the soup served on the Monday pointed to the presence of arsenic being present in the soup.

At the inquest on the body of Mrs. Sydney, which was held separately, Dr. Southgate gave evidence of his bacteriological examination of certain of the organs but he found nothing abnormal.

Dr. Bronte who was also called, said the findings of Dr. Ryffel the analyst for the Home Office, were entirely consistent with acute arsenical poisoning caused by doses of arsenic taken by Mrs. Sydney about six hours before death. Dr. Ryffel had found arsenic in the nails and a trace in the hair, and he was of the opinion that she must have had arsenic from five to seven days before her death.

He based this on the finding of arsenic in the top of the finger nails. The average growth of the nail in a healthy person, he explained, was an eighth of an inch a week. In an old person and an ill person, the growth was not so rapid. Arsenic had to be brought from the blood into the skin and so into the nail. As the nail grew at the rate of an eighth of an inch a week, it would therefore take between five and seven days to reach the part of the nail examined.

One single fatal dose of arsenic could not account for arsenic being found in the hair or nails, he contended. He was satisfied that the arsenic taken by Mrs. Sydney before the fatal dose was not taken in toxic doses. The fact that anyone showed arsenic in the hair or nails did not necessarily mean there was any arsenical poisoning. It might have been taken medicinally. Two grains was a minimum fatal dose of arsenious oxide.

The doctors who had attended both Mrs. and Miss Sydney stated that they had never prescribed or administered arsenic to them in any form.

A bottle containing the remains of metatone, a medicinal preparation, which Mrs. Sydney had been taking on the advice of her doctor, was submitted to analysis by Dr. Ryffel who stated in evidence that when the bottle of metatone was handed to him it contained some deep red liquid and a sediment. The red liquid contained arsenic in strong solution, the strength of which being such that if Mrs. Sydney were taking doses of tea-spoonfuls at a time, the dose before the last must have produced obvious symptoms of poisoning.

At this stage of the proceedings, a Home Office order was obtained for the exhumation of the body of Mr. Duff on whom a fresh inquest was held.

Dr. Binning, who had been called in when Mr. Duff was taken ill, described his symptoms and his collapse and death. He had never administered or prescribed any arsenic for him. He had also attended both Miss and Mrs. Sydney in their last illnesses. Miss Sydney who was taken ill on February 14th died on the following day.

Sir Bernard Spilsbury, who made second examination of the body of Mr. Duff on May 18th, 1929, said a remarkable feature was the degree of preservation, in view of the fact that death had occurred so long before.

Arsenic had been found in every tissue he had examined and the total amount he estimated at 0.815 of a grain.

Dr. Roche Lynch said he was of opinion that Mr. Duff had died from acute arsenical poisoning, and he must have had a fatal dose one day before his death.

The Coroner in summing up, first dealt with the case of Miss Vera Sydney.

He said the evidence suggested that the arsenic was in the soup consumed at Wednesday's lunch, but apart from the evidence that arsenic was taken in the soup, there was no direct information as to how or by whom it was administered. There were three alternatives. First, that she took it herself to commit suicide. Second, that the arsenic got into the soup accidentally. Third, that Miss Sydney was poisoned by someone who put the arsenic into the soup in order to kill her. She was a cheerful, affectionate woman, perfectly sane, devoted to her mother and living on terms of the greatest affection with her sister, her brother and her family. She had never been known to threaten her life and there is no known reason why she should do so. There was no evidence of any arsenic being on the premises, except a few specks of powdered rust in an old empty weed-killer tin found in a shed in Mrs. Sydney's garden.

He suggested that there were several points to be considered in reviewing the three deaths: 1 : That they all happened in the same family within a year or two. 2 : All were from the same poison. 3 : In every case the victim was suffering from some slight illness at the time when the poison was taken. 4 : In Miss Sydney's case, there was reason to believe that the poison was in the soup which she alone in the household was in the habit of taking. In Mrs. Sydney's case, the poison was in her special medicine. In Mr. Duff's case there was evidence that the arsenic was probably taken in liquid form, and that he took beer and had whisky before he became poisoned. He was the only member of the household who took beer or whisky. 6 : The deaths occurred in two different houses and in each house the side, or back door was usually kept unlocked in the day-time. It was easy of access at any time of the day and was quite near the pantry in which the food and drink was kept.

Arsenic might get into the soup by accident, although in the circumstances of this case it would be an extraordinary or unusual accident. But would it get into something which Mr. Duff drank ten months before by accident also, and, also by accident, into Mrs. Sydney's medicine bottle, ten months later ? And if it were accidental—what an extraordinary coincidence that all three cases should have in common the points enumerated. The suicide and accident theories were difficult to accept.

The gravest suggestion was that Miss Sydney was poisoned by someone else.

There was absolutely not a tittle of evidence of administration and in his judgment no evidence to single out anyone as the poisoner.

The jury after seventeen minutes deliberation returned the verdict that : " Vera Sydney was murdered by arsenic, wilfully administered by some person or persons unknown."

At the conclusion of the inquest on Mrs. Sydney who died eighteen days after the death of her daughter, the jury found that " Mrs. Sydney died about 7 p.m. on March 5th, 1929, from acute arsenical poisoning, and that there is not sufficient evidence to show whether she killed herself or whether she was murdered by some person or persons unknown."

The second inquest on the body of Mr. Duff was not concluded until August 6th, 1929.

Sir Bernard Spilsbury was recalled and gave further evidence as to Mr. Duff's first symptoms, which he thought were due to a feverish chill from which he was suffering when he arrived home.

If it had been due to the action of a poisonous dose of arsenic, the taking of food would have produced immediate vomiting.

He thought the dose was taken probably with the evening meal or shortly afterwards. The beer was the most likely vehicle in which the poisonous dose of arsenic was taken.

The coroner in addressing the jury, drew their attention to the fact that Mr. Edmund Creighton Duff was a member of a family, three of which had died within a year, each with symptoms of acute arsenical poisoning. Sir Bernard Spilsbury had told them that the beer would disguise the taste of liquid arsenic, which had practically no taste and that white arsenic could not make the beer flat.

There was no evidence that anyone outside had doctored the bottle. It would have to be someone who knew the ways and habits of the household, the easy access to the house and where the food was kept.

After deliberating twenty minutes, a verdict was returned that " Mr. Duff died on April 27th, 1928, from acute arsenical poisoning, wilfully administered by some person or persons unknown."

The Coroner dismissed the idea of accidental poisoning or suicide, so it would appear most probable that the same person was responsible for the three murders.

The form in which the arsenic was administered and where and how it was obtained, are equally involved in mystery.

In Mr. Duff's case, the actual cause of his death, in spite of an inquest and post-mortem having been held, was only discovered after two other murders had been committed. If the poisonous dose was contained in the beer he drank the evening of his arrival home as suggested by Sir Bernard Spilsbury, it must have been placed in it within the space of a few hours after his return from his holiday.

In Miss Sydney's case, the soup it was known she would probably take was evidently doctored twice, as if to make sure of the victim, and in that of Mrs. Sydney the murderer took the risk of adding the arsenic to a bottle of colourless medicine and so changing its appearance and taste.

The entire absence of motive for these crimes points to the conclusion that they were probably the work of a homicidal maniac to whom the ways and habits of the families were known.

They must have been plotted with extraordinary cunning, by someone who carefully watched and took the opportunity when it offered, of introducing the arsenic into the food, drink and medicine.

CHAPTER LII

SOME IRISH POISON MYSTERIES

A CURIOUS case which had many unusual features was investigated at Armagh in June, 1905, when two women named Pearson and Black were charged with murdering Alice Pearson, aged seventy-four, the mother-in-law of the former and mother of the latter, insurance benefits being alleged as the motive for the crime.

The case came to be investigated through the statement of one of the women while she was in gaol. Sarah Pearson, one of the accused, was arrested in Montreal, and made a confession of the crime, implicating herself, her husband and her sister-in-law. She said she bought three pennyworth of strychnine in Armagh and mixed it with mashed potatoes and eggs. When her mother-in-law was eating the meal she said that it tasted sour and she did not like it. Both she and her sister had also partaken of the food.

Evidence went to prove that systematic attempts were made to kill the old woman for the sake of the little money, some forty pounds, which she possessed; that Pearson and Black had first tried metallic mercury, but eventually put strychnine into the meal of potatoes and eggs which caused her death. According to the evidence of a witness, one of the accused women came to his house and said she had seen " Old Alice's ghost," and added that her husband had dreamed that his mother was going to die.

The analyst who made an examination of the organs said that he discovered two hundred and ninety-six grains of pure metallic mercury in the body and had not been able to trace any record of a case where mercury in such large quantities had been found in any human body. The mercury, however, was not the cause of death and did not act as a poison while in a metallic state. He found one-seventh of a grain of strychnine in the stomach, liver and kidneys and there was little doubt that strychnine had been the cause of death.

The jury found Sarah Pearson guilty and she was sentenced to death.

Perhaps one of the most curious defences to a charge of poisoning that has ever been put forward in court, was that advanced in a case which was tried in Ireland, where a woman was charged with murdering her husband.

The victim was a farmer who was taken ill after eating a supper prepared by his wife, which consisted of a poached egg. He died the following morning apparently from the effects of strychnine poisoning.

A week later, one of his daughters, a child of three, also died from the effects of strychnine poisoning after drinking some milk. A post-mortem examination was made on both bodies, which led to the discovery of half a grain of strychnine in the stomach of each.

At the trial, the counsel for the defence declared that he could satisfy the jury that no human hand was laid upon the egg eaten from the moment it was broken in the pan until it reached the deceased man. He contended that the poison had *fallen from the rafters*, and *accidentally dropped on the egg*, portions of which he could prove the accused woman had also eaten. Her husband before he died had expressed this view, and it was proved that some strychnine to poison rats had been placed on the floor of the loft immediately above the kitchen, and some of it had fallen from the rafters on to the egg as it was being removed from the fire to the table. Although the Crown contended this accident could not have happened, the jury found the accused " not guilty," and she was acquitted.

CHAPTER LIII

AMERICAN POISON MYSTERIES
THE MOLINEUX CASE—THE POISONED KISS MYSTERY

ONE of the most carefully planned murders by means of poison in the annals of crime in America was investigated at the trial of Roland B. Molineux, who was charged with causing the death of Mrs. Catherine J. Adams in New York in 1899.

On November 10th, 1898, Mr. Henry C. Barnett, a produce broker, who was a member of the Knickerbocker Athletic Club, one of the most prominent social organizations in New York, received by post at the Club a sample box of Kutnow's Powder. He was in the habit of taking this and similar preparations for simple ailments, and soon after receiving the box he took a dose of its contents. He became ill immediately afterwards, and was thought to be suffering from diphtheria. That he had a slight attack of this disease there is little doubt, as the fact was proved from a bacteriological examination made by his medical attendant. He left his bed earlier than the doctor advised, and died presumably of heart failure.

The contents of the box, however, were examined, which led to the discovery that the powder had been tampered with and mixed with cyanide of mercury, and although Mr. Barnett had died from natural causes, it seemed clear that an attempt had been made to poison him by someone who knew he was in the habit of taking this powder. The investigation, however, does not appear to have been carried further.

The next chapter in the story occurred in connexion with a Mr. Harry Cornish, who occupied the position of physical director to the Knickerbocker Athletic Club.

A day or two before Christmas in the same year, a packet directed to him was delivered by post at his address. It contained a box in which, on opening, he found at one end a silver article for holding matches and toothpicks ; at the other end was a bottle labelled " Emerson's Bromo-seltzer," and between the two was packed some soft tissue paper.

Mr. Cornish was at first under the impression that someone had sent him the packet as a present. After removing the articles from the box, he threw it and the wrapper into his wastepaper basket, but on second thoughts he cut the address from the wrapper and kept it.

The bottle, labelled " Bromo-seltzer," which is a saline preparation well-known in America, was sealed over the top and bore the usual revenue stamp. After tearing off the outside wrapper, Mr. Cornish placed the bottle and the silver holder on his desk.

On the following Sunday he remarked to his aunt, Mrs. Catherine Adams, that he had received a present. Mrs. Adams and her daughter, Mrs. Rogers, joked him about it, saying he must have some admirer, and was afraid to bring his present home, as the sender's name was probably on it. On Tuesday night, Mr. Cornish took the bottle and the silver holder home with him and presented them to Mrs. Rogers, saying they were no use to him and she might have them.

The next morning Mrs. Adams complained of a headache, and her daughter suggested a dose of the Bromo-seltzer. Mr. Cornish was present, and mixed a teaspoonful of the preparation from the bottle with a glass of water, and gave it to his aunt. After drinking it she at once exclaimed : " My, how bitter that is ! "

" Why, that's all right ! " said Mr. Cornish, as he took a drink from the glass.

A few moments afterwards Mrs. Adams collapsed, and died within a short time. Mr. Cornish was seized with violent vomiting, which doubtless saved his life, and he recovered.

A post-mortem examination revealed the fact that Mrs. Adams had died from cyanide poisoning, and on the bottle of Bromo-seltzer being analysed, the contents were found to have been mixed with cyanide of mercury.

For a long time the affair seemed a complete mystery, and the police investigations appeared likely to be fruitless. Then the particulars of the death of Mr. Barnett, who was Chairman of the House Committee of the Knickerbocker Club, were recalled. Connecting them with the fact that Mr. Cornish was also a prominent member of the club, and had received the bottle of Bromo-seltzer by post in the same manner, it seemed highly probable that both the poisoned packets which contained cyanide of mercury had been sent by the same person.

Further examination proved that the bottle used was not a genuine Bromo-seltzer one, and that the label had been removed from a genuine bottle and carefully pasted on that sent to Mr. Cornish.

A firm of druggists in Cincinnati then came forward and stated that as far back as May 31st, 1898, they had received a written application signed " H. C. Barnett " for a sample box of pills, and another similar application on December 21st, 1898, which was signed " H. Cornish."

Both these applications were found to be in the same hand-writing, which was also strikingly similar to the address on the packet sent to Mr. Cornish, which he had fortunately kept. The address given by the applicant who called himself " H. C. Barnett," was 257, West Forty-second Street, New York, a place where private letter-boxes are rented for callers. The address given by the applicant signing himself " H. Cornish," was a similar place at 1,620, Broadway, in the same city. From these facts it seemed evident that an attempt had been made to poison both Barnett and Cornish by someone who knew them, and the poisoner had concealed his identity by employing the names of his intended victims.

The nature of the poison used, cyanide of mercury, was also a slight clue, as it is a substance which is not used in medicine and must in all probability have been specially prepared for the purpose by someone with a knowledge of chemistry.

At the coroner's inquest, which began on February 9th, 1899, certain facts were elicited that tended to bring suspicion on Roland B. Molineux, who was also a member of the Knickerbocker Club and well acquainted with Barnett and Cornish. He was also known to have quarrelled with the latter. At the close of the inquest Molineux was arrested and removed to the Tombs prison.

Owing to legal technicalities in the original indictment, which charged him with the murder of both Mr. Barnett and Mrs. Adams, he was twice liberated, and then for the third time arrested.

The trial of Molineux for the murder of Mrs. Adams was a memorable one, and lasted nearly three months. It began on November 14th, 1899, at the Central Criminal Court, New York, and was not concluded till February 11th, 1900.

The evidence was entirely circumstantial. Most of the experts in handwriting who were examined declared that the address on the packet sent to Mr. Cornish was in Molineux's handwriting, and that he had also written both applications to the druggists in Cincinnati. Further, Molineux was engaged as a chemist to a colour factory in which cyanide of mercury was used, which would enable him either to make or procure that special poison, from which only three other fatal cases had been recorded.

No witnesses were called for the defence, and the jury found Roland B. Molineux guilty of " murder in the first degree," which, according to American law, is murder with premeditation.

In January, 1911, a mysterious case that for some time baffled the united exertions of the police, occurred in Cumberland, Maryland, U.S.A. On Christmas Eve of 1910, the night before their wedding, a Mr. Trigg and Miss Grace Loeser, who were well known in Maryland, were found sitting together in an upright position on a sofa in the drawing-room of Miss Loeser's home, both apparently dead. An hour before they were thus discovered, Mrs. Loeser had seen them sitting exactly in the same position full of life and animation and talking over the arrangements for their wedding on the following day.

Returning an hour later, she found them still both sitting in the same position but lifeless. Nothing was found in the room to indicate the cause of death.

Before the ghastly discovery Mrs. Loeser had heard them laughing and talking in the drawing-room ; then she heard the telephone bell ring, and heard her daughter go to it and speak to a friend at the other end of the wire about the final arrangements for the wedding.

A doctor who was immediately summoned and examined the bodies, noticed that the lips of both the man and the woman were burned, and in the mouth of the man was found a piece of chewing-gum, which he believed might contain poison. According to the doctor, Mr. Trigg had apparently taken poison and then kissed his fiancée and poisoned her in doing so.

A post-mortem examination was held and revealed traces of potassium cyanide in the organs of both young people, but how the poison came to be swallowed there was nothing to indicate, beyond the fact that the tongues of both were burned and there was a larger quantity of the poison found in the stomach of Trigg.

The chewing-gum habit is very common in America and a package of it with one stick missing and the wrapper on the floor, was found in Mr. Trigg's bedroom. The questions that arose were : was the chewing-gum the cause of death, and had they divided the one stick missing from the packet between them, or if the gum was poisoned, why had they thus decided to take their lives ?

Mrs. Loeser protested against the theory of suicide as being beyond all reason, as both young people were absolutely devoted to each other and had never even quarrelled.

A younger sister of Miss Loeser's, to whom Mr. Trigg is said to have first paid attentions before he became engaged to Grace Loeser, in giving evidence said that she also had symptoms of cyanide poisoning. She was upstairs when Trigg came to the house that afternoon, and the first she knew of the tragedy was her mother screaming. She swore that she had no poison in her possession, and had never heard of cyanide or hydrocyanic acid before her sister's death.

Mrs. Loeser when brought to the court to give evidence was practically in a state of collapse, but she swore that no poison of any kind was kept in the house and that both her daughters were on friendly terms.

Dr. Foard, the medical man first called in, described how he found the young couple sitting upright together on the sofa ; the woman was breathing stertorously, with her teeth clenched and the pupils of her eyes dilated. A slight froth issued from her lips, all of which, said the doctor, were symptomatic of hydrocyanic acid or cyanide poisoning.

Dr. Broadrup, another medical practitioner, corroborated Dr. Foard's statements. When he visited the house, he was called upstairs to see Miss May Loeser who was in her room and when he got there, he found the bedroom was full of a strong odour of gas.

The evidence went to prove that Trigg at the last moment did not wish to carry out the marriage with Miss Loeser, and it was suggested that he may have poisoned her with the chewing-gum, only swallowing a small portion himself in the belief that he would easily have survived the effects.

At the coroner's inquiry, it was stated that cyanide of potassium was found in the chewing-gum, and the jury returned a verdict that both persons had died of cyanide poisoning " administered in an unknown manner."

CHAPTER LIV

SOME FRENCH POISON MYSTERIES

A POISONER FOR PLEASURE

As a general rule some motive is to be found in cases of criminal poisoning and the poisoner has some definite object in view before carrying out his or her secret plans. This motive usually distinguishes the sane from the homicidal criminal. It is rare therefore in the annals of criminal poisoning to find a case in which the accused has admittedly killed her victims for pleasure.

Such a case however was brought to light in the summer of 1851, when a medical practitioner living at Rennes, in Brittany, reported to the authorities that a domestic servant employed in the house of M. Bidard had died suddenly, and that he and a colleague who had been called in were satisfied that she had been poisoned.

A police magistrate proceeded to the house and on the servants being summoned before him and questioned, one of them at once hotly declared that she was innocent.

" Innocent of what ? " asked the magistrate. " No one has accused you."

She was a common, hard-featured woman, of repulsive and brutal appearance, with dull expressionless eyes, named Hélène Jegado.

The magistrate's suspicions were aroused as he looked at her intently and on his return to his office he at once caused inquiries to be made as to her previous history.

A striking feature of the facts disclosed by the inquiry was that wherever she had been employed, some mysterious deaths had occurred. When she was thirty years of age, she had been in a situation as cook and during the time she was employed in the house, seven people had died in agonies after suffering terrible sickness.

She had been a most devoted nurse to them all and after each death she had been heard to say : " This will not be the last."

And so it had proved.

After taking another situation, again there would be sudden and mysterious deaths in the family she served. She professed to be a very religious woman and on leaving one situation she entered a convent but had not been there long before several of the inmates were seized with illnesses which ended fatally.

Between 1833 and 1841 she was suspected of having caused the deaths of twenty-three persons as well as having committed numerous thefts.

When she came to Rennes, she first entered the service of a M. Rabot and had not been there long when it was found she was stealing the wine and was given notice to leave. Immediately afterwards several members of the family were seized with violent pains and sickness but none of the cases proved fatal.

On leaving there she took service in an inn and soon afterwards the child of her employer suddenly died in great agony. Later on, a fellow servant and the landlord's wife were taken ill in a similar manner and both died. She was a consummate hypocrite and escaped suspicion until she was again found stealing the wine, when she was discharged by the inn-keeper.

Her next situation was at the house of M. Bidard in Rennes, where after a while, a fellow servant was suddenly taken ill and died in great agony.

She was arrested on suspicion of poisoning this girl and was brought to trial in December, 1851.

The evidence was entirely circumstantial, as no one had ever seen her in possession of arsenic which was shown to be the poison used and it could not be ascertained where she had obtained it.

The only fact elicited was that a long time previously to her arrest, three packets of a white powder which she said were powdered gum, were seen in her box.

She persistently denied the charges brought against her and declared that she knew nothing of arsenic and no one had ever seen her with it. No apparent motive could be found for the series of murders and she seems to have been irresistibly impelled to crime by her evil-disposition and the pleasure in seeing her victims suffer. She had no jealousy against anyone she declared to the President of the Court. She hated no one and her only mistake was that she was too fond of her victims. She still professed her religious principles and regularly attended Mass while planning her crimes.

She was found guilty on all the charges made and sentenced to death on the guillotine.

CHAPTER LV

THE CANABY CASE—THE STRANGE CASE OF JEANNE GILBERT—" GENTLEMAN GIRARD "

FOR centuries past, poison has played a prominent part in love intrigues which form so common a feature in French life. Such crimes are generally incited by jealousy or the desire to remove some obstacle that obstructs the path of the ardent lover. A typical case of this character and one which caused a great sensation at the time, occurred at Bordeaux in 1906, when Madame Canaby was tried for attempting to poison her husband. Monsieur and Madame Canaby were people of good position and well known in Bordeaux society. The arrest of the lady, therefore, caused considerable excitement. The story begins early in 1906 when Monsieur Canaby was taken ill with influenza. On the 27th of that month, his cook called at a pharmacy in the city with a prescription which contained a large quantity of aconitine and digitalin, two very powerful poisons. The prescription was signed by a Dr. Gaube. The pharmacist, who happened to be the uncle of Madame Canaby, knew that his niece and her husband were friendly with Dr. Gaube, who lived some distance away from Bordeaux. His natural surprise at the large quantity of the poisons ordered was somewhat allayed by a note which accompanied the prescription, stating that Dr. Gaube required the poisons for experimental purposes. M. Fouries, the pharmacist, then wrote a note to his niece, whom he had not seen for three years, explaining that although he had dispensed this prescription he could not in future deliver such dangerous drugs by a messenger. He further cautioned the servant, saying : " Be careful ; there is enough there to poison thirty men ! "

On May 1st, M. Erny, the pharmacist who usually dispensed for Madame Canaby, received a prescription for one gramme of digitalin, signed by Dr. Gaube, also accompanied by a note similar to that presented to M. Fouries. This was followed by another prescription on May 4th for one gramme of aconitine and five centigrams of digitalin. Five days afterwards a third prescription was presented for one gramme of potassium cyanide and one gramme of digitalin, both of which are extremely virulent poisons. The pharmacist's suspicions now being aroused, he refused to dispense the last prescription, and on May 11th he called on Dr. Guérin, whom he knew to be attending M. Canaby, and showed him the prescription. The following day Dr. Guérin called in four physicians, and after a consultation, it was decided to remove M. Canaby to a private hospital under the charge of Dr. Villar. Here, carefully watched, M. Canaby gradually made some progress towards recovery.

Meanwhile, the doctors submitted the prescriptions to Dr. Gaube, who at once pronounced them forgeries and lodged a complaint with the Procureur of the Republic. A police inquiry followed, and a search was made in the Canaby's house, which resulted in the discovery of a large number of empty bottles which had formerly contained Fowler's solution of arsenic. An analysis made of the hair of M. Canaby revealed the presence of arsenic to the extent of forty milligrams per kilo, and in hair from his beard twenty-six milligrams.

The arrest of Madame Canaby quickly followed, and she was committed for trial on the charge of attempting to poison her husband. The motive was assigned to an intimacy Madame had formed with a Monsieur Rabot, a friend of the family.

At the trial, M. Canaby, still weak and ill, was brought to the Court and strongly affirmed his wife's innocence. He stated his belief that a discharged servant had by means of anonymous letters instigated the prosecution. He ascribed the presence of arsenic in his beard to patent medicines, which he said he had been in the habit of taking in large doses. M. Rabot, whose intimacy with Madame Canaby had given rise to some scandal, denied that any improper relations existed between him and the lady. The onus of proving the case then rested with the medical men who had been in attendance on M. Canaby. Beyond a few explanations, however, they declined to say anything, stating that they could not say more without betraying the secrets of their patients, which professional usage forbade.

The President of the Court informed Dr. Villar, the chief medical witness, that his refusal to speak would probably tell against the prisoner.

" I will ask her to release you from your pledge," continued the President.

" I want the truth to be told ; I don't want anyone to keep silence on my account," broke in Madame Canaby.

" So now you can speak," remarked the President.

" Not at all," replied the doctor. " No one can release us from our pledge of secrecy, and certainly not Madame Canaby, who was not our patient."

" But every good citizen under pain of punishment is bound to disclose any criminal act that is known to have been committed by another," said the President sharply.

" On the contrary," replied the witness, " the law punishes

those who violate professional secrecy and did so recently in Paris. Even if we know an accused person guilty, we would refuse to speak."

For the defence, evidence was adduced that M. Canaby was in the habit of taking a certain patent medicine that contained arsenic. Of the three experts who were called to give an opinion on the writing of the prescriptions, one declared the writing resembled that of M. Rabot, while the others averred that it was unquestionably that of Madame Canaby who had attempted to disguise her hand-writing.

Madame Canaby declared that the poisons when received had been handed to her by a fair young man, who came presumably from Dr. Gaube, but as to his identity she could trace nothing.

In the end, Madame Canaby was acquitted on the charge of attempting to poison her husband, but was found guilty of forging medical prescriptions, by which poison was fraudulently obtained by her. For this she was sentenced to fifteen months imprisonment and a fine of a hundred francs.

Another strange case, apparently due to homicidal mania occurred in Varennes, a village near Saint Amand-Montroud. In April, 1905, a well-to-do farmer named Gilbert died suddenly, and six months afterwards his wife expired in a similar manner. In September of the following year, another farmer in the same district, called Renaud, died very suddenly and within a month his wife also succumbed to a mysterious illness. In the meantime, one of their farm labourers also died from an unexplained cause, and a young man, who was steward of a neighbouring château, together with his little daughter, was likewise fatally attacked. No suspicions of foul play were apparently aroused until a considerable time afterwards, when Madame Pallot, a villager, found a small cheese on her window-sill which she took to be a present from a neighbour. She ate some of it with her lunch, and in less than three hours she was dead.

The origin of the cheese, which on analysis proved to be strongly impregnated with arsenic, was traced to a young married woman named Jeanne Gilbert, the daughter of the farmer Renaud and the daughter-in-law of M. and Mme Gilbert, all of whom had died in a similar manner. She was arrested and charged with the murder of Madame Pallot.

M. Bouillot, a pharmacist of Saint Amand, was able to prove from his poison register that Jeanne Gilbert had bought arsenic by the half-pound from him, stating that she required it for poisoning rats on the farm. She might have had two pounds of the poison in her possession at one time. Jeanne at first stoutly denied that she had purchased the arsenic and declared she did not even know the pharmacist. Even when confronted with the *juge d'instruction* she continued her denials, but the pharmacist had been careful to make her sign his register on the occasion of each purchase. The judge required her to sign her name, with the result that the identity of the writing was at once established.

When compared, the dates of sales and the deaths of the woman's relatives practically corresponded. She subsequently admitted the purchases of the arsenic, but adhered to her original assertion that she used it for destroying rats. Altogether, it was suspected that Jeanne Gilbert had poisoned no fewer than eleven persons.

The most extraordinary feature of the case was that she appeared to have no possible motive for committing these terrible crimes as she was comfortably settled in life. Her parents were in good circumstances and she could expect no advantages to accrue from their deaths, or that of her mother-in-law and the other persons she is believed to have poisoned. The only explanation offered is the statement of her husband, that her mind may have been affected by an illness after which he had noticed that she sometimes acted strangely.

A more recent case which excited great interest throughout France was that of Henri Girard, who died in prison while awaiting trial. About 1909, this man, who passed as an insurance agent, was living at Montreuil-sous-Bois. Well educated, of good appearance, and apparently a cultured person with a leaning towards music, literature and science, he soon became popular among a wide circle in the district in which he lived and also in Paris. Among his acquaintances was a wealthy man named Pernotte, who after some persuasion consented to have his life insured in two different companies for a total sum of £8,400, which was to be payable to Girard in case of Pernotte's death.

A short time afterwards, all the members of Pernotte's family were stricken with typhoid fever, but in the course of time they recovered and went away for a holiday. On their return, however, as M. Pernotte was still feeling weak, his friend Girard, who claimed to have some medical knowledge and was interested in science, gave him a hypodermic injection which he said would speedily put him on his feet again. Pernotte died soon afterwards and the physicians who examined the body declared that death had resulted from poison.

Girard, it was afterwards discovered, had made an entry in his diary as follows : " Poisons ; prepare bottle, tubes, rubber gloves ; buy microbe books."

Police inquiries were set on foot and disclosed the fact that Girard at this time was studying bacteriology and had actually bought cultures of typhoid bacilli, and a selection of toxic organisms and poisons were found at his house.

Meanwhile Girard calmly took possession of the £8,400 for which he had insured the life of M. Pernotte.

He appears to have been a man possessed of the most extraordinary power of attraction for both men and women ;
his manners are said to have been charming and the courtly
tone of his conversation gave him the name among his acquaintances of " Gentleman Girard."

Once his intimate friends came within the sphere of his
magnetic personality they seem to have surrendered their wills
entirely to his.

In 1913 he became very friendly with a M. Godel and the
latter agreed, at the suggestion of Girard, to take out a joint
life insurance for £8,000. In case of the death of one, the money
was to go to the survivor. M. Godel after lunching one day
with Girard was taken ill with typhoid fever ; he eventually
recovered, but becoming suspicious, he refused to see Girard
again, to which decision he no doubt owed his life.

Girard was mobilized during the Great War and served in the
automobile service in Paris where he made the acquaintance of
a soldier called Delmas. Delmas became very friendly with
Girard, and after having signed bills in favour of the insurance
agent he developed typhoid fever. He was sent to a military
hospital and ultimately recovered.

It is stated that Girard meanwhile was experimenting with
micro-organisms and had bought quantities of typhoid cultures
from wholesale druggists. At this time, too, he fitted up a
bacteriological laboratory in the house of a woman with whom
he lived at Neuilly.

Finding that his efforts in using pathogenic organisms had
proved so uncertain in effects, he next turned his attention
to the study of poisonous fungi and tried the resulting poison
on his next victim, a M. Duroux, a post-office employee, whose
life he had insured for a large sum without the latter's knowledge.

Having invited him to dine at his house, he took the opportunity of placing the poison in his food. The servants,
it is alleged, were told not to wash up, and they said that Girard
and one of his mistresses washed the plates, knives and forks
in a bath full of antiseptic solution. Duroux, however, was
none the worse. Girard's notebook at this time showed the
following entry : " Mimiche Dinner—mushrooms," opposite
the dates May 10th and 11th, 1917. The dinner took place on
May 14th. In December of the same year Duroux went twice
to a café with Girard and each time was taken violently ill
afterwards.

The next victim was a Madame Monin, a widow, with whom
Girard had become very intimate. Having taken out four insurance policies on her life, he decided to poison her. He persuaded
her to come to the house of his future wife, a Mlle Drouhin to
see some hats, and while Mme Monin was so engaged, Girard
offered her some refreshment and wine was brought into the

room. The hat having been selected, the lady partook of a
glass of wine handed to her by Girard, which is said to have
contained a poison he had specially prepared from fungi for this
purpose.

It acted very rapidly, as the unfortunate lady was taken ill
in the street almost directly afterwards and after being taken
by two policemen to her home, she died three hours later. A
post-mortem examination revealed the fact that she died from
mushroom poisoning. Girard, however, was bold enough to
make a claim on the insurance policies, but owing to the refusal
of one of the companies to pay £400, the amount of one policy
he had taken out on the life of Mme Monin, he was arrested.

It was then discovered that two other insurance companies
had already handed over to Girard or his accomplices, over
£800 without inquiries. Girard, as agent, having secured the
business in each case, had according to custom, been paid the
first premium as his commission.

After his arrest, on his house being searched, in his laboratory,
which was completely equipped, were found a considerable
number of poisons and a number of glass jars containing typhoid
cultures and other organisms. Inquiries revealed other
mysterious cases on which Girard had operated back to 1913,
including that of a man who he had invited to dinner and who
had died after drinking an apéritif which had been offered to him
by Girard.

The preliminary legal investigation into this remarkable
series of crimes lasted nearly three years and in the end, Girard
was sent before the Chamber of Criminal Indictment, but before
the trial took place at the Paris Assizes, death had cheated the
guillotine for Girard died in prison after he had made, it is said,
a full confession of his crimes.

CHAPTER LVI

THE STRANGE CASE OF DR. BOUGRAT

IN 1925, a bank cashier named Rumebe, of Marseilles mysteriously disappeared together with 85,000 francs which he was supposed to have collected and had in his possession.

Every effort was made to trace him without avail, until some two months afterwards it was discovered that he paid a visit to Dr. Bougrat one of the best known specialists in the city.

Rumebe had been seen to enter the doctor's house and it was proved that he never left it alive. The police decided to search the apartments, and in a cupboard in the doctor's surgery or consulting room, they discovered the decomposed body of the missing man, after which Dr. Bougrat was arrested on the charge of murder.

After being confined in prison for two years, his trial, which is said to have been one of the most remarkable in French judicial records, was opened at Marseilles, in March 1927.

The prosecution charged the doctor with the murder of Rumebe and the theft of the money he carried. They also sought to prove that he was heavily in debt and had been leading a life of great extravagance.

His servants gave evidence as to the arrival of Rumebe at his house and a footman declared that after his master had closed the surgery and left, he looked through the keyhole and on the edge of the couch, just within the range of sight, he saw a man's boot.

On being interrogated by the President of the Court, Dr. Bougrat stated : " I knew Rumebe very well when we were in the French Army at Salonika. He was due to see me for a hypodermic injection at half-past two. He arrived at seven o'clock after I had closed my surgery and he rushed in looking most disturbed.

" He explained that he was £800 short on his account and begged me to lend him the money to put it right. He said he had been robbed.

" When I told him that I had not that sum to lend him he broke down and declared that he was ruined. I then promised to go out and see if I could raise the money and did so but without success.

" When I returned, I found my poison chest broken open with

the tubes scattered about and Rumebe lying on the floor purple in the face. I did all I could to revive him but he died.

" There he was lying dead on the couch and it was 4 o'clock in the morning. I realised my danger—Rumebe, a bank cashier.

" I must have gone mad with fear and I determined to hide the body till I found some definite proof of the robbery which would be evidence in my behalf.

" I was never able to find evidence to protect myself and therefore the body remained in its insecure hiding place."

Several people who were awaiting trial and had been confined in the same prison as Dr. Bougrat were called, one of whom alleged that the doctor had confessed to him that he had killed Rumebe by pressing a handkerchief soaked in prussic acid to his face.

Bougrat however totally denied this statement and protested his innocence of the crime.

Dr. Barral, professor of toxicology at Lyons University who was called for the defence said, that he had made an autopsy on the body of Rumebe and as the result of his investigations he was of the opinion that Rumebe was not poisoned but that he had died as the result of a therapeutic accident after receiving an injection of arseno-benzol which is normally harmless if properly used.

Dr. Desgrez, professor of chemistry of the Faculty of Medicine of Paris, in giving evidence, agreed with Dr. Barral's conclusions.

He maintained that there could be no question as to the cause of Rumebe's death. It was perfectly obvious that it was the result of an accident arising out of the use of arseno-benzol which had been known to have fatal results. He declared the alleged statement that Dr. Bougrat had killed Rumebe by holding a handkerchief soaked in prussic acid to his face, was absurd. It was an obvious lie. No other poison had been used by Dr. Bougrat and he was prepared to swear that on his most solemn oath.

On examination Dr. Desgrez admitted that there were supposed to be poisons which left no trace behind in the body, but he had made conclusive tests by trying varying extracts on animals and frogs, and had any such poisons been used there would have been a reaction and there was none. He was of the opinion that Rumebe died as the result of a normal injection and he most certainly was not wilfully murdered. " I believe," he concluded, " we have here one of those therapeutic accidents which have been under observation by medical men in recent years but which are not yet explained."

Questioned by the Public Prosecutor, if he did not consider it was unnatural on the part of the doctor to place in a cupboard the body of one of his patients who had fallen a victim in his consulting-room to a therapeutic accident ? Dr. Desgrez replied : " It is possible that Dr. Bougrat would not be the first to undergo such a disagreeable experience.

" I remember the case of a doctor in Paris who once placed the body of a patient who died in his consulting-room in a trunk, immediately after he had succumbed following an injection. When such a terrible thing happens and other patients may be waiting outside in the ante-room, in a moment of madness the irretrievable concealment is resorted to."

Both Professor Barral and Dr. Desgrez agreed that it was possible that Rumebe might have died suddenly from the effects of a hypodermic injection administered perhaps a week before.

The trial lasted eight days and after deliberating for an hour, in spite of the medical evidence, the jury found Dr. Bougrat guilty of murder but recommended him to mercy.

The President of the Court taking the extenuating circumstances into consideration, pronounced sentence on the doctor of penal servitude for life.

Dr. Bougrat, in the course of time, was sent to the French Penal Settlement on Devil's Island, French Guiana and is said to have escaped some time ago. He reached Irapa, a town in Venezuela where he settled and commenced practice as a doctor. He re-married and became very popular owing to his organization of relief measures which are said to have saved hundreds of lives in the town of his adoption when it was visited by a pestilence.

CHAPTER LVII

A FIENDISH GERMAN POISONER

OF the poisoners who utterly regardless of human life had no compunction in removing anyone who stood between them and their objective, Anna Maria Schonleben or Zwanizer was a type. Like Hélène Jegado she appears to have had an irresistible impulse towards crime.

She was the daughter of an inn-keeper at Nuremberg and in early life had an extraordinarily chequered career.

Before she was twenty she married a notary addicted to drink and after his death she became, in turn, a confectioner, doll-maker, housekeeper and cook to a travelling circus.

After this she led a wandering life in the country, going from place to place and taking various domestic situations.

Eventually at Rosendorf in Bavaria, she obtained a post as housekeeper to a Judge Glaser, who was then living apart from his wife. Schonleben, as she then called herself, laid a deep plan to get rid of this lady with the object of marrying the judge and making her position secure.

In order to carry this out, she first brought about a reconciliation between the husband and wife and succeeded in getting the latter to return to her home. Within a week, she began to carry out her nefarious plan by administering small doses of arsenic to Frau Glaser in her tea. She gradually increased the quantity until the unfortunate woman became seriously ill and eventually died after three days sickness.

Apparently no suspicion fell on the housekeeper, although several people who had stayed at the house were seized with severe pains and vomiting. She did not, however, succeed in carrying out her plan to marry the judge, for she left his service to take a situation in the same capacity with a Judge Grohmann at Sanspareil.

He was thirty-eight years of age and a sufferer from chronic gout. Soon after his new housekeeper had taken up her position, he became engaged to be married which by no means suited Schonleben's plan as she had resolved to marry him herself. Determined that he should not marry the lady of his choice, she began to dose him with arsenic and soon afterwards he became very ill. She nursed him with the greatest care and attention, which averted suspicion, but the violent sickness and internal pains continued until she gave him the last fatal dose which ended his sufferings.

After Judge Grohmann's death her capabilities as a nurse so impressed Frau Gebhardt the wife of a local magistrate who was a chronic invalid, that she engaged her in that capacity, but Schonleben was not contented with her new situation for long. Without any apparent motive, she resolved to murder her mistress and she too was taken ill with violent internal pains and vomiting, to which eventually she succumbed. Herr Gebhardt far from suspecting the nurse, who was generally regarded as a " pious, worthy creature," retained her as his housekeeper after his wife's death.

She remained in his employ for several months but at length several of the servants having been seized with mysterious attacks of vomiting and pain after partaking of coffee and other beverages given to them by Schonleben, he at last became suspicious of her and although he had no evidence to support it, he dismissed her with a good character.

Furious and filled with resentment owing to her plans having been again upset, Schonleben resolved to wreak her revenge on the whole household.

On the morning of her departure she prepared coffee for the maids to which she added arsenic, and then mixed a quantity of the poison with the salt kept in the kitchen salt-box.

When she was about to enter the carriage at the door which had been hired to take her to Bayreuth, she took Herr Gebhardt's infant child in her arms and caressed it with affection and at the same time gave it a biscuit which she had prepared soaked in milk impregnated with arsenic, then, waving good-bye to all, she drove off.

Half an hour after she had gone, the baby and the whole household were taken ill with pains and vomiting.

The magistrate's suspicions were now thoroughly aroused and he communicated with the police. The contents of the salt-box were analysed and found to contain a large proportion of arsenic. From the contents of another salt barrel kept in the kitchen containing three pounds of salt, thirty grains of arsenic were obtained.

The authorities then had the body of Frau Glaser exhumed and it was found wonderfully preserved, which was attributed to the presence of a considerable quantity of arsenic. Frau Gebhardt's body was also examined and was discovered in the same condition and arsenic was found in the intestines. Lastly, Judge Grohmann's remains were exhumed and found in a similar state of preservation.

Meanwhile, Schonleben who was unaware of the investigations and the incriminating discoveries that had been made, had visited several places and at length found a post in Nuremberg where she was arrested on October 18th, 1809.

When she was searched by the police, arsenic was found in her pocket and when it was shown to her, it is said that she "trembled with pleasure and gazed upon the deadly white powder with eyes beaming with rapture."

"Poison," says Feuerbach, in commenting on this remarkable case, "enabled her to deal death, sickness and torture to all who offended her or stood in her way. It removed all obstacles from her path and opened the road to her fondest hopes. She was afforded amusement by the sufferings of her victims. In fact, the mixing and giving of poison became her constant occupation, she practised it in jest and earnest and at last with real passion for poison itself, without reference to the object for which it was given."

A contemporary description gives us some idea of the appearance of this fiend in human shape at the age of fifty. "She was a short, thin woman, almost deformed, with a sallow meagre face, deeply furrowed by passion and from age. Her eyes glittered with malice, her brow was clouded, her manner was cringing and servile but affected, and she was consumed with a fierce craving for admiration."

At her trial, she denied any knowledge of the crimes with which she was charged and for six months she constantly declared she knew nothing of poisons. She had never used arsenic, but the evidence accumulated against her was so strong that in July, 1811, nearly two years after her arrest, she was found guilty and sentenced to death by decapitation with the sword and her body afterwards exposed on the wheel.

After the sentence, she confessed to the Judge that her death was fortunate for mankind, as it would have been impossible for her to abandon the practice of poisoning.

CHAPTER LVIII

THE GREAT HUNGARIAN POISON MYSTERIES

IN 1929, a medical student was called on to make an analysis and examination of the body of a supposed suicide that had been washed up by the river Tisza, near the village of Nagyrev in Hungary. To his surprise, he discovered a large quantity of arsenic in the stomach and communicated with the police, and in this way one of the greatest poison mysteries known in Europe for centuries was brought to light.

The suspicions of the police were further aroused by the sudden and mysterious deaths of two men, named Josef Nadarasz and Michael Szabo, who had lived in the village and been recently buried in the grave-yard. Their bodies were exhumed and an analysis of their organs also revealed the presence of arsenic in large quantities.

From further inquiries it was found that a local midwife named Susanne Fazekas, had been in the habit of supplying poison to women in the district for some years, by means of which many had got rid of unwanted husbands and brothers. Through this woman an amazing and extensive epidemic of poisoning was revealed which has only been equalled by the crimes of the infamous Toffana in the eighteenth century.

In the remote parts of Hungary to-day, there is usually neither doctor or nurse with any training and in the country villages the midwife practically occupies the position of the tribal wise-woman of primitive times.

She is the confidante of all and is usually present at every birth and death in the district. She gathers and sells medicinal and other herbs, the remedial properties of which she is supposed to have a special knowledge. She supplies the love-sick with philtres and others with counter potions for spells while the ignorance of the superstitious villagers and local officials renders her nefarious trade and operations an easy matter.

The confessions of nine women that they had obtained poison from Susanne Fazekas a midwife of Nagyrev, led to the discovery that she had carried on a trade in arsenic for twenty years and was probably responsible for over a hundred deaths.

It is said that she even tried to poison the police who were engaged in the investigation, and before they could arrest her she committed suicide. Another midwife, who was an accomplice, hanged herself when she heard of Susanne's death.

On searching the cottages occupied by these women, the police discovered piles of arsenical fly-papers from which the poison had been extracted and it was found they had sold it at exorbitant prices.

A thorough investigation was ordered by the authorities and the bodies of fifty suspected cases were exhumed in the cemetery of Nagyrev. Policemen had to be posted to guard the graves at night to prevent the terrified women of the village from removing incriminating tombstones and obliterating their inscriptions. Midnight battles were fought between the police and the suspects and in spite of the guard many stones were secretly removed.

An analysis of the organs of the bodies of forty-four of the suspected cases disclosed the presence of arsenic in large quantities in most of them.

One of the widows in her endeavour to get rid of the superfluous poison, had actually buried a bottle containing a solution of arsenic in her husband's grave, where it was found by the police at the foot of the coffin.

After the results of the examination of the bodies were known the suspected persons were arrested, thirty-one being women whose ages ranged from twenty to seventy years.

The ambition and desire to obtain property and land appears to have been the chief motive for these crimes. The ancient custom of single inheritance, common in this part of the country, renders more than one child in the family superfluous, thus the sudden death of old people or children often leads to wealth for the women left behind, as only death transfers ownership of land.

The habit of killing appears to have become part of the life of this village and even young women, who had been forced to marry rich old peasants, set about poisoning their husbands on the first opportunity.

Tragedies soon followed the arrests and five of the suspected women committed suicide, among whom was Frau Szabai whose husband's body was one of the forty-four exhumed on suspicion. On analysis, no trace of arsenic was discovered in it but when the police called to inform her of the result she thought they had come to arrest her and locking the door of her cottage she hanged herself.

The authorities decided to try the accused, who numbered fifty-three, in groups and the trials which were held at Szolnok began on December 13th, 1929, when thirty of the prisoners were placed in the dock.

The mentality of some of them is shown in the statement made by one old woman, who calmly replied to the charge by saying : " we are no murderers. We have not beaten, stabbed or drowned our husbands. They died of poison and for them it was a pleasant and painless death." Another declared that she had

simply received a bottle of colourless medicine from Suzanne
Fazekas to give to her sick husband.

One of the accused named Holyba, said she had been advised
by another woman to apply to Fazekas for some medicine to
poison her husband which later she put into his coffee.

The trial of the first group of prisoners resulted in one
being sentenced to death and the others to imprisonment
for life. In these cases, the acquisition of the dead man's land
or the desire to replace aged husbands by young ones, were the
motives for the crimes. The use of arsenic in the food to effect
the object recalls the popularity of the *poudre d' inheritance* employed in France in the seventeenth century for the same
purpose.

At the trial of the next group on January 17th, 1930, Maria
Szendi and Julia Dari, both belonging to the wealthy peasant
class, were among the prisoners. The former, an old woman,
had in her youth been the village beauty and been the idol of
the district.

She confessed that she had connived at the death of her only
son, who was only twenty-three, " because he drank and played
cards."

When charged with the knowledge that Fazekas was trying to
poison him she said : " We cooked a nice supper and put
arsenic in it. I paid nearly two pounds to Suzanne, and Handor
died."

Questioned as to how her husband had met his death, she
replied : " Four weeks before he died, we put some arsenic
in his brandy. It had no effect. Then I watched Suzanne put
a large spoonful of poison in his soup but again with no success.
My husband was a strong man, but we gave him a third dose
and that finished him."

Julia Dari, who was charged with poisoning two husbands and
her mother, pleaded not guilty. " I never put poison in my
husband's wine," she declared. " I sent him to Budapeste to
recover from his weakness resulting from wounds received in
the War. I have not the slightest idea how the arsenic got into
his body. I never put it there, I loved him far too much for
that."

" You loved him so much," said counsel for the prosecution,
" that you married another man six months later."

" I loved him also and only married so that I would be able
to look after my parents."

" Yet," said the counsel, " your mother soon died under
tragic circumstances and her death was followed by that of
your second husband."

" His death was unfortunate," responded the prisoner. " He
ate some soup, had terrible convulsions and died."

Among the third group tried on February 7th, 1930, was

Maria Varga, aged forty-one, who was charged with poisoning her husband who was blinded during the War, her lover named Michael Ambrus, and the latter's grandfather.

She admitted that the apparently fatal doses had been administered by Suzanne Fazekas the midwife, but declared that she had simply asked her for her advice and had no knowledge whatever of the medicine she had supplied for him. The facts that she did not inherit as the result of the death of the grandfather of Ambrus and a doctor who had visited her husband said that he might have died from the result of a stroke, told in her favour, until she was confronted with Maria Szendi who had been already tried and condemned.

This once beautiful woman was brought into court guarded by a policeman and calmly taking the oath spoke direct to the accused woman, who was obviously disconcerted when confronted.

" You know very well," she cried dramatically to the prisoner in dock, " that it is not true to tell the court this nonsense about Suzanne. The whole village knew her evil reputation and we all knew when she darkened the door of any house, some unwanted man or woman very soon died.

" I have killed my own husband and my own son," she calmly continued, " I have no ulterior motive or intent. I have been condemned to death for my crime and I am simply here to tell the truth. I want no other murderess to escape."

She then described to the startled listeners the agonies in which Maria Varga's husband died, and so convinced the Court of her guilt that she was sentenced to imprisonment for life with hard labour for the murder of her husband, but was acquitted on the other charges.

In all, thirty-six of the women tried were found guilty and sentenced to death including Marie Kardos who was a woman of wealth.

She was found guilty of the most heartless of all these revolting peasant crimes. It was proved that she murdered her second husband and her eldest son, and it was also probable that she had killed her first husband.

She callously said in court : " After my son Sandor had swallowed the poison I remembered how beautifully he sang in the church choir and begged him to sing my favourite hymn. He did so, but suddenly stopped, screamed ' Mother ! ' and fell dead. I crossed his hands according to the dictates of religion and put on mourning clothes."

CHAPTER LIX

THE LEWANNICK MYSTERY

ABOUT five o'clock on the afternoon of October 16th, 1930, three people were seated at a table taking tea in a café at Bude. They were Mr. and Mrs. Thomas who lived at Trenhorne Farm, Lewannick, near Launceston, and their friend Mrs. Sarah Ann Hearn, who also came from Lewannick. Mr. Thomas had driven the party over in his car with his mother who had been left at her home at Bude. A pot of tea, some cakes and bread and butter were ordered, but while the meal was in progress, Mrs. Hearn produced some sandwiches which she had brought with her and placed them on the table. Each of the party ate one.

They left the café together when Mr. Thomas went for a stroll and arranged to meet the others at the hotel to drive back home. Shortly afterwards, Mr. Thomas began to feel unwell and he took some whisky. Before they left for home, Mrs. Thomas complained that she had a " sweety " taste in her mouth and asked her husband to get her some fruit, and he bought her some bananas. On their way back, she was seized with an attack of violent vomiting and they had to get out of the car for about half an hour. On their arrival at Trenhorne Farm she seemed very weak and ill and was put to bed and attended to by Mrs. Hearn. Later in the evening Mr. Thomas summoned a doctor, who saw his wife and judged she was suffering from the effects of food or ptomaine poisoning, and it transpired that the sandwiches of which they had each partaken, had been made with tinned salmon.

For several days Mrs. Thomas remained ill and was nursed by Mrs. Hearn who also did all the cooking, and on November 1st she appeared to be getting better, but two or three days later, she again became very ill and Dr. Lister, a consultant from Plymouth, was called in and diagnosed arsenical poisoning. He ordered her removal to the Plymouth Hospital where he saw her at 1.30 a.m. on November 4th ; she died later that morning. A post-mortem examination was made and the organs removed for analysis. When Mr. Thomas returned to his farm on November 11th, he received a letter from Mrs. Hearn in which she said : " Good-bye. I am going out if I can. I cannot forget that awful man and the things he said. I am innocent. Innocent. But she is dead and it was my lunch she ate. I cannot bear it. When I am dead they will be sure I am guilty and you at least will be clear. May your dear wife's presence guard and comfort you still. Yours A.H."

On receiving this, Mr. Thomas went to Trenhorne House where Mrs. Hearn lived, but he was unable to get in, so he took the letter to the police who returned with him, and they entered the house through a window, to find it unoccupied. Mrs. Hearn had completely disappeared.

An inquest was opened on the body of Mrs. Thomas on November 24th at which evidence was given that Mrs. Hearn had purchased some weed-killer from a firm in Launceston on July 13th, 1926. It also transpired that after the funeral the brother of the dead woman, when talking in the dining-room at the farm, had said : " This is poison. It must be cleared up," and this was the man Mrs. Hearn had alluded to in her letter.

Another witness said that Mrs. Hearn had told her she could stay no longer at Trenhorne Farm as " they seem to think I have poisoned Mrs. Thomas with the sandwiches."

Mr. Tickle, the public analyst for Devonshire deposed that he had found arsenic in each organ that he had examined and in the liver two-thirds of a grain. He could say there must have been sufficient in the body to cause death.

The coroner's jury returned a verdict that " the cause of death was arsenical poisoning but there was not sufficient evidence to show by whom or by what means the arsenic was administered."

Subsequently, Mrs. Hearn's coat was found on the cliffs at Looe, and a hat believed to have been hers was picked up in a field about three miles away. Meanwhile, all trace of her had been lost.

Suspicions having been aroused respecting the deaths of Miss Mary Ann Everard and Mrs. Lydia Maria Everard, a sister and an aunt of Mrs. Hearn, who had died at her house some months previously, the Home Office authorised the exhumation of their bodies which were buried in Lewannick Churchyard.

On January 13th, Mrs. Hearn was recognized at Torquay, where she had been working as a cook-general under the name of Mrs. Faithful since her disappearance.

She was arrested and charged before the magistrates at Launceston with the murder of Alice Thomas on November 4th 1930 and of Lydia Maria Everard, her sister, who had lived with her at Lewannick, on July 21st, 1930.

A statement made by Mrs. Hearn to the Superintendent of police after her arrest at Torquay was read, in which she said that when asked by Mr. Thomas to accompany them to Bude, she made some sandwiches and used a tin of salmon which she had previously purchased, and also took with her some chocolate cakes she had made herself. In the café she placed the six sandwiches on the table. Mrs. Thomas took the first, she took the second and Mr. Thomas the third. When she disappeared she went to Looe with the intention of taking her life but could not do it and she then made her way to Torquay.

After the evidence of the medical men who had attended Mrs. Thomas and Miss Everard, Mrs. Hearn was committed for trial on both charges. The trial was opened before Mr. Justice Roche at Cornwall Assizes at Bodmin on June 15th, 1931. Mr. H. du Parcq K.C., conducted the case for the Crown and Mr. Norman Birkett K.C., M.P., appeared for the defence. Mr. du Parcq recounted the story of the case of Mrs. Thomas and submitted that in addition to the poison in the sandwiches, a second dose was subsequently administered. With respect to Miss Everard, he contended that Mrs. Hearn had been administering arsenic to her sister over a period of seven months with the intention of killing her.

During the evidence of Mr. Thomas, the Judge interposed with the question : " Did you from first to last, ever yourself give your wife any arsenic ? "

" No, sir, never in all my life," replied the witness.

Dr. Eric Wordley, pathologist to Plymouth Hospital said he had made a number of tests to find if there was any evidence of poisoning by food but the results were all negative. In his opinion some arsenic was given in Mrs. Thomas's case from perhaps three to five days before death.

Mr. Tickle, the County analyst, said he found a total amount of .85 of a grain of arsenic in the organs of Mrs. Thomas's body, and the stomach was empty except for natural juices.

Dr. C. G. Gibson said he had treated Miss Everard since 1922 largely for stomach trouble. None of the medicines he gave her contained arsenic. He certified the cause of her death as chronic gastric catarrh and colitis.

Dr. Gerald Roche Lynch, senior analyst to the Home Office, in the course of his evidence said in his opinion, on the day of the alleged taking of the sandwiches, a dose, quite possibly in the region of ten grains, might have been administered to Mrs. Thomas. He thought that she received one or more doses of arsenic between October 18th and November 4th, and that these were not administered within about four or five days of her death.

In the case of Miss Everard, the body was in a good state of preservation, though emaciated. He found arsenic in every organ submitted to him ; the total amount in the body being 0.776 of a grain and eighty or ninety per cent of it was found in the muscle. The amount of arsenic in the skin, nails and heart was considerable, especially the nails, in which he found forty parts per million. He concluded that Miss Everard had been taking arsenic for a period of at least seven months. He took a lock of her hair and divided it into three parts, and as the approximate growth of hair per month was half an inch, the presence of arsenic in each part established his conclusion. He said that the amount of arsenic found in the muscles and tissues of the liver and heart showed that no dose had been administered for several days prior to death.

At a rough guess he thought Mrs. Thomas received about ten grains of arsenic in the sandwich ; that would mean 14.3 grains of weed-killer. He said that white arsenic was practically tasteless and, as an experiment, he had put in a sandwich the amount of the harmless residuum contained in 14.3 grains of weed-killer, and could detect no taste.

In his examination of the hair of Miss Everard, he found arsenic to the extent of sixteen parts per million. He also found that soil from the top of the coffin contained 125 parts per million of arsenic and the soil from the bottom sixty-two parts per million. According to the tests, practically all the arsenic was in an insoluble form.

Asked by Mr. Birkett if he could exclude the possibility of contamination of the hair by absorption, Dr. Lynch replied that he thought he could.

" Did you find anything which could enable you to say that arsenic did not soak into the hair ? " asked Mr. Birkett.

Dr. Lynch replied : " Evidence points to the fact that no water did soak into the coffin."

Mr. Birkett then suggested that the possibility of contamination of the hair and organs by diffusion from the surface of Lewannick Churchyard could not be excluded, to which Dr. Lynch agreed but thought it was extremely unlikely.

Mrs. Hearn was then called and examined by her counsel.

Leaning towards her with outstretched finger Mr. Birkett asked :

" Mrs. Hearn, have you ever at any time or in any form given arsenic to Mrs. Thomas ? "

" No, sir," replied Mrs. Hearn.

" Have you ever at any time or in any form given arsenic to your dead sister, Minnie ? "

" No, sir," again answered Mrs. Hearn.

Counsel then questioned Mrs. Hearn on her history, her sister's illness and her friendship with Mr. and Mrs. Thomas, down to the day of their visit to Bude.

Questioned about the sandwiches, Mrs. Hearn said the ingredients were bread and butter and salmon, and there might have been a little salad cream which she had made herself. She put them on the table. Mrs. Thomas, she thought, took the first one. The sandwiches which were not eaten were given to her dog which had not become ill.

In cross-examination by the counsel for the Crown, Mr. du Parcq asked : " Is it not a fact that you did put some weed-killer in that sandwich ? "

" No, it is not a fact," replied Mrs. Hearn with great emphasis. In his speech for the defence Mr. Norman Birkett said Mrs. Hearn was being charged on one indictment and the jury must determine that they were satisfied beyond all reasonable doubt that Mrs. Hearn had murdered Mrs. Thomas. With the exception of the fanciful and fantastic suggestion put forward at the last moment, that Mrs. Hearn had conceived some kind of idea that if Mrs. Thomas were not there Mr. Thomas might marry her, there was not a breath or a hint of motive.

The case for the Crown rested on the blue weed-killer bought in 1926, yet there were some worm-tablets in that house which contained arsenic and copper, and in the organs of Mrs. Thomas there was found copper. The Crown said that for seven months Mrs. Hearn had been poisoning her sister and watching her dying in pain and misery. " It is not a woman who does that, but a fiend incarnate."

Mr. Justice Roche in his summing up said : " In this case the evidence is of necessity circumstantial because most crimes as far as possible are done in secret, and poisoning throughout all the ages of the world has been the most secret and, therefore, one of the most dangerous of crimes.

" That which is thus done in secret cannot be deposed to as a rule by human testimony. It is traces alone of the poison which are, as a rule, available for the detection of the crime.

" Poisoners employ the methods of the laboratory and the results of the laboratory. The crime and the doings with regard to it can only be investigated by those methods.

" The first question to answer is : Was death caused by arsenical poisoning ? If you are of opinion that it was, the second question is : Was it the act of Mrs. Hearn ? If you decide it was not arsenical poisoning the second question does not arise."

The Judge reviewed at length the visit to Bude and said : " The sandwiches are the very kernel of this case. If you are not satisfied that the arsenic was put in the sandwich by Mrs. Hearn, you should acquit her."

The jury after deliberating fifty-four minutes returned with a verdict of not guilty and the other charge was not proceeded with.

It will be gathered from the survey of the history of criminal poisoners recorded in the preceding pages, that the toxicologist and pathologist are their most formidable enemies.

It may be safely said that the days have gone by when poison could be administered by the criminal with intent to murder without much fear of detection.

The advance of our knowledge of pathology, chemistry and pharmacology, have all contributed to make criminal poisoning more difficult, and although in some cases the identity of the poisoner may baffle the police, the secret weapon employed is inevitably revealed by the aid of analysis.

As new poisonous substances have been discovered, so the chemist by patient research has been able to find methods of detecting them.

Even in cases where the poisoner has been one with skilled knowledge and had the means of choosing the most subtle weapon known and has employed it with the greatest cunning, scientific experts have been able to bring it to light and reveal the cause of death.

Thus the chance of the poisoner successfully evading detection is gradually being reduced to a minimum and in the course of time, it is hoped, will be brought to a practical impossibility.

INDEX